# Embedded System Design

# Embedded System Design

## A Unified Hardware/Software Introduction

### Frank Vahid
Department of Computer Science and Engineering
University of California, Riverside

### Tony Givargis
Department of Information and Computer Science
University of California, Irvine

John Wiley & Sons, Inc.

ACQUISITIONS EDITOR          Bill Zobrist

SENIOR MARKETING MANAGER  Katherine Hepburn

PRODUCTION EDITOR            Caroline Sieg

COVER DESIGNER               Madelyn Lesure

COVER ILLUSTRATOR          Fanny Berry, represented by Anita Grien

This book was set in 10/12 Times Roman by the authors and printed and bound by Malloy Lithographing. The cover was printed by Phoenix Color Corp.

This book is printed on acid free paper. $\infty$

To order books or for customer service please, call 1(800)-CALL-WILEY (225-5945).

ISBN 978-0-471-38678-0

Printed in the United States of America

*To my world: Amy, Eric, Kelsi and Maya, and to the memory of our sixth member, Vahid Aminian.  —  FV*


*To my family: Neli, Fredrick, Odet, and Edvin. — TG*

# *Preface*

## Purpose

Embedded computing systems have grown tremendously in recent years, not only in their popularity, but also in their complexity. This complexity demands a new type of designer, one who can easily cross the traditional border between hardware design and software design. After investigating the availability of courses and textbooks, we felt a new course and accompanying textbook were necessary to introduce embedded computing system design using a unified view of software and hardware. This textbook portrays hardware and software not as different domains, but rather as two implementation options along a continuum of options varying in their design metrics, like cost, performance, power, size, and flexibility.

Three important trends have made such a unified view possible. First, integrated circuit (IC) capacities have increased to the point that both software processors and custom hardware processors now commonly coexist on a single IC. Second, quality compilers and program size increases have led to the common use of processor-independent C, C++, and Java compilers and integratcd design environments (IDEs) in embedded system design, significantly decreasing the importance of the focus on microprocessor internals and assembly language programming that dominate most existing embedded system courses and textbooks. Third, synthesis technology has advanced to the point that synthesis tools have become commonplace in the design of digital hardware. Synthesis tools achieve nearly the same for hardware design as compilers achieve in software design: They allow the designer to describe desired functionality in a high-level programming language, and they then automatically generate an efficient custom-hardware processor implementation. The first trend makes the past separation of software and hardware design nearly impossible. Fortunately, the second and third trends enable their unified design, by turning embedded system design, at its highest level, into the problem of selecting and programming (for software), designing (for hardware), and integrating "processors."

## Coverage

The first four chapters of this book strive to achieve the goal of presenting hardware and software in a unified way. These chapters stress that computations are carried out by processors. Many types of processors are available, including general-purpose processors (software), custom single-purpose processors (hardware), standard single-purpose processors (peripherals), and so on. But nevertheless, they are all just processors, differing in their cost, power, performance, design time, flexibility, and so on, but essentially doing the same thing. Chapter 1 provides an overview of embedded systems and their design challenges. We introduce custom single-purpose processors in Chapter 2, emphasizing a top-down technique to digital design amenable to synthesis, picking up where many textbooks on digital design leave off. We introduce general-purpose processors and their use in Chapter 3, expecting this chapter to be mostly review for many readers, and ending by showing how to design a general-purpose processor using the techniques of Chapter 2. Chapter 4 describes numerous standard single-purpose processors (peripherals) common in embedded systems. Chapters 5 and 6 introduce memories and interfacing concepts, respectively, to complete the fundamental knowledge necessary to build basic embedded systems. Chapter 7 provides a digital camera example, showing how we can trade off among hardware, software, and peripherals to achieve implementations that vary in their power, performance, and size. These seven chapters form the core of this book.

Freed from the necessity of covering the nitty-gritty details of a particular microprocessor's internals and assembly language programming, this book includes coverage of some additional embedded systems topics. Chapter 8 describes advanced state machine computation models that are becoming popular when describing complex embedded system behavior. It also introduces the concurrent process model and real-time systems. Chapter 9 gives a basic introduction to control systems, enough to make students aware that a rich theory exists for control systems, and to enable students to determine when an embedded system is an example of a control system. Chapter 10 introduces a variety of popular IC technologies, from which a designer may choose for system implementation. Finally, Chapter 11 highlights various design technologies for building embedded systems, including discussion of hardware/software codesign, a user's introduction to synthesis (from behavioral down to logic levels), and the major trend toward design based on intellectual property (IP).

## How to Use This Book

We use this book at the University of California, Riverside, in a one-quarter course called Introduction to Embedded Systems, which follows our introductory course on logic design, and which is taken by all computer science, computer engineering, and electrical engineering students at roughly the sophomore level. This early placement of the course in our curriculum represents our belief that an early unified view of hardware and software can be very beneficial to a student's mindset when later taking more specialized courses. The suggested placement of the course in an undergraduate curriculum is shown in Figure P.1. Our one-quarter course covers Chapters 1–7. We have a second quarter course on embedded systems that covers Chapters 8–12, supplemented with a textbook on real-time systems. A one-semester course might cover Chapters 1–7 plus two or three additional chapters of the instructor's choice.

We anticipate that in most electrical and computer engineering/science curricula, this textbook could be used in place of a processor-specific textbook in an existing course on microprocessor-based system design or microprocessor interfacing, as the lab components of

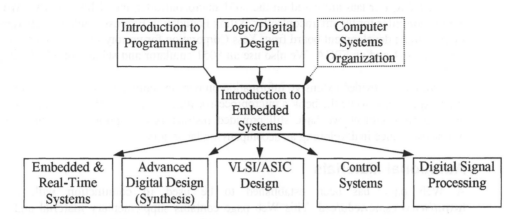

Figure P.1: Embedded systems design placement in a curriculum to create a unified view of hardware and software early.

those courses shift away from assembly-level programming to the use of more modern tools and to the integration of microprocessors and custom hardware (e.g., FPGAs). In other curricula, a new course on embedded systems may be necessary; we observe that numerous universities are introducing such courses, often converting a second course in digital design to a course on embedded systems (as we did at UCR). The book could also be used in a capstone senior design course as a text that brings together and organizes much of what students may have been exposed to already – such courses often do not even have a textbook. The book should also be useful at the graduate level for an introductory embedded systems course.

## Laboratory

Ideally, a course using this book should have an accompanying laboratory. The ideal lab setup would include both software development on an embedded microprocessor or microcontroller platform and hardware development on an FPGA platform (or even in a simulation environment).

We intentionally created this book to be independent from any particular microprocessor. One reason is because embedded system tools and products are evolving rapidly, and thus we consider the ability to change lab environments without having to change textbooks an important one. A second reason is because the embedded system field has evolved sufficiently to warrant a book based on principles. However, a course with a hands-on lab may supplement this book with a processor-specific databook, which is typically low cost or even free, or with one of many commonly available "extended databook" processor-specific textbooks in wide use today.

Likewise, the book is independent of any particular hardware description language, synthesis tool, simulator, or FPGA. Supplements that describe the particular hardware environment, again usually available for free or at low cost, may be useful.

At UCR, our labs are based on the 8051 microcontroller and Xilinx FPGAs. We use the Keil C compiler for the microcontroller, Xilinx Foundation Express synthesis software for the FPGA, and a development board from Xess Corporation for prototyping — the board contains both an 8051 and an FPGA. We also use an 8051 emulator and stand-alone 8051 chips from Philips.

We have provided extensive information on our lab setup and assignments on the book's Web page. Thus, while the book's microprocessor independence enables instructors to choose any lab environment, we have still provided instructors the option of obtaining extensive online assistance in developing an accompanying laboratory.

## Additional Materials

A Web page has been established to be used in conjunction with the book: **http://www.cs.ucr.edu/esd**. This Web page contains supplementary material and links for each chapter. It also contains a set of lecture slides in Microsoft PowerPoint format; because the book itself was done entirely in Microsoft Word, the figures in the PowerPoint slides are PowerPoint drawings (rather than imported graphics), and thus can be modified as desired by instructors.

Furthermore, the Web page contains an extensive lab curriculum to accompany this textbook. Over 30 lab exercises, including detailed descriptions, schematics, and complete or partial solutions, can be found there. The exercises are organized by chapter, starting with very simple exercises and leading to progressively more complex ones. For example, Chapter 2's exercises start with a simple blinking light, and end with a soda machine controller and a calculator. Appendix A provides further information on our Web page.

## Acknowledgments

We are grateful to numerous individuals for their assistance in developing this book. Sharon Hu of Notre Dame, Nikil Dutt of UC Irvine, and Smita Bakshi of UC Davis and Synplicity provided excellent reviewer feedback. Sharon Hu, Jan Madsen of the Technical University of Denmark, and Enoch Hwang of UC Riverside used early drafts of this book in their embedded systems courses. Susan Cotterell provided numerous contributions to the book, including several examples, much of the accompanying lab materials, and the Web site setup. Jason Villarreal and Kris Miller helped with proofreading at various stages. Jay Farrell of UC Riverside contributed much of the chapter on control systems. Karen Schechter converted our cover design idea into the initial 3-D scene. The generous donations of 8051 equipment from Philips Semiconductors and of FPGA equipment from Xilinx were a big assistance. Likewise, a National Science Foundation CAREER award supported some of this book's development. We thank Caroline Sieg at Wiley for overseeing the book's production and Madelyn Lesure for overseeing the cover design. Finally, we are deeply grateful to Bill Zobrist of Wiley, for believing in this project from its onset, for arranging the reviews of the book, and for overseeing various aspects of its production.

## About the Authors

**Frank Vahid** is an Associate Professor in the Department of Computer Science and Engineering at the University of California, Riverside, which he joined in 1994. He is also a faculty member of the Center for Embedded Computer Systems at the University of California, Irvine. He received his B.S. in Computer Engineering from the University of Illinois, Urbana/Champaign, and his M.S. and Ph.D. degrees in Computer Science from the University of California, Irvine, where he was recipient of the Semiconductor Research Corporation Graduate Fellowship. He was an engineer at Hewlett Packard and has consulted for numerous companies, including NEC and Motorola. He is co-author of the graduate-level textbook *Specification and Design of Embedded Systems* (Prentice-Hall, 1994). He has been program chair and general chair for both the International Symposium on System Synthesis and for the International Symposium on Hardware/Software Codesign. He has been an active researcher in embedded system design since 1988, with more than 50 publications and several best paper awards, including an IEEE Transactions on VLSI best paper award in 2000. His research interests are in embedded system architectures, low-power design, and design methods for system-on-a-chip.

**Tony Givargis** is an Assistant Professor in the Department of Information and Computer Science and a member of the Center for Embedded Computer Systems at the University of California, Irvine. He received his B.S. and Ph.D. degrees from the University of California, Riverside, where he received the Department of Computer Science Best Thesis award and the UCR College of Engineering Outstanding Student award, and where he was recipient of the GAANN Graduate Fellowship, a MICRO fellowship, and a Design Automation Conference scholarship. As a consultant, he has developed numerous embedded systems for several companies, ranging from an irrigation management system to a GPS-guided, self-navigating automobile. He has published more than 20 research papers in the embedded systems field. His research interests include embedded and real-time system design, low power design, and processor/system-on-a-chip architectures.

# *Contents*

# Contents

# CHAPTER 1: *Introduction*

## 1.1  Embedded Systems Overview

Computing systems are everywhere. It is probably no surprise that millions of computing systems are built every year, destined for desktop computers like personal computers, laptops, workstations, mainframes, and servers. What may be surprising is that billions of computing systems are built every year for a very different purpose: They are embedded within larger electronic devices, repeatedly carrying out a particular function, often going completely unrecognized by the device's user. Creating a precise definition of such embedded computing systems, or simply *embedded systems*, is not an easy task. We might try the following definition: an embedded system is nearly any computing system other than a desktop computer. That definition isn't perfect, but it may be as close as we'll get. We can better understand such systems by examining common examples and common characteristics. Such examination will reveal major challenges facing designers of embedded systems.

Embedded systems are found in a variety of common electronic devices, such as consumer electronics (cell phones, pagers, digital cameras, camcorders, videocassette recorders, portable video games, calculators, and personal digital assistants), home appliances (microwave ovens, answering machines, thermostats, home security systems, washing machines, and lighting systems), office automation (fax machines, copiers, printers, and scanners), business equipment (cash registers, curbside check-in, alarm systems, card readers,

| | |
|---|---|
| Anti-lock brakes | Modems |
| Auto-focus cameras | MPEG decoders |
| Automatic teller machines | Network cards |
| Automatic toll systems | Network switches/routers |
| Automatic transmission | On-board navigation |
| Avionic systems | Pagers |
| Battery chargers | Photocopiers |
| Camcorders | Point-of-sale systems |
| Cell phones | Portable video games |
| Cell phone base stations | Printers |
| Cordless phones | Satellite phones |
| Cruise control | Scanners |
| Curbside check-in systems | Smart ovens/dishwashers |
| Digital cameras | Speech recognizers |
| Disk drives | Stereo systems |
| Electronic card readers | Teleconferencing systems |
| Electronic instruments | Televisions |
| Electronic toys/games | Temperature controllers |
| Factory control | Theft tracking systems |
| Fax machines | TV set-top boxes |
| Fingerprint identifiers | VCR's, DVD players |
| Home security systems | Video game consoles |
| Life-support systems | Video phones |
| Medical testing systems | Washers and dryers |

Figure 1.1: A short list of embedded systems.

product scanners, and automated teller machines), and automobiles (transmission control, cruise control, fuel injection, antilock brakes, and active suspension). Figure 1.1 is a short list of embedded system examples; a more complete list would require many pages. One might say that nearly any device that runs on electricity either already has or will soon have a computing system embedded within it. Although embedded computers typically cost far less than desktop computers, their quantities are huge. For example, in 1999 a typical American household may have had one desktop computer, but each one had between 35 and 50 embedded computers, with that number expected to rise to nearly 300 by 2004. Furthermore, the average 1998 car had 50 embedded computers costing several hundred dollars in all, with an annual cost growth rate of 17%. Several billion embedded microprocessor units were sold annually in recent years, compared to a few hundred million desktop microprocessor units.

Embedded systems have several common characteristics that distinguish such systems from other computing systems:

1. *Single-functioned*: An embedded system usually executes a specific program repeatedly. For example, a pager is always a pager. In contrast, a desktop system executes a variety of programs, like spreadsheets, word processors, and video games, with new programs added frequently. Of course, there are exceptions. One case is where an embedded system's program is updated with a newer program version. For example, some cell phones can be updated in such a manner. A second case is where

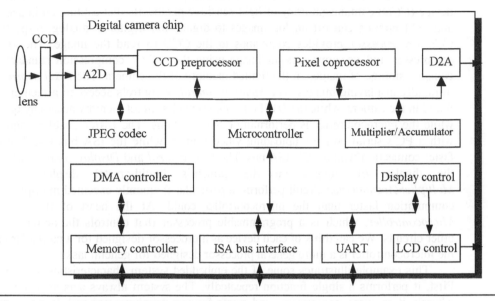

Figure 1.2: An embedded system example — a digital camera.

several programs are swapped in and out of a system due to size limitations. For example, some missiles run one program while in cruise mode, then load a second program for locking onto a target. Nevertheless, we can see that even these exceptions represent systems with a specific function.

2. *Tightly constrained*: All computing systems have constraints on design metrics, but those on embedded systems can be especially tight. A design metric is a measure of an implementation's features, such as cost, size, performance, and power. Embedded systems often must cost just a few dollars, must be sized to fit on a single chip, must perform fast enough to process data in real time, and must consume minimum power to extend battery life or prevent the necessity of a cooling fan.

3. *Reactive and real time*: Many embedded systems must continually react to changes in the system's environment and must compute certain results in real time without delay. For example, a car's cruise controller continually monitors and reacts to speed and brake sensors. It must compute acceleration or deceleration amounts repeatedly within a limited time; a delayed computation could result in a failure to maintain control of the car. In contrast, a desktop system typically focuses on computations, with relatively infrequent (from the computer's perspective) reactions to input devices. In addition, a delay in those computations, while perhaps inconvenient to the computer user, typically does not result in a system failure.

For example, consider the digital camera chip shown in Figure 1.2. The charge-coupled device (*CCD*) contains an array of light-sensitive photocells that capture an image. The *A2D* and *D2A* circuits convert analog images to digital and digital to analog, respectively. The *CCD preprocessor* provides commands to the *CCD* to read the image. The *JPEG codec* compresses and decompresses an image using the *JPEG*[1] compression standard, enabling compact storage of images in the limited memory of the camera. The *Pixel coprocessor* aids in rapidly displaying images. The *Memory controller* controls access to a memory chip also found in the camera, while the *DMA controller* enables direct memory access by other devices while the microcontroller is performing other functions. The *UART* enables communication with a PC's serial port for uploading video frames, while the ISA bus interface enables a faster connection with a PC's ISA bus. The *LCD control* and *Display control* circuits control the display of images on the camera's liquid-crystal display device. The *Multiplier/Accumulator* circuit performs a particular frequently executed multiply/accumulate computation faster than the microcontroller could. At the heart of the system is the *Microcontroller*, which is a programmable processor that controls the activities of all the other circuits. We can think of each device as a processor designed for a particular task, while the microcontroller is a more general processor designed for general tasks.

This example illustrates some of the embedded system characteristics described earlier. First, it performs a single function repeatedly. The system always acts as a digital camera, wherein it captures, compresses, and stores frames, decompresses and displays frames, and uploads frames. Second, it is tightly constrained. The system must be low cost since consumers must be able to afford such a camera. It must be small so that it fits within a standard-sized camera. It must be fast so that it can process numerous images in milliseconds. It must consume little power so that the camera's battery will last a long time. However, this particular system does not possess a high degree of the characteristic of being reactive and real time, as it responds only to the pressing of buttons by a user, which, even in the case of an avid photographer, is still quite slow with respect to processor speeds.

## 1.2  Design Challenge — Optimizing Design Metrics

The embedded-system designer must of course construct an implementation that fulfills desired functionality, but a difficult challenge is to construct an implementation that simultaneously optimizes numerous design metrics.

### Common Design Metrics

For our purposes, an implementation consists either of a microprocessor with an accompanying program, a connection of digital gates, or some combination thereof. A *design metric* is a measurable feature of a system's implementation. Commonly used metrics include:

---

[1] *JPEG* is short for *Joint Photographic Experts Group*. "Joint" refers to the group's status as a committee working on both ISO and ITU-T standards. Their best-known standard is for still-image compression.

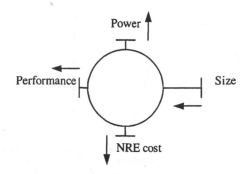

Figure 1.3: Design metric competition — improving one may worsen others.

- *NRE cost* (nonrecurring engineering cost): The one-time monetary cost of designing the system. Once the system is designed, any number of units can be manufactured without incurring any additional design cost; hence the term *nonrecurring*.
- *Unit cost*: The monetary cost of manufacturing each copy of the system, excluding NRE cost.
- *Size*: The physical space required by the system, often measured in bytes for software, and gates or transistors for hardware.
- *Performance*: The execution time of the system.
- *Power*: The amount of power consumed by the system, which may determine the lifetime of a battery, or the cooling requirements of the IC, since more power means more heat.
- *Flexibility*: The ability to change the functionality of the system without incurring heavy NRE cost. Software is typically considered very flexible.
- *Time-to-prototype*: The time needed to build a working version of the system, which may be bigger or more expensive than the final system implementation, but it can be used to verify the system's usefulness and correctness and to refine the system's functionality.
- *Time-to-market*: The time required to develop a system to the point that it can be released and sold to customers. The main contributors are design time, manufacturing time, and testing time.
- *Maintainability*: The ability to modify the system after its initial release, especially by designers who did not originally design the system.
- *Correctness*: Our confidence that we have implemented the system's functionality correctly. We can check the functionality throughout the process of designing the system, and we can insert test circuitry to check that manufacturing was correct.
- *Safety*: The probability that the system will not cause harm.

Metrics typically compete with one another: Improving one often leads to worsening of another. For example, if we reduce an implementation's size, the implementation's performance may suffer. Some observers have compared this phenomenon to a wheel with numerous pins, as illustrated in Figure 1.3. If you push one pin in, such as size, then the other

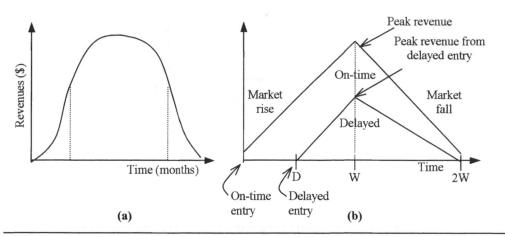

Figure 1.4: Time-to-market: (a) market window, (b) simplified revenue model for computing revenue loss from delayed entry.

pins pop out. To best meet this optimization challenge, the designer must be comfortable with a variety of hardware and software implementation technologies, and must be able to migrate from one technology to another, in order to find the best implementation for a given application and constraints. Thus, a designer cannot simply be a hardware expert or a software expert, as is commonly the case today; the designer must have expertise in both areas.

## The Time-to-Market Design Metric

Most of these metrics are heavily constrained in an embedded system. The time-to-market constraint has become especially demanding in recent years. Introducing an embedded system to the marketplace early can make a big difference in the system's profitability, since market windows for products are becoming quite short, with such windows often measured in months. For example, Figure 1.4(a) shows a sample market window during which time a product would have highest sales. Missing this window, which means that the product begins being sold further to the right on the time scale, can mean significant loss in sales. In some cases, each day that a product is delayed from introduction to the market can translate to a one-million-dollar loss. The average time-to-market constraint has been reported as having shrunk to only 8 months!

Adding to the difficulty of meeting the time-to-market constraint is the fact that embedded system complexities are growing due to increasing IC capacities, as we will see later in this chapter. Such rapid growth in IC capacity translates into pressure on designers to add more functionality to a system. Thus, designers today are being asked to do more in less time.

Let's investigate the loss of revenue that can occur due to delayed entry of a product in the market. We'll use a simplified model of revenue that is shown in Figure 1.4(b). This model assumes the peak of the market occurs at the halfway point, denoted as $W$, of the product life, and that the peak is the same even for a delayed entry. The revenue for an

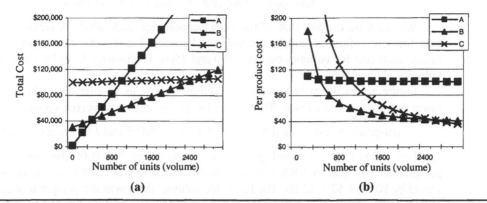

Figure 1.5: Costs for technologies A, B, and C as a function of volume: (a) total cost, (b) per-product cost.

on-time market entry is the area of the triangle labeled *On-time*, and the revenue for a delayed entry product is the area of the triangle labeled *Delayed*. The revenue loss for a delayed entry is just the difference of these two triangles' areas. Let's derive an equation for percentage revenue loss, which equals ((*On-time* – *Delayed*) / *On-time*) * 100%. For simplicity, we'll assume the market rise angle is 45 degrees, meaning the height of the triangle is $W$, and we leave as an exercise the derivation of the same equation for any angle. The area of the *On-time* triangle, computed as ½ * *base* * *height*, is thus ½ * 2$W$ * $W$, or $W^2$. The area of the *Delayed* triangle is ½($W$ – $D$ + $W$) * ($W$ – $D$). After algebraic simplification, we obtain the following equation for percentage revenue loss:

$$\text{percentage revenue loss} = (D(3W - D) / 2W^2) * 100\%$$

Consider a product whose lifetime is 52 weeks, so $W = 26$. According to the preceding equation, a delay of just $D = 4$ weeks results in a revenue loss of 22%, and a delay of $D = 10$ weeks results in a loss of 50%. Some studies claim that reaching market late has a larger negative effect on revenues than development cost overruns or even a product price that is too high.

## The NRE and Unit Cost Design Metrics

As another exercise, let's consider NRE cost and unit cost in more detail. Suppose three technologies are available for use in a particular product. Assume that implementing the product using technology A would result in an NRE cost of $2,000 and unit cost of $100, that technology B would have an NRE cost of $30,000 and unit cost of $30, and that technology C would have an NRE cost of $100,000 and unit cost of $2. Ignoring all other design metrics, like time-to-market, the best technology choice will depend on the number of units we plan to produce. We illustrate this concept with the plot of Figure 1.5(a). For each of the three technologies, we plot total cost versus the number of units produced, where:

$$\text{total cost} = \text{NRE cost} + \text{unit cost} * \text{\# of units}$$

We see from the plot that, of the three technologies, technology A yields the lowest total cost for low volumes, namely for volumes between 1 and 400. Technology B yields the lowest total cost for volumes between 400 and 2500. Technology C yields the lowest cost for volumes above 2500.

Figure 1.5(b) illustrates how larger volumes allow us to amortize NRE costs such that lower per-product costs result. The figure plots per-product cost versus volume, where:

$$\text{per-product cost} = \text{total cost} / \text{\# of units} = \text{NRE cost} / \text{\# of units} + \text{unit cost}$$

For example, for technology C and a volume of 200,000, the contribution to the per-product cost due to NRE cost is $100,000 / 200,000, or $0.50. So the per-product cost would be $0.50 + $2 = $2.50. The larger the volume, the lower the per-product cost, since the NRE cost can be distributed over more products. The per-product cost for each technology approaches that technology's unit cost for very large volumes. So for very large volumes, numbering in the hundreds of thousands, we can approach a per-product cost of just $2 — quite a bit less than the per-product cost of over $100 for small volumes.

Clearly, one must consider the revenue impact of both time-to-market and per-product cost, as well as all the other relevant design metrics when evaluating different technologies.

## The Performance Design Metric

Performance of a system is a measure of how long the system takes to execute our desired tasks. Performance is perhaps the most widely used design metric in marketing an embedded system, and also one of the most abused. Many metrics are commonly used in reporting system performance, such as clock frequency or instructions per second. However, what we really care about is how long the system takes to execute our application. For example, in terms of performance, we care about how long a digital camera takes to process an image. The camera's clock frequency or instructions per second are not the key issues — one camera may actually process images faster but have a lower clock frequency than another camera.

With that said, there are several measures of performance. For simplicity, suppose we have a single task that will be repeated over and over, such as processing an image in a digital camera. The two main measures of performance are:

- *Latency*, or *response time*: The time between the start of the task's execution and the end. For example, processing an image may take 0.25 second.
- *Throughput*: The number of tasks that can be processed per unit time. For example, a camera may be able to process 4 images per second.

However, note that throughput is not always just the number of tasks times latency. A system may be able to do better than this by using parallelism, either by starting one task before finishing the next one or by processing each task concurrently. A digital camera, for example, might be able to capture and compress the next image, while still storing the previous image to memory. Thus, our camera may have a latency of 0.25 second but a throughput of 8 images per second.

In embedded systems, performance at a very detailed level is also often of concern. In particular, two signal changes may have to be generated or measured within some number of nanoseconds.

*Speedup* is a common method of comparing the performance of two systems. The speedup of system A over system B is determined simply as:

speedup of A over B = performance of A / performance of B.

Performance could be measured either as latency or as throughput, depending on what is of interest. Suppose the speedup of camera A over camera B is 2. Then we also can say that A is 2 times faster than B and B is 2 times slower than A.

# 1.3   Processor Technology

We can define *technology* as a manner of accomplishing a task, especially using technical processes, methods, or knowledge. This book takes the perspective that three types of technologies are central to embedded system design: processor technologies, IC technologies, and design technologies. We describe all three briefly in this chapter and provide further details in subsequent chapters.

Processor technology relates to the architecture of the computation engine used to implement a system's desired functionality. Although the term *processor* is usually associated with programmable software processors, we can think of many other, nonprogrammable, digital systems as being processors also. Each such processor differs in its specialization towards a particular function (e.g., image compression), thus manifesting design metrics different than other processors. We illustrate this concept graphically in Figure 1.6. The application requires a specific embedded functionality, symbolized as a cross, such as the summing of the items in an array, as shown in Figure 1.6(a). Several types of processors can implement this functionality, each of which we now describe. We often use a collection of such processors to optimize a system's design metrics, as in our digital camera example.

## General-Purpose Processors — Software

The designer of a *general-purpose processor*, or *microprocessor*, builds a programmable device that is suitable for a variety of applications to maximize the number of devices sold. One feature of such a processor is a program memory — the designer of such a processor does not know what program will run on the processor, so the program cannot be built into the digital circuit. Another feature is a general datapath — the datapath must be general enough to handle a variety of computations, so such a datapath typically has a large register file and one or more general-purpose arithmetic-logic units (ALUs). An embedded system designer, however, need not be concerned about the design of a general-purpose processor. An embedded system designer simply uses a general-purpose processor, by programming the processor's memory to carry out the required functionality. Many people refer to this part of an implementation as the "software" portion.

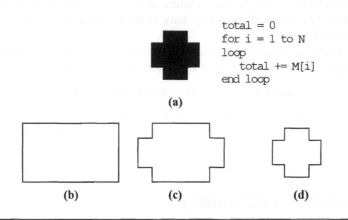

```
total = 0
for i = 1 to N
loop
    total += M[i]
end loop
```

(a)

(b)          (c)          (d)

Figure 1.6: Processors vary in their customization for the problem at hand: (a) desired functionality, (b) general-purpose processor, (c) application-specific processor, (d) single-purpose processor.

Using a general-purpose processor in an embedded system may result in several design metric benefits. Time-to-market and NRE costs are low because the designer must only write a program but not do any digital design. Flexibility is high because changing functionality requires changing only the program. Unit cost may be low in small quantities compared with designing our own processor, since the general-purpose processor manufacturer sells large quantities to other customers and hence distributes the NRE cost over many units. Performance may be fast for computation-intensive applications, if using a fast processor, due to advanced architecture features and leading-edge IC technology.

However, there are also some design-metric drawbacks. Unit cost may be relatively high for large quantities, since in large quantities we could design our own processor and amortize our NRE costs such that our unit cost is lower. Performance may be slow for certain applications. Size and power may be large due to unnecessary processor hardware.

For example, we can use a general-purpose processor to carry out our array-summing functionality from the earlier example. Figure 1.6(b) illustrates that a general-purpose processor covers the desired functionality but not necessarily efficiently. Figure 1.7(a) shows a simple architecture of a general-purpose processor implementing the array-summing functionality. The functionality is stored in a program memory. The controller fetches the current instruction, as indicated by the program counter (PC), into the instruction register (IR). It then configures the datapath for this instruction and executes the instruction. It then determines the next instruction address, sets the PC to this address, and fetches again.

## Single-Purpose Processors — Hardware

A *single-purpose processor* is a digital circuit designed to execute exactly one program. For example, consider the digital camera example of Figure 1.2. All of the components other than the microcontroller are single-purpose processors. The JPEG codec, for example, executes a single program that compresses and decompresses video frames. An embedded system

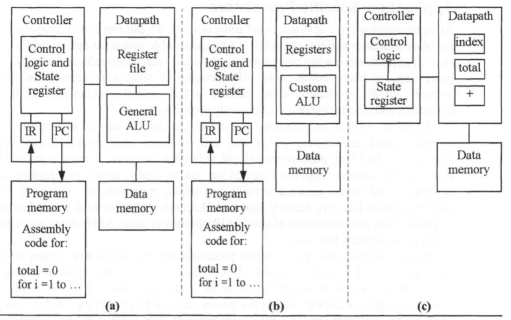

Figure 1.7: Implementing desired functionality on different processor types: (a) general-purpose, (b) application-specific, (c) single-purpose.

designer may create a single-purpose processor by designing a custom digital circuit, as discussed in later chapters. Alternatively, the designer may purchase a predesigned single-purpose processor. Many people refer to this part of the implementation simply as the "hardware" portion, although even software requires a hardware processor on which to run. Other common terms include *coprocessor*, *accelerator*, and *peripheral*.

Using a single-purpose processor in an embedded system results in several design-metric benefits and drawbacks, which are essentially the inverse of those for general-purpose processors. Performance may be fast, size and power may be small, and unit cost may be low for large quantities, while design time and NRE costs may be high, flexibility low, unit cost high for small quantities, and performance may not match general-purpose processors for some applications.

For example, Figure 1.6(d) illustrates the use of a single-purpose processor in our embedded system example, representing an exact fit of the desired functionality, nothing more, nothing less. Figure 1.7(c) illustrates the architecture of such a single-purpose processor for the example. The datapath contains only the essential components for this program: two registers and one adder. Since the processor only executes this one program, we hardwire the program's instructions directly into the control logic and use a state register to step through those instructions, so no program memory is necessary.

## Application-Specific Processors

An *application-specific instruction-set processor* (ASIP) can serve as a compromise between the other processor options. An ASIP is a programmable processor optimized for a particular class of applications having common characteristics, such as embedded control, digital-signal processing, or telecommunications. The designer of such a processor can optimize the datapath for the application class, perhaps adding special functional units for common operations and eliminating other infrequently used units.

Using an ASIP in an embedded system can provide the benefit of flexibility while still achieving good performance, power, and size. However, such processors can require large NRE cost to build the processor itself and to build a compiler, if these items don't already exist. Much research currently focuses on automatically generating application-specific processors and their associated compile and debug environments, and some commercial products that do this have recently appeared. However, due to the lack of good compilers that can exploit the unique features of most ASIPs, designers using ASIPs often write much of the software in assembly language.

Microcontrollers and digital signal processors are two well-known types of ASIPs that have been used for several decades. A *microcontroller* is a microprocessor that has been optimized for embedded control applications. Such applications typically monitor and set numerous single-bit control signals but do not perform large amounts of data computations. Thus, microcontrollers tend to have simple datapaths that excel at bit-level operations and at reading and writing external bits. Furthermore, they tend to incorporate on the microprocessor chip several peripheral components common in control applications, like serial communication peripherals, timers, counters, pulse-width modulators, and analog-digital converters, all of which will be covered in a later chapter. Such incorporation of peripherals enables single-chip implementations and hence smaller and lower-cost products.

*Digital-signal processors* (DSPs) are another common type of ASIP. A DSP is a microprocessor designed to perform common operations on digital signals, which are the digital encodings of analog signals like video and audio. These operations carry out common signal processing tasks like signal filtering, transformation, or a combination. Such operations are usually math-intensive, including operations like multiply and add or shift and add. To support such operations, a DSP may have special-purpose datapath components such as a multiply-accumulate unit, which can perform a computation like $T = T + M[i] * k$ using only one instruction. Because DSP programs often manipulate large arrays of data, a DSP may also include special hardware to fetch sequential data memory locations in parallel with other operations, to further speed execution.

Although microcontrollers and DSPs represent widely used types of ASIPs, the term *ASIP* has really been used only in the past few years, as a result of recent attention given to creating ASIPs for much smaller application classes, some as small as just a handful of programs.

Figure 1.6(c) illustrates the use of an ASIP for our example. Although partially customized to the desired functionality, the ASIP yields some inefficiency since it also contains features to support reprogramming. Figure 1.7(b) shows the general architecture of an ASIP for the example. The datapath may be customized for the example. It may have an autoincrementing register, a path that allows us to add a register with a memory location in one instruction, fewer registers, and a simpler controller.

# 1.4   IC Technology

Every processor must eventually be implemented on an integrated circuit (IC). IC technology involves the manner in which we map a digital (gate-level) implementation onto an IC. An IC, often called a "chip," is a semiconductor device consisting of a set of connected transistors and other devices. A number of different processes exist to build semiconductors, the most popular of which is complementary metal oxide semiconductor (CMOS).

IC technologies differ by how customized the IC is for a particular design. IC technology is independent from processor technology; any type of processor can be mapped to any type of IC technology, as illustrated in Figure 1.14.

To understand the differences among IC technologies, we must first recognize that semiconductors consist of numerous layers as illustrated in Figure 1.8. The bottom layers form the transistors. The middle layers form logic components. The top layers connect these components with wires. One way to create these layers is by depositing photo-sensitive chemicals on the chip surface and then shining light through masks to change regions of the chemicals. Thus, the task of building the layers is actually one of designing appropriate masks. A set of masks is often called a *layout*. The narrowest line that we can create on a chip is called the *feature size*, which today is well below one micrometer (submicron). For each IC technology, all layers must eventually be built to get a working IC; the question is who builds each layer and when.

## Full-Custom/VLSI

In a full-custom IC technology, we optimize all layers for a particular embedded system's digital implementation. Such optimization includes placing the transistors to minimize interconnection lengths, sizing the transistors to optimize signal transmissions and routing wires among the transistors. Once we complete all the masks, we send the mask specifications to a fabrication plant that builds the actual ICs. Full-custom IC design, often referred to as very large scale integration (VLSI) design, has a very high NRE cost and long turnaround times, typically many months before the IC becomes available, but can yield excellent performance with small size and power. It is usually used only in high-volume or extremely performance-critical applications.

## Semicustom ASIC (Gate Array and Standard Cell)

In an application-specific IC (ASIC) technology, the lower layers are fully or partially built, leaving us to finish the upper layers. In a gate-array ASIC technology, the masks for the transistor and gate levels are already built (i.e., the IC already consists of arrays of gates). The remaining task is to connect these gates to achieve our particular implementation. In a standard-cell ASIC technology, logic-level cells, such as an AND gate or an

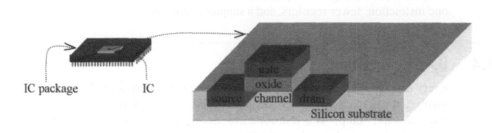

Figure 1.8: ICs consist of several layers. Shown is a simplified CMOS transistor; an IC may possess millions of these, connected above by many layers of metal (not shown).

AND-OR-INVERT combination, the mask portions are predesigned, usually by hand. Thus, the remaining task is to arrange these portions into complete masks for the gate level, and then to connect the cells. ASICs are by far the most popular IC technology, as they provide for good performance and size, with much less NRE cost than full-custom ICs. However, ASICs still require weeks or even months to manufacture.

## PLD

In a programmable logic device (PLD) technology, all layers already exist, so we can purchase the actual IC before finishing our design. The layers implement a programmable circuit, where programming has a lower-level meaning than a software program. The programming that takes place may consist of creating or destroying connections between wires that connect gates, either by blowing a fuse, or setting a bit in a programmable switch. Small devices called programmers, connected to a desktop computer, typically perform such programming. We can divide PLDs into two types, simple and complex. One type of simple PLD is a programmable logic array (PLA), which consists of a programmable array of AND gates and a programmable array of OR gates. Another type is a programmable array logic (PAL), which uses just one programmable array to reduce the number of expensive programmable components. One type of complex PLD, growing very rapidly in popularity over the past decade, is the field programmable gate array (FPGA). FPGAs offer more general connectivity among blocks of logic, rather than just arrays of logic as with PLAs and PALs, and are thus able to implement far more complex designs. PLDs offer very low NRE cost and almost instant IC availability. However, they are typically bigger than ASICs, may have higher unit cost, may consume more power, and may be slower (especially FPGAs). They still provide reasonable performance, though, so they are especially well-suited to rapid prototyping.

## Trends

We should be aware of what is by far the most important trend in embedded systems, a trend related to ICs: *IC transistor capacity has doubled roughly every 18 months for the past several decades.*

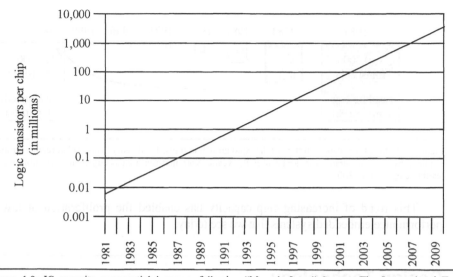

Figure 1.9: IC capacity exponential increase, following "Moore's Law." Source: The International Technology Roadmap for Semiconductors.

This trend, illustrated in Figure 1.9, was actually predicted way back in 1965 by Intel co-founder Gordon Moore. He predicted that semiconductor transistor density would double every 18 to 24 months. The trend is therefore known as *Moore's Law*. Moore recently predicted about another decade before such growth slows down. The trend is mainly caused by improvements in IC manufacturing that result in smaller parts, such as transistor parts and wires, on the surface of the IC. The minimum part size, commonly known as feature size, for a CMOS IC in 2002 is about 130 nanometers.

Figure 1.9 shows leading-edge chip approximate capacity per year from 1981 to 2010, using predicted data for years 2000–2010. Note that chip capacity, shown in millions of transistors per chip, is plotted on a logarithmic scale. People often underestimate and are somewhat amazed by the actual growth of something that doubles over short time periods, in this case 18 months. For example, this underestimation in part explains the popularity of so-called pyramid schemes. It is the key to the popular trick question of asking someone to choose between a salary of $1,000/day for a year, or a penny on day one, 2 pennies on day two, with continued doubling each day for a year. While many people would choose the first option, the second option results in more money than exists in the world. Many people are also surprised to discover that just 20 generations ago, meaning a few hundred years, we find that we each have one million ancestors.

Figure 1.10 shows that in 1981, a leading-edge chip could hold about 10,000 transistors, which is roughly the complexity of an 8-bit microprocessor. In 2002, a leading-edge chip can hold about 150,000,000 transistors, the equivalent of 15,000 8-bit microprocessors! For comparison, if automobile fuel efficiency had improved at this rate since 1981, cars in 2002 would get about 500,000 miles per gallon.

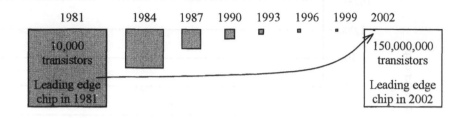

Figure 1.10: Graphical demonstration of the rapid growth in transistor density. The shaded region symbolizes the area required by a 10,000-transistor design over the years. Note that the area occupies an incredibly tiny portion of a leading edge chip in 2002.

This trend of increasing chip capacity has enabled the proliferation of low-cost, high-performance embedded systems that we see today.

## 1.5 Design Technology

Design technology involves the manner in which we convert our concept of desired system functionality into an implementation. We must not only design the implementation to optimize design metrics, but we must do so quickly. As described earlier, the designer must be able to produce larger numbers of transistors every year to keep pace with IC technology. Hence, improving design technology to enhance productivity has been a key focus of the software and hardware design communities for decades.

To understand how to improve the design process, we must first understand the design process itself. Variations of a *top-down design* process have become popular in the past decade, an ideal form of which is illustrated in Figure 1.11. The designer refines the system through several abstraction levels. At the system level, the designer describes the desired functionality in some language, often a natural language like English, but preferably an executable language like C; we shall call this the *system specification*. The designer refines this specification by distributing portions of it among several general and/or single-purpose processors, yielding *behavioral specifications* for each processor. The designer refines these specifications into *register-transfer* (RT) *specifications* by converting behavior on general-purpose processors to assembly code, and by converting behavior on single-purpose processors to a connection of register-transfer components and state machines. The designer then refines the register-transfer-level specification of a single-purpose processor into a *logic specification* consisting of Boolean equations; no refinement of a general-purpose processor's assembly code is done at this level. Finally, the designer refines the remaining specifications into an implementation, consisting of machine code for general-purpose processors and a gate-level netlist for single-purpose processors.

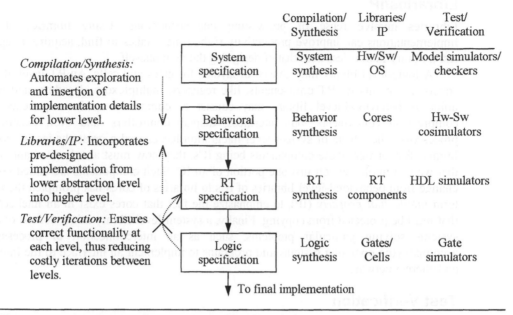

| | | Compilation/<br>Synthesis | Libraries/<br>IP | Test/<br>Verification |
|---|---|---|---|---|
| *Compilation/Synthesis:*<br>Automates exploration<br>and insertion of<br>implementation details<br>for lower level. | System<br>specification | System<br>synthesis | Hw/Sw/<br>OS | Model simulators/<br>checkers |
| *Libraries/IP:* Incorporates<br>pre-designed<br>implementation from<br>lower abstraction level<br>into higher level. | Behavioral<br>specification | Behavior<br>synthesis | Cores | Hw-Sw<br>cosimulators |
| *Test/Verification:* Ensures | RT<br>specification | RT<br>synthesis | RT<br>components | HDL simulators |
| correct functionality at<br>each level, thus reducing<br>costly iterations between<br>levels. | Logic<br>specification | Logic<br>synthesis | Gates/<br>Cells | Gate<br>simulators |

To final implementation

Figure 1.11: Ideal top-down design process, and productivity improvers.

There are three main approaches to improving the design process for increased productivity, which we label as compilation/synthesis, libraries/IP, and test/verification. Several other approaches also exist. We will discuss all of these approaches. Each approach can be applied at any of the four abstraction levels.

## Compilation/Synthesis

Compilation/synthesis lets a designer specify desired functionality in an abstract manner and automatically generates lower-level implementation details. Describing a system at high abstraction levels can improve productivity by reducing the amount of details, often by an order of magnitude, that a designer must specify.

A logic synthesis tool converts Boolean expressions into a connection of logic gates, called a netlist. A register-transfer (RT) synthesis tool converts finite-state machines and register transfers into a datapath of RT components and a controller of Boolean equations. A behavioral synthesis tool converts a sequential program into finite-state machines and register transfers. Likewise, a software compiler converts a sequential program to assembly code, which is essentially register-transfer code. Finally, a system synthesis tool converts an abstract system specification into a set of sequential programs on general- and single-purpose processors.

## Libraries/IP

Libraries involve reuse of preexisting implementations. Using libraries of existing implementations can improve productivity if the time it takes to find, acquire, integrate, and test a library item is less than that of designing the item oneself.

A logic-level library may consist of layouts for gates and cells. An RT-level library may consist of layouts for RT components, like registers, multiplexors, decoders, and functional units. A behavioral-level library may consist of commonly used components, such as compression components, bus interfaces, display controllers, and even general-purpose processors. The advent of system-level integration has caused a great change in this level of library. Rather than these components being ICs, they now must also be available in a form that we can implement on just one portion of an IC. Such components are called *cores*. This change from behavioral-level libraries of ICs to libraries of cores has prompted the use of the term *intellectual property* (IP), to emphasize the fact that cores exist in an intellectual form that must be protected from copying. Finally, a system-level library might consist of complete systems solving particular problems, such as an interconnection of processors with accompanying operating systems and programs to implement an interface to the Internet over an Ethernet network.

## Test/Verification

Test/verification involves ensuring that functionality is correct. Such assurance can prevent time-consuming debugging at low abstraction levels and iterating back to high abstraction levels.

Simulation is the most common method of testing for correct functionality, although more formal verification techniques are growing in popularity. At the logic level, gate-level simulators provide output signal timing waveforms given input signal waveforms. Likewise, general-purpose processor simulators execute machine code. At the RT-level, hardware description language (HDL) simulators execute RT-level descriptions and provide output waveforms given input waveforms. At the behavioral level, HDL simulators simulate sequential programs, and cosimulators connect HDL and general-purpose processor simulators to enable hardware/software coverification. At the system level, a model simulator simulates the initial system specification using an abstract computation model, independent of any processor technology, to verify correctness and completeness of the specification. Model checkers can also verify certain properties of the specification, such as ensuring that certain simultaneous conditions never occur or that the system does not deadlock.

## More Productivity Improvers

There are numerous additional approaches to improving designer productivity. Standards focus on developing well-defined methods for specification, synthesis, and libraries. Such standards can reduce the problems that arise when a designer uses multiple tools, or retrieves or provides design information from or to other designers. Common standards include language standards, synthesis standards, and library standards.

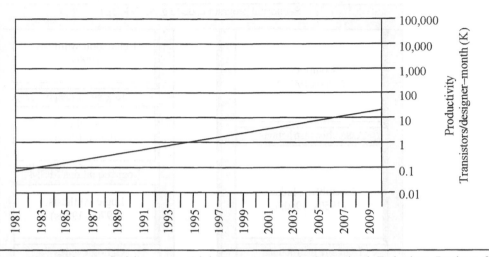

Figure 1.12: Design productivity exponential increase. Source: The International Technology Roadmap for Semiconductors.

Languages focus on capturing desired functionality with minimum designer effort. For example, the sequential programming language of C is giving way to the object-oriented language of C++, which in turn has given some ground to Java. As another example, state-machine languages permit direct capture of functionality as a set of states and transitions, which can then be translated to other languages like C.

Frameworks provide a software environment for the application of numerous tools throughout the design process and management of versions of implementations. For example, a framework might generate the UNIX directories needed for various simulators and synthesis tools, supporting application of those tools through menu selections in a single graphical user interface.

### Trends

The combination of compilation/synthesis, libraries/IP, test/verification, standards, languages, and frameworks has improved designer productivity over the past several decades, as shown in Figure 1.12. Productivity is measured as the number of transistors that one designer can produce in one month. As the figure shows, the growth has been impressive. A designer in 1981 could produce only about 100 transistors per month, whereas in 2002 a designer should be able to produce about 5,000 transistors per month.

## 1.6 Trade-offs

Perhaps the key embedded system design challenge is the simultaneous optimization of competing design metrics. To address this challenge, the designer trades off among the

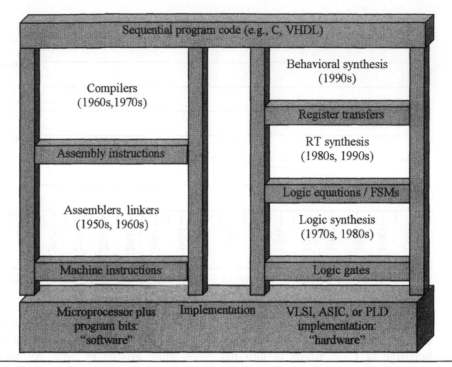

Figure 1.13: The co-design ladder: recent maturation of synthesis enables a unified view of hardware and software.

advantages and disadvantages of the various available processor technologies and IC technologies. To optimize a system, the designer must therefore be familiar with and comfortable with the various technologies — the designer must be a "renaissance engineer," in the words of some. In the past and to a large extent in the present, however, most designers had expertise with either general-purpose processors or with single-purpose processors but not both — they were either software designers or hardware designers. Because of this separation of design expertise, systems had to be separated into the software and hardware subsystems very early in the design process, separately designed, and then integrated near the end of the process. However, such early and permanent separation clearly doesn't allow for the best optimization of design metrics. Instead, being able to move functions between hardware and software, at any stage of the design process, provides for better optimization.

The relatively recent maturation of RT and behavioral synthesis tools has enabled a unified view of the design process for hardware and software. In the past, the design processes were radically different — software designers wrote sequential programs, while hardware designers connected components. But today, synthesis tools have changed the hardware designer's task essentially into one of writing sequential programs, albeit with some knowledge of how the hardware will be synthesized from such programs. We can think of abstraction levels as being the rungs of a ladder, and compilation and synthesis as enabling us to step up the ladder and hence enabling designers to focus their design efforts at higher levels

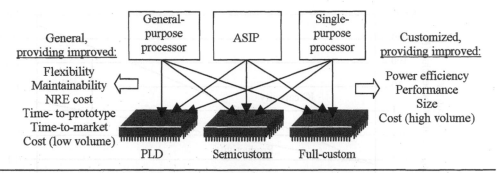

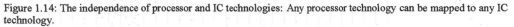

Figure 1.14: The independence of processor and IC technologies: Any processor technology can be mapped to any IC technology.

of abstraction, as illustrated in Figure 1.13. Thus, the starting point for either hardware or software is sequential programs, enhancing the view that system functionality can be implemented in hardware, software, or some combination thereof, leading to the following important point:

> *The choice of hardware versus software for a particular function is simply a trade-off among various design metrics, like performance, power, size, NRE cost, and especially flexibility; there is no fundamental difference between what hardware or software can implement.*

*Hardware/software codesign* is the field that emphasizes a unified view of hardware and software, and develops synthesis tools and simulators that enable the co-development of systems using both hardware and software.

In general, we can view the basic design trade-off as general versus customized implementation, with respect to either processor technology or IC technology, as illustrated in Figure 1.14. The more general, programmable technologies on the left of the figure provide greater flexibility (a design can be reprogrammed relatively easily), reduced NRE cost (designing using those technologies is generally cheaper), faster time-to-prototype and time-to-market (since designing takes less time), and lower cost in low volumes (since the IC manufacturer distributes its IC NRE cost over large quantities of ICs). On the other hand, more customized technologies provide for better power efficiency, faster performance, reduced size, and lower cost in high volumes.

Recall that each of the three processor technologies can be implemented in any of the three IC technologies. For example, a general-purpose processor can be implemented on a PLD, semicustom, or full-custom IC. In fact, a company marketing a product, such as a set-top box or even a general-purpose processor, might first market a semicustom implementation to reach the market early, and then later introduce a full-custom implementation. They might also first map the processor to an older but more reliable technology, like 0.2 micron, and then later map it to a newer technology, like 0.08 micron. These two evolutions of mappings to a large extent explain why a general-purpose processor's

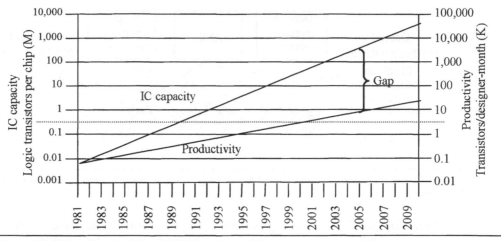

Figure 1.15: The growing "design productivity gap."

clock speed improves on the market over time. Likewise, a designer of an embedded system may use PLDs for prototyping a product, and even for the first few hundred instances of the product to speed its time-to-market, switching to ASICs for larger-scale production.

Furthermore, we often implement multiple processors of different types on the same IC. Figure 1.2 was an example of just such a situation — the digital camera included a microcontroller plus numerous single-purpose processors on the same IC. A single chip with multiple processors is often referred to as a *system-on-a-chip*. In fact, we can even implement more than one IC technology on a single IC — a portion of the IC may be custom, another portion semicustom, and yet another portion programmable logic. The need for designers comfortable with the variety of processor and IC technologies thus becomes evident.

## Design Productivity Gap

While designer productivity has grown at an impressive rate over the past decades, the rate of improvement has not kept pace with chip capacity growth. Figure 1.15 shows the productivity growth plot superimposed on the chip capacity growth plot, illustrating the growing design productivity gap. For example, in 1981, a leading-edge chip required about 100 designer-months to design, since 100 designer-months * 100 transistors/designer-month = 10,000 transistors. However, in 2002, a leading-edge chip would require about 30,000 designer months, since 30,000 designer-months * 5,000 transistors/designer-month = 150,000,000 transistors. So the design productivity gap has resulted in an increase from 100 to 30,000 designer-months to build a leading-edge chip. Assuming a designer costs $10,000 per month, the cost of building a leading-edge chip has risen from $1,000,000 in 1981 to an incredible $300,000,000 in 2002. Few products can justify such large investment in a chip. Thus, most designs do not even come close to using potential chip capacity.

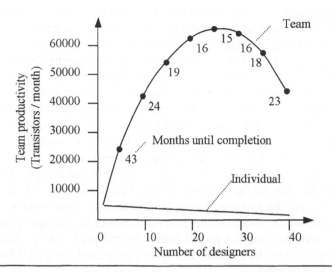

Figure 1.16: The "mythical man-month": Adding designers can decrease individual productivity and at some point can actually delay the project completion time.

The situation is even worse than stated before, because the discussion assumes that designer productivity is independent of project team size, whereas in reality adding more designers to a project team can actually decrease productivity. Suppose 10 designers work together on a project, and each produces 5,000 transistors/month, so that their combined output is 10 * 5,000 = 50,000 transistors/month. Would 100 designers on a project then produce 100 * 5,000 = 500,000 transistors/month? Probably not. The complexity of having 100 designers work together is far greater than having 10 designers work together. Even calling a meeting of 100 designers is a fairly complex task, whereas a 10-designer meeting is quite straightforward. Furthermore, a 100-designer team would likely be decomposed into groups, each group having a group leader that meets with other group leaders and reports back to his or her group, thus introducing extra layers of communication and hence more likelihood of misunderstandings and time-consuming mistakes.

This decrease in productivity as designers are added to a project was reported by Frederick Brooks in his classic 1975 book entitled *The Mythical Man-Month*. His book focused on writing software, but the same principle applies to designing hardware. The decrease in productivity due to team-size complexity can at some point actually lengthen the time to complete a project. For example, consider a hypothetical 1,000,000 transistor project, in which a designer working alone can produce 5,000 transistors per month, and each additional designer added to the project results in a productivity decrease of 100 transistors per designer, due to the added complexities of team communication and management. So a designer can complete the project in 1,000,000 / 5,000 = 200 months. 10 designers can produce 4,100 transistors per month each, meaning 10 * 4,100 = 41,000 transistors per month total, requiring 1,000,000 / 41,000 = 24.3 months to complete the project. Figure 1.16 plots individual designer productivity as designers are added to the project. The figure also plots team productivity, computed simply as the number of designers multiplied by their individual productivity. Project completion times for different team sizes, computed as 1,000,000 transistors divided by team-transistors/month, are also shown. A 25-designer team can produce 25 * 2,600 = 65,000 transistors per month, requiring 1,000,000/65,000 = 15.3 months to complete the project. However, a 26-designer team also produces 26 * 2,500 = 65,000 transistors per month, so adding a $26^{th}$ designer doesn't help. Furthermore, a 27-designer team produces only 27 * 2,400 = 64,800 transistors per month, thus actually delaying the project completion time to 15.4 months. Adding more designers beyond 26 only worsens the project completion time. Hence, man-months are in a sense mythical: We cannot always add designers to a project to decrease the project completion time.

Therefore, the growing gap between IC capacity and designer productivity in Figure 1.15 is even worse than the figure shows. Designer productivity decreases as we add designers to a project, making the gap even larger. Furthermore, at some point we simply cannot decrease project completion time no matter how much money we can spend on designers, since adding designers will decrease the project team's overall productivity. And therefore, leading-edge chips cannot always be designed in a given time period, no matter how much money we have to spend on designers.

Thus, a pressing need exists for new design technologies that will shrink the design gap. One partial solution proposed by many people is to educate designers not just in one subarea of embedded systems, like hardware design or software design, but instead to educate them to be comfortable with both hardware and software design. This book is intended to contribute to this solution.

## 1.7   Summary and Book Outline

The number of embedded systems is growing every year as electronic devices gain computational elements. Embedded systems possess several common characteristics that differentiate them from desktop systems and pose several challenges to designers. The key challenge is to optimize design metrics, which is particularly difficult since those metrics compete with one another. One particularly difficult design metric to optimize is time-to-market, because embedded systems are growing in complexity at a tremendous rate, and the rate at which productivity improves every year is not keeping up with that growth. This book seeks to help improve productivity by presenting a unified view of software and hardware design. This goal is worked toward by presenting three key technologies for embedded systems design: processor technology, IC technology, and design technology. Processor technology is divided into general-purpose, application-specific, and single-purpose processors. IC technology is divided into custom, semicustom, and programmable logic ICs. Design technology is divided into compilation/synthesis, libraries/IP, and test/verification.

This book focuses on processor technology (both hardware and software), with the last several chapters providing introductions to topics in IC and design technologies.

Chapters 2–7 discuss processor technology. Chapter 2 describes digital design techniques for building custom single-purpose processors. Chapter 3 covers general-purpose processors.

The chapter is mostly a review of the features of such processors; we assume the reader already has familiarity with programming such processors using structured languages. Chapter 4 covers standard single-purpose processors, describing a number of common peripherals used in embedded systems. Chapter 5 describes memories, which are components necessary to store data for processors. Chapter 6 describes buses, components necessary to communicate data among processors and memories, beginning with basic interfacing concepts, and introducing more advanced concepts and describing common buses. Chapter 7 provides an example of using processor technology to build an embedded system, a digital camera, illustrating the trade-offs of several different implementations.

Chapter 8 introduces some advanced techniques for programming embedded systems, including state machine models, and concurrent process models. It also introduces real-time systems. Chapter 9 discusses the very common class of embedded systems known as control systems, and introduces some design techniques used for such systems.

Chapter 10 describes the three main IC technologies with which we can implement the processor-based designs we learn to create in the earlier chapters. Finally, Chapter 11 summarizes key tools and advances in design technology and emphasizes the need for a new breed of engineers for embedded systems proficient with both software and hardware design.

## 1.8 References and Further Reading

- Brooks Jr., F.P., *The Mythical Man-Month*, anniversary edition. Reading, MA: Addison-Wesley, 1995. Original edition published in 1975.
- *EE Times*, Oct 11, 1999. Embedded Systems section.
- Midyear forecast – CEO Perspectives, *EE Times*, May 27, 1998, Issue 1009.
- Semiconductor Industry Association. *International Technology Roadmap for Semiconductors: 1999 edition*. Austin, TX: International SEMATECH, 1999.
- Debardelaben, J., Madisetti, V.K., and Gadient, A.J., Incorporating Cost Modeling into Embedded System Design, *IEEE Design and Test of Computers*, July 1997, pp. 24-35. Includes discussion of revenue model.

## 1.9 Exercises

1.1 What is an embedded system? Why is it so hard to define?

1.2 List and define the three main characteristics of embedded systems that distinguish such systems from other computing systems.

1.3 What is a design metric?

1.4 List a pair of design metrics that may compete with one another, providing an intuitive explanation of the reason behind the competition.

1.5 What is a "market window" and why is it so important for products to reach the market early in this window?

1.6   Using the revenue model of Figure 1.4(b), derive the percentage revenue loss equation for any rise angle, rather than just for 45 degrees (*Hint*: you should get the same equation).

1.7   Using the revenue model of Figure 1.4(b), compute the percentage revenue loss if $D = 5$ and $W = 10$. If the company whose product entered the market on time earned a total revenue of $25 million, how much revenue did the company that entered the market 5 months late lose?

1.8   What is NRE cost?

1.9   The design of a particular disk drive has an NRE cost of $100,000 and a unit cost of $20. How much will we have to add to the cost of each product to cover our NRE cost, assuming we sell: (a) 100 units, and (b) 10,000 units?

1.10  Create a graph with the $x$-axis the number of units and the $y$-axis the product cost. Plot the per-product cost function for an NRE of $50,000 and a unit cost of $5.

1.11  For a particular product, you determine the NRE cost and unit cost to be the following for the three listed IC technologies: FPGA: ($10,000, $50); ASIC: ($50,000, $10); VLSI: ($200,000, $5). Determine precise volumes for which each technology yields the lowest total cost.

1.12  Give an example of a recent consumer product whose prime market window was only about one year.

1.13  Create an equation for total revenue that combines time-to-market and NRE/unit cost considerations. Use the revenue model of Figure 1.4(b). Assume a 100-month product lifetime, with peak revenue of $100,000 month. Compare use of a general-purpose processor having an NRE cost of $5,000, a unit cost of $30, and a time-to-market of 12 months (so only 88 months of the product's lifetime remain), with use of a single-purpose processor having an NRE cost of $20,000, a unit cost of $10, and a time-to-market of 24 months. Assume the amount added to each unit for profit is $5.

1.14  Using a spreadsheet, develop a tool that allows us to plug in any numbers for problem 1.13 and generates a revenue comparison of the two technologies.

1.15  List and define the three main processor technologies. What are the benefits of using each of the three different processor technologies?

1.16  List and define the three main IC technologies. What are the benefits of using each of the three different IC technologies?

1.17  List and define the three main design technologies. How are each of the three different design technologies helpful to designers?

1.18  Create a 3*3 grid with the three processor technologies along the $x$-axis, and the three IC technologies along the $y$-axis. For each axis, put the most programmable form closest to the origin, and the most customized form at the end of the axis. Explain features and possible occasions for using each of the combinations of the two technologies.

1.19  Redraw Figure 1.9 to show the transistors per IC from 1990 to 2000 on a linear, not logarithmic, scale. Draw a square representing a 1990 IC and another representing a 2000 IC, with correct relative proportions.

1.20  Provide a definition of Moore's law.

1.21 Compute the annual growth rate of (a) IC capacity, and (b) designer productivity.

1.22 If Moore's law continues to hold, predict the approximate number of transistors per leading edge IC in (a) 2030, (b) 2050.

1.23 Explain why single-purpose processors (hardware) and general-purpose processors are essentially the same, and then describe how they differ in terms of design metrics.

1.24 What is a "renaissance engineer," and why is it so important in the current market?

1.25 What is the design gap?

1.26 Compute the rate at which the design productivity gap is growing per year. What is the implication of this growing gap?

1.27 Define what is meant by the "mythical man-month."

1.28 Assume a designer's productivity when working alone on a project is 5,000 transistors per month. Assume that each additional designer reduces productivity by 5%. (And keep in mind this is an extremely simplified model of designer productivity!) (a) Plot team monthly productivity versus team size for team sizes ranging from 1 to 40 designers. (b) Plot on the same graph the project completion time versus team size for projects of sizes 100,000 and 1,000,000 transistors. (c) Provide the "optimal" number of designers for each of the two projects, indicating the number of months required in each case.

# CHAPTER 2: *Custom Single-Purpose Processors: Hardware*

## 2.1    Introduction

A *processor* is a digital circuit designed to perform computation tasks. A processor consists of a datapath capable of storing and manipulating data and a controller capable of moving data through the datapath. A general-purpose processor is designed such that it can carry out a wide variety of computation tasks, which are described by a set of programmer-provided instructions. In contrast, a single-purpose processor is designed specifically to carry out a particular computation task. While some tasks are so common that we can purchase standard single-purpose processors to implement those tasks, others are unique to a particular embedded system. Such custom tasks may be best implemented using custom single-purpose processors that we design ourselves.

An embedded system designer may obtain several benefits by choosing to use a custom single-purpose processor rather than a general-purpose processor to implement a computation task.

First, performance may be faster, due to fewer clock cycles resulting from a customized datapath, and due to shorter clock cycles resulting from simpler functional units, fewer multiplexors, or simpler controller logic. Second, size may be smaller, due to a simpler

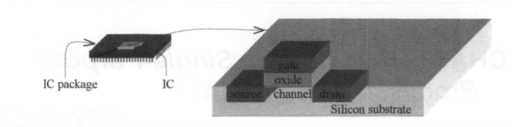

Figure 2.1: A simplified view of a CMOS transistor on silicon.

datapath and no program memory. Third, power consumption may be less, due to more efficient computation.

However, cost could be higher because of high NRE costs. Since we may not be able to afford to invest as much NRE cost as can designers of a mass-produced general-purpose processor, performance and size could actually be worse. Time-to-market may be longer, and flexibility reduced, compared to general-purpose processors.

In this chapter, we describe basic techniques for designing custom processors. We start with a review of combinational and sequential design, and we describe methods for converting programs to custom single-purpose processors.

## 2.2 Combinational Logic

### Transistors and Logic Gates

A transistor is the basic electrical component in digital systems. Combinations of transistors form more abstract components called logic gates, which designers use when building digital systems. Thus, we begin with a short description of transistors before discussing logic design.

A transistor acts as a simple on/off switch. One type of transistor, complementary metal oxide semiconductor (CMOS), is shown in Figure 2.1. Figure 2.2(a) shows the schematic of a transistor. The *gate*, not to be confused with logic gate, controls whether or not current flows from the *source* to the *drain*. We can apply either low or high voltage levels to the gate. The high level may be, for example, +3 or +5 volts, which we'll refer to as logic 1. The low voltage is typically ground, drawn as several horizontal lines of decreasing width, which we'll refer to as logic 0. When logic 1 is applied to the gate, the transistor conducts and so current flows. When logic 0 is applied to the gate, the transistor does not conduct. We can also build a transistor with the opposite functionality, illustrated in Figure 2.2(b). When logic 0 is applied to the gate, the transistor conducts. When logic 1 is applied, the transistor does not conduct.

Given these two basic transistors, we can easily build a circuit whose output inverts its gate input, as shown in Figure 2.2(c). When the input $x$ is logic 0, the top transistor conducts and the bottom transistor does not conduct, so logic 1 appears at the output $F$. We can also easily build a circuit whose output is logic 1 when at least one of its inputs is logic 0, as shown in Figure 2.2(d). When at least one of the inputs $x$ and $y$ is logic 0, then at least one of

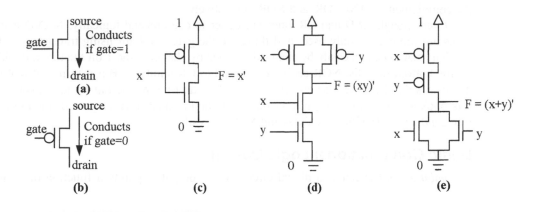

Figure 2.2: CMOS transistor implementations of some basic logic gates: (a) nMOS transistor, (b) pMOS transistor, (c) inverter, (d) NAND gate, (e) NOR gate.

the top transistors conducts and the bottom transistors do not conduct, so logic 1 appears at $F$. If both inputs are logic 1, then neither of the top transistors conducts, but both of the bottom transistors do, so logic 0 appears at $F$. Likewise, we can easily build a circuit whose output is logic 1 when both of its inputs are logic 0, as illustrated in Figure 2.2(e). The three circuits shown implement three basic logic gates: an inverter, a NAND gate, and a NOR gate.

Digital system designers usually work at the abstraction level of logic gates rather than transistors. Figure 2.3 describes eight basic logic gates. Each gate is represented symbolically, with a Boolean equation, and with a truth table. The truth table has inputs on the left and an output on the right. The AND gate outputs 1 if and only if both inputs are 1. The OR gate outputs 1 if and only if at least one of the inputs is 1. The XOR (exclusive-OR) gate outputs 1

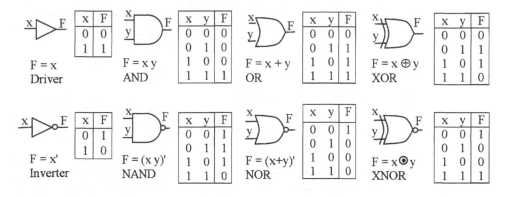

Figure 2.3: Basic logic gates.

if and only if exactly one of its two inputs is 1. The NAND, NOR, and XNOR gates output the complement of AND, OR, and XOR, respectively.

Even though AND and OR gates are easier to comprehend logically, NAND and NOR gates are more commonly used, and those are the gates we built using transistors in Figure 2.2. The NAND could easily be changed to AND by changing the 1 on the top to 0 and the 0 on the bottom to 1; the NOR could be changed to OR similarly. But it turns out that pMOS transistors don't conduct 0s very well, though they do fine conducting 1s, for reasons beyond this book's scope. Likewise, nMOS transistors don't conduct 1s very well, though they do fine conducting 0s. Hence, NANDs and NORs prevail.

## Basic Combinational Logic Design

A *combinational* circuit is a digital circuit whose output is purely a function of its present

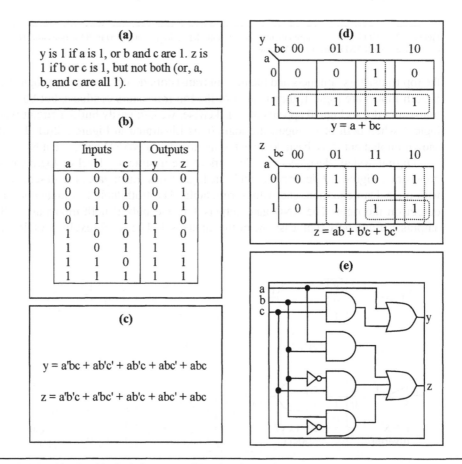

Figure 2.4: Combinational logic design.: (a) problem description, (b) truth table, (c) output equations, (d) minimized output equations, (e) final circuit.

inputs. Such a circuit has no memory of past inputs. We can use a simple technique to design a combinational circuit from our basic logic gates, as illustrated in Figure 2.4. We start with a problem description, which describes the outputs in terms of the inputs, as in Figure 2.4(a). We translate that description to a truth table, with all possible combinations of input values on the left and desired output values for each combination on the right, as in Figure 2.4(b). For each output column, we can derive an output equation, with one equation term per row, as in Figure 2.4(c). We can then translate these equations to a circuit diagram. However, we usually want to minimize the logic gates in the circuit. We can minimize the output equations by algebraically manipulating the equations. Alternatively, we can use Karnaugh maps, as shown in Figure 2.4(d). Once we've obtained the desired output equations, we can draw the circuit diagram, as shown in Figure 2.4(e).

## RT-Level Combinational Components

Although we can design all combinational circuits in this manner, large circuits would be very complex to design. For example, a circuit with 16 inputs would have $2^{16}$, or 64K, rows in its truth table. One way to reduce the complexity is to use combinational components that are more powerful than logic gates. Figure 2.5 shows several such combinational components, often called *register–transfer*, or RT, level components. We now describe each briefly.

A *multiplexor*, sometimes called a *selector*, allows only one of its data inputs $Im$ to pass through to the output $O$. Thus, a multiplexor acts much like a railroad switch, allowing only one of multiple input tracks to connect to a single output track. If there are $m$ data inputs, then there are $\log_2(m)$ select lines $S$. We call this an $m$-by-1 multiplexor, meaning $m$ data inputs, and 1 data output. The binary value of $S$ determines which data input passes through; 00...00 means $I0$ passes through, 00...01 means $I1$ passes through, 00...10 means $I2$ passes through, and so on. For example, an $8\times1$ multiplexor has eight data inputs and thus three select lines. If those three select lines have values of 110, then $I6$ will pass through to the output. So if $I6$ were 1, then the output would be 1; if $I6$ were 0, then the output would be 0. We commonly use a more complex device called an $n$-bit multiplexor, in which each data input as well as the output consist of $n$ lines. Suppose the previous example used a 4-bit $8\times1$ multiplexor. Thus, if $I6$ were 1110, then the output would be 1110. Note that $n$ is independent of the number of select lines.

Another combinational component is a decoder. A *decoder* converts its binary input $I$ into a one-hot output $O$. "One-hot" means that exactly one of the output lines can be 1 at a given time. Thus, if there are $n$ outputs, then there must be $\log_2(n)$ inputs. We call this a $\log_2(n)\times n$ decoder. For example, a $3\times8$ decoder has three inputs and eight outputs. If the input were 000, then the output $O0$ would be 1 and all other outputs would be 0. If the input were 001, then the output $O1$ would be 1, and so on. A common feature on a decoder is an extra input called *enable*. When enable is 0, all outputs are 0. When enable is 1, the decoder functions as before.

An *adder* adds two $n$-bit binary inputs $A$ and $B$, generating an $n$-bit output sum along with an output carry. For example, a 4-bit adder would have a 4-bit $A$ input, a 4-bit $B$ input, a 4-bit *sum* output, and a 1-bit *carry* output. If $A$ were 1010 and $B$ were 1001, then *sum* would be 0011 and *carry* would be 1. An adder often comes with a carry input also, so that such adders can be cascaded to create larger adders.

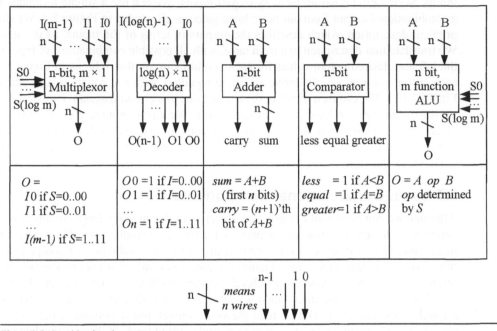

Figure 2.5: Combinational components.

A *comparator* compares two $n$-bit binary inputs $A$ and $B$, generating outputs that indicate whether $A$ is less than, equal to, or greater than $B$. If $A$ were 1010 and $B$ were 1001, then *less* would be 0, *equal* would be 0, and *greater* would be 1.

An *arithmetic-logic unit* (ALU) can perform a variety of arithmetic and logic functions on its $n$-bit inputs $A$ and $B$. The select lines $S$ choose the current function; if there are $m$ possible functions, then there must be at least $\log_2(m)$ select lines. Common functions include addition, subtraction, AND, and OR.

Another common RT-level component, not shown in the figure, is a shifter. An $n$-bit input $I$ can be shifted left or right and then output to an output $O$. For example, a 4-bit shifter with an input 1010 would output 0101 when shifting right one position. Shifters usually come with an additional input indicating what value should be shifted in and an additional output indicating the value of the bit being shifted out.

## 2.3   Sequential Logic

### Flip-Flops

A *sequential circuit* is a digital circuit whose outputs are a function of the present as well as previous input values. In other words, sequential logic possesses memory. One of the most

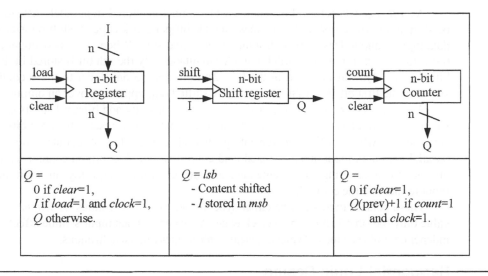

Figure 2.6: Sequential components.

basic sequential circuits is a *flip-flop*. A flip-flop stores a single bit. The simplest type is the *D* flip-flop. It has two inputs: *D* and *clock*. When *clock* is 1, the value of *D* is stored in the flip-flop, and that value appears at the output *Q*. When *clock* is 0, the value of *D* is ignored, and the output *Q* continues to reflect the stored value. Another type of flip-flop is the *SR* flip-flop, which has three inputs: *S*, *R*, and *clock*. When *clock* is 0, the previously stored bit is maintained and appears at output *Q*. When *clock* is 1, the inputs *S* and *R* are examined. If *S* is 1, a 1 is stored. If *R* is 1, a 0 is stored. If both are 0, there's no change. If both are 1, behavior is undefined. Thus, *S* stands for set to 1, and *R* for reset to 0. Another flip-flop type is a *JK* flip-flop, which is the same as an *SR* flip-flop except that when both *J* and *K* are 1, the stored bit toggles from 1 to 0 or 0 to 1. To prevent unexpected behavior from signal glitches, flip-flops are typically designed to be *edge-triggered*, meaning they examine their non-clock inputs when *clock* is rising from 0 to 1, or alternatively when *clock* is falling from 1 to 0.

## RT-Level Sequential Components

Just as we used more abstract combinational components to implement complex combinational systems, we also use more abstract sequential components for complex sequential systems. Figure 2.6 illustrates several sequential components, which we describe.

A *register* stores *n* bits from its *n*-bit data input *I*, with those stored bits appearing at its output *Q*. A register usually has at least two control inputs, *clock* and *load*. For a rising-edge-triggered register, the inputs *I* are only stored when *load* is 1 and *clock* is rising from 0 to 1. The clock input is usually drawn as a small triangle, as shown in the figure. Another common register control input is *clear*, which resets all bits to 0, regardless of the value of *I*. Because all *n* bits of the register can be stored in parallel, we often refer to this type of register as a *parallel-load* register, to distinguish it from a shift register.

A *shift register* stores $n$ bits, but these bits cannot be stored in parallel. Instead, they must be shifted into the register serially, meaning one bit per clock edge. A shift register has a 1-bit data input $I$, and at least two control inputs *clock* and *shift*. When *clock* is rising and *shift* is 1, the value of $I$ is stored in the $n$th bit, while simultaneously the $n$th bit is stored in the $(n-1)$th bit, the $(n-1)$th bit is stored in the $(n-2)$th bit, and so on, down to the second bit being stored in the first bit. The first bit is typically shifted out, appearing over an output $Q$.

A *counter* is a register that can also increment, meaning add binary 1, to its stored binary value. In its simplest form, a counter has a clear input, which resets all stored bits to 0, and a count input, which enables incrementing on each clock edge. A counter often also has a parallel load data input and associated load control signal. A common counter feature is both up and down counting or incrementing and decrementing, requiring an additional control input to indicate the count direction.

These control inputs can be either synchronous or asynchronous. A *synchronous* input's value only has an effect during a clock edge. An asynchronous input's value affects the circuit independent of the clock. Typically, clear control lines are asynchronous.

## Sequential Logic Design

Sequential logic design can be achieved using a straightforward technique, whose steps are illustrated in Figure 2.7. We again start with a problem description, shown in Figure 2.7(a). We translate this description to a state diagram, also called a finite state machine (FSM), as in Figure 2.7(b). We describe FSMs further in a later chapter. Briefly, each state represents the current "mode" of the circuit, serving as the circuit's memory of past input values. The desired output values are listed next to each state. The input conditions that cause a transition from one state to another are shown next to each arc. Each arc condition is implicitly "ANDed" with a rising (or falling) clock edge. In other words, all inputs are synchronous. All inputs and outputs must be Boolean, and all operations must be Boolean operations. FSMs can also describe asynchronous systems, but we do not cover such systems in this book, since they are not very common.

We will implement this FSM using a register to store the current state, and combinational logic to generate the output values and the next state, as shown in Figure 2.7(c). We assign to each state a unique binary value, and we then create a truth table for the combinational logic, as in Figure 2.7(d). The inputs for the combinational logic are the state bits coming from the state register, and the external inputs, so we list all combinations of these inputs on the left side of the table. The outputs for the combinational logic are the state bits to be loaded into the register on the next clock edge (the next state), and the external output values, so we list desired values of these outputs for each input combination on the right side of the table. Because we used a state diagram for which outputs were a function of the current state only, and not of the inputs, we list an external output value only for each possible state, ignoring the external input values. Now that we have a truth table, we proceed with combinational logic design as described earlier, by generating minimized output equations as shown in Figure 2.7(e), and then drawing the combinational logic circuit as in Figure 2.7(f). As you can see, sequential logic design is very much like combinational logic design, as long as we draw the state table in such a way that it can be used as a combinational logic truth table also.

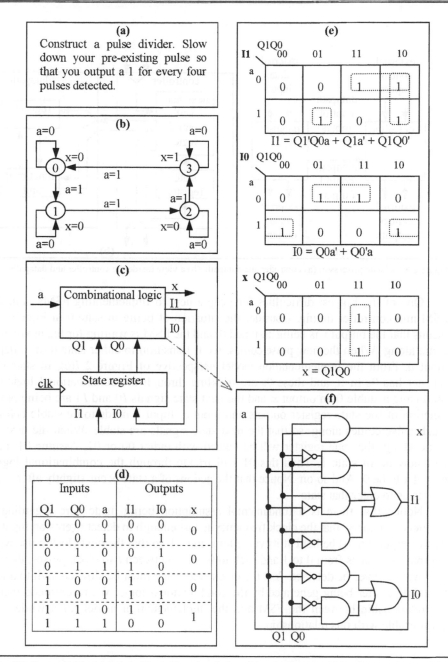

**(a)**
Construct a pulse divider. Slow down your pre-existing pulse so that you output a 1 for every four pulses detected.

**(b)**

**(c)**

**(d)**

| Inputs | | | Outputs | | |
|---|---|---|---|---|---|
| Q1 | Q0 | a | I1 | I0 | x |
| 0 | 0 | 0 | 0 | 0 | |
| 0 | 0 | 1 | 0 | 1 | 0 |
| 0 | 1 | 0 | 0 | 1 | |
| 0 | 1 | 1 | 1 | 0 | 0 |
| 1 | 0 | 0 | 1 | 0 | |
| 1 | 0 | 1 | 1 | 1 | 0 |
| 1 | 1 | 0 | 1 | 1 | |
| 1 | 1 | 1 | 0 | 0 | 1 |

**(e)**

I1 = Q1'Q0a + Q1a' + Q1Q0'

I0 = Q0a' + Q0'a

x = Q1Q0

**(f)**

Figure 2.7: Sequential logic design: (a) problem description, (b) state diagram, (c) implementation model, (d) state table (Moore-type), (e) minimized output equations, (f) combinational logic.

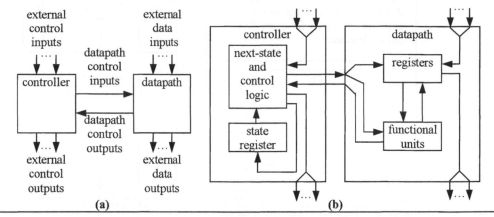

Figure 2.8: A basic processor: (a) controller and datapath, (b) a view inside the controller and datapath.

One of the biggest difficulties for people new to implementing FSMs is understanding FSM and controller timing. Consider the situation of being in state 0 in Figure 2.7(b). This means that the output $x$ is being assigned 0, and the FSM is waiting for the next clock pulse to come along. When the new pulse comes, we'll transition to either state 0 or 1, depending on input $a$. From the implementation model perspective of Figure 2.7(c), in state 0, the state register has 0s in it, and these 0s are trickling through the combinational logic, eventually producing a stable 0 on output $x$, and the next state signals $I0$ and $I1$ are being produced as a function of the state register outputs and input $a$. Input $a$ needs to be stable before the next clock pulse comes along, so that the next state signals are stable. When the next pulse does come along, the state register will be loaded with either 00 or 01. Assume 01, meaning we will now be in state 1. Then this 01 will trickle through the combinational logic, causing output $x$ to be 0. And so on. Notice that the actions of a state occur slightly after a clock pulse causes us to enter that state.

Notice that there is a fundamental assumption being made here regarding the clock frequency, namely, that the clock frequency is fast enough to detect events on input $a$. In other words, input $a$ must be held at its value long enough so that the next clock pulse will detect it. If input a switches from 0 to 1 and back to 0, all in between two clock pulses, then the switch to 1 would never be detected. Yet the clock frequency must be slow enough to allow outputs to stabilize after being generated by the combinational logic. We recommend that one study the relationship between the FSM and the implementation model for a while, until one is comfortable with this relationship.

## 2.4 Custom Single-Purpose Processor Design

We now have the knowledge needed to build a basic processor. A basic processor consists of a controller and a datapath, as illustrated in Figure 2.8. The *datapath* stores and manipulates a system's data. Examples of data in an embedded system include binary numbers representing external conditions like temperature or speed, characters to be displayed on a screen, or a digitized photographic image to be stored and compressed. The datapath contains register units, functional units, and connection units like wires and multiplexors. The datapath can be configured to read data from particular registers, feed that data through functional units configured to carry out particular operations like add or shift, and store the operation results back into particular registers. A *controller* carries out such configuration of the datapath. It sets the datapath control inputs, like register load and multiplexor select signals, of the register units, functional units, and connection units to obtain the desired configuration at a particular time. It monitors external control inputs as well as datapath control outputs, known as status signals, coming from functional units, and it sets external control outputs as well.

We can apply the combinational and sequential logic design techniques described earlier to build a controller and a datapath. Therefore, we now describe a technique to convert a computation task into a custom single-purpose processor consisting of a controller and a datapath.

We begin with a sequential program describing the computation task that we wish to implement. Figure 2.9 provides an example task of computing a greatest common divisor (GCD). Figure 2.9(a) shows a black-box diagram of the desired system, having $x\_i$ and $y\_i$ data inputs and a data output $d\_o$. The system's functionality is straightforward: the output should represent the GCD of the inputs. Thus, if the inputs are 12 and 8, the output should be 4. If the inputs are 13 and 5, the output should be 1. Figure 2.9(b) provides a simple program with this functionality. The reader might trace this program's execution on these examples to verify that the program does indeed compute the GCD.

To begin building our single-purpose processor implementing the GCD program, we first convert our program into a complex state diagram, in which states and arcs may include arithmetic expressions, and those expressions may use external inputs and outputs as well as variables. In contrast, our earlier state diagrams included only Boolean expressions, and those expressions could use only external inputs and outputs, not variables. This more complex state diagram is essentially a sequential program in which statements have been scheduled into states. We'll refer to a complex state diagram as a *finite state machine with data* (FSMD).

We can use templates to convert a program to an FSMD, as illustrated in Figure 2.10. First, we classify each statement as an assignment statement, loop statement, or branch (if-then-else or case) statement. For an assignment statement, we create a single state with that statement as its action, and we add an arc from this state to the first state of the next statement, as shown in Figure 2.10(a). For a loop statement, we create a condition state $C$ and a join state $J$, both with no actions, as shown in Figure 2.10(b). We add an arc with the loop's condition from the condition state to the first statement in the loop body. We add a second arc with the complement of the loop's condition from the condition state to the next statement after the loop body. We also add an arc from the join state back to the condition state. For a branch statement, we create a condition state $C$ and a join state $J$, both with no actions, as shown in Figure 2.10(c). We add an arc with the first branch's condition from the condition state to the branch's first statement. We add another arc with the complement of the first branch's condition ANDed with the second branch's condition from the condition state to the branch's

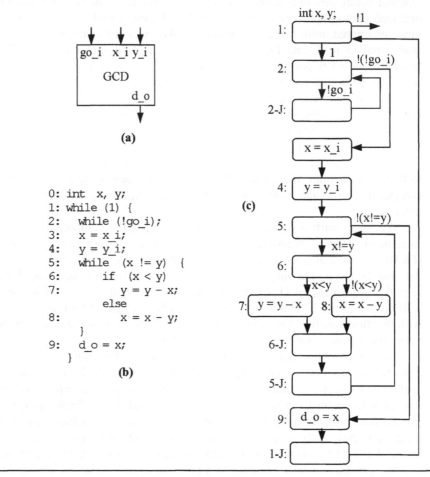

```
0: int  x, y;
1: while (1) {
2:    while (!go_i);
3:    x = x_i;
4:    y = y_i;
5:    while  (x != y)  {
6:        if  (x < y)
7:            y = y - x;
       else
8:            x = x - y;
       }
9:    d_o = x;
   }
```

**(b)**

Figure 2.9: Example program – Greatest Common Divisor (GCD): (a) black-box view, (b) desired functionality, (c) state diagram.

first statement. We repeat this for each branch. Finally, we connect the arc leaving the last statement of each branch to the join state, and we add an arc from this state to the next statement's state.

Using this template approach, we convert our GCD program to the FSMD of Figure 2.9(c). Notice that variables are being assigned in some of the states, such as the action $x = x - y$, which also includes an arithmetic operation. Again, variables and arithmetic operations/conditions are what make FSMDs more powerful than FSMs.

We are now well on our way to designing a custom single-purpose processor that executes the GCD program. Our next step is to divide the functionality into a datapath part

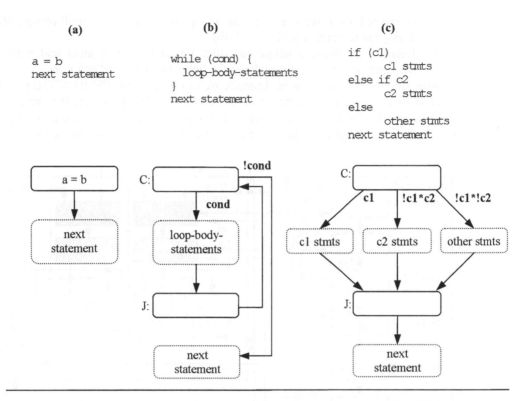

Figure 2.10: Templates for creating a state diagram from program statements: (a) assignment, (b) loop, (c) branch.

and a controller part, as shown in Figure 2.11. The datapath part should consist of an interconnection of combinational and sequential components. The controller part should consist of a pure FSM (i.e., one containing only Boolean actions and conditions.)

We construct the datapath through a four-step process:

1. First, we create a register for any declared variable. In the example, the variables are $x$ and $y$. We treat an output port as an implicit variable, so we create a register $d$ and connect it to the output port. We also draw the input and output ports. Figure 2.11(b) shows these three registers as light-gray rectangles.

2. Second, we create a functional unit for each arithmetic operation in the state diagram. In the example, there are two subtractions, one comparison for less than, and one comparison for inequality, yielding two subtractors and two comparators, shown as white rectangles in Figure 2.11(b).

3. Third, we connect the ports, registers, and functional units. For each write to a variable in the state diagram, we draw a connection from the write's source to the variable's register. A source may be an input port, a functional unit, or another register. For each arithmetic and logical operation, we connect sources to an input of the operation's corresponding functional unit. When more than one source is

connected to a register, we add an appropriately sized multiplexor, shown as dark-gray rectangles in Figure 2.11(b).

4. Finally, we create a unique identifier for each control input and output of the datapath components. Examples in the figure include $x\_sel$ and $x\_neq\_y$.

Now that we have a complete datapath, we can modify our FSMD of Figure 2.9(c) into the FSM of Figure 2.11(a) representing our controller. The FSM has the same states and transitions as the FSMD. However, we replace complex actions and conditions by Boolean ones, making use of our datapath. We replace every variable write by actions that set the

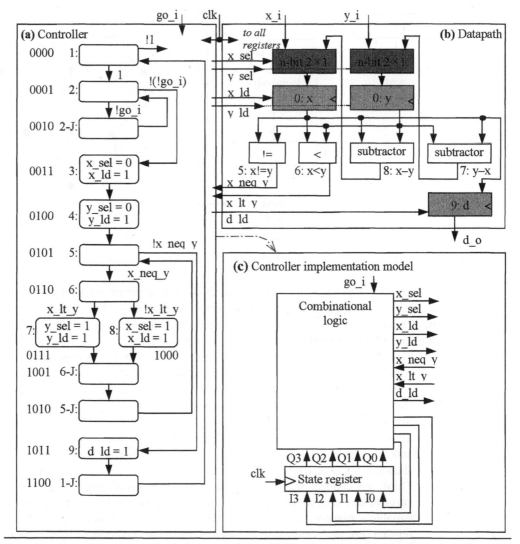

Figure 2.11: Example program — Greatest Common Divisor (GCD): (a) controller, (b) datapath, (c) controller model.

State table

| Inputs | | | | | | | Outputs | | | | | | | | |
|---|---|---|---|---|---|---|---|---|---|---|---|---|---|---|---|
| Q3 | Q2 | Q1 | Q0 | x_neq_y | x_lt_y | go_i | I3 | I2 | I1 | I0 | x_sel | y_sel | x_ld | y_ld | p_ld |
| 0 | 0 | 0 | 0 | * | * | * | 0 | 0 | 0 | 1 | X | X | 0 | 0 | 0 |
| 0 | 0 | 0 | 1 | * | * | 0 | 0 | 0 | 1 | 0 | X | X | 0 | 0 | 0 |
| 0 | 0 | 0 | 1 | * | * | 1 | 0 | 0 | 1 | 1 | X | X | 0 | 0 | 0 |
| 0 | 0 | 1 | 0 | * | * | * | 0 | 0 | 0 | 1 | X | X | 0 | 0 | 0 |
| 0 | 0 | 1 | 1 | * | * | * | 0 | 1 | 0 | 0 | 0 | X | 1 | 0 | 0 |
| 0 | 1 | 0 | 0 | * | * | * | 0 | 1 | 0 | 1 | X | 0 | 0 | 1 | 0 |
| 0 | 1 | 0 | 1 | 0 | * | * | 1 | 0 | 1 | 1 | X | X | 0 | 0 | 0 |
| 0 | 1 | 0 | 1 | 1 | * | * | 0 | 1 | 1 | 0 | X | X | 0 | 0 | 0 |
| 0 | 1 | 1 | 0 | * | 0 | * | 1 | 0 | 0 | 0 | X | X | 0 | 0 | 0 |
| 0 | 1 | 1 | 0 | * | 1 | * | 0 | 1 | 1 | 1 | X | X | 0 | 0 | 0 |
| 0 | 1 | 1 | 1 | * | * | * | 1 | 0 | 0 | 1 | X | 1 | 0 | 1 | 0 |
| 1 | 0 | 0 | 0 | * | * | * | 1 | 0 | 0 | 1 | 1 | X | 1 | 0 | 0 |
| 1 | 0 | 0 | 1 | * | * | * | 1 | 0 | 1 | 0 | X | X | 0 | 0 | 0 |
| 1 | 0 | 1 | 0 | * | * | * | 0 | 1 | 0 | 1 | X | X | 0 | 0 | 0 |
| 1 | 0 | 1 | 1 | * | * | * | 1 | 1 | 0 | 0 | X | X | 0 | 0 | 1 |
| 1 | 1 | 0 | 0 | * | * | * | 0 | 0 | 0 | 0 | X | X | 0 | 0 | 0 |
| 1 | 1 | 0 | 1 | * | * | * | 0 | 0 | 0 | 0 | X | X | 0 | 0 | 0 |
| 1 | 1 | 1 | 0 | * | * | * | 0 | 0 | 0 | 0 | X | X | 0 | 0 | 0 |
| 1 | 1 | 1 | 1 | * | * | * | 0 | 0 | 0 | 0 | X | X | 0 | 0 | 0 |

\* - indicates all possible combinations of 0s and 1s
X - indicates don't cares

Figure 2.12: State table for the GCD example.

select signals of the multiplexor in front of the variable's register such that the write's source passes through, and we assert the load signal of that register. We replace every logical operation in a condition by the corresponding functional unit control output. In this FSM, any signal not explicitly assigned in a state is implicitly assigned a 0. For example, *x_ld* is implicitly assigned 0 in every state except for 3 and 8, where *x_ld* is explicitly assigned 1.

We can then complete the controller design by implementing the FSM using our sequential design technique described earlier and illustrated in Figure 2.4. Figure 2.11(c) shows the controller implementation model. Figure 2.12 shows a state table for the controller. Note that there are seven inputs to the controller, resulting in 128 rows for the state table. We reduced rows in the state table of the figure by using * for some input combinations, but we can still see that optimizing the design using hand techniques could be quite tedious. For this reason, computer-aided design (CAD) tools that automate both the combinational and the sequential logic design can be very helpful; we'll introduce some CAD tools in the last chapter. CAD tools that automatically generate digital gates from sequential programs, FSMDs, FSMs, or logic equations are known as synthesis tools.

Also, note that we could perform significant amounts of optimization to both the datapath and the controller. For example, we could merge functional units in the datapath, resulting in fewer units at the expense of more multiplexors. We could also merge a number of states into a single state, reducing the size of the controller. Interested readers might examine the textbook by Gajski referred to at the end of this chapter for an introduction to these optimizations.

Note that we could alternatively implement the GCD program by programming a general-purpose processor, thus eliminating the need for this design process, but possibly yielding a slower and bigger design.

Finally, we once again discuss timing, this time for FSMDs rather than FSMs. When in a particular state, all actions internal to that state are considered to be concurrent to one another. Those actions are very different from a sequential program, in which statements are executed in sequence. So, if $x = 0$ before entering a state $A$ in an FSMD, and state $A$'s actions are "$x = x + 1$" and "$y = x$," then $y$ will equal 0, not 1, after exiting state $A$. This concurrency of actions also implies that the order in which we write the actions in the state does not matter.

Furthermore, note that actions consisting of writes to variables do not actually update those variables until the next clock pulse, because those variables are implemented as registers. However, arcs leaving a state may use those variables in their conditions. Thus, an arc leaving state $A$, but using variable $x$, is using the old value of $x$, 0 in our example in the previous paragraph. Assuming an outgoing arc is using the new value assigned in the arc's source state is by far the most common mistake that people make when creating FSMDs. If we wish to assign a value to variable $x$ and then branch to different states depending on that value, then we must insert an additional state before branching.

## 2.5   RT-Level Custom Single-Purpose Processor Design

Section 2.4 described a basic technique for converting a sequential program into a custom single-purpose processor, by first converting the program to an FSMD using the provided templates for each language construct, splitting the FSMD into a simple FSM controlling a datapath, and performing sequential logic design on the FSM. However, in many cases, we prefer not to start with a program, but instead directly with an FSMD. The reason is that often the cycle-by-cycle timing of a system is central to the design, but programming languages don't typically support cycle-by-cycle description. FSMDs, in contrast, make cycle-by-cycle timing explicit.

For example, consider the design problem in Figure 2.13(a). We want one device (the sender) to send an 8-bit number to another device (the receiver). The problem is that while the receiver can receive all 8 bits at once, the sender sends 4 bits at a time; first it sends the low-order 4 bits, then the high-order 4 bits. So we need to design a bridge that will enable to two devices to communicate.

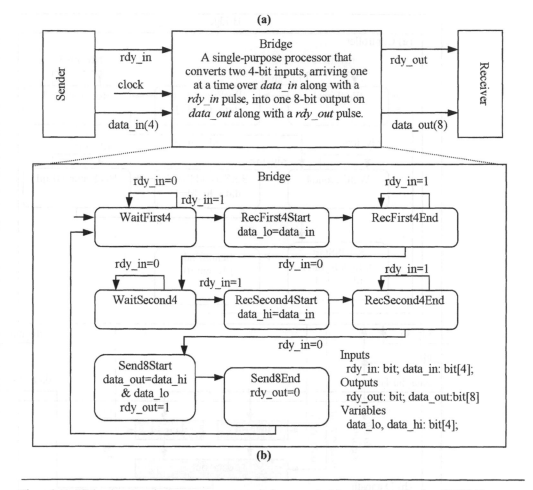

**(a)**

**(b)**

Figure 2.13: RT-level custom single-purpose processor design example: (a) problem specification, (b) FSMD.

Different designers might attack this problem at different levels of abstraction. One designer might start thinking in terms of registers, multiplexors, and flip-flops. Another might try to describe the bridge as a sequential program. But perhaps the most natural level is to describe the bridge as an FSMD, as shown in Figure 2.13(b). We begin by creating a state *WaitFirst4* that waits for the first 4 bits, whose presence on *data_in* will be indicated by a pulse on *rdy_in*. Once the pulse is detected, we transition to a state *RecFirst4Start* that saves the contents of *data_in* in a variable called *data_lo*. We then wait for the pulse on *rdy_in* to end, and then wait for the other 4 bits, indicated by a second pulse on *rdy_in*. We save the contents of *data_in* in a variable called *data_hi*. After waiting for the second pulse on *rdy_in* to end, we write the full 8 bits of data to the output *data_out*, and we pulse *rdy_out*. We

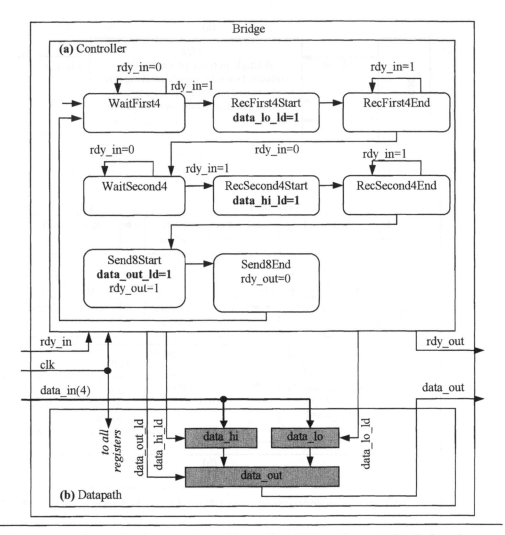

Figure 2.14: RT-level custom single-purpose processor design example continued: (a) controller, (b) datapath.

assume we are building a synchronous circuit, so the bridge has a clock input — in our FSMD, every transition is implicitly ANDed with the clock.

We apply the same methods as before to convert this FSMD to a controller and a datapath implementation, as illustrated in Figure 2.14. We build a datapath, shown in Figure 2.14(b), using the four-step process outlined before. We add registers for *data_hi* and *data_lo*, as well as for the output *data_out*. We don't add any functional units since there are no arithmetic operations. We connect the registers according to the assignments in the FSMD; no multiplexors are necessary. We create unique identifiers for the register control signals. Having completed the datapath, we convert the FSMD into an FSM that uses the datapath, as shown in Figure 2.14(a). This conversion requires only three simple changes, as shown in bold in the figure. Having obtained the FSM, we can convert the FSM into a state-register and combinational logic using the same technique as in Figure 2.7; we omit this conversion here.

This example demonstrates how a problem that consists mostly of waiting for or making changes on signals, rather than consisting mostly of performing computations on data, might most easily be described as an FSMD. The FSMD would be even more appropriate if specific numbers of clock cycles were specified (e.g., the input pulse would be held high exactly two cycles and the output pulse would have to be held high for three cycles). On the other hand, if a problem consists mostly of an algorithm with lots of computations, the detailed timing of which are not especially important, such as the GCD computation in the earlier example, then a program might be the best starting point.

The FSMD level is often referred to as the register-transfer (RT) level, since an FSMD describes in each state which registers should have their data transferred to which other registers, with that data possibly being transformed along the way. The RT-level is probably the most common starting point for custom single-purpose processor design today.

Some custom single-purpose processors do not manipulate much data. These processors consist primarily of a controller, with perhaps no datapath or a trivial one with just a couple registers or counters, as in our bridge example of Figure 2.14. Likewise, other custom single-purpose processors do not exhibit much control. These processors consist primarily of a datapath configured to do one or a few things repeatedly, with no controller or a trivial one with just a couple flip-flops and gates. Nevertheless, we can still think of these circuits as processors.

## 2.6   Optimizing Custom Single-Purpose Processors

You may have noticed in the GCD example of Figure 2.11 that we ignored several opportunities to simplify the resulting design. For example, the FSM had several states that obviously do nothing and could have been removed. Likewise, the datapath has two adders whereas one would have been sufficient. We intentionally did not perform such optimizations so as not to detract from the basic idea that programs can be converted to custom single-purpose processors through a series of straightforward steps. However, when we really design such processors, we will usually also want to optimize them whenever possible. Optimization is the task of making design metric values the best possible. Optimization is an extensive subject, and we do not intend to cover it in depth here. Instead, we point out some simple optimizations that can be applied, and refer the reader to textbooks on the subject.

### Optimizing the Original Program

Let us start with optimizing the initial program, such as the GCD program in Figure 2.9. At this level, we can analyze the number of computations and size of variables that are required by the algorithm. In other words, we can analyze the algorithm in terms of time complexity and space complexity. We can try to develop alternative algorithms that are more efficient. In the GCD example, if we assume we can make use of a modulo operation %, we could write an algorithm that would use fewer steps. In particular, we could use the following algorithm:

```
int  x, y, r;
while (1) {
   while (!go_i);
   if (x_i >= y_i)    {x=x_i; y=y_i;}
   else {x=y_i; y=x_i;} // x must be the larger number
   while  (y != 0)  {
      r = x % y;
      x = y;
      y = r;
   }
   d_o = x;
}
```

Let us compare this second algorithm with the earlier one when computing the GCD of 42 and 8. The earlier algorithm would step through its inner loop with x and y values as follows: (42,8), (34,8), (26,8), (18,8), (10,8), (2,8), (2,6), (2,4), (2,2), thus outputting 2. The second algorithm would step through its inner loop with x and y values as follows: (42,8), (8,2), (2,0), thus outputting 2. The second algorithm is far more efficient in terms of time. Analysis of algorithms and their efficient design is a widely researched area. The choice of algorithm can have perhaps the biggest impact on the efficiency of the designed processor.

## Optimizing the FSMD

Once an algorithm is settled upon, we convert the program describing that algorithm to an FSMD. Use of the template-based method introduced in this chapter will result in a rather inefficient FSMD. In particular, many states in the resulting FSMD could likely be merged into fewer states.

*Scheduling* is the task of assigning operations from the original program to states in an FSMD. The scheduling obtained using the template-based method can be improved. Consider the original FSMD for the GCD, which is redrawn in Figure 2.15(a). State 1 is clearly not necessary since its outgoing transitions have constant values. States 2 and 2-J can be merged into a single state since there are no loop operations in between them. States 3 and 4 can be merged since they perform assignment operations that are independent of one another. States 5 and 6 can be merged. States 6-J and 5-J can be eliminated, with the transitions from states 7 and 8 pointing directly to state 5. Likewise, state 1-J can be eliminated. The resulting reduced FSMD is shown in Figure 2.15(b). We reduced the FSMD from thirteen states to only six states. Be careful, though, to avoid the common mistake of assuming that a variable assigned in a state can have the newly assigned value read on an outgoing arc of that state!

The original FSMD could also have had too few states to be efficient in terms of hardware size. Suppose a particular program statement had the operation $a = b * c * d * e$. Generating a single state for this operation will require us to use three multipliers in our datapath. However, multipliers are expensive, and thus we might instead want to break this

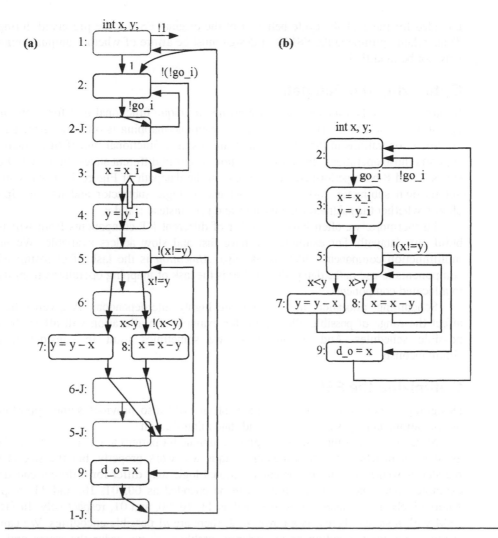

Figure 2.15: Optimizing the FSMD for the GCD example: (a) original FSMD and optimizations, and (b) optimized FSMD.

operation down into smaller operations, like $t1 = b * c$, $t2 = d * e$, and $a = t1 * t2$, with each smaller operation having its own state. Thus, only one multiplier would be needed in the datapath, since the three multiplications could share multiplier; sharing will be discussed in the next section.

In this scenario, we assumed that the timing of output operations could be changed. For example, the reduced FSMD will generate the GCD output in fewer clock cycles than the original FSMD. In many cases, changing the timing is not acceptable. For example, in our earlier clock divider example, changing the timing clearly would not be acceptable, since we intended for the cycle-by-cycle behavior of the original FSM to be preserved during design. Thus, when optimizing the FSMD, a design must be aware of whether output timing may or may not be modified.

## Optimizing the Datapath

In our four-step datapath approach, we created a unique functional unit for every arithmetic operation in the FSMD. However, such a one-to-one-mapping is often not necessary. Many arithmetic operations in the FSMD can share a single functional unit if that functional unit supports those operations, and those operations occur in different states. In the GCD example, states 7 and 8 both performed subtractions. In the datapath of Figure 2.11, each subtraction got its own subtractor. Instead, we could use a single subtractor and use multiplexors to choose whether the subtractor inputs are $x$ and $y$, or instead $y$ and $x$.

Furthermore, we often have a number of different RT components from which we can build our datapath. For example, we have fast and slow adders available. We may have multifunction components, like ALUs, also. *Allocation* is the task of choosing which RT components to use in the datapath. *Binding* is the task of mapping operations from the FSMD to allocated components.

Scheduling, allocation, and binding are highly interdependent. A given schedule will affect the range of possible allocations, for example. An allocation will affect the range of possible schedules. And so on. Thus, we sometimes want to consider these tasks simultaneously.

## Optimizing the FSM

Designing a sequential circuit to implement an FSM also provides some opportunities for optimization, namely, state encoding and state minimization.

*State encoding* is the task of assigning a unique bit pattern to each state in an FSM. Any assignment in which the encodings are unique will work properly, but the size of the state register as well as the size of the combinational logic may differ for different encodings. For example, four states $A$, $B$, $C$, and $D$ can be encoded as 00, 01, 10, and 11, respectively. Alternatively, those states can be encoded as 11, 10, 00, and 01, respectively. In fact, for an FSM with $n$ states where $n$ is a power of 2, there are $n!$ possible encodings. We can see this easily if we treat encoding as an ordering problem — we order the states and assign a straightforward binary encoding, starting with $00...00$ for the first state, $00...01$ for the second state, and so on. There are $n!$ possible orderings of $n$ items, and thus $n!$ possible encodings. $n!$ is a very large number for large $n$, and thus checking each encoding to determine which yields the most efficient controller is a hard problem. Even more encodings are possible, since we can use more than $\log_2(n)$ bits to encode $n$ states, up to $n$ bits to achieve a one-hot encoding. CAD tools are therefore a great aid in searching for the best encoding.

*State minimization* is the task of merging equivalent states into a single state. Two states are equivalent if, for all possible input combinations, those two states generate the same outputs and transition to the same next state. Such states are clearly equivalent, since merging them will yield exactly the same output behavior.

The state merging that we did when optimizing our FSMD was not the same as state minimization as defined here. The reason is that our state merging in the FSMD actually changed the output behavior, in particular the output timing, of the FSMD. Typically, by the time we arrive at an FSM, we assume output timing cannot be changed. State minimization does not change the output behavior in any way.

## 2.7 Summary

Designing a custom single-purpose processor for a given program requires an understanding of various aspects of digital design. Design of a circuit to implement Boolean functions requires combinational design, which consists of building a truth table with all possible inputs and desired outputs, optimizing the output functions, and drawing a circuit. Design of a circuit to implement a state diagram requires sequential design, which consists of drawing an implementation model with a state register and a combinational logic block, assigning a binary encoding to each state, drawing a state table with inputs and outputs, and repeating our combinational design process for this table. Finally, design of a single-purpose processor circuit to implement a program requires us to first schedule the program's statements into a complex state diagram, construct a datapath from the diagram, create a new state diagram that replaces complex actions and conditions by datapath control operations, and then design a controller circuit for the new state diagram using sequential design. The register-transfer level is the most common starting point of design today. Much optimization can be performed at each level of design, but such optimization is hard, so CAD tools would be a great designer's aid.

## 2.8 References and Further Reading

- De Micheli, Giovanni, *Synthesis and Optimization of Digital Circuits*. New York: McGraw-Hill, 1994. Covers synthesis techniques from sequential programs down to gates.
- Gajski, Daniel D., *Principles of Digital Design*. Englewood Cliffs, NJ: Prentice-Hall, 1997. Describes combinational and sequential logic design, with a focus on optimization techniques, CAD, and higher levels of design.
- Gajski, Daniel D., Nikil Dutt, Allen Wu, and Steve Lin, *High-Level Synthesis: Introduction to Chip and System Design*. Norwell, MA: Kluwer Academic Publishers, 1992. Emphasizes optimizations when converting sequential programs to a custom single-purpose processor.
- Katz, Randy, *Contemporary Logic Design*. Redwood City, CA: Benjamin/Cummings, 1994. Describes combinational and sequential logic design, with a focus on logic and sequential optimization and CAD.

## 2.9  Exercises

2.1   What is a single-purpose processor? What are the benefits of choosing a single-purpose processor over a general-purpose processor?

2.2   How do nMOS and pMOS transistors differ?

2.3   Build a 3-input NAND gate using a minimum number of CMOS transistors.

2.4   Build a 3-input NOR gate using a minimum number of CMOS transistors.

2.5   Build a 2-input AND gate using a minimum number of CMOS transistors.

2.6   Build a 2-input OR gate using a minimum number of CMOS transistors.

2.7   Explain why NAND and NOR gates are more common than AND and OR gates.

2.8   Distinguish between a combinational circuit and a sequential circuit.

2.9   Design a 2-bit comparator (compares two 2-bit words) with a single output "less-than," using the combinational design technique described in the chapter. Start from a truth table, use K-maps to minimize logic, and draw the final circuit.

2.10  Design a 3×8 decoder. Start from a truth table, use K-maps to minimize logic and draw the final circuit.

2.11  Describe what is meant by edge-triggered and explain why it is used.

2.12  Design a 3-bit counter that counts the following sequence: 1, 2, 4, 5, 7, 1, 2, etc. This counter has an output "odd" whose value is 1 when the current count value is odd. Use the sequential design technique of the chapter. Start from a state diagram, draw the state table, minimize the logic, and draw the final circuit.

2.13  Four lights are connected to a decoder. Build a circuit that will blink the lights in the following order: 0, 2, 1, 3, 0, 2, .... Start from a state diagram, draw the state table, minimize the logic, and draw the final circuit.

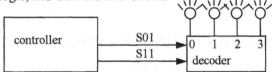

2.14  Design a soda machine controller, given that a soda costs 75 cents and your machine accepts quarters only. Draw a black-box view, come up with a state diagram and state table, minimize the logic, and then draw the final circuit.

2.15  What is the difference between a synchronous and an asynchronous circuit?

2.16  Determine whether the following are synchronous or asynchronous: (a) multiplexor, (b) register, (c) decoder.

2.17  What is the purpose of the datapath? of the controller?

2.18  Compare the GCD custom-processor implementation to a software implementation (a) Compare the performance. Assume a 100-ns clock for the microcontroller, and a 20-ns clock for the custom processor. Assume the microcontroller uses two operand instructions, and each instruction requires four clock cycles. Estimates for the microcontroller are fine. (b) Estimate the number of gates for the custom design, and compare this to 10,000 gates for a simple 8-bit microcontroller. (c) Compare the custom GCD with the GCD running on a 300-MHz processor with 2-operand instructions and one clock cycle per instruction (advanced processors use parallelism to meet or exceed one cycle per instruction). (d) Compare the estimated gates with 200,000 gates, a typical number of gates for a modern 32-bit processor.

2.19 Design a single-purpose processor that outputs Fibonacci numbers up to $n$ places. Start with a function computing the desired result, translate it into a state diagram, and sketch a probable datapath.

2.20 Design a circuit that does the matrix multiplication of matrices $A$ and $B$. Matrix $A$ is $3 \times 2$ and matrix $B$ is $2 \times 3$. The multiplication works as follows:

$$
\begin{array}{ccc}
A & B & C \\
\begin{bmatrix} a & b \\ c & d \\ e & f \end{bmatrix} & \bullet \ \begin{bmatrix} g & h & i \\ j & k & l \end{bmatrix} & = \ \begin{bmatrix} a*g + b*j & a*h + b*k & a*i + b*l \\ c*g + d*j & c*h + d*k & c*i + d*l \\ e*g + f*j & e*h + f*k & e*i + f*l \end{bmatrix}
\end{array}
$$

2.21 An algorithm for matrix multiplication, assuming that we have one adder and one multiplier, follows. (a) Convert the matrix multiplication algorithm into a state diagram using the template provided in Figure 2.10. (b) Rewrite the matrix multiplication algorithm given the assumption that we have three adders and six multipliers. (c) If each multiplication takes two cycles to compute and each addition takes one cycle compute, how many cycles does it take to complete the matrix multiplication given one adder and one multiplier? Three adders and six multipliers? Nine adders and 18 multipliers? (d) If each an adder requires 10 transistors to implement and each multiplier requires 100 transistors to implement, what is the total number of transistor needed to implement the matrix multiplication circuit using one adder and one multiplier? Three adders and six multipliers? Nine adders and 18 multipliers? (e) Plot your results from parts (c) and (d) into a graph with latency along the $x$-axis and size along the $y$-axis.

```
main( ) {
        int A[3][2] = { {1, 2}, {3,4}, {5,6} };
        int B[2][3] = { {7, 8, 9}, {10, 11, 12} };
        int C[3][3];
        int i, j, k;

for (i=0; i < 3; i++){
        for ( j=0; j < 3; j++){
                C[i][j]=0;
                for (k=0; k < 2; k++){
                        C[i][j] += A[i][k] * B[k][j];
                }
        }
}
```

2.22 A subway has an embedded system controlling the turnstile, which releases when two tokens are deposited. (a) Draw the FSMD state diagram for this system. (b) Separate the FSMD into an FSM+D. (c) Derive the FSM logic using truth tables and K-maps to minimize logic. (d) Draw your FSM and datapath connections.

# CHAPTER 3: *General-Purpose Processors: Software*

## 3.1   Introduction

A general-purpose processor is a programmable digital system intended to solve computation problems in a large variety of applications. Copies of the same processor may solve computation problems in applications as diverse as communication, automotive, and industrial embedded systems. An embedded-system designer choosing to use a general-purpose processor to implement part of a system's functionality may achieve several benefits.

First, the unit cost of the processor may be very low, often a few dollars or less. One reason for this low cost is that the processor manufacturer can spread its NRE cost for the processor's design over large numbers of units, often numbering in the millions or billions. For example, Motorola sold nearly half a billion 68HC05 microcontrollers in 1996 alone (source: Motorola 1996 Annual Report).

Second, because the processor manufacturer can spread NRE cost over large numbers of units, the manufacturer can afford to invest large NRE cost into the processor's design, without significantly increasing the unit cost. The processor manufacturer may thus use

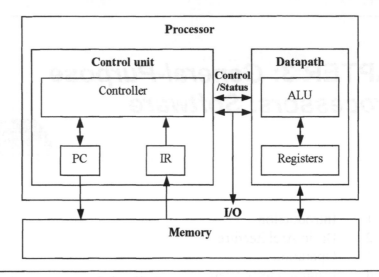

Figure 3.1: General-purpose processor basic architecture.

experienced computer architects who incorporate advanced architectural features, and may use leading-edge optimization techniques, state-of-the-art IC technology, and handcrafted VLSI layouts for critical components. These factors can improve design metrics like performance, size and power.

Third, the embedded system designer may incur low NRE cost, since the designer need only write software, and then apply a compiler and/or an assembler, both of which are mature and low-cost design technologies. Likewise, time-to-prototype and time-to-market will be short, since processor ICs can be purchased and then programmed in the designer's own lab. Flexibility will be great, since the designer can perform software rewrites in a straightforward manner.

## 3.2   Basic Architecture

A general-purpose processor, sometimes called a CPU (central processing unit) or a microprocessor, consists of a datapath and a control unit, tightly linked with a memory. We now discuss these components briefly. Figure 3.1 illustrates the basic architecture.

### Datapath

The datapath consists of the circuitry for transforming data and for storing temporary data. The datapath contains an arithmetic-logic unit (ALU) capable of transforming data through operations such as addition, subtraction, logical AND, logical OR, inverting, and shifting. The ALU also generates status signals, often stored in a status register (not shown), indicating particular data conditions. Such conditions include indicating whether data is zero or whether an addition of two data items generates a carry. The datapath also contains registers capable of storing temporary data. Temporary data may include data brought in from memory but not yet sent through the ALU, data coming from the ALU that will be needed for later ALU operations or will be sent back to memory, and data that must be moved from one memory location to another. The internal data bus carries data within the datapath, while the external data bus carries data to and from the data memory.

We typically distinguish processors by their size, and we usually measure size as the bit-width of the datapath components. A *bit*, which stands for binary digit, is the processor's basic data unit, representing either a 0 (low or false) or a 1 (high or true), while we refer to 8 bits as a *byte*. An *N-bit* processor may have N-bit-wide registers, an N-bit-wide ALU, an N-bit-wide internal bus over which data moves among datapath components, and an N-bit wide external bus over which data is brought in and out of the datapath. Common processor sizes include 4-bit, 8-bit, 16-bit, 32-bit, and 64-bit. However, in some cases, a particular processor may have different sizes among its registers, ALU, internal bus, or external bus, so the processor-size definition is not an exact one. For example, a processor may have a 16-bit internal bus, ALU and registers, but only an 8-bit external bus to reduce pins on the processor's IC.

## Control Unit

The control unit consists of circuitry for retrieving program instructions and for moving data to, from, and through the datapath according to those instructions. The control unit has a program counter (PC) that holds the address in memory of the next program instruction to fetch, and an instruction register (IR) to hold the fetched instruction. The control unit also has a controller, consisting of a state register plus next-state and control logic, as we saw in Chapter 2. This controller sequences through the states and generates the control signals necessary to read instructions into the IR, and control the flow of data in the datapath. Such flows may include inputting two particular registers into the ALU, storing ALU results into a particular register, or moving data between memory and a register. The controller also determines the next value of the PC. For a nonbranch instruction, the controller increments the PC. For a branch instruction, the controller looks at the datapath status signals and the IR to determine the appropriate next address.

The PC's bit-width represents the processor's address size. The address size is independent of the data word size; the address size is often larger. The address size determines the number of directly accessible memory locations, referred to as the *address space* or *memory space*. If the address size is $M$, then the address space is $2^M$. Thus, a processor with a 16-bit PC can directly address $2^{16} = 65,536$ memory locations. We would typically refer to this address space as 64K, although if 1K = 1,000, this number would represent 64,000, not the actual 65,536. Thus, in computer-speak, 1K = 1,024.

For each instruction, the controller typically sequences through several stages, such as fetching the instruction from memory, decoding it, fetching operands, executing the instruction in the datapath, and storing results. Each stage may consist of one or more clock cycles. A clock cycle is usually the longest time required for data to travel from one register to another. The path through the datapath or controller that results in this longest time (e.g., from a datapath register through the ALU and back to a datapath register) is called the *critical*

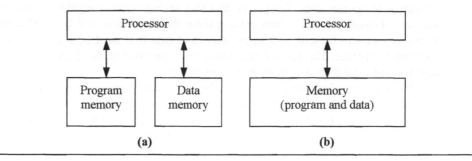

Figure 3.2: Two memory architectures: (a) Harvard, (b) Princeton.

*path*. The inverse of the clock cycle is the clock frequency, measured in cycles per second, or Hertz (Hz). For example, a clock cycle of 10 nanoseconds corresponds to a frequency of $1/10 \times 10^{-9}$ Hz, or 100 MHz. The shorter the critical path, the higher the clock frequency. We often use clock frequency as a means of comparing processors, especially different versions of the same processor, with higher clock frequency implying faster program execution. However, using clock frequency is not always an accurate method for comparing processor speeds.

## Memory

While registers serve a processor's short-term storage requirements, memory serves the processor's medium- and long-term information-storage requirements. We can classify stored information as either program or data. Program information consists of the sequence of instructions that cause the processor to carry out the desired system functionality. Data information represents the values being input, output and transformed by the program.

We can store program and data together or separately. In a *Princeton architecture*, data and program words share the same memory space. In a *Harvard architecture*, the program memory space is distinct from the data memory space. Figure 3.2 illustrates these two methods. The Princeton architecture may result in a simpler hardware connection to memory, since only one connection is necessary. A Harvard architecture, while requiring two connections, can perform instruction and data fetches simultaneously, so may result in improved performance. Most machines have a Princeton architecture. The Intel 8051 is a well-known Harvard architecture.

Memory may be read-only memory (ROM) or readable and writable memory (RAM). ROM is usually much more compact than RAM. An embedded system often uses ROM for program memory, since, unlike in desktop systems, an embedded system's program does not change. Constant data may be stored in ROM, but other data of course requires RAM.

Memory may be on-chip or off-chip. On-chip memory resides on the same IC as the processor, while off-chip memory resides on a separate IC. The processor can usually access on-chip memory much faster than off-chip memory, perhaps in just one cycle, but finite IC capacity of course implies only a limited amount of on-chip memory.

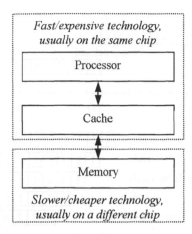

Figure 3.3: Cache memory.

To reduce the time needed to access (read or write) memory, a local copy of a portion of memory may be kept in a small but especially fast memory called *cache*, as illustrated in Figure 3.3. Cache memory often resides on-chip and often uses fast but expensive static RAM technology rather than slower but cheaper dynamic RAM (see Chapter 5). Cache memory is based on the principle that if at a particular time a processor accesses a particular memory location, then the processor will likely access that location and immediate neighbors of the location in the near future. Thus, when we first access a location in memory, we copy that location and some number of its neighbors (called a *block*) into cache, and then access the copy of the location in cache. When we access another location, we first check a cache table to see if a copy of the location resides in cache. If the copy does reside in cache, we have a *cache hit*, and we can read or write that location very quickly. If the copy does not reside in cache, we have a *cache miss*, so we must copy the location's block into cache, which takes a lot of time. Thus, for a cache to be effective in improving performance, the ratio of hits to misses must be very high, requiring intelligent caching schemes. Caches are used for both program memory (often called instruction cache, or *I-cache*) as well as data memory (often called *D-cache*).

## 3.3  Operation

### Instruction Execution

We can think of a microprocessor's execution of instructions as consisting of several basic stages:

1.  *Fetch instruction*: the task of reading the next instruction from memory into the instruction register.

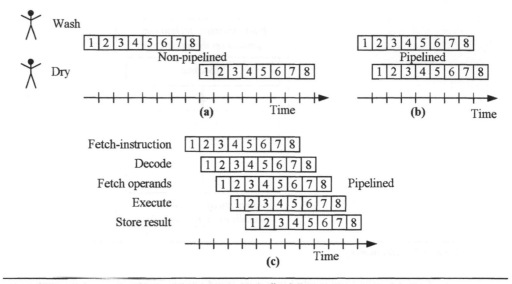

Figure 3.4: Pipelining: (a) nonpipelined dish cleaning, (b) pipelined dish cleaning, (c) pipelined instruction execution.

2. *Decode instruction*: the task of determining what operation the instruction in the instruction register represents (e.g., add, move, etc.).
3. *Fetch operands*: the task of moving the instruction's operand data into appropriate registers.
4. *Execute operation*: the task of feeding the appropriate registers through the ALU and back into an appropriate register.
5. *Store results*: the task of writing a register into memory.

If each stage takes one clock cycle, then we can see that a single instruction may take several cycles to complete.

## Pipelining

Pipelining is a common way to increase the instruction throughput of a microprocessor. We first make a simple analogy of two people approaching the chore of washing and drying eight dishes. In one approach, the first person washes all eight dishes, and then the second person dries all eight dishes. Assuming 1 minute per dish per person, this approach requires 16 minutes. The approach is clearly inefficient since at any time only one person is working and the other is idle. Obviously, a better approach is for the second person to begin drying the first dish immediately after it has been washed. This approach requires only 9 minutes — 1 minute for the first dish to be washed, and then 8 more minutes until the last dish is finally dry . We refer to this latter approach as "pipelined."

Each dish is like an instruction, and the two tasks of washing and drying are like the five stages listed earlier. By using a separate unit (each akin to a person) for each stage, we can pipeline instruction execution. After the instruction fetch unit fetches the first instruction, the decode unit decodes it while the instruction fetch unit simultaneously fetches the next instruction. The idea of pipelining is illustrated in Figure 3.4. Note that for pipelining to work well, instruction execution must be decomposable into roughly equal length stages, and instructions should each require the same number of cycles.

Branches pose a problem for pipelining, since we don't know the next instruction until the current instruction has reached the execute stage. One solution is to stall the pipeline when a branch is in the pipeline, waiting for the execute stage before fetching the next instruction. An alternative is to guess which way the branch will go and fetch the corresponding instruction next; if right, we proceed with no penalty, but if we find out in the execute stage that we were wrong, we must ignore all the instructions fetched since the branch was fetched, thus incurring a penalty. Modern pipelined microprocessors often have very sophisticated branch predictors built in.

## Superscalar and VLIW Architectures

We can use multiple ALUs to further speed up a processor. A *superscalar* micprocessor can execute two or more scalar operations in parallel, requiring two or more ALUs. A scalar operation transforms one or two numbers, as opposed to vector or matrix operations that transform entire sets of numbers. Some superscalar microprocessors require that the instructions be ordered statically (at compile time), while others may reorder the instructions dynamically (during runtime) to make use of the additional ALUs. A *VLIW* (very long instruction word) architecture is a type of static superscalar architecture that encodes several (perhaps four or more) operations in a single machine instruction.

## 3.4  Programmer's View

A programmer writes the program instructions that carry out the desired functionality on the general-purpose processor. The programmer may not actually need to know detailed information about the processor's architecture or operation, but instead may deal with an architectural abstraction, which hides much of that detail. The level of abstraction depends on the level of programming. We can distinguish between two levels of programming. The first is assembly-language programming, in which one programs in a language representing processor-specific instructions as mnemonics. The second is structured-language programming, in which one programs in a language using processor-independent instructions. A compiler automatically translates those instructions to processor-specific instructions. Ideally, the structured-language programmer would need no information about the processor architecture, but in embedded systems, the programmer must usually have at least some awareness, as we shall discuss.

Actually, we can define an even lower programming level, machine-language programming, in which the programmer writes machine instructions in binary. This level has become extremely rare due to the advent of assemblers. Machine-language–programmed computers often had rows of lights representing to the programmer the current binary instructions being executed. Today's computers look more like boxes or refrigerators, but

| Instruction 1 | opcode | operand1 | operand2 |
|---|---|---|---|
| Instruction 2 | opcode | operand1 | operand2 |
| Instruction 3 | opcode | operand1 | operand2 |
| Instruction 4 | opcode | operand1 | operand2 |
| | ... | | |

Figure 3.5: Instructions stored in memory.

they do not make for interesting movie props, so you may notice that in the movies, computers with rows of blinking lights live on.

## Instruction Set

The assembly-language programmer must know the processor's instruction set. The instruction set describes the bit configurations allowed in the IR, indicating the atomic processor operations that the programmer may invoke. Each such configuration forms an assembly instruction, and a sequence of such instructions forms an assembly program, stored in a processor's memory, as illustrated in Figure 3.5.

An instruction typically has two parts, an opcode field and operand fields. An opcode specifies the operation to take place during the instruction. We can classify instructions into three categories. Data-transfer instructions move data between memory and registers, between input/output channels and registers, and between registers themselves. Arithmetic/logical instructions configure the ALU to carry out a particular function, move data from the registers through the ALU, and move data from the ALU back to a particular register. Branch instructions determine the address of the next program instruction, based possibly on datapath status signals.

Branches can be further categorized as being unconditional jumps, conditional jumps or procedure call and return instructions. Unconditional jumps always determine the address of the next instruction, while conditional jumps do so only if some condition evaluates to true, such as a particular register containing zero. A call instruction, in addition to indicating the address of the next instruction, saves the address of the current instruction so that a subsequent return instruction can jump back to the instruction immediately following the most recent invoked call instruction. This pair of instructions facilitates the implementation of procedure/function call semantics of high-level programming languages .

An operand field specifies the location of the actual data that takes part in an operation. Source operands serve as input to the operation, while a destination operand stores the output. The number of operands per instruction varies among processors. Even for a given processor, the number of operands per instruction may vary depending on the instruction type.

| Addressing mode | Operand field | Register-file contents | Memory contents |
|---|---|---|---|

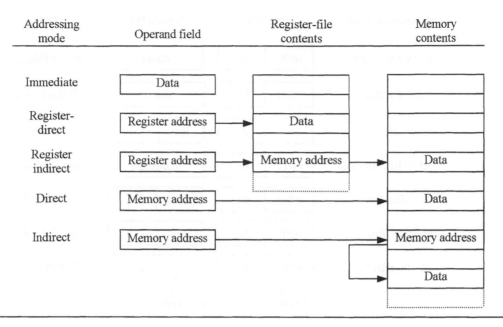

Figure 3.6: Addressing modes.

The operand field may indicate the data's location through one of several addressing modes, illustrated in Figure 3.6. In *immediate* addressing, the operand field contains the data itself. In *register* addressing, the operand field contains the address of a datapath register in which the data resides. In *register-indirect* addressing, the operand field contains the address of a register, which in turn contains the address of a memory location in which the data resides. In *direct* addressing, the operand field contains the address of a memory location in which the data resides. In *indirect* addressing, the operand field contains the address of a memory location, which in turn contains the address of a memory location in which the data resides. Those familiar with structured languages may note that direct addressing implements regular variables, and indirect addressing implements pointers. In *inherent* or *implicit* addressing, the particular register or memory location of the data is implicit in the opcode; for example, the data may reside in a register called the "accumulator." In *indexed* addressing, the direct or indirect operand must be added to a particular implicit register to obtain the actual operand address. Jump instructions may use *relative* addressing to reduce the number of bits needed to indicate the jump address. A relative address indicates how far to jump from the current address, rather than indicating the complete address. Such addressing is very common since most jumps are to nearby instructions.

Ideally, the structured-language programmer would not need to know the instruction set of the processor. However, nearly every embedded system requires the programmer to write at least some portion of the program in assembly language. Those portions may deal with low-level input/output operations with devices outside the processor, like a display device.

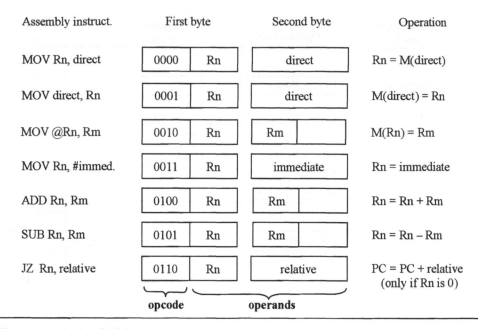

| Assembly instruct. | First byte | | Second byte | Operation |
|---|---|---|---|---|
| MOV Rn, direct | 0000 | Rn | direct | Rn = M(direct) |
| MOV direct, Rn | 0001 | Rn | direct | M(direct) = Rn |
| MOV @Rn, Rm | 0010 | Rn | Rm | M(Rn) = Rm |
| MOV Rn, #immed. | 0011 | Rn | immediate | Rn = immediate |
| ADD Rn, Rm | 0100 | Rn | Rm | Rn = Rn + Rm |
| SUB Rn, Rm | 0101 | Rn | Rm | Rn = Rn – Rm |
| JZ Rn, relative | 0110 | Rn | relative | PC = PC + relative (only if Rn is 0) |

opcode      operands

Figure 3.7: A simple (trivial) instruction set.

Such a device may require specific timing sequences of signals in order to receive data, and the programmer may find that writing assembly code achieves such timing most conveniently. A *driver* routine is a portion of a program written specifically to communicate with, or drive, another device. Since drivers are often written in assembly language, the structured-language programmer may still require some familiarity with at least a subset of the instruction set.

Figure 3.7 shows a (trivial) instruction set with four data transfer instructions, two arithmetic instructions, and one branch instruction, for a hypothetical processor. Figure 3.8(a) shows a program written in C that adds the numbers 1 through 10. Figure 3.8(b) shows that same program written in assembly language using the given instruction set.

## Program and Data Memory Space

The embedded systems programmer must be aware of the size of the available memory for program and for data. For example, a particular processor may have a 64K program space, and a 64K data space. The programmer must not exceed these limits. In addition, the programmer will probably want to be aware of on-chip program and data memory capacity, taking care to fit the necessary program and data in on-chip memory if possible.

## Registers

Assembly-language programmers must know how many registers are available for general-purpose data storage. They must also be familiar with other registers that have special

|  |  |  |  |
|---|---|---|---|
| int total = 0;<br>for (int i=10; i!=0; i—)<br>    total += i;<br>// next instructions... | 0 | MOV R0, #0; | // total = 0 |
|  | 1 | MOV R1, #10; | // i = 10 |
|  | 2 | MOV R2, #1; | // constant 1 |
|  | 3 | MOV R3, #0; | // constant 0 |
|  | Loop: | JZ R1, Next; | // Done if i=0 |
|  | 5 | ADD R0, R1; | // total += i |
|  | 6 | SUB R1, R2; | // i-- |
|  | 7 | JZ R3, Loop; | // Jump always |
|  | Next: | // next instructions... | |
| **(a)** | | **(b)** | |

Figure 3.8: Sample programs: (a) C program, (b) equivalent assembly program.

functions. For example, a base register may exist, which permits the programmer to use a data-transfer instruction where the processor adds an operand field to the base register to obtain an actual memory address.

Other special-function registers must be known by both the assembly-language and the structured-language programmer. Such registers may be used for configuring built-in timers, counters, and serial communication devices, or for writing and reading external pins.

## I/O

The programmer should be aware of the processor's input and output (I/O) facilities, with which the processor communicates with other devices. One common I/O facility is parallel I/O, in which the programmer can read or write a port (a collection of external pins) by reading or writing a special-function register. Another common I/O facility is a system bus, consisting of address and data ports that are automatically activated by certain addresses or types of instructions. I/O methods will be discussed further in Chapter 6.

## Interrupts

An *interrupt* causes the processor to suspend execution of the main program and jump to an *interrupt service routine* (ISR) that fulfills a special, short-term processing need. In particular, the processor stores the current PC and sets it to the address of the ISR. After the ISR completes, the processor resumes execution of the main program by restoring the PC. The programmer should be aware of the types of interrupts supported by the processor (described in Chapter 6), and must write ISRs when necessary. The assembly-language programmer places each ISR at a specific address in program memory. The structured-language programmer must do so also; some compilers allow a programmer to force a procedure to

```
CheckPort        proc
        push     ax              ; save the content
        push     dx              ; save the content
        mov      dx, 3BCh + 1    ; base + 1 for register #1
        in       al, dx          ; read register #1
        and      al, 10h         ; mask out all but bit # 4
        cmp      al, 0           ; is it 0?
        jne      SwitchOn        ; if not, we need to turn the LED on

SwitchOff:
        mov      dx, 3BCh + 0    ; base + 0 for register #0
        in       al, dx          ; read the current state of the port
        and      al, feh         ; clear first bit (masking)
        out      dx, al          ; write it out to the port
        jmp      Done            ; we are done

SwitchOn:
        mov      dx, 3BCh + 0    ; base + 0 for register #0
        in       al, dx          ; read the current state of the port
        or       al, 01h         ; set first bit (masking)
        out      dx, al          ; write it out to the port

Done:   pop      dx              ; restore the content
        pop      ax              ; restore the content
CheckPort        endp

extern "C" CheckPort(void);      // defined in assembly above
void main(void) {
        while( 1 )
                CheckPort();
}
```

Figure 3.9: PC parallel port example.

start at a particular memory location, while others recognize predefined names for particular ISRs.

For example, we may need to record the occurrence of an event from a peripheral device, such as the pressing of a button. We record the event by setting a variable in memory when that event occurs, although the user's main program may not process that event until later. Rather than requiring the user to insert checks for the event throughout the main program, the programmer merely writes an interrupt service routine and associates it with an input pin connected to the button. The processor will then call the routine automatically when the button is pressed.

## Example: Assembly-Language Programming of Device Drivers

This example provides an application of assembly language programming of a low-level driver, showing how the parallel port of a PC can be used to perform digital I/O. The code is

| LPT Connector Pin | I/O Direction | Register Address |
|---|---|---|
| 1 | Output | $0^{th}$ bit of register #2 |
| 2-9 | Output | $0^{th}$-$7^{th}$ bit of register #0 |
| 10, 11, 12, 13,15 | Input | 6,7,5,4,$3^{th}$ bit of register #1 |
| 14,16,17 | Output | 1,2,$3^{st}$ bit of register #2 |

Figure 3.10: PC parallel port signals and associated registers.

given in Figure 3.9. Writing and reading three special registers accomplishes parallel communication on the PC. Those three registers are actually in an 8255A Peripheral Interface Controller chip. In unidirectional mode, (default power-on-reset mode), this device is capable of driving 12 output and 5 input lines. In Figure 3.10, we give the parallel port (known as LPT) connector pin numbers and the corresponding register location.

A switch is connected to input pin number 13 of the parallel port. A light-emitting diode (LED) is connected to output pin number 2. Our program, running on the PC, should monitor the input switch and turn the LED on/off accordingly.

Figure 3.9 gives the code for such a program, in x86 assembly language. Note that the *in* and *out* assembly instructions read and write the internal registers of the 8255A. Both instructions take two operands, address and data. The address specifies the register we are trying to read or write. This address is calculated by adding the address of the device, called the *base address*, to the address of the particular register as given in Figure 3.9. In most PCs, the base address of LPT1 is at 3BC hex (though not always). The second operand is the data. For the *in* instruction, the content of this 8-bit operand will be written to the addressed register. For the *out* instruction, the content of the addressed 8-bit register will be read into this operand.

The program makes use of masking, something quite common during low-level I/O. A *mask* is a bit-pattern designed such that ANDing it with a data item D yields a specific part of D. For example, a mask of 00001111 can be used to yield bits 3 through 0 (e.g., 00001111 AND 10101010 yields 00001010). A mask of 00010000, or 10h in hexadecimal format, would yield bit 4.

In Figure 3.9, we have broken our program in two source files, assembly and C. The assembly program implements the low-level I/O to the parallel port and the C program implements the high-level application.

## Operating System

An *operating system* is a layer of software that provides low-level services to the application layer, a set of one or more programs executing on the CPU consuming and producing input and output data. The task of managing the application layer involves the loading and executing of programs, sharing and allocating system resources to these programs, and

```
DB file_name "out.txt"    - store file name

MOV R0, 1324              - system call "open" id
MOV R1, file_name         - address of file-name
INT 34                    - cause a system call
JZ  R0, L1                - if zero -> error

   . . . read the file
JMP L2                    - bypass error condition
L1:
   . . . handle the error

L2:
```

Figure 3.11: System call invocation.

protecting these allocated resources from corruption by non-owner programs. One of the most important resource of a system is the central processing unit (CPU), which is typically shared among a number of executing programs. The operating system is responsible for deciding what program is to run next on the CPU and for how long. This is called *process* (or *task*) *scheduling* and it is determined by the operating system's preemption policy. Another very important resource is memory, including disk storage, which is also shared among the applications running on the CPU.

In addition to implementing an environment for management of high-level application programs, the operating system provides the software required for servicing various hardware-interrupts, and provides device drivers for driving the peripheral devices present in the system. Typically, on startup, an operating system initializes all peripheral devices, such as disk controllers, timers, and input/output devices and installs hardware interrupt service routines (ISRs) to handle various signals generated by these devices. Then it installs software interrupts (interrupts generated by the software) to process system calls (calls made by high-level applications to request operating system services) as described next.

A *system call* is a mechanism for an application to invoke the operating system. It is analogous to a procedure or function call, as in high-level programming languages. When a program requires some service from the operating system, it generates a predefined software interrupt that is serviced by the operating system. Parameters specific to the requested services are typically passed from (to) the application program to (from) the operating system through CPU registers. Figure 3.11 illustrates how the file "open" system call may be invoked, in assembly, by a program. Languages like C and Pascal provide wrapper functions around the system-calls to provide a high-level mechanism for performing system calls.

In summary, the operating system abstracts away the details of the underlying hardware and provides the application layer an interface to the hardware through the system call mechanism.

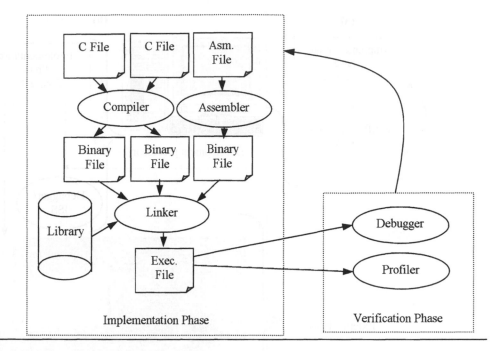

Figure 3.12: Software development process.

## 3.5 Development Environment

In this section, we take a look at the general software design tools that are used by embedded system designers in design, test, and debugging of embedded software.

### Design Flow and Tools

Several software and hardware tools commonly support the programming of general-purpose processors. First, we must distinguish between two processors we deal with when developing an embedded system. One processor is the *development processor*, on which we write and debug our program. This processor is part of our desktop computer. The other processor is the *target processor*, to which we will send our program and which will form part of our embedded system's implementation. For example, we may develop our system on a Pentium processor but use a Motorola 68HC11 as our target processor. Of course, sometimes the two processors happen to be the same, but this is mostly a coincidence.

Programming of an embedded system's processor is similar to writing a program that runs on your desktop computer, with some subtle but important differences. Figure 3.12 depicts the standard software development process. The general design flow for programming

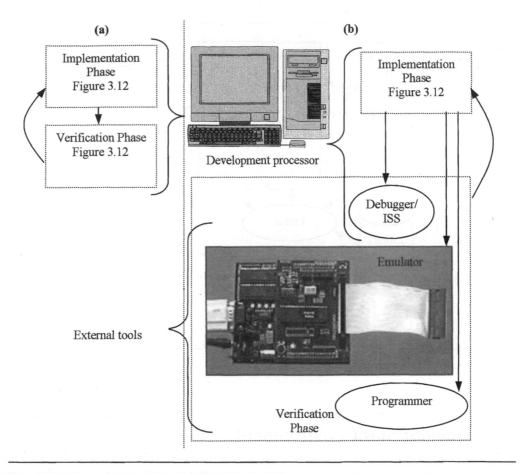

Figure 3.13: Software design process: (a) desktop, (b) embedded.

applications that run on a desktop computer starts with writing our source code, possibly organized in a number of files for modularity, using an editor. Then we compile or assemble the code in each file, using a compiler or assembler, into corresponding binary files. Next, using a linker, we combine these binary files into a final executable. These tasks, collectively, can be considered as the implementation phase. Next, we test our program by running the executable file under the command of a debugger. Sometimes we may use a profiler to pinpoint the performance bottlenecks of your program. During this phase, if we discover errors or performance bottlenecks, we return to the implementation phase, make improvements, and repeat the process.

Typically, all of these tools have been combined into a single *integrated development environment* (IDE), which greatly simplifies the design process. Figure 3.13(b) shows the design flow for embedded software development, in contrast to the design flow for desktop applications in Figure 3.13(a). Here, the implementation phase, which is the process of editing, compiling, assembling, and linking our program, is the same as that used for designing applications intended for our desktop computer. We perform these on our development computer using cross-compilers, cross-assemblers, etc. It is the verification phase (i.e., the process of testing the final executable) that is greatly different in embedded systems. In the following paragraphs, we will describe each of the development tools in greater detail.

*Assemblers* translate assembly instructions to binary machine instructions. In addition to just replacing opcode and operand mnemonics by binary equivalents, an assembler may also translate symbolic labels into actual addresses. For example, a programmer may add a symbolic label *END* to an instruction *A* and may reference *END* in a branch instruction. The assembler determines the actual binary address of *A* and replaces references to *END* by this address. The mapping of assembly instructions to machine instructions is one-to-one.

*Compilers* translate structured programs into machine (or assembly) programs. Structured programming languages possess high-level constructs that greatly simplify programming, such as loop constructs, so each high-level construct may translate to several or tens of machine instructions. Compiler technology has advanced tremendously over the past decades, applying numerous program optimizations, often yielding very size and performance efficient code. A *cross compiler* executes on one processor (our development processor) but generates code for a different processor (our target processor). Cross compilers are extremely common in embedded system development.

A *linker* allows a programmer to create a program in separately assembled or compiled files; it combines the machine instructions of each into a single program, perhaps incorporating instructions from standard library routines. A linker designed for embedded processors will also try to eliminate binary code associated with uncalled procedures and functions as well as memory allocated to unused variables in order to reduce the overall program footprint.

## Example: Instruction-Set Simulator for a Simple Processor

An *instruction-set simulator* is a program that runs on one processor and executes the instructions of another processor. In this example, we design an instruction-set simulator for the simple processor of Figure 3.7. Our program takes as input a file name containing binary instructions of our simple processor. The code for this instruction-set simulator is given in Figure 3.14.

## Testing and Debugging

Generally, the testing and debugging phase of developing programs is a major part of the overall design processes. This is especially true when the program is being developed to run in an embedded system. For example, it is not acceptable for your car's engine management system to require occasional rebooting because of a software hang up. Programming is an error prone activity, and it is inevitable that there will exist errors and bugs in writing any reasonably large program. The most common method of verifying the correctness of a program is running (executing) it with ample input data that check the program's behavior,

```
#include <stdio.h>
typedef struct {
        unsigned char first_byte, second_byte;
} instruction;
instruction program[1024];// this is our instruction memory
unsigned char memory[256];// this is our data memory
void run_program(int num_bytes) {
        int pc = -1;
        unsigned char reg[16], fb, sb;
        while( ++pc < (num_bytes / 2) ) {
                fb = program[pc].first_byte;
                sb = program[pc].second_byte;
                switch( fb >> 4 ) {
                    case 0: reg[fb & 0x0f] = memory[sb]; break;
                    case 1: memory[sb] = reg[fb & 0x0f]; break;
                    case 2: memory[reg[fb & 0x0f]] = reg[sb >> 4]; break;
                    case 3: reg[fb & 0x0f] = sb; break;
                    case 4: reg[fb & 0x0f] += reg[sb >> 4]; break;
                    case 5: reg[fb & 0x0f] -= reg[sb >> 4]; break;
                    case 6: if(reg[fb & 0x0f] == 0) pc += sb; break;
                    default: return -1;
                }
        }
        return 0;
}

int main(int argc, char *argv[]) {
        FILE* ifs;
        If( argc != 2 || (ifs = fopen(argv[1], "rb") == NULL ) return -1;
        if (run_program(fread(program, sizeof(program) == 0) {
                print_memory_contents();
                return(0);
        }
        else return(-1);
}
```

Figure 3.14: Instruction-set simulator implementation.

especially using boundary cases. This is relatively easy to do when developing programs that run on your desktop computer.

For embedded system programmers, this task is a little more challenging. Specifically, a program running in an embedded system most often needs to be real-time. For example, our engine management program must generate pulses that actuate the fuel-injectors with a timely and calculated pattern. A distinguishing characteristic of a real-time system is that it must compute correct results within a predetermined amount of time, while a non–real-time system only needs to compute correct results. In addition, a program running in an embedded system works in conjunction with many other components of that system as well as interacts with the environment where the embedded system is to function. Hence, debugging a program running in an embedded system requires having control over time, as well as control over the environment and the ability to trace or follow the execution of the program, in order to detect errors. In the remaining paragraphs, we take a look at some tools and methods to help us do just that. These tools, for the most part, enable us to execute and observe the behavior of our programs.

*Debuggers* help programmers evaluate and correct their programs. They run on the development processor and support stepwise program execution, executing one instruction and then stopping, proceeding to the next instruction when instructed by the user. They permit execution up to user-specified breakpoints, which are instructions that when encountered cause the program to stop executing. Whenever the program stops, the user can examine values of various memory and register locations. A source-level debugger enables step-by-step execution in the source program language, whether assembly language or a structured language. A good debugging capability is crucial, as today's programs can be quite complex and hard to write correctly. Since debuggers are programs that run on your development processor but execute code designed for your target processor, they always mimic or simulate the function of the target processor. These debuggers are also known as instruction-set simulators (ISS) or virtual machines (VM).

*Emulators* support debugging of the program while it executes on the target processor. An emulator typically consists of a debugger coupled with a board connected to the desktop processor via a cable. The board consists of the target processor plus some support circuitry (often another processor). The board may have another cable with a device having the same pin configuration as the target processor, allowing one to plug the device into a real embedded system. Such an in-circuit emulator enables one to control and monitor the program's execution in the actual embedded system circuit. In-circuit emulators are available for nearly any processor intended for embedded use, although they can be quite expensive if they are to run at real speeds.

*Device programmers* download a binary machine program from the development processor's memory into the target processor's memory. Once the target processor has been programmed, the entire embedded system can be tested in its most realistic form (i.e., it can be executed in its environment and the behavior observed in a realistic way). For example, a car equipped with our engine management system can be taken out for a drive!

Revisiting Figure 3.12, we see that programs intended for embedded systems can be tested in three ways, namely, debugging using an ISS, emulation using an emulator, and field testing by downloading the program directly into the target processor. The difference between these three methods is as follows. The design cycle using a debugger based on an ISS running on the development computer is fast, but it is inaccurate since it can only interact with the rest of the system and the environment to a limited degree. The design cycle using an emulator is a little longer, since the code must be downloaded into the emulator hardware; however, the emulator hardware can interact with the rest of the system, hence can allow for more accurate testing. The design cycle using a programmer to download the program into the target processor is the longest of all. Here, the target processor must be removed from its system and put into the programmer, programmed, and returned to the system. However, this method will enable the system to interact with its environment more freely, hence provides the highest execution accuracy but little debug control.

The availability of low-cost or high-quality development environments for a processor often heavily influences the choice of a processor.

## 3.6 Application-Specific Instruction-Set Processors (ASIPs)

Today's embedded applications, such as high definition TV, require high computing power and very specific functionality. The performance, power, cost, or size demands of these applications cannot always be dealt with efficiently by using general-purpose processors. Nonetheless, the inflexibility of custom single-purpose processors is often too prohibitive. A solution is to use an instruction-set processor that is specific to that application or application domain. Because these ASIPs are instruction-set processors, they can be programmed by writing software, resulting in short time-to-market and good flexibility, while the performance and other constraints may be efficiently satisfied.

As with most other aspects of embedded systems design, there is a trade-off here. Instruction-set processors and the associated software tools (compilers, linkers, etc.) are very expensive to develop; therefore, they are expensive to integrate into low-cost embedded systems. In contrast, the large applicability and resulting cost amortization of general-purpose processors make them very cost effective solutions in most embedded systems. ASIPs tend to come in three major varieties, namely, microcontrollers, which are specific to applications that perform a large amount of control-oriented tasks, digital signal processors (DSPs), which are specific to applications that process large amounts of data, and everything else, which are less general ASIPs.

### Microcontrollers

Numerous processor IC manufacturers market devices specifically for the control-dominated embedded systems domain. These devices may include several features. First, they may include several peripheral devices, such as timers, analog-to-digital converters, and serial communication devices, on the same IC as the processor. Second, they may include some program and data memory on the same IC. Third, they may provide the programmer with direct access to a number of pins of the IC. Fourth, they may provide specialized instructions for common embedded system control operations, such as bit-manipulation operations. A *microcontroller* is a device possessing some or all of these features.

Incorporating peripherals and memory onto the same IC reduces the number of required ICs, resulting in compact and low-power implementations. Providing pin access allows programs to easily monitor sensors, to set actuators, and to transfer data with other devices. Providing specialized instructions improves performance for embedded systems applications. Thus, microcontrollers can be considered ASIPs to some degree.

Many manufacturers market devices referred to as "embedded processors." The difference between embedded processors and microcontrollers is not clear, although we note that the former term seems to be used more for large (32-bit) processors.

### Digital Signal Processors (DSP)

*Digital signal processors* (DSPs) are processors that are highly optimized for processing large amounts of data. The source of this large amount of data is some form of digitized signal, like a photo image captured by a digital camera, a voice packet going through a network router, or an audio clip played by a digital keyboard. A DSP may contain numerous register files, memory blocks, multipliers, and other arithmetic units. In addition, DSPs often provide instructions that are central to digital signal processing, such as filtering and transforming vectors or metrics of data. In a DSP, frequently used arithmetic functions, such as multiply-and-accumulate, are implemented in hardware and thus execute orders of magnitude faster than a software implementation running on a general-purpose processor. In addition, DSPs may allow for execution of some functions in parallel, resulting in a boost in performance.

As with microcontrollers, DSPs also tend to incorporate many peripherals that are useful in signal processing on a single IC. As an example, a DSP device may contain a number of analog-to-digital and digital-to-analog converters, pulse-width-modulators, direct-memory-access controllers, timers, and counters.

Many companies offer a variety of commonly used DSPs that are well supported in terms of compiler and other development tools, making them easy and cheap to integrate into most embedded systems.

### Less-General ASIP Environments

In contrast to microcontrollers and DSPs, which can be used in a variety of embedded systems, IC manufacturers have designed ASIPs that are less general in nature. These ASIPs are designed to perform some very domain specific processing while allowing some degree of programmability. For example, an ASIP designed for networking hardware may be designed to be programmable with different network routing, checksum, and packet processing protocols.

## 3.7 Selecting a Microprocessor

The embedded system designer must select a microprocessor for use in an embedded system. The choice of a processor depends on technical and nontechnical aspects. From a technical perspective, one must choose a processor that can achieve the desired speed within certain power, size and cost constraints. Nontechnical aspects may include prior expertise with a processor and its development environment, special licensing arrangements, and so on.

Speed is a particularly difficult processor aspect to measure and compare. We could compare processor clock speeds, but the number of instructions per clock cycle may differ greatly among processors. We could instead compare instructions per second, but the complexity of each instruction may also differ greatly among processors. For example, one processor may require 100 instructions while another processor may require 300 instructions to perform the same computation.

| Processor | Clock Speed | Peripherals | Bus Width | MIPS | Power | Transistors | Price |
|---|---|---|---|---|---|---|---|
| General Purpose Processors | | | | | | | |
| Intel PIII | 1GHz | 2x16 K L1,256K L2, MMX | 32 | ~900 | 97 W | ~7 M | $900 |
| IBM PowerPC 750X | 550 MHz | 2x32K L1, 256K L2 | 32/64 | ~1300 | 5 W | ~7 M | $900 |
| MIPS R5000 | 250 MHz | 2x32K, 2 way set assoc. | 32/64 | NA | NA | 3.6 M | NA |
| StrongARM SA-110 | 233 MHz | None | 32 | 268 | 1 W | 2.1 M | NA |
| Microcontrollers | | | | | | | |
| Intel 8051 | 12 MHz | 4K ROM, 128 RAM, 32 I/O, Timer, UART | 8 | ~1 | ~0.2 W | ~10 K | $7 |
| Motorola 68HC811 | 3 MHz | 4K ROM, 192 RAM, 32 I/O, Timer, WDT, SPI | 8 | ~.5 | ~0.1 W | ~10 K | $5 |
| Digital Signal Processors | | | | | | | |
| TI C5416 | 160 MHz | 128K SRAM, 3 T1 Ports, DMA, 13 ADC, 9 DAC | 16/32 | ~600 | NA | NA | $34 |
| Lucent DSP32C | 80 MHz | 16K Inst., 2K Data, Serial Ports, DMA | 32 | 40 | NA | NA | $75 |

*Sources: Intel, Motorola, MIPS, ARM, TI, and IBM Websites/Datasheets; Embedded Systems Programming, Nov. 1998.*

Figure 3.15: General-purpose processors.

One attempt to provide a means for a fairer comparison is the *Dhrystone benchmark*. A benchmark is a program intended to be run on different processors to compare their performance. The Dhrystone benchmark was originally developed in 1984 by Reinhold Weicker specifically as a performance benchmark; it performs no useful work. It focuses on exercising a processor's integer arithmetic and string-handling capabilities. Its current version is written in C and is in the public domain. Because most processors can execute it in milliseconds, it is typically executed thousands of times, and thus a processor is said to be able to execute so many Dhrystones per second.

Another commonly used speed comparison unit, which happens to be based on the Dhrystone, is MIPS. One might think that MIPS simply means millions of instructions per second, but actually the common use of the term is based on a somewhat more complex notion. Specifically, its origin is based on the speed of Digital's VAX 11/780, thought to be the first computer able to execute one million instructions per second. A VAX 11/780 could execute 1,757 Dhrystones/second. Thus, for a VAX 11/780, 1 MIPS = 1,757 Dhrystones/second. This unit for MIPS is the one commonly used today, and it is sometimes referred to as *Dhrystone MIPS*. So if a machine today is said to run at 750 MIPS, that actually means it can execute 750 * 1,757 = 1,317,750 Dhrystones/second.

The use and validity of benchmark data is a subject of great controversy. There is also a clear need for benchmarks that measure performance of embedded processors. An effort underway in this area is EEMBC (pronounced "embassy"), the EDN Embedded Benchmark Consortium. The EEMBC has five benchmarking suites of programs corresponding to different embedded applications: automotive/industrial, consumer electronics, networking, office automation, and telecommunications. Each suite consists of several common algorithms found in the suite's application area. For example, two of the programs in the consumer electronics suite are JPEG compression and decompression (JPEG is a standard for still digital image compression). Another program in that suite involves infrared signal transmission and reception.

Numerous general-purpose processors have evolved in the recent years and are in common use today. In Figure 3.15, we summarize some of the features of several popular processors.

# 3.8 General-Purpose Processor Design

A general-purpose processor is really just a single-purpose processor whose purpose is to process instructions stored in a program memory. Therefore, we can design a general-purpose processor using the single-purpose processor design technique described in Chapter 2. While real microprocessors intended for mass production are more commonly designed using custom methods rather than the general technique of this section, using the the general technique here may prove a useful exercise that will illustrate the basic unity between single-purpose and general-purpose processors.

Suppose we want to design a general-purpose processor having the basic architecture of Figure 3.1 and supporting the instruction set of Figure 3.7. We can begin by creating the FSMD shown in Figure 3.16(a), which describes the desired processor's behavior. The FSMD declares several variables for storage: a 16-bit program counter $PC$, a 16-bit instruction register $IR$, a 64K × 16 bit memory $M$, and a 16 × 16 bit register file $RF$. The FSMD's initial state, *Reset*, clears $PC$ to 0. The *Fetch* state reads $M[PC]$ into $IR$. The *Decode* state does nothing but adds the extra cycle necessary for $IR$ to get updated so we can then read it on an arc. Each arc leaving the *Decode* state detects a particular instruction opcode, causing a transition to the corresponding execute state for that opcode. Each execute state, like *Mov1*,

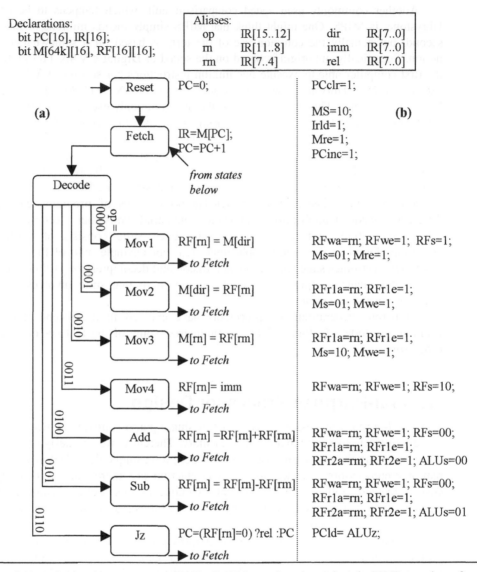

Declarations:
bit PC[16], IR[16];
bit M[64k][16], RF[16][16];

| Aliases: | | | |
|---|---|---|---|
| op | IR[15..12] | dir | IR[7..0] |
| rn | IR[11..8] | imm | IR[7..0] |
| rm | IR[7..4] | rel | IR[7..0] |

**(a)**

Reset — PC=0;                    PCclr=1;

**(b)**

Fetch — IR=M[PC];               MS=10;
        PC=PC+1                 Irld=1;
                                Mre=1;
        *from states*           PCinc=1;
        *below*

Decode

op = 0000
Mov1 — RF[rn] = M[dir]          RFwa=rn; RFwe=1; RFs=1;
       *to Fetch*               Ms=01; Mre=1;

0001
Mov2 — M[dir] = RF[rn]          RFr1a=rn; RFr1e=1;
       *to Fetch*               Ms=01; Mwe=1;

0010
Mov3 — M[rn] = RF[rm]           RFr1a=rn; RFr1e=1;
       *to Fetch*               Ms=10; Mwe=1;

0011
Mov4 — RF[rn]= imm              RFwa=rn; RFwe=1; RFs=10;
       *to Fetch*

0100
Add — RF[rn] =RF[rn]+RF[rm]     RFwa=rn; RFwe=1; RFs=00;
      *to Fetch*                RFr1a=rn; RFr1e=1;
                                RFr2a=rm; RFr2e=1; ALUs=00

0101
Sub — RF[rn] = RF[rn]-RF[rm]    RFwa=rn; RFwe=1; RFs=00;
      *to Fetch*                RFr1a=rn; RFr1e=1;
                                RFr2a=rm; RFr2e=1; ALUs=01

0110
Jz — PC=(RF[rn]=0) ?rel :PC     PCld= ALUz;
     *to Fetch*

Figure 3.16: A simple microprocessor: (a) FSMD, (b) FSM operations that replace the FSMD operations after we create the datapath of Figure 3.17.

*Add*, and *Jz*, carries out the actual instruction operations by moving data between storage devices, modifying data, or updating *PC*.

We can now build a datapath that can carry out the operation of this FSMD, as described in Chapter 2. The datapath we create using the following steps is shown in Figure 3.17. The first step is to instantiate a storage device for each declared variable, so we instantiate

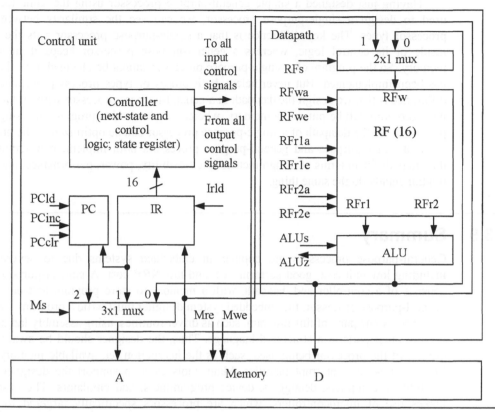

Figure 3.17: Architecture of a simple microprocessor.

registers *PC* and *IR*, memory *M*, and register file *RF*. The second step is to instantiate functional units to carry out the FSMD operations. We'll use a single ALU capable of carrying out all the operations. The third step is to add the connections among the components' ports as required by the FSMD operations, adding multiplexors when there is more than one connection being input to a port. Finally, we create unique identifiers for every control signal.

Given this datapath, we can now rewrite the FSMD as an FSM representing the datapath's controller. Each FSMD operation must be replaced by binary operations on control signals, as shown in Figure 3.16(b). The states and arcs are identical for the FSMD and FSM, and only the operations change, so we do not redraw the states and arcs in the figure. As an example of operation replacement, we replace the assignment *PC* = 0 in state *Reset* by the control signal setting *PCclr* = 1.

We can use the FSM design technique of Chapter 2 to design a controller, consisting of a state register and next-state/control logic. We omit this step here.

Having just designed a simple general-purpose processor using the same technique we used to design a single-purpose processor, we can see the similarity between the two processor types. The key difference is that a single-purpose processor puts the "program" inside of its control logic, whereas a general-purpose processor keeps it in an external memory. So the program of a single-purpose processor cannot be changed once the processor has been implemented. But nevertheless, both processor types process programs. A second difference is that we design the datapath in a general-purpose processor without knowledge of what program will be put in the memory, whereas we know this program in a single-purpose processor. So the datapath of a single-purpose processor can be optimized to the program. We see that single-purpose and general-purpose processors both implement programs. Though they may differ in terms of design metrics like flexibility, power, performance, and cost, they fundamentally do the same thing.

## 3.9 Summary

General-purpose processors are popular in embedded systems due to several features, including low unit cost, good performance, and low NRE cost. A general-purpose processor consists of a controller and datapath, with a memory to store program and data. To use a general-purpose processor, the embedded system designer must write a program. The designer may write some parts of this program, such as driver routines, using assembly language, while writing other parts in a structured language. Thus, the designer should be aware of several aspects of the processor being used, such as the instruction set, available memory, registers, I/O facilities, and interrupt facilities. Many tools exist to support the designer, including assemblers, compilers, debuggers, device programmers, and emulators. The designer often makes use of microcontrollers, which are processors specifically targeted to embedded systems. These processors may include on-chip peripheral devices and memory, additional I/O ports, and instructions supporting common embedded system operations. The designer has a variety of processors from which to choose.

## 3.10 References and Further Reading

* Philips semiconductors, *80C51-based 8-bit Microcontrollers Databook*, Philips Electronics North America, 1994. Provides an overview of the 8051 architecture and on-chip peripherals, describes a large number of derivatives each with various features, describes the I2C and CAN bus protocols, and highlights development support tools.
* Rafiquzzaman, Mohamed. *Microprocessors and Microcomputer-Based System Design*. Boca Raton: CRC Press, 1995. Provides an overview of general-purpose processor architecture, along with detailed descriptions of various Intel 80xx and Motorola 68000 series processors.
* *Embedded Systems Programming*, Miller Freeman Inc., San Francisco, 1999. A monthly publication covering trends in various aspects of general-purpose processors for

embedded systems, including programming, compilers, operating systems, emulators, device programmers, microcontrollers, PLDs, and memories. An annual buyer's guide provides tables of vendors for these items, including 8/16/32/64-bit microcontrollers/microprocessors and their features.

- *Microprocessor Report*, MicroDesign Resources, California, 1999. A monthly report providing in-depth coverage of trends, announcements, and technical details, for desktop, mobile, and embedded microprocessors.
- www.eembc.org. The Web site for the EEMBC benchmark consortium.
- SIGPLAN Notices 23,8 (Aug. 1988), 49-62. Provides source for the Dhrystone benchmark version 2. Online source can be found at ftp.nosc.mil:pub/aburto.

## 3.11 Exercises

3.1 Describe why a general-purpose processor could cost less than a single-purpose processor you design yourself.

3.2 Detail the stages of executing the MOV instructions of Figure 3.7, assuming an 8-bit processor and a 16-bit IR and program memory following the model of Figure 3.1. For example, the stages for the ADD instruction are (1) fetch M[PC] into IR, (2) read Rn and Rm from register file through ALU configured for ADD, storing results back in Rn.

3.3 Add one instruction to the instruction set of Figure 3.7 that would reduce the size of our summing assembly program by 1 instruction. *Hint*: add a new branch instruction. Show the reduced program.

3.4 Create a table listing the address spaces for the following address sizes: (a) 8-bit, (b) 16-bit, (c) 24-bit, (d) 32-bit, (e) 64-bit.

3.5 Illustrate how program and data memory fetches can be overlapped in a Harvard architecture.

3.6 Read the entire problem before beginning. (a) Write a C program that clears an array "short int M[256]." In other words, the program sets every location to 0. *Hint*: your program should only be a couple lines long. (b) Assuming M starts at location 256 (and thus ends at location 511), write the same program in assembly language using the earlier instruction set. (c) Measure the time it takes you to perform parts a and b, and report those times.

3.7 Acquire a databook for a microcontroller. List the features of the basic version of that microcontroller, including key characteristics of the instruction set (number of instructions of each type, length per instruction, etc.), memory architecture and available memory, general-purpose registers, special-function registers, I/O facilities, interrupt facilities, and other salient features.

3.8 For the microcontroller in the previous excercise, create a table listing five existing variations of that microcontroller, stressing the features that differ from the basic version.

# CHAPTER 4: *Standard Single-Purpose Processors: Peripherals*

## 4.1   Introduction

A single-purpose processor is a digital system intended to solve a specific computation task, as opposed to a general-purpose processor, which is intended to solve a wide variety of computation tasks. The single-purpose processor may be a custom one that we design ourselves, as discussed in Chapter 2. However, some computation tasks are so common that *standard* single-purpose processors have evolved. These processors can be purchased "off the shelf." The manufacturer of such an off-the-shelf processor sells the device in large quantities.

An embedded system designer choosing to use a standard single-purpose processor to implement a specific computation task, as opposed to choosing to design a custom single-purpose processor, may achieve several benefits. First, NRE cost will be low, since the processor is predesigned. Second, unit cost may be low, since the standard processor is mass-produced and hence the manufacturer can amortize NRE costs.

Using a standard single-purpose processor also provides benefits over using a general-purpose processor. Performance may be faster, power may be lower, and size may be smaller, all due to the fact that the standard single-purpose processor is customized for the particular task. Even if a general-purpose processor will exist in a system, adding single-purpose processors can free the general-purpose processor for other tasks.

There are of course trade-offs. If we are already using a general-purpose processor, then implementing a task on an additional single-purpose processor rather than in software may add to the system size and power consumption.

In this chapter, we describe the basic functionality of several standard single-purpose processors commonly found in embedded systems. The level of detail of the description is intended to be enough to enable use of such processors but not necessarily the design of one.

We refer to standard single-purpose processors as *peripherals* because they usually exist on the periphery of the CPU. However, microcontrollers tightly integrate these peripherals with the CPU, often placing them on-chip, and even assigning peripheral registers to the CPU's own register space. The result is the common term *on-chip peripherals*, which some may consider somewhat of an oxymoron.

## 4.2   Timers, Counters, and Watchdog Timers

### Timers and Counters

A *timer* is an extremely common peripheral device that can measure time intervals. Such a device can be used to either generate events at specific times, or to determine the duration between two external events. Example applications that require generating events include keeping a traffic light green for a specified duration, or communicating bits serially between devices at a specific rate. An example of an application that determines inter-event duration is that of computing a car's speed by measuring the time the car takes to pass over two separated sensors in a road.

A timer measures time by counting pulses that occur on an input clock signal having a known period. For example, if a particular clock's period is 1 microsecond, and we've counted 2,000 pulses on the clock signal, then we know that 2,000 microseconds have passed.

A *counter* is a more general version of a timer. Instead of counting clock pulses, a counter counts pulses on some other input signal. For example, a counter may be used to count the number of cars that pass over a road sensor, or the number of people that pass through a turnstile. We often combine counters and timers to measure rates, such as counting the number of times a car wheel rotates in one second, in order to determine a car's speed.

To use a timer, we must configure its inputs and monitor its outputs. Such use often requires or can be greatly aided by an understanding of the internal structure of the timer. The internal structure can vary greatly among manufacturers. We provide a few common features of such internal structures in Figure 4.1.

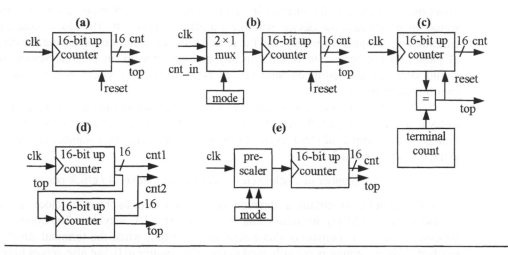

Figure 4.1: Timer structures: (a) a basic timer, (b) a timer/counter, (c) a timer with a terminal count, (d) a 16/32-bit timer, (e) a timer with a prescaler.

Figure 4.1(a) provides the structure of a very simple timer. This timer has an internal 16-bit up counter, which increments its value on each clock pulse. Thus, the output value *cnt* represents the number of pulses since the counter was last reset to zero. To interpret this number as a time interval, we must know the frequency or period of the clock signal *clk*. For example, suppose we wish to measure the time that passes between two button presses. In this case, we could reset the timer on the occurrence of the first press, and then read the timer output on the second press. Suppose the frequency of *clk* were 100 MHz, meaning the period would be 1 / (100 MHz) = 10 nanoseconds, and that *cnt* = 20,000 at the time of the second button press. We would then compute the time that passed between the first and second button presses as 20,000 * 10 nanoseconds = 200 microseconds. We note that since this timer's counter can count from 0 to 65,535, this particular timer has a measurement range of 0 to 65,535 * 10 nanoseconds = 655.35 microseconds, with a resolution of 10 nanoseconds. We define a timer's *range* as the maximum time interval the timer can measure. A timer's *resolution* is the minimum interval it can measure.

The timer in Figure 4.1(a) has an additional output *top* that indicates when the top value of its range has been reached, also known as an overflow occurring, in which case the timer rolls over to 0. When we use a timer in conjunction with a general-purpose processor, and we expect time intervals to exceed the timer range, we typically connect the *top* signal to an interrupt pin on the processor. We create a corresponding interrupt service routine that counts the number of times the routine is called, thus effectively extending the range we can measure. Many microcontrollers that include built-in timers will have special interrupts just for its timers, with those interrupts distinct from external interrupts.

Figure 4.1(b) provides the structure of a more advanced timer that can also be configured as a counter. A *mode* register holds a bit, which the user sets, that uses a 2 × 1 multiplexor to select the clock input to the internal 16-bit up counter. The clock input can be the external *clk* signal, in which case the device acts like a timer. Alternatively, the clock input can be the external *cnt_in* signal, in which case the device acts like a counter, counting the occurrences of pulses on *cnt_in*. *cnt_in* would typically be connected to an external sensor, so pulses would occur at indeterminate intervals. In other words, we could not measure time by counting such pulses.

Figure 4.1(c) provides the structure of a timer that can inform us whenever a particular interval of time has passed. A *terminal count* register holds a value, which the user sets, indicating the number of clock cycles in the desired interval. This number can be computed using the simple formula:

$$\text{number of clock cycles} = \text{desired time interval} / \text{clock period}$$

For example, to obtain a duration of 3 microseconds from a clock cycle of 10 nanoseconds (100 MHz), we must count: $3 \times 10^{-6}$ s $/ 10 \times 10^{-9}$ s/cycle = 300 cycles. The timer structure includes a comparator that asserts its *top* output when the terminal count has been reached. This *top* output is not only used to reset the counter to 0, but also serves to inform the timer user that the desired time interval has passed. As mentioned earlier, we often connect this signal to an interrupt. The corresponding interrupt service routine would include the actions that must be taken at the specified time interval.

To improve efficiency, instead of counting up from 0 to terminal count, a timer could instead count down from terminal count to 0, meaning we would load terminal count rather than 0 into the 16-bit counter upon reset, and the counter would be a down counter rather than an up counter. The efficiency comes from the simplicity by which we can check if our count has reached 0 — we simply input the count into a 16-bit NOR gate. A single 16-bit NOR gate is far more area- and power-efficient than a 16-bit comparator.

Figure 4.1(d) provides the structure of a timer that can be configured as a 16-bit or 32-bit timer. The timer simply uses the *top* output of its first 16-bit up counter as the clock input of its second 16-bit counter. These are known as cascaded counters.

Finally, Figure 4.1(e) shows a timer with a prescaler. A *prescaler* is essentially a configurable clock-divider circuit. Depending on the mode bits being input to the prescaler, the prescaler output signal might be the same as the input signal, or it may have half the frequency (double the period), one-fourth the frequency, one-eighth the frequency, etc. Thus, a prescaler can be used to extend a timer's range, by reducing the timer's resolution. For example, consider a timer with a resolution of 10 ns and a range of 65,535 * 10 nanoseconds = 655.35 microseconds. If the prescaler of such a timer is configured to divide the clock frequency by eight, then the timer will have a resolution of 80 ns and a range of 65,535 * 80 nanoseconds = 5.24 milliseconds.

Many timers will combine the above features, plus adding other configurable features. One such feature is a mode bit or additional input that enables or disables counting. Another feature is a mode bit that enables or disables interrupt generation when top count is reached.

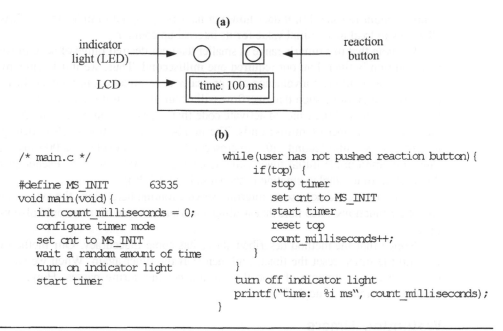

(a)

(b)

```
/* main.c */                           while(user has not pushed reaction button){
                                         if(top) {
#define MS_INIT      63535                 stop timer
void main(void){                           set cnt to MS_INIT
   int count_milliseconds = 0;             start timer
   configure timer mode                    reset top
   set cnt to MS_INIT                      count_milliseconds++;
   wait a random amount of time          }
   turn on indicator light             }
   start timer                         turn off indicator light
                                       printf("time:   %i ms", count_milliseconds);
                                     }
```

Figure 4.2: Reaction timer: (a) LED, LCD, and button, (b) pseudo-code.

Note that we could use a general-purpose processor to implement a timer. Knowing the number of cycles that each instruction requires, we could write a loop that executes the desired number of instructions; when this loop completes, we know that the desired time passed. This implementation of a timer on a dedicated general-purpose processor is obviously quite inefficient in terms of size. One could alternatively incorporate the timer functionality into a main program, but the timer functionality then occupies much of the program's run time, leaving little time for other computations. Thus, the benefit of assigning timer functionality to a special-purpose processor becomes evident.

## Example: Reaction Timer

A reaction timer is an application that measures the time a person takes to respond to a visual or audio stimulus. In this example, the application turns on an LED, then measures the time a person takes to push a button in response, and displays this time on an LCD, as illustrated in Figure 4.2. We expect reaction times to be on the order of seconds, and we want to display reaction times to millisecond precision.

In this example, we'll use a microcontroller with a built-in 16-bit timer. The timer is incremented once every instruction-cycle, where one instruction cycle for this microcontroller equals six clock cycles. The clock frequency is 12 MHz, meaning the period is 83.333 nanoseconds. Thus, this timer has a resolution of 1 instruction-cycle = 6 clock cycles = 6 * 83.333 nanoseconds = 0.5 microsecond. Furthermore, since the timer has 16 bits, its range is 65,535 * 0.5 microsecond = 32.77 milliseconds. This timer does not have a prescaler or a terminal count register, but it does however have a *top* signal to indicate overflow, and it also allows us to load in an initial value for its internal up counter.

We note that this timer's range is smaller than our desired range of several seconds, while its resolution is finer than our required one millisecond. Thus, we must somehow extend the range, but without the convenience of a prescaler or terminal count register. Instead, we'll set the initial timer value such that overflow will occur after 1 millisecond, and then monitor the *top* output signal of the timer to activate code that keeps a count of the number of overflows, meaning the number of milliseconds. The number of instruction cycles corresponding to 1 millisecond is 1 millisecond / (0.5 microsecond/instruction-cycle) = 2,000 instruction cycles. Thus, the appropriate initial timer value is 65,535 – 2,000 = 63,535. Pseudocode describing the reaction timer implementation is shown in Figure 4.2(b).

Note that we did not use an interrupt service routine here, since the system does not have any other functions. Also note that waiting a random amount of time could also make use of a timer.

Notice that the method described above has some inaccuracy. Our method requires that we stop the timer, reset the timer, and then start the timer again. When we stop the timer to reset it, a certain amount of time that we are not measuring passes. However, this time is small so we treat it as negligible.

## Watchdog Timers

A special type of timer is a watchdog timer. We configure a watchdog timer with a real-time value, just as with a regular timer. However, instead of the timer generating a signal for us every $X$ time units, we must generate a signal for the timer every $X$ time units. If we fail to generate this signal in time, then the timer "times out" and generates a signal indicating that we failed.

One common use of a watchdog timer is to enable an embedded system to restart itself in case of a failure. In such use, we modify the system's program to include statements that reset the watchdog timer. We place these statements such that the watchdog timer will be reset at least once during every time out interval if the program is executing normally. We connect the fail signal from the watchdog timer to the microprocessor's reset pin. Now suppose the program has an unexpected failure, such as entering an undesired infinite loop, or waiting for an input event that never arrives. The watchdog timer will time out, and thus the microprocessor will reset itself, starting its program from the beginning. In systems where such a full reset during system operation is not practical, we might instead connect the fail signal to an interrupt pin, and create an interrupt service routine that jumps to some safe part of the program. We might even combine these two responses, first jumping to an interrupt service routine to test parts of the system and record what went wrong, and then resetting the system. The interrupt service routine may record information as to the number of failures and the causes of each, so that a service technician may later evaluate this information to determine if a particular part requires replacement. Note that an embedded system often must self-recover from failures whenever possible, as the user may not have the means to reboot the system in the same manner that he/she might reboot a desktop system.

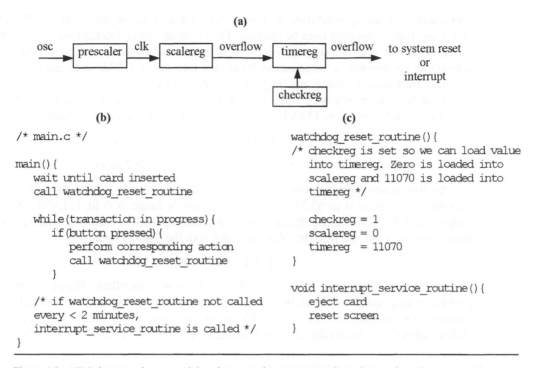

Figure 4.3: ATM timeout using a watchdog timer: (a) timer structure, (b) main pseudo-code, (c) watchdog reset routine.

Another common use is to support time outs in a program while keeping the program structure simple. For example, we may desire that a user respond to questions on a display within some time period. Rather than sprinkling response-time checks throughout our program, we can use a watchdog timer to check for us, thus keeping our program neater. An example in this chapter illustrates such use of a watchdog timer.

## Example: ATM Timeout Using a Watchdog Timer

In this example, a watchdog timer is used to implement a timeout for an automatic teller machine, or ATM. A normal ATM session involves a user inserting a bank card, typing in a personal identification number, and then answering questions about whether to deposit or withdraw money, which account will be involved, how much money will be involved, whether another transaction is desired, and so on. We want to design the ATM such that it will terminate the session if at any time the user does not press any button for 2 minutes. In this case, the ATM will eject the bank card and terminate the session.

We will use a watchdog timer with the internal structure shown in Figure 4.3(a). An oscillator signal *osc* is connected to a prescaler that divides the frequency by 12 to generate a signal *clk*. The signal *clk* is connected to an 11-bit up-counter *scalereg*. When *scalereg* overflows, it rolls over to 0, and its overflow output causes the 16-bit up-counter *timereg* to increment. If *timereg* overflows, it triggers the system reset or an interrupt. To reset the watchdog timer, *checkreg* must be enabled. Then a value can be loaded into *timereg*. When a value is loaded into *timereg*, the *checkreg* register is automatically reset. If the *checkreg* register is not enabled, a value cannot be loaded into *timereg*. This is to prevent erroneous software from unintentionally resetting the watchdog timer.

Now let's determine what value to load into *timereg* to achieve a timeout of 2 minutes. The *osc* signal frequency is 12 MHz. *timereg* is incremented at every $t$ seconds where:

$$t = 12 * 2^{11} * 1/(\text{osc frequency}) = 12 * 2^{11} * 1/(12 * 10^6)$$

$$= 12 * 2{,}048 * (8.33 * 10^{-8}) = 0.002 \text{ second}$$

So this watchdog timer has a resolution of 2 milliseconds. Since *timereg* is a 16-bit register, its range is 0 to 65,535, and thus the timer's range is 0 to 131,070 milliseconds (approximately 2.18 minutes). Because *timereg* counts up, then to attain the watchdog interval time $X$ milliseconds, we load the following value into the *timereg* register:

$$\text{timereg value} = 131{,}070 - X$$

If *timereg* is not reset within $X$ milliseconds, it will overflow. Figure 4.3(b) and (c) provide pseudo-code for the main routine and the watchdog reset routine to implement the timeout functionality of the ATM. We want the timeout to be 2 minutes (120,000 milliseconds). This means the value of $X$ should be 11,070 (i.e., 131,070 − 120,000).

## 4.3   UART

A universal asynchronous receiver/transmitter (*UART*) receives serial data and stores it as parallel data, usually one byte. It also takes parallel data and transmits it as serial data. Such serial communication is beneficial when we need to communicate bytes of data between devices that are separated by long distances, or when those devices simply have few available I/O pins. Advanced principles and protocols of serial communication will be discussed in a later chapter. For our purpose in this section, we will look at the basics of serial communication using UARTs.

Internally, a simple UART may possess some configuration registers, and two independently operating processors, one for receiving and the other for transmitting. The transmitter may possess a register, often called a *transmit buffer*, that holds data to be sent. This register is a shift register, so the data can be transmitted one bit at a time by shifting at the appropriate rate. Likewise, the receiver receives data into a shift register, and then this data can be read in parallel. This is illustrated in Figure 4.4(a). Note that in order to shift at the appropriate rate based on the configuration register, a UART requires a timer.

The receiver is constantly monitoring the *receive* pin (*rx*) for a start bit. The start bit is typically signaled by a high to low transition on the *rx* pin. After the start bit has been detected, the receiver starts sampling the *rx* pin at predetermined intervals, shifting each sampled bit into the receive shift register. If configured to do so, the receiver also reads an additional bit called *parity* which it uses to determine if the received data is correct. For

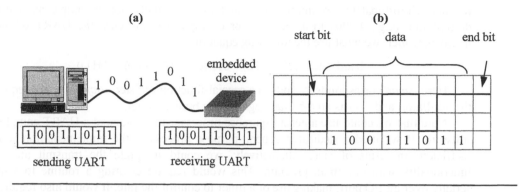

Figure 4.4: Serial transmission using UARTs, (a) A PC communicating serially with an embedded device, (b) transmission protocol used by the two UARTs.

example, using odd parity, if the number of 1s in the received data add up to an even number, and the parity bit is 1, the data is assumed to be valid, otherwise it is assumed to be erroneous. Likewise, the UART can be configured to check for even parity or no parity at all. Once data is received, the UART signals its host processor. The host processor in turn reads the byte out of the receive shift register. The receiver is now ready to receive more data.

The transmitter works as follows. After the host processor writes a byte to the transmit buffer of the UART, the transmitter sends a start bit over its *transmit pin* (*tx*), signaling the beginning of a transmission to the remote UART. Then, the transmitter shifts out the data in its *tx* pin at a predetermined rate. If configured to do so, the transmitter also transmits an additional parity bit used as discussed previously. At this point, the UART processor signals its host processor, indicating that it is ready to send more data if available.

In order for two serially connected UARTs to communicate with each other, they must agree on the transmission protocol in use. A sample transmission protocol is illustrated in Figure 4.4(b). The transmission protocol used by UART's determines the rate at which bits are sent and received. This is called the *baud rate*. The protocol also specifies the number of bits of data and the type of parity sent during each transmission. Finally, the protocol specifies the minimum number of bits used to separate two consecutive data transmissions. Stop bits are important in serial communication as they are used to give the receiving UART a chance to prepare itself prior to the reception of the next data transmission.

The baud rate determines the speed at which data is exchanged between two serially connected UARTs. Common baud rates include 2,400, 4,800, 9,600, and 19.2K. There is a great deal of misuse of the term *baud rate*, often assumed to be just the same as the term *bit rate*. In fact, bit rate is a true measure of the number of bits that are sent over a connection in one second, while baud rate is the measure of the number of signal changes that are transmitted over a connection in 1 second. Some clever techniques can be used to achieve a bit rate higher than the baud rate.

To use a UART, we must configure its baud rate by writing to the configuration register, and then we must write data to the transmit register and/or read data from the received register. Unfortunately, configuring the baud rate is usually not as simple as writing the desired rate (e.g., 4,800) to a register. For example, to configure the UART of an 8051 microcontroller, we must use the following equation:

$$\text{baud rate} = (2^{smod} / 32) * \text{oscfreq} / (12 * (256 - \text{TH1})).$$

Here, *smod* corresponds to 2 bits in a special-function register, *oscfreq* is the frequency of the oscillator, and *TH1* is an 8-bit rate register of a built-in timer.

Note that we could use a general-purpose processor to implement a UART completely in software. If we used a dedicated general-purpose processor, the implementation would be inefficient in terms of size. Alternatively, we could integrate the transmit and receive functionality with our main program. This would require creating a routine to send data serially over an I/O port, making use of a timer to control the rate. It would also require using an interrupt service routine to capture serial data coming from another I/O port whenever such data begins arriving. However, as with the timer functionality, adding send and receive functionality can detract from time for other computations.

## 4.4   Pulse Width Modulators

### Overview

A *pulse width modulator* (PWM) generates an output signal that repeatedly switches between high and low values. We control the duration of the high value and of the low value by indicating the desired period, and the desired *duty cycle*, which is the percentage of time the signal is high compared to the signal's period. A *square wave* has a duty cycle of 50%. The pulse's width corresponds to the pulse's time high, as shown in Figure 4.5.

Again, PWM functionality could be implemented on a dedicated general-purpose processor, or integrated with another program's functionality, but the single-purpose processor approach has the benefits of efficiency and simplicity.

A common use of a PWM is to generate a clock-like signal to another device. For example, a PWM can be used to blink a light at a specific rate.

Another common use of a PWM is to control the average current or voltage input to a device. For example, a DC (direct current) electric motor rotates when its input voltage is set high, with the rotation speed proportional to the input voltage level. Suppose the revolutions per minute (rpm) equals 10 times the input voltage. To achieve a desired rpm of 125, we would need to set the input voltage to 1.25 V, whereas achieving 250 rpm would require an input voltage of 2.50 V.

One approach to control the average input voltage to a DC motor uses a DC-to-DC converter circuit, which converts some reference voltage to a desired voltage. However, these circuits can be expensive. Another approach uses a digital-to-analog converter. A third approach, perhaps the simplest, uses a PWM. The PWM approach makes use of the fact that a DC motor does not come to an immediate stop when its input voltage is lowered to 0, but rather it coasts, much like a bicycle coasts when we stop pedaling. Thus, we need only set the

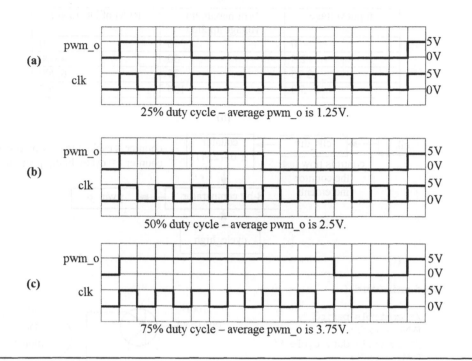

Figure 4.5: Operation of a PWM, (a) 25% duty cycle, (b) 50% duty cycle, (c) 75% duty cycle. In the diagrams, logic high is 5V, low is 0V.

average input voltage appropriately to obtain the desired speed. Using a PWM, we set the duty cycle to achieve the appropriate average voltage, and we set the period small enough for smooth operation of the motor (i.e., so the motor does not noticeably speed up and slow down). Assuming the PWM's output is 5 V when high and 0 V when low, then we can obtain an average output of 1.25 V by setting the duty cycle to 25%, since 5 V * 25% = 1.25 V. This duty cycle is shown in Figure 4.5(a). Likewise, we can obtain an average output of 2.50 V by setting the duty cycle to 50%, as shown in Figure 4.5(b). A duty cycle of 75% would result in average output of 3.75 V, as shown in Figure 4.5(c). This duty cycle adjustment principle applies to the control of a wide variety of electric devices, such as dimmer lights.

Another use of a PWM is to encode control commands in a single signal for use by another device. For example, we may control a radio-controlled car by sending pulses of different widths. Perhaps a width of 1 ms corresponds to a turn left command, a 4-ms width to turn right, and an 8-ms width to forward. The receiver can use a timer to measure the pulse width, by starting a timer when the pulse starts and stopping the timer when the pulse ends, and thus determining how much time elapsed.

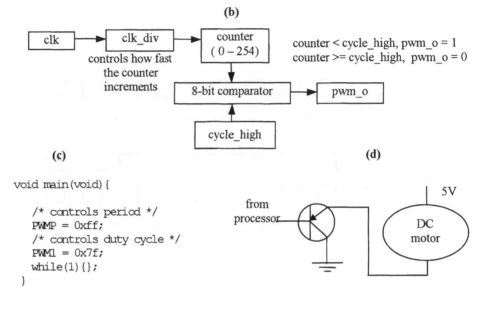

**(a)**

| input voltage | % of maximum voltage applied | RPM of DC motor |
|---|---|---|
| 0 | 0 | 0 |
| 2.5 | 50 | 4,600 |
| 3.75 | 75 | 6,900 |
| 5.0 | 100 | 9,200 |

**(b)**

counter < cycle_high, pwm_o = 1
counter >= cycle_high, pwm_o = 0

**(c)**

```
void main(void) {

    /* controls period */
    PWMP = 0xff;
    /* controls duty cycle */
    PWM1 = 0x7f;
    while(1){};
}
```

**(d)**

Figure 4.6: Controlling a DC motor with a PWM: (a) relationship between applied voltage and DC motor speed, (b) internal PWM structure, (c) pseudo-code, (d) connection to DC motor.

## Example: Controlling a DC Motor Using a PWM

In this example, we wish to control the speed of a direct-current (DC) electric motor using a PWM. The speed of the DC motor is proportional to the voltage applied to the motor. Suppose that for a fixed load, the motor yields the revolutions per minute (rpm) shown in Figure 4.6(a) for the given input voltages. We must set the duty cycle of a PWM such that the average output voltage equals the desired voltage.

Suppose that we use a PWM as part of a system that includes two 8-bit registers called *clk_div* and *cycle_high*, an 8-bit counter, and an 8-bit comparator, as shown in Figure 4.6(b). The PWM works as follows. Initially, the value of *clk_div* is loaded into the register. The *clk_div* register works as a clock divider. After a specified amount of time has elapsed, a pulse is sent to the *counter* register. This causes the counter to increment itself. The comparator then looks at the values in the *counter* register and the *cycle_high* register. When the counter value is less than *cycle_high*, a 1 (+5V) is outputted. When the value in counter is lower than the value in the *cycle_high* register a 0 (0V) is outputted. When the counter value reaches 254, *counter* is reset to 0 and the process repeats. Thus, we see that *clk_div* determines the PWM's period, specifying the number of cycles in the period. The register *cycle_high* determines the duty cycle, indicating how many of a period's cycles should output a 1. Note that if *cycle_high* is set to 255 (FFh), the output signal is always high resulting in a duty cycle of 100%. Conversely, if *cycle_high* is set to 0 (00h), the output signal is always low resulting in a duty cycle of 0%.

To determine the value of *clk_div*, we can try various values and test to see if the frequency is too fast or too slow for our particular motor. If the value of *clk_div* is too low, the value outputted by the comparator oscillates too quickly. The comparator never outputs zeros long enough for the DC motor to slow down, causing the DC motor to continuously run at full speed. Setting the value of *clk_div* to FFh in this case worked best. Once this value is set, the only register that needs to be considered is *cycle_high*.

For the motor to run at 4,600 RPM, we need a duty cycle of 50%. To compute the value needed in *cycle_high* for a 50% duty cycle, we multiply 254 by 0.50, yielding 127. Thus, putting 7Fh (127 in hexadecimal) into the *cycle_high* register should cause the motor to run at about 4,600 RPM. For the motor to run at 6,900 RPM, we need a 75% duty cycle. We compute 254 * 0.75, yielding 191. Thus, putting BFh (191 in hexadecimal) into *cycle_high* should cause the DC motor to run at about 6,900 RPM.

We cannot just connect the DC motor to the PWM because the PWM does not provide enough current to run the DC motor. To remedy this problem, we use an NPN transistor to drive the DC motor. The code and schematic used for this example are found in Figure 4.6(c) and (d). In the figure, the name of the *clk_div* register is *PWMP* and *cycle_high* is *PWM1*.

## 4.5 LCD Controllers

### Overview

A *liquid crystal display* (LCD) is a low-cost, low-power device capable of displaying text and images. LCDs are extremely common in embedded systems, since such systems often do not have video monitors like those that come standard with desktop systems. LCDs can be found in numerous common devices like watches, fax and copy machines, and calculators.

The basic principle of one type of LCD, a reflective LCD, works as follows. First, incoming light passes through a polarizing plate. Next, that polarized light encounters liquid crystal material. If we excite a region of this material, we cause the material's molecules to align, which in turn causes the polarized light to pass through the material. Otherwise, the light does not pass through. Finally, light that has passed through hits a mirror and reflects back, so the excited region appears to light up. Another type of LCD, an absorption LCD, works similarly, but uses a black surface instead of a mirror. The surface below the excited region absorbs light, thus appearing darker than the other regions.

**(a)**

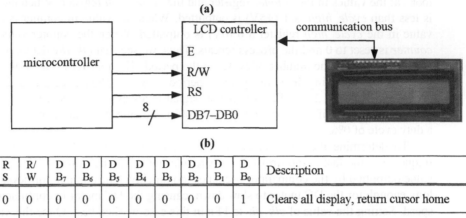

**(b)**

| R S | R/ W | D B₇ | D B₆ | D B₅ | D B₄ | D B₃ | D B₂ | D B₁ | D B₀ | Description |
|---|---|---|---|---|---|---|---|---|---|---|
| 0 | 0 | 0 | 0 | 0 | 0 | 0 | 0 | 0 | 1 | Clears all display, return cursor home |
| 0 | 0 | 0 | 0 | 0 | 0 | 0 | 0 | 1 | * | Returns cursor home |
| 0 | 0 | 0 | 0 | 0 | 0 | 0 | 1 | I/ D | S | Sets cursor move direction and specifies or not to shift display |
| 0 | 0 | 0 | 0 | 0 | 0 | 1 | D | C | B | ON/ OFF of all display (D), cursor ON/ OFF (D), and blink cursor position (B) |
| 0 | 0 | 0 | 0 | 0 | 1 | S/ C | R/ L | * | * | Move cursor and shifts display |
| 0 | 0 | 0 | 0 | 1 | D L | N | F | * | * | Sets interface data length, number of display lines, and character font |
| 1 | 0 | DATA | | | | | | | | Writes DATA |

**(c)**

| Codes | |
|---|---|
| I/D = 1  cursor moves left | DL = 1  8-bit |
| I/D = 0  cursor moves right | DL = 0  4-bit |
| S = 1  with display shift | N = 1  2 rows |
| S/C = 1  display shift | N = 0  1 row |
| S/C = 0  cursor movement | F = 1  5 × 10 dots |
| R/L = 1  shift to right | F = 0  5 × 7 dots |
| R/L = 0  shift to left | |

**(d)**

```
void WriteChar(char c){
    /* indicate data being sent */
    RS = 1;
    /* send data to LCD */
    DATA_BUS = c;
    /* toggle LCD with delay */
    EnableLCD(45);
}
```

Figure 4.7: Example of LCD initialization: (a) components, (b) initialization sequence, (c) control codes, (d) microcontroller pseudocode.

One of the simplest LCDs is a seven-segment LCD. Each of the seven segments can be activated, enabling the display of any digit character or one of several letters and symbols. Such an LCD may have seven inputs, each corresponding to a segment, or it may have only four inputs to represent the numbers 0 through 9. An LCD driver converts these inputs to the electrical signals necessary to excite the appropriate LCD segments.

A dot-matrix LCD consists of a matrix of dots that can display alphanumeric characters (letters and digits) as well as other symbols. A common dot-matrix LCD has five columns and eight rows of dots for one character. An LCD driver converts input data into the appropriate electrical signals necessary to excite the appropriate LCD dots.

Each type of LCD may be able to display multiple characters. In addition, each character may be displayed in normal or inverted fashion. The LCD may permit a character to be blinking (cycling through normal and inverted display) or may permit display of a cursor (such as a blinking underscore) indicating the "current" character. Such functionality would be difficult for us to implement using software. Thus, we use an LCD *controller* to provide us with a simple interface to an LCD, perhaps eight data inputs and one enable input. To send a byte to the LCD, we provide a value to the eight inputs and pulse the enable. This byte may be a control word, which instructs the LCD controller to initialize the LCD, clear the display, select the position of the cursor, brighten the display, and so on. Alternatively, this byte may be a data word, such as an ASCII character, instructing the LCD to display the character at the currently-selected display position.

### Example: LCD Initialization

In this example, a microprocessor is connected to an LCD controller, which in turn is connected to an LCD, as illustrated in Figure 4.7. The LCD controller receives control words from the microcontroller, it decodes the control words and performs the corresponding actions on the LCD.

Once the initialization sequence is done, we can send control words or send actual data to be displayed. *RS* is set to low to indicate that the data sent is a control word. When *RS* is high, this indicates that the data sent over the communication bus corresponds to a character that is to be displayed. Every time data is sent, whether it is a control word or data, the enable bit E must be toggled. Below are some of the corresponding control words that can be sent.

Using the initialization codes of Figure 4.7(d), the LCD has been set with an 8-bit interface. In addition, the display has been cleared, the cursor is in the home position, and the cursor moves to the right as data is displayed (as opposed to the actual data shifting when we write to the LCD). The LCD is now ready to be written to. Using the table of Figure 4.7(c), we see that in order to write data, we set *RS* = 1. The actual data we want to write is present on *DB7-DB0*. The *WriteChar* function, shown in Figure 4.7(d), accepts a character which will be sent to the LCD controller to display on the LCD. The *EnableLCD* function toggles the enable bit and acts as a delay so that the command can be processed and executed.

## 4.6  Keypad Controllers

A *keypad* consists of a set of buttons that may be pressed to provide input to an embedded system. Again, keypads are extremely common in embedded systems, since such systems may lack the keyboard that comes standard with desktop systems.

A simple keypad has buttons arranged in an $N$-column by $M$-row grid as illustrated in Figure 4.8. The device has $N$ outputs, each output corresponding to a column, and another $M$

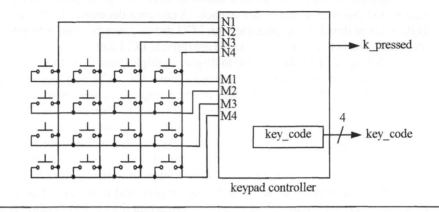

Figure 4.8: Internal keypad structure, with $N = 4$ and $M = 4$.

outputs, each output corresponding to a row. When we press a button, one column output and one row output go high, uniquely identifying the pressed button. To read such a keypad from software, we must scan the column and row outputs. The scanning may be performed by a *keypad controller*. Actually, such a device decodes rather than controls, but we'll call it a "controller" for consistency with the other peripherals discussed. A simple form of such a controller, as shown in Figure 4.8, scans the column and row outputs of the keypad. When the controller detects a button press, it stores a code corresponding to that button into a register, *key_code*, and sets an output high, *k_pressed*, indicating that a button has been pressed. Our software may poll this output every 100 milliseconds or so, and read the register when the output is high. Alternatively, this output can generate an interrupt on our general-purpose processor, eliminating the need for polling.

## 4.7   Stepper Motor Controllers

### Overview

A *stepper motor* is an electric motor that rotates a fixed number of degrees whenever we apply a "step" signal. In contrast, a regular electric motor rotates continuously whenever power is applied, coasting to a stop when power is removed. We specify a stepper motor either by the number of degrees in a single step of the motor, such as 1.8 degrees, or by the number of steps required to move 360 degrees, such as 200 steps. Stepper motors are common in embedded systems with moving parts, such as disk drives, printers, photocopy and fax machines, robots, camcorders, and VCRs.

Internally, a stepper motor typically has four coils. To rotate the motor one step, we pass current through one or two of the coils; which particular coil or coils depends on the present

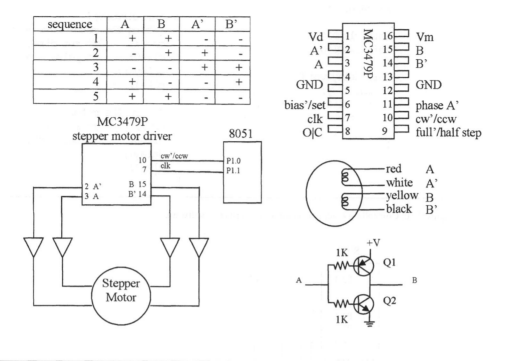

| sequence | A | B | A' | B' |
|----------|---|---|----|----|
| 1 | + | + | - | - |
| 2 | - | + | + | - |
| 3 | - | - | + | + |
| 4 | + | - | - | + |
| 5 | + | + | - | - |

Figure 4.9: Controlling a stepper motor using a driver — hardware.

orientation of the motor. Thus, rotating the motor 360 degrees requires applying current to the coils in a specified sequence. Applying the sequence in reverse causes reversed rotation.

In some cases, the stepper motor comes with four inputs corresponding to the four coils, and with documentation that includes a table indicating the proper input sequence. To control the motor from software, we must maintain this table in software, and write a step routine that applies high values to the inputs based on the table values that follow the previously applied values.

In other cases, the stepper motor comes with a built-in controller, which is an instance of a special-purpose processor, implementing this sequence. Thus, we merely create a pulse on an input signal of the motor, causing the controller to generate the appropriate high signals to the coils that will cause the motor to rotate one step.

## Example: Using a Stepper Motor Driver

Controlling a stepper motor requires applying a series of voltages to the four (typically) coils of the stepper motor. The coils are energized one or two at a time causing the motor to rotate one step. In this example, we are using a 9-volt, 2-phase bipolar stepper motor. Figure 4.9 shows a table indicating the input sequence required to rotate the motor. The entire sequence

```
/* main.c */

sbit clk=P1^1;
sbit cw=P1^0;

void delay(void) {
    int i, j;
    for (i=0; i<1000; i++)
        for (j=0; j<50; j++)
            i = i + 0;
}
```

```
void main(void) {
    */turn the motor forward */
    cw=0;       /* set direction */
    clk=0;      /* pulse clock */
    delay();
    clk=1;

    /*turn the motor backwards */
    cw=1;       /* set direction */
    clk=0;      /* pulse clock */
    delay();
    clk=1;
}
```

Figure 4.10: Controlling a stepper motor using a driver — software.

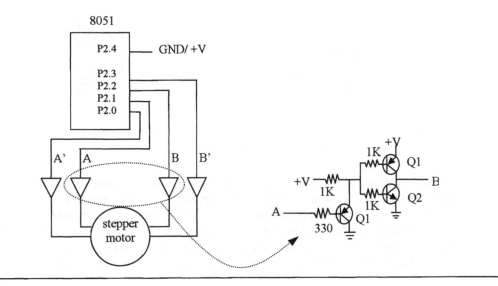

Figure 4.11: Controlling a stepper motor directly — hardware.

must be applied to get the motor to rotate 7.5 degrees. To rotate the motor in the opposite direction, we simply apply the sequence in reverse order.

We can use an 8051 microcontroller and a stepper motor driver (MC3479P) chip to control the stepper motor. We need only worry about setting the direction on the clockwise/counterclockwise pin (*cw'/ccw*) and pulsing the clock pin (*clk*) on the stepper motor driver chip using the 8051 microcontroller. Figure 4.9 gives the schematic showing how to connect the stepper motor to the driver, and the driver to the 8051. Figure 4.10 gives some sample code to run the stepper motor.

```
sbit notA=P2^0;
sbit isA=P2^1;
sbit notB=P2^2;
sbit isB=P2^3;
sbit dir=P2^4;
void delay(){
   int a, b;
   for(a=0; a<5000; a++)
      for(b=0; b<10000; b++);
}
void move(int dir, int steps) {
   int y, z;
   if(dir == 1){
      for(y=0; y<=steps; y++){
         for(z=0; z<=19; z+=4){
            isA=lookup[z];
            isB=lookup[z+1];
            notA=lookup[z+2];
            notB=lookup[z+3];
            delay();
         }
      }
   }
}
```

```
if(dir==0){
   for(y=0;   y<=step; y++){
      for(z=19; z>=0; z -= 4){
         isA=lookup[z];
         isB=lookup[z-1];
         notA=lookup[z -2];
         notB=lookup[z-3];
         delay( );
      }
   }
}
}
int lookup[20] = {
   1,  1,  0,  0,  0,  1,  1,  0,  0,  0,
   1,  1,  1,  0,  0,  1,  1,  1,  0,  0 };
void main( ){
   while(1){
      /* move forward 15 degrees */
      move(1, 2);
      /* move backwards 7.5 degrees */
      move(0, 1);
   }
}
```

Figure 4.12: Controlling a stepper motor directly — software.

## Example: Controlling a Stepper Motor Directly

In the second example, the stepper motor driver is eliminated. The stepper motor is connected directly to the 8051 microcontroller. Figure 4.11 gives the schematic showing how to connect the stepper motor to the 8051. The direction of the stepper motor is controlled maually. If P2.4 is grounded, the motor rotates counterclockwise, otherwise the motor rotates clockwise. Figure 4.12 gives the code required to execute the input sequence from the table in Figure 4.9 to turn the motor.

Note that the 8051 ports are unable to directly supply the current needed to drive the motor. This can be solved by adding buffers. A possible way to implement the buffers is show in Figure 4.11. The 8051 alone cannot drive the stepper motor, so several transistors were added to increase the current going to the stepper motor. Q1 are MJE3055T NPN transistors and Q2 is an MJE2955T PNP transistor. A is connected to the 8051 microcontroller and B is connected to the stepper motor.

## 4.8 Analog-to-Digital Converters

An *analog-to-digital converter* (ADC, A/D, or A2D) converts an analog signal to a digital signal, and a *digital-to-analog converter* (DAC, D/A, or D2A) does the opposite. Such conversions are necessary because, while embedded systems deal with digital values, an embedded system's surroundings typically involve many analog signals. *Analog* refers to a continuously valued signal, such as temperature or speed, with infinite possible values in between. *Digital* refers to discretely valued signals, such as integers, and in computing systems, these signals are encoded in binary. By converting between analog and digital signals, we can use digital processors in an analog environment.

For example, consider an analog input signal whose value could range from 0 to 7.5 volts. We want to represent each possible voltage in this range using a 4-bit binary number. Clearly, 0000 would be the most obvious encoding for 0 V, and 1111 for 7.5 V. The encodings between 0000 and 1111 would then be evenly distributed to the range between 0 and 7.5 V, as shown in Figure 4.13(a).

Now suppose that for a particular time interval, the analog input signal's values were those shown in Figure 4.13(b), ranging from 1 V up to 4 V and then down to just over 2 V. The digital encoding of this signal, sampled at times $t1$, $t2$, $t3$ and $t4$, into four bits is shown beneath the figure's $x$-axis. Conversely, suppose that for a time interval, we want to output an analog signal corresponding to the digital encodings shown at the bottom of Figure 4.13(c). The analog signal is shown in the figure.

More generally, we can compute the digital values from the analog values, and vice versa, using the following ratio:

$$e / V_{max} = d / (2^n - 1)$$

Here, $V_{max}$ is the maximum voltage that the analog signal can assume, $n$ is the number of bits available for the digital encoding, $d$ is the present digital encoding, and $e$ is the present analog voltage. In our example of Figure 4.13, suppose $V_{max}$ is 7.5 V. Then for $e = 3$ V, we have the following ratio: $3 / 7.5 = d / 15$, resulting in $d = 6$, or 0110.

We can define the *resolution* of a DAC or ADC as $V_{max} / (2^n - 1)$, representing the number of volts between successive digital encodings. In Figure 4.13(a), we see graphically that the resolution is 0.5 V between successive encodings.

The above discussion assumes a minimum voltage of 0 V. The equations can easily be extended to any voltage range.

Internally, DACs possess simpler designs than ADCs. A DAC has $n$ inputs for the digital encoding $d$, a $V_{max}$ analog input, and an analog output $e$. A fairly straightforward circuit, involving resistors and an op-amp, can be used to convert $d$ to $e$.

ADCs, on the other hand, require designs that are more complex, for the following reason. Given a $V_{max}$ analog input and an analog input $e$, how does the converter know what binary value to assign in order to satisfy the above ratio? Unlike DACs, there is no simple analog circuit to compute $d$ from $e$. Instead, an ADC may itself contain a DAC also connected to $V_{max}$. The ADC "guesses" an encoding $d$, and then evaluates its guess by inputting $d$ into the DAC, and comparing the generated analog output $e'$ with the original analog input $e$

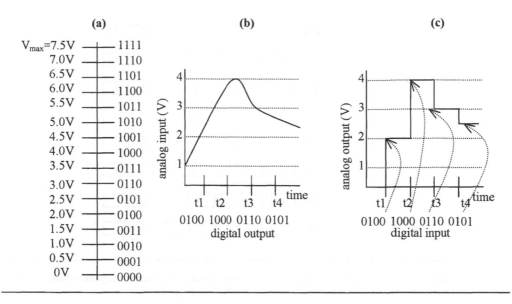

Figure 4.13: Conversion: (a) proportionality, (b) analog-to-digital, (c) digital-to-analog.

(using an analog comparator). If the two sufficiently match, then the ADC has found a proper encoding. So now the question remains: how do we guess the correct encoding?

This problem is analogous to the common computer-programming problem of finding an item in a list. One approach is sequential search, or "counting-up" in analog-digital terminology. In this approach, we start with an encoding of 0, then 1, then 2, etc., until we find a match. Unfortunately, while simple, this approach (in the worst case) requires $2^n$ comparisons (where $n$ was the number of bits in the encoding), so it may be quite slow.

A faster solution uses what programmers call binary search, or "successive approximation" in analog-digital terminology. We start with an encoding corresponding to half of the maximum. We then compare the resulting analog value with the original; if the resulting value is greater (less) than the original, we set the new encoding to halfway between this one and the maximum (minimum). We continue this process, dividing the possible encoding range in half at each step, until the compared voltages are equal. This technique requires at most $n$ comparisons, which is significantly better than $2^n$. However, it requires a more complex converter.

Because ADCs must guess the correct encoding, they require some time. Thus, in addition to the analog input and digital output, they include a *start* input that starts the conversion, and a *done* output to indicate that the conversion is complete.

## Example: Successive Approximation

Given an analog input signal whose voltage should range from 0 to 15 V, and an 8-bit digital encoding, we are to calculate the correct encoding of 5 V. Let us trace through the successive-

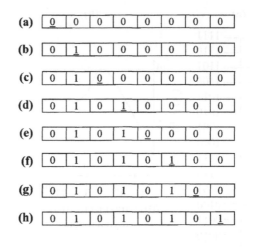

Figure 4.14: Successive approximation: given an analog input signal whose voltage should range from 0 to 15 V, and 8 bits for digital encoding, we are to calculate the correct encoding of 5 V.

approximation approach to find the correct encoding. We already know that the encoding should be:

$$5/15 = d/(2^8-1)$$

$$d = 85$$

Applying the successive approximation method we start by finding the halfway point between the maximum and minimum voltages, where $V_{max} = 15$ V and $V_{min} = 0$ V:

7.5 V

Since the above voltage is higher than the input voltage we insert a zero into the highest bit, as shown in Figure 4.14(a). We also know that the highest possible value is 7.5 V, so we set $V_{max} = 7.5$ V. Next, we plug into the formula again and compute the next approximation:

$$\tfrac{1}{2}(7.5 + 0)$$

3.75 V

Since the above voltage is lower then the input voltage, we insert a one into the next most significant bit, as shown in Figure 4.14(b). We know the lowest possible value is 3.75 V, so $V_{min}$ is set to 3.75 V. Next, we plug into the formula and compute the next approximation:

$$\tfrac{1}{2}(7.5 + 3.75)$$

5.63 V

Since the above value is higher than the input voltage, we insert a zero into the next bit, as shown in Figure 4.14(c). Note that $V_{max}$ is set to 5.63 V. Now we plug into the formula and compute the next approximation:

$$½(5.63 + 3.75)$$

$$4.69 \text{ V}$$

Since the above value is lower than the input voltage, we insert a one into the next most significant bit, as shown in Figure 4.14(d). Note that $V_{min}$ is set to 4.69 V. Now we plug into the formula and compute the next approximation:

$$½(5.63 + 4.69)$$

$$5.16 \text{ V}$$

Since the above value is higher than the input voltage, we insert a zero into the next most significant bit, as shown in Figure 4.14(e). Note that $V_{max}$ is set to 5.16 V. Now we plug into the formula and compute the next approximation:

$$½(5.16 + 4.69)$$

$$4.93 \text{ V}$$

Since the above value is lower then the input voltage, we insert a one into the next bit, as shown in Figure 4.14(f). Note that $V_{min}$ is set to 4.93 V. Now we plug into the formula and compute the next approximation:

$$½(5.16 + 4.93)$$

$$5.05 \text{ V}$$

Since the above voltage is higher than the input voltage, we insert a zero into the next bit, as shown in Figure 4.14(g). Note that $V_{max}$ is set to 5.05 V. Now we plug into the formula and compute the next approximation:

$$½(5.05 + 4.93)$$

$$4.99 \text{ V}$$

Since the above voltage is less than the input voltage, we insert a one into the next bit, as shown in Figure 4.14(h).

The encoding is now done. Note that the division by ½ can be done efficiently in binary arithmetic by simply shifting the number to right. The resulting value, shown in Figure 4.14(h), is 01010101 = 85, as expected.

# 4.9  Real-Time Clocks

Much like a digital wristwatch, a *real-time clock* (RTC) keeps the time and date in an embedded system. Real-time clocks are typically composed of a crystal-controlled oscillator, numerous cascaded counters, and a battery backup. The crystal-controlled oscillator generates a very consistent high-frequency digital pulse that feeds the cascaded counters. The first counter, typically, counts these pulses up to the oscillator frequency, which corresponds to exactly one second. At this point, it generates a pulse that feeds the next counter. This counter counts up to 59, at which point it generates a pulse feeding the minute counter. The hour, date, month, and year counters work in a similar fashion. In addition, real-time clocks adjust for leap years. The rechargeable back-up battery is used to keep the real-time clock running while the system is powered off.

From the microcontroller's point of view, the content of these counters can be set to a desired value, which corresponds to setting the clock, and retrieved. Communication between the microcontroller and a real-time clock is typically accomplished through a serial bus, such as $I^2C$. It should be noted that, given a timer peripheral, it is possible to implement a real-time clock in software running on a processor. In fact, many systems use this approach to maintain the time. However, the drawback of such systems is that when the processor is shut down or reset, the time is lost.

## 4.10 Summary

Numerous single-purpose processors are manufactured to fulfill a specific function in a variety of embedded systems. These standard single-purpose processors may be fast and small, and they have low unit and NRE costs. A timer informs us when a particular interval of time has passed, while a watchdog timer requires us to signal it within a particular interval to indicate that a program is running without error. A counter informs us when a particular number of pulses have occurred on a signal. A UART converts parallel data to serial data, and vice versa. A PWM generates pulses on an output signal, with specific high and low times. An LCD controller simplifies the writing of characters to an LCD. A keypad controller simplifies capture and decoding of a button press. A stepper-motor controller assists us to rotate a stepper motor a fixed amount forward or backward. ADCs and DACs convert analog signals to digital, and vice versa. A real-time clock keeps track of date and time. Most of these single-purpose processors could be implemented as software on a general-purpose processor, but such implementation can be burdensome. These standard single-purpose processors thus simplify embedded system design tremendously. Many microcontrollers integrate these processors on-chip.

## 4.11 References and Further Reading

- *Embedded Systems Programming*. Includes information on a variety of single-purpose processors, such as programs for implementing or using timers and UARTs on microcontrollers.

- Spasov, Peter, *Microcontroller Technology: The 68HC11*, 2nd edition. Englewood Cliffs, NJ: Prentice Hall, 1996. Contains descriptions of principles and details for common 68HC11 peripherals.

# 4.12 Exercises

4.1 Given a timer structured as in Figure 4.1(c) and a clock frequency of 10 MHz: (a) Determine its range and resolution. (b) Calculate the terminal count value needed to measure 3 ms intervals. (c) If a prescaler is added, what is the minimum division needed to measure an interval of 100 ms? (Divisions should be in powers of 2.) Determine this design's range and resolution. (d) If instead of a prescaler a second 16-bit up-counter is cascaded as in Figure 4.1(d), what is the range and resolution of this design?

4.2 A watchdog timer that uses two cascaded 16-bit up-counters as in Figure 4.1(d) is connected to an 11.981 MHz oscillator. A timeout should occur if the function *watchdog_reset* is not called within 5 minutes. What value should be loaded into the up-counter pair when the function is called?

4.3 Given a controller with two built-in timers designed as in Figure 4.1(b), write C code for a function "double *RPM*" that returns the revolutions per minute of some device or −1 if a timer overflows. Assume all inputs to the timers have been initialized and the timers have been started before entering *RPM*. *Timer1's cnt_in* is connected to the device and is pulsed once for each revolution. *Timer2's clk* input is connected to a 10 MHz oscillator. The timers have the outputs *cnt*1, *cnt*2, *top*1, and *top*2, which were initialized to 0 when their respective timer began. What is the minimum (other than 0) and maximum revolutions per minute that can be measured if *top* is not used?

4.4 Given a 100 MHz crystal-controlled oscillator and a 32-bit and any number of 16-bit terminal-count timers, design a real-time clock that outputs the date and time down to milliseconds. You can ignore leap years. Draw a diagram and indicate terminal-count values for all timers.

4.5 Determine the values for *smod* and *TH*1 to generate a baud rate of 9,600 for the 8051 baud rate equation in the chapter, assuming an 11.981 MHz oscillator. Remember that *smod* is 2 bits and *TH*1 is 8 bits. There is more than one correct answer.

4.6 A particular motor operates at 10 revolutions per second when its controlling input voltage is 3.7 V. Assume that you are using a microcontroller with a PWM whose output port can be set high (5 V) or low (0 V). (a) Compute the duty cycle necessary to obtain 10 revolutions per second. (b) Provide values for a pulse width and period that achieve this duty cycle. You do not need to consider whether the frequency is too high or too low although the values should be reasonable. There is no one correct answer.

4.7 Using the PWM described in Figure 4.6 compute the value assigned to PWM1 to achieve an RPM of 8,050 assuming the input voltage needed is 4.375 V.

4.8 Write a function in pseudocode that initializes the LCD described in Figure 4.7. After initialization, the display should be clear with a blinking cursor. The initialization should set the following data to shift to the left, have a data length of 8-bits and a font of 5 × 10 dots, and be displayed on one line.

4.9 Given a 120-step stepper motor with its own controller, write a C function *Rotate (int degrees)*, which, given the desired rotation amount in degrees (between 0 and 360), pulses a microcontroller's output port the correct number of times to achieve the desired rotation.

4.10 Modify only the *main* function in Figure 4.12 to cause a 240-step stepper motor to rotate forward 60 degrees followed by a backward rotation of 33 degrees. This stepper motor uses the same input sequence as the example for each step. In other words, do not change the lookup table.

4.11 Extend the ratio and resolution equations of analog-to-digital conversion to any voltage range between $V_{min}$ to $V_{max}$ rather than 0 to $V_{max}$.

4.12 Given an analog output signal whose voltage should range from 0 to 10 V, and an 8-bit digital encoding, provide the encodings for the following desired voltages: (a) 0 V, (b) 1 V, (c) 5.33 V, (d) 10 V, (e) What is the resolution of our conversion?

4.13 Given an analog input signal whose voltage ranges from 0 to 5 V, and an 8-bit digital encoding, calculate the correct encoding for 3.5 V, and then trace the successive-approximation approach (i.e., list all the guessed encodings in the correct order) to find the correct encoding.

4.14 Given an analog input signal whose voltage ranges from –5 to 5 V, and a 8-bit digital encoding, calculate the correct encoding 1.2 V, and then trace the successive-approximation approach to find the correct encoding.

4.15 Compute the memory needed in bytes to store a 4-bit digital encoding of a 3-second analog audio signal sampled every 10 milliseconds.

# CHAPTER 5: *Memory*

5.1    Introduction
5.2    Memory Write Ability and Storage Permanence
5.3    Common Memory Types
5.4    Composing Memory
5.5    Memory Hierarchy and Cache
5.6    Advanced RAM
5.7    Summary
5.8    References and Further Reading
5.9    Exercises

## 5.1    Introduction

Any embedded system's functionality consists of three aspects: processing, storage, and communication. Processing is the transformation of data, storage is the retention of data for later use, and communication is the transfer of data. Each of these aspects must be implemented. We use *processors* to implement processing, *memory* to implement storage, and *buses* to implement communication. The earlier chapters described common processor types: custom single-purpose processors, general-purpose processors, and standard single-purpose processors. This chapter describes memory.

Let's start by describing some basic memory concepts. A memory stores large numbers of bits. These bits can be viewed as $m$ words of $n$ bits each, for a total of $m * n$ bits, as illustrated in Figure 5.1(a). We refer to a memory as an $m \times n$ ("$m$-by-$n$") memory. Figure 5.1(b) shows an external view of a memory. $Log_2(m)$ address input signals are required to identify a particular word. Stated another way, if a memory has $k$ address inputs, it can have up to $2^k$ words. $n$ data signals are required to output (and possibly input) a selected word. For example, a 4,096-by-8 memory can store 32,768 bits, and requires 12 address signals and eight input/output data signals. To read a memory means to retrieve the word of a particular address, while to write a memory means to store a word in a particular address. A *memory access* refers to either a read or write. A memory that can be both read and written requires an

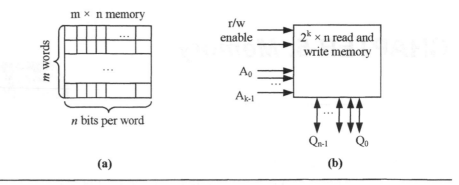

Figure 5.1: Memory: (a) words and bits per word, (b) memory block diagram.

additional control input, labeled *r/w* in Figure 5.1(b), to indicate which access to perform. Most memory types have an enable control input, which when deasserted, causes the memory to ignore the address, such that data is neither written to or read from the memory. Some types of memory, known as *multiport* memory, support multiple accesses to different locations simultaneously. Such a memory has multiple sets of control lines, address lines, and data lines, where one set of address and corresponding data and control lines is known as a *port*.

Memory has evolved very rapidly over the past few decades. The main advancement has been the trend of memory-chip bit-capacity doubling every 18 months, following Moore's Law. The importance of this trend in enabling today's sophisticated embedded systems should not be underestimated. No matter how fast and complex processors become, those processors still need memories to store programs and to store data to operate on. For example, a digital camera is possible not only because of fast A2D and compression processors but also because of memories capable of storing sufficient quantities of bits to represent quality pictures.

Further advancements to memory have blurred the distinction between the two traditional memory categories of ROM and RAM, providing designers with the benefit of more choice. Traditionally, the term *ROM* has referred to a memory that a processor can only read, and which holds its stored bits even without a power source. The term *RAM* has referred to a memory that a processor can both read and write but loses its stored bits if power is removed. However, processors can not only read, but also write to advanced ROMs, like EEPROM and Flash, although such writing may be slow compared to writing RAMs. Furthermore, advanced RAMs, like NVRAMs, can hold their bits even when power is removed.

Thus, in this chapter, we depart from the traditional ROM/RAM distinction, and instead distinguish among memories using two characteristics, namely write ability and storage permanence. We then introduce forms of memories commonly found in embedded systems. We describe techniques for the common task of composing memories to build bigger memories. We describe the use of memory hierarchy to improve memory access speed.

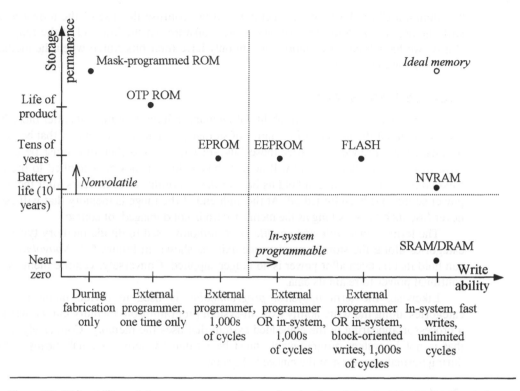

Figure 5.2: Write ability and storage permanence of memories, showing relative degrees along each axis (not to scale).

## 5.2 Memory Write Ability and Storage Permanence

### Write Ability

We use the term *write ability* to refer to the manner and speed that a particular memory can be written. All types of memory can be read from by a processor, since otherwise their stored bits would serve little purpose in an embedded system. Likewise, all types of memory can be written, since otherwise we would have no way to store bits in such a memory. However, the manner and speed of such writing varies greatly among memory types.

At the high end of the range of write ability, we have types of memory that a processor can write to simply and quickly by setting such a memory's address lines, data input bits, and control lines appropriately. Toward the middle of the range, we have types of memory that are slower to write by a processor. Toward the lower end of the range, we have types of memory that can only be written to by a special piece of equipment called a "programmer." This device must apply special voltage levels to write to the memory, also known as "programming" or "burning" the memory. Do not confuse this use of the term *programmer* with the use referring to someone who writes software. At the low end of the range of write ability, we have types of memory that can only have their bits stored when the memory chip itself is being fabricated.

## Storage Permanence

*Storage permanence* refers to the ability of memory to hold its stored bits after those bits have been written. At the low end of the range of storage permanence is memory that begins to lose its bits almost immediately after those bits are written, and therefore must be continually refreshed. Next is memory that will hold its bits as long as power is applied to the memory. Next comes memory that can hold its bits for days, months, or even years after the memory's power source has been turned off. At the high-end of the range is memory that will essentially never lose its bits — as long as the memory chip is not damaged, of course.

The terms *nonvolatile* and *volatile* are commonly used to divide memory types into two categories along the storage permanence axis, as shown in Figure 5.2. *Nonvolatile* memory can hold its bits even after power is no longer supplied. Conversely, volatile memory requires continual power to retain its data.

Likewise, the term *in-system programmable* is used to divide memories into two categories along the write ability axis. In-system programmable memory can be written to by a processor appearing in the embedded system that uses the memory. Conversely, a memory that is not in-system programmable must be written by some external means, rather than during normal operation of the embedded system.

## Trade-offs

As described in Chapter 1, design metrics often compete with one another. Memory write ability and storage permanence are two such metrics. Ideally, we want a memory with the highest write ability and the highest storage permanence, as illustrated by the ideal memory point in Figure 5.2. Unfortunately, write ability and storage permanence tend to be inversely proportional to one another. Furthermore, highly writable memory typically requires more area and/or power than less-writable memory.

## 5.3 Common Memory Types

### Introduction to "Read-Only" Memory — ROM

ROM, or read-only memory, is a nonvolatile memory that can be read from, but not written to, by a processor in an embedded system. Of course, there must be a mechanism for setting the bits in the memory, but we call this programming, not writing. For traditional types of ROM, such programming is done off-line, when the memory is not actively serving as a memory in an embedded system. We program such a ROM before inserting it into the embedded system. Figure 5.3(a) provides an external block diagram of a ROM.

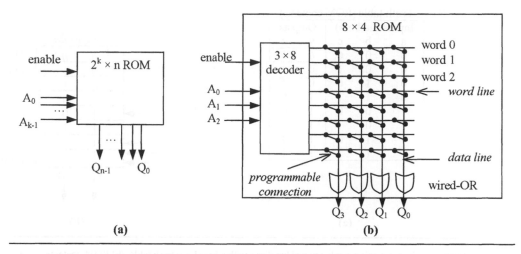

Figure 5.3: ROM: (a) external block diagram, (b) internal view of an $8 \times 4$ ROM.

We can use ROM for various purposes. One use is to store a software program for a general-purpose processor. We may write each program instruction to one ROM word. For some processors, we write each instruction to several ROM words. For other processors, we may pack several instructions into a single ROM word. A related use is to store constant data, like large lookup tables of strings or numbers.

A second common use is to store constant data needed by a system. A third, less common, use is to implement a combinational circuit. We can implement any combinational function of $k$ variables by using a $2^k \times 1$ ROM, and we can implement $n$ functions of the same $k$ variables using a $2^k \times n$ ROM. We simply program the ROM to implement the truth table for the functions, as shown in Figure 5.4.

Figure 5.3(b) provides a symbolic view of the internal design of an $8 \times 4$ ROM. To the right of the $3 \times 8$ decoder in the figure is a grid of lines, with word lines running horizontally and data lines vertically; lines that cross without a circle in the figure are not connected. Thus, word lines only connect to data lines via the programmable connection lines shown. The figure shows all connection lines in place except for two connections in word 2. To see how this device acts as a read-only memory, consider an input address of 010. The decoder will thus set word 2's line to 1. Because the lines connecting this word line with data lines 2 and 0 do not exist, the ROM output will read 1010. Note that if the ROM *enable* input were 0, then no word would be read, since all decoder outputs would be 0. Also note that each data line is shown as a wired-OR, meaning that the wire itself acts to logically OR all the connections to it.

How do we program the programmable connections? The answer depends on the type of ROM being used. Common types include mask-programmed ROM, one-time programmable ROM, erasable programmable ROM, electrically erasable programmable ROM, and Flash, in order of increasing write ability. In terms of write ability, the latter two have such a high

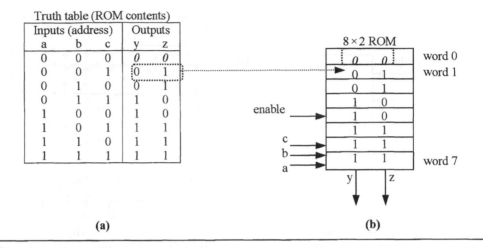

Figure 5.4: Implementing combinational functions with a ROM: (a) truth table, (b) ROM contents.

degree of write ability that calling them read-only memory is not really accurate. In terms of storage permanence, all ROMs have high storage permanence, and in fact, all are nonvolatile. We now describe each ROM type briefly.

## Mask-Programmed ROM

In a *mask-programmed* ROM, the connection is programmed when the chip is being fabricated by creating an appropriate set of masks. Mask-programmed ROM obviously has extremely low write ability, as illustrated in Figure 5.2, but has the highest storage permanence of any memory type, since the stored bits will never change unless the chip is damaged. Such ROM types are typically only used after a final design has been determined, and only in high-volume systems, for which the NRE costs can be amortized to result in a lower unit cost than other ROM types.

## OTP ROM — One-Time Programmable ROM

Many systems use some form of user-programmable ROM device, meaning the ROM can be programmed by a designer in the lab, long after the chip has been manufactured. User-programmable ROMs are generally referred to as *programmable* ROMs, or PROMs. These devices are better suited to prototyping and to low-volume applications than are mask-programmed ROM. The most basic PROM uses a fuse for each programmable connection. To program a PROM device, the user provides a file that indicates the desired ROM contents. A piece of equipment called a ROM programmer then configures each programmable connection according to the file. Note that here the programmer is a piece of equipment, not a person who writes software. The ROM programmer blows fuses by passing a large current wherever a connection should not exist. However, once a fuse is blown, the connection can never be reestablished. For this reason, basic PROM is often referred to as one-time-programmable ROM, or OTP ROM.

OTP ROMs have the lowest write ability of all PROMs, as illustrated in Figure 5.2, since they can only be written once, and they require a programmer device. However, they have very high storage permanence, since their stored bits won't change unless someone reconnects the device to a programmer and blows more fuses. Because of their high storage permanence, OTP ROMs are commonly used in final products, versus other PROMs, which are more susceptible to having their contents inadvertently modified from radiation, maliciousness, or just the mere passage of many years.

OTP ROMs are also cheaper per chip than other PROMs, often costing under a dollar each. This also makes them more attractive in final products versus other types of PROM, and also versus mask-programmed ROM when time-to-market constraints or unit costs make them a better choice. Because the chips are so cheap, some designers even use OTP ROMs during design development. Those designers simply throw away the used chips as they program new ones.

## EPROM — Erasable Programmable ROM

Another type of PROM is an *erasable* PROM, or EPROM. This device uses a MOS transistor as its programmable component. The transistor has a "floating gate," shown in Figure 5.5(a), meaning the transistor's gate is not connected and is instead surrounded by insulator. An EPROM programmer injects electrons into the floating gate, using higher than normal voltage (usually 12 V to 25 V) that causes electrons to tunnel through the insulator into the gate, as in Figure 5.5(b). When that high voltage is removed, the electrons cannot escape, and hence the gate has been charged and programming has occurred. Reading an EPROM is much faster than writing, since reading doesn't require programming. To erase the program, the electrons must be excited enough to escape from the gate. Ultraviolet (UV) light is used to fulfill this role of erasing, as shown in Figure 5.5(c). The device must be placed under a UV eraser for a period of time, typically ranging from 5 to 30 minutes, after which the device can be programmed again. For the UV light to reach the chip, EPROMs come with a small quartz window in the package through which the chip can be seen, as shown in Figure 5.5(d). For this reason, EPROM is often referred to as a *windowed* ROM device. EPROMs can typically be erased and reprogrammed thousands of times, and standard EPROMs are guaranteed to hold their programs for at least 10 years.

Compared with OTP ROM, EPROMs have improved write ability, as illustrated in Figure 5.2, since they can be erased and reprogrammed thousands of times. However, they have reduced storage permanence, since they are guaranteed to hold a program only for about 10 years, and their stored bits are susceptible to undesired changes if the chip is used in environments with much electrical noise or radiation. Thus, use of EPROMs in production parts is limited. If used in production, EPROMs should have their windows covered by a sticker to reduce the likelihood of undesired changes of the memory.

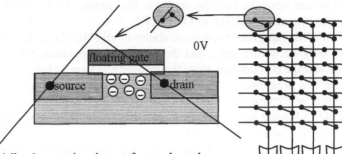

0V

**(a)** Initially, the negative charges form a channel between the source and drain of the transistor storing a logic 1 at that cell's location.

+15V

**(b)** By applying a large positive voltage at the gate of the transistor, the negative charges move out of the channel area and get trapped in the floating gate, storing a logic 0 at that cell's location.

5-30 min

**(c)** By shining UV rays on the surface of the floating-gate, the negative charges move down into the channel restoring the logic 1 at the cell's location.

**(d)** An EPROM package with a quartz window through which UV light can pass.

Figure 5.5: EPROM internals.

## EEPROM — Electrically Erasable Programmable ROM

*Electrically erasable* PROM, or EEPROM, developed in the early 1980s, was designed to eliminate the time-consuming and sometimes impossible requirement of exposing an EPROM to UV light to erase the ROM. An EEPROM is not only programmed electronically, but it is also erased electronically, typically by using higher than normal voltage. Such electronic erasing typically only requires seconds, rather than the many minutes required for EPROMs. Furthermore, EEPROMs can have individual words erased and reprogrammed, whereas

EPROMs can only be erased in their entirety. EEPROMs are typically more expensive than EPROMs, but far more convenient to use. EEPROMs are often called $E^2$s, pronounced "E-squareds."

Because EEPROMs can be erased and programmed electronically, we can build the circuit providing the higher-than-normal voltage levels for such electronic erasing and programming right into the embedded system in which the EEPROM is being used. Thus, we can treat this as a memory that can be both read and written — a write to a particular word would consist of erasing that word followed by programming that word. Thus, an EEPROM is in-system programmable. We can use it to store data that an embedded system should save after power is shut off. For example, EEPROM is typically used in telephones that can store commonly dialed phone numbers in memory for speed-dialing. If you unplug the phone, thus shutting off power, and then plug it back in, the numbers will still be in memory. EEPROMs can typically hold data for 10 years and can be erased and programmed tens of thousands of times before losing their ability to store data.

In-system programming of EEPROMs has become so common that many EEPROMs come with a built-in memory controller. A *memory controller* hides internal memory-access details from the memory user, and provides a simple memory interface to the user. In this case, the memory controller would contain the circuitry and single-purpose processor necessary for erasing the word at the user-specified address, and then programming the user-specified data into that word.

While read accesses may require only tens of nanoseconds, writes may require tens of microseconds or more, because of the necessary erasing and programming. Thus, EEPROMs with built-in memory controllers will typically latch the address and data, so that the writing processor can move on to other tasks. Furthermore, such an EEPROM would have an extra "busy" pin to indicate to the processor that the EEPROM is busy writing, meaning that a processor wanting to write to the EEPROM must check the value of this busy pin before attempting to write. Some EEPROMs support read accesses even while the memory is busy writing.

A common use of EEPROM is to serve as the program memory for a microprocessor. In this case, we may want to ensure that the memory cannot be in-system programmed. Thus, EEPROM typically comes with a pin that can be used to disable programming.

EEPROMs are more writable than EPROMs, as illustrated in Figure 5.2, since EEPROMs can be programmed in-system, and they are easier to erase. EEPROM is where the distinction between ROM and RAM begins to blur, since EEPROMs are in-system programmable and thus writable directly by a processor. Thus, the term "read-only-memory" for EEPROM is really a misnomer, since the processor can in fact write to an EEPROM. Such writes are slow compared to reads and are limited in number, but nevertheless, EEPROMs can and are commonly written by a processor during normal system operation.

## Flash Memory

Flash memory is an extension of EEPROM that was developed in the late 1980s. While also using the floating-gate principle of EEPROM, flash memory is designed such that large blocks of memory can be erased all at once, rather than just one word at a time as in traditional EEPROM. A block is typically several thousand bytes large. This fast erase ability can vastly improve the performance of embedded systems where large data items must be stored in nonvolatile memory, systems like digital cameras, TV set-top boxes, cell phones, and medical monitoring equipment. It can also speed manufacturing throughput, since programming the complete contents of flash may be faster than programming a similar-sized EEPROM.

Like EEPROM, each block in a flash memory can typically be erased and reprogrammed tens of thousands of times before the block loses its ability to store data, and can store its data for 10 years or more.

A drawback of flash memory is that writing to a single word in flash may be slower than writing to a single word in EEPROM, since an entire block will need to be read, the word within it updated, and than the block written back.

## Introduction to Read-Write Memory — RAM

We now turn our attention to a type of memory referred to as RAM. RAM, or random-access memory, is a memory that can be both read and written easily. Writing to a RAM is about as fast as reading from a RAM, in contrast to in-system programmable ROMs where writes take much longer than reads. Furthermore, RAM is typically volatile. Unlike forms of ROM, RAM never contains data when inserted in an embedded system. Instead, the system writes data to and then reads data from the RAM during its execution. Figure 5.1(b) provides a block diagram of a RAM.

A common question is, where does the term *random-access* come from in the name random-access memory? RAM should really be called read-write memory, to contrast it from read-only memory. However, when RAM was first introduced, it was in stark contrast to the then-common sequentially accessed memory media, like magnetic tapes or drums. These media required that the particular location to be accessed be positioned under an access device (e.g., a head). To access another location not immediately adjacent to the current location on

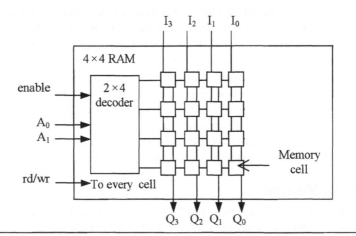

Figure 5.6: RAM internals.

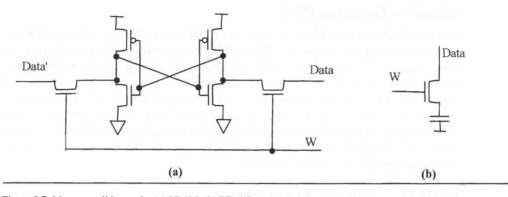

Figure 5.7: Memory cell internals: (a) SRAM, (b) DRAM.

the media, one would have to sequence through a number of other locations. For example, a tape would have to be rewound or fast-forwarded. In contrast, with RAM, any "random" memory location could be accessed in the same amount of time as any other location, regardless of the previously accessed location. This random-access feature was the key distinguishing feature of this memory type at the time of its introduction, and the name has stuck even today.

A RAM's internal structure is somewhat more complex than a ROM's, as shown in Figure 5.6, which illustrates a 4 × 4 RAM. (*Note*: RAMs typically have thousands of words, not just four as in the figure.) Each word consists of a number of memory cells, each storing 1 bit. In the figure, each input data line connects to every cell in its column. Likewise, each output data line connects to every cell in its column, with the output of a memory cell being ORed with the output data line from above. Each word enable line from the decoder connects to every cell in its row. The read/write input (*rd/wr*) is assumed to be connected to every cell. The memory cell must possess logic such that it stores the input data bit when *rd/wr* indicates write and the row is enabled, and such that it outputs this bit when *rd/wr* indicates read and the row is enabled.

There are two basic types of RAM, static and dynamic. Static RAM is faster but larger than dynamic RAM. Furthermore, static RAM is easily implemented on the same IC as processors, whereas dynamic RAM is usually implemented on a separate IC.

## SRAM — Static RAM

*Static* RAM, or SRAM, uses a memory cell, shown in Figure 5.7(a), consisting of a flip-flop to store a bit. Each bit thus requires about six transistors. This RAM type is called static because it will hold its data as long as power is supplied, in contrast to dynamic RAM. Static RAM is typically used for high-performance parts of a system (e.g., cache).

## DRAM — Dynamic RAM

*Dynamic* RAM, or DRAM, uses a memory cell, shown in Figure 5.7(b), consisting of a MOS transistor and capacitor to store a bit. Each bit thus requires only one transistor, resulting in more compact memory than SRAM. However, the charge stored in the capacitor leaks gradually, leading to discharge and eventually to loss of data. To prevent loss of data, each cell must regularly have its charge "refreshed." A typical DRAM cell's minimum refresh rate is once every 15.625 microseconds. Because of the way DRAMs are designed, reading a DRAM word refreshes that word's cells. In particular, accessing a DRAM word results in the word's data being stored in a buffer and then being written back to the word's cells. DRAMs tend to be slower to access than SRAMs.

## PSRAM — Pseudo-Static RAM

Many RAM variations exist. *Pseudo-static* RAMs, or PSRAMs, are DRAMs with a memory refresh controller built-in. Thus, since the RAM user need not worry about refreshing, the device appears to behave much like an SRAM. However, in contrast to true SRAM, a PSRAM may be busy refreshing itself when accessed, which could slow access time and add some system complexity. Nevertheless, PSRAM is a popular low-cost high-density memory alternative to SRAM in many embedded systems.

## NVRAM — Nonvolatile RAM

*Nonvolatile* RAM, or NVRAM, is a special RAM variation that is able to hold its data even after external power is removed. There are two common types of NVRAM.

One type, often called *battery-backed RAM*, contains a static RAM along with it own permanently connected battery. When external power is removed or drops below a certain threshold, the internal battery maintains power to the SRAM, and thus the memory continues to store its bits. Compared with other forms of nonvolatile memory, battery-backed RAM is far more writable, as illustrated in Figure 5.2. Since no special programming is necessary, writes are done in nanoseconds, just like reads. Furthermore, unlike ROM-based forms of nonvolatile memory, battery-backed RAM imposes no limits on the number of times it can be written to. Storage permanence is obviously better than SRAM or DRAM, with many NVRAMs having batteries that can last for 10 years. However, NVRAMs are more susceptible to having bits changed inadvertently due to noise than are EEPROM or flash.

A second type of NVRAM contains a static RAM as well as an EEPROM or flash having the same capacity as the static RAM. This type of NVRAM stores its complete RAM contents into the EEPROM just before power is turned off, or whenever instructed to store the data, and then reloads that data from EEPROM into RAM after power is turned back on.

## Example: HM6264 and 27C256 RAM/ROM Devices

In this example, we introduce a pair of low-cost low-capacity memory devices, shown in Figure 5.8(a), commonly used in 8-bit microcontroller-based embedded systems. The first two numeric digits in these devices indicate whether the device is RAM (62) or ROM (27).

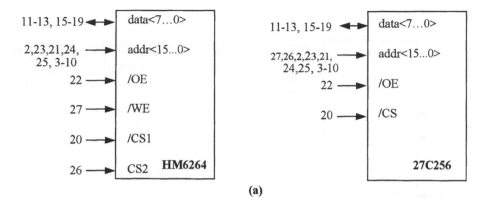

**(a)**

| Device | Access Time (ns) | Standby Pwr. (mW) | Active Pwr. (mW) | Vcc Voltage (V) |
|--------|------------------|-------------------|------------------|-----------------|
| HM6264 | 85-100 | .01 | 15 | 5 |
| 27C256 | 90 | .5 | 100 | 5 |

**(b)**

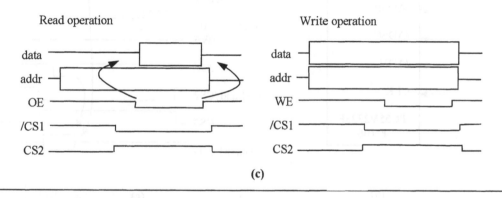

**(c)**

Figure 5.8: HM6264 and 27C256 RAM/ROM devices: (a) block diagram, (b) characteristics, (c) timing diagrams.

Subsequent digits give the memory capacity in kilobits. Both these devices are available in 4, 8, 16, 32, and 64 kilobytes, so the part numbers 62 or 27 would be followed by the number of kilobits, which may be 32, 64, 128, 256, or 512. Figure 5.8(b) summarizes some of the characteristics of these devices.

Memory access to and from these devices is performed through an 8-bit parallel protocol. Placing a memory address on the address-bus and asserting the read signal output enable (*OE*) performs a read operation. Placing some data and a memory address on the data and address busses and asserting the write signal write enable (*WE*) performs a write operation. The read and write timing is given in Figure 5.8(c).

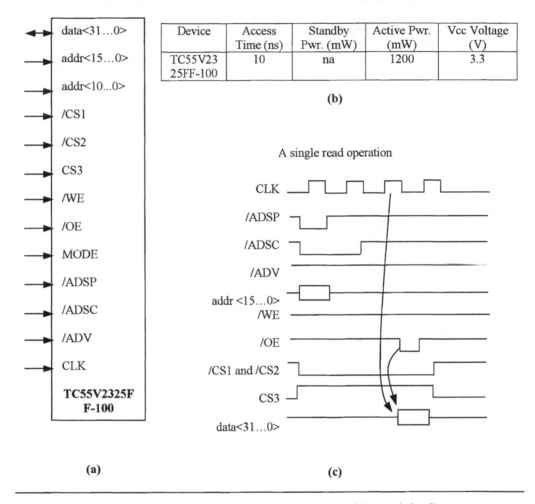

| Device | Access Time (ns) | Standby Pwr. (mW) | Active Pwr. (mW) | Vcc Voltage (V) |
|---|---|---|---|---|
| TC55V23 25FF-100 | 10 | na | 1200 | 3.3 |

(b)

(a)

(c)

Figure 5.9: TC55V2325FF-100 RAM devices: (a) block diagram, (b) characteristics, (c) timing diagrams.

## Example: TC55V2325FF-100 Memory Device

In this example, we introduce a 2-megabit synchronous pipelined burst SRAM memory device, shown in Figure 5.9(a), designed to be interfaced with 32-bit processors. This device, made by Toshiba Inc., is organized as 64K × 32 bits. Figure 5.9(b) summarizes some of the characteristics of this device.

In Figure 5.9(c), we present the timing diagram for a single read operation. Write operation is similar. This device is capable of fast sequential reads and writes as well as single byte I/O. The interested reader should refer to the manufacturer's datasheets for complete timing information. The read operation can be initiated with either the address status processor (*ADSP*) input or the address status controller (*ADSC*) input. Here, we have asserted both. Subsequent burst addresses can be generated internally and are controlled by the address advance (*ADV*) input. In other words, as long as *ADV* is asserted, the device will keep incrementing its address register and output the corresponding data on the next clock cycle.

## 5.4 Composing Memory

An embedded system designer is often faced with the situation of needing a particular-sized memory (ROM or RAM), but having readily available memories of a different size. For example, the designer may need a $2^k \times 8$ ROM, but may have $4^k \times 16$ ROMs readily available. Alternatively, the designer may need a $4^k \times 16$ ROM, but may have $2^k \times 8$ ROMs available for use.

The case where the available memory is larger than needed is easy to deal with. We simply use the needed lower words in the memory, thus ignoring unneeded higher words and their high-order address bits, and we use the lower data input/output lines, thus ignoring unneeded higher data lines. Of course, we could use the higher data lines and ignore the lower lines instead.

The case where the available memory is smaller than needed requires more design effort. In this case, we must compose several smaller memories to behave as the larger memory we need. Suppose the available memories have the correct number of words, but each word is not wide enough. In this case, we can simply connect the available memories side-by-side. For example, Figure 5.10(a) illustrates the situation of needing a ROM three-times wider than that available. We connect three ROMs side-by-side, sharing the same address and enable lines among them, and concatenating the data lines to form the desired word width.

Suppose instead that the available memories have the correct word width, but not enough words. In this case, we can connect the available memories top to bottom. For example, Figure 5.10(b) illustrates the situation of needing a ROM with twice as many words, and hence needing one extra address line, than that available. We connect the ROMs top to bottom, ORing the corresponding data lines of each. We use the extra high-order address line to select the higher or lower ROM using a $1 \times 2$ decoder, and the remaining address lines to offset into the selected ROM. Since only one ROM will ever be enabled at a time, the ORing of the data lines never actually involves more than one nonzero data line.

If we instead needed four times as many words, and hence two extra address lines, we would instead use four ROMs. A $2 \times 4$ decoder having the two high-order address line as input would select one of the four ROMs to access.

Suppose the available memories have a smaller word width as well as fewer words than necessary. We then combine the above two techniques, first creating the number of columns of memories necessary to achieve the needed word width, and then creating the number of rows of memories necessary, along with a decoder, to achieve the needed number of words. The approach is illustrated in Figure 5.10(c).

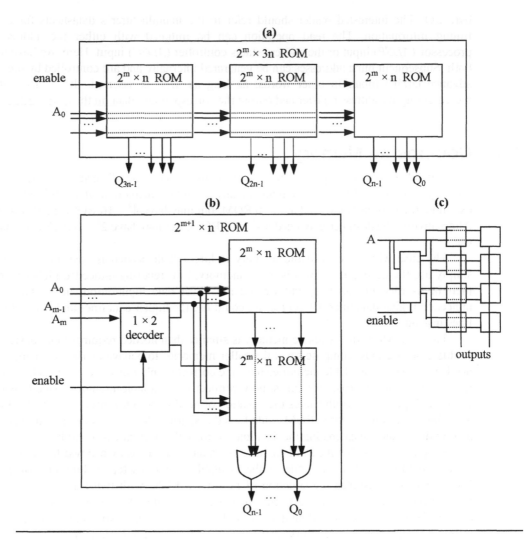

Figure 5.10: Composing smaller memory parts into larger memory.

Note that, when composing memories to increase the number of words, we don't necessarily have to use the highest-order address lines to select the appropriate memory, although these are the most logical choice. Sometimes, especially when we are composing just two memories, we use the lowest order bit to select among memories — thus, one memory represents "odd" addresses, and the other represents "even" addresses.

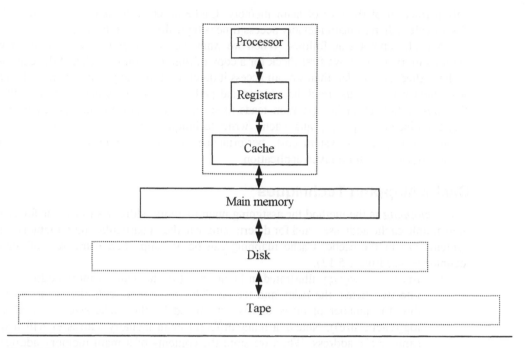

Figure 5.11: An example memory hierarchy.

## 5.5   Memory Hierarchy and Cache

When we design a memory to store an embedded system's program and data, we are often faced with a dilemma: We want an inexpensive and fast memory, but inexpensive memory tends to be slow, whereas fast memory tends to be expensive. The solution to this problem is to create a memory hierarchy, as illustrated in Figure 5.11. We use an inexpensive but slow main memory to store all of the program and data. We use a small amount of fast but expensive cache memory to store copies of likely accessed parts of main memory. Using cache is analogous to posting on a wall near a telephone a short list of important phone numbers rather than posting the entire phonebook.

Some systems include even larger and less expensive forms of memory, such as disk and tape, for some of their storage needs. However, we do not consider these further as they are not especially common in embedded systems. Also, although the figure shows only one cache, we can include any number of levels of cache, those closer to the processor being smaller and faster than those closer to main memory. A two-level cache scheme is common.

Cache is usually designed using static RAM rather than dynamic RAM, which is one reason that cache is more expensive but faster than main memory. Because cache usually appears on the same chip as a processor, where space is very limited, cache size is typically only a fraction of the size of main memory. Cache access time may be as low as just one clock cycle, whereas main memory access time is typically several cycles.

A cache operates as follows. When we want the processor to access (read or write) a main memory address, we first check for a copy of that location in cache. If the copy is in the cache, called a *cache hit*, then we can access it quickly. If the copy is not there, called a *cache miss*, then we must first read the address and perhaps some of its neighbors into the cache. This description of cache operation leads to several cache design choices: cache mapping, cache replacement policy, and cache write techniques. These design choices can have significant impact on system cost, performance, as well as power, and thus should be evaluated carefully for a given application.

## Cache Mapping Techniques

*Cache mapping* is the method for assigning main memory addresses to the far fewer number of available cache addresses, and for determining whether a particular main memory address's contents are in the cache. Cache mapping can be accomplished using one of three basic techniques (see Figure 5.12):

1. In *direct mapping*, illustrated in Figure 5.12(a), the main memory address is divided into two fields, the index and the tag. The *index* represents the cache address, and thus the number of index bits is determined by the cache size (i.e., index size = $\log_2$(cache size)). Note that many different main memory addresses will map to the same cache address. When we store the contents of a main memory address in the cache, we also store the *tag*. To determine if a desired main memory address is in the cache, we go to the cache address indicated by the index, and compare the tag there with the desired tag. If the tags match, then we check the valid bit. The *valid bit* indicates whether the data stored in that cache slot has previously been loaded into the cache from the main memory. We use the *offset* portion of the memory address to grab a particular word within the cache line. A cache *line*, also known as a cache *block*, is the number of (inseparable) adjacent memory addresses loaded from or stored into main memory at a time. A typical block size is four or eight addresses.

2. In *fully associative mapping*, illustrated in Figure 5.12(b), each cache address contains not only the contents of a main memory address, but also the complete main memory address. To determine if a desired main memory address is in the cache, we simultaneously (associatively) compare all the addresses stored in the cache with the desired address.

3. In *set-associative mapping*, illustrated in Figure 5.12(c), a compromise is reached between direct and fully associative mapping. As in direct mapping, an index maps each main memory address to a cache address, but now each cache address contains the content and tags of two or more memory locations, namely, a set of entries. To determine if a desired main memory address is in the cache, we go to the cache address indicated by the index, and we then simultaneously (associatively) compare all the tags at that location (i.e., of that set) with the desired tag. A cache with a set of size $N$ is called an $N$-way set-associative cache; 2-way, 4-way, and 8-way set associative caches are common.

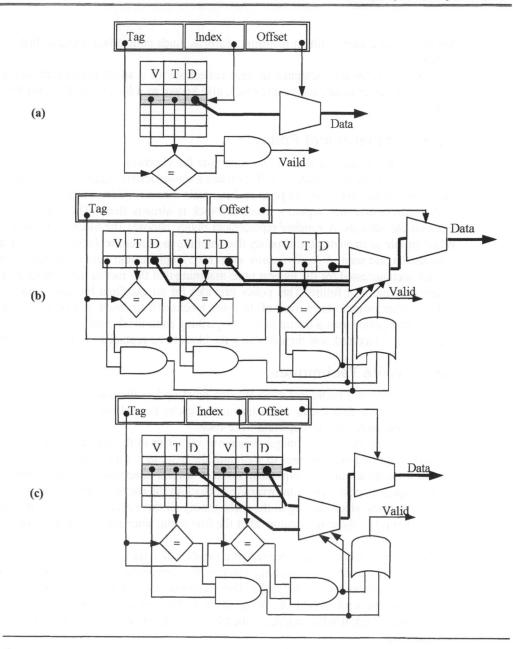

**(a)**

**(b)**

**(c)**

Figure 5.12: Cache mapping techniques: (a) direct-mapped, (b) fully associative, (c) two-way set associative.

Direct-mapped caches are easy to implement, but may result in numerous misses if two or more words with the same index are accessed frequently, since each will bump the other out of the cache. Fully associative caches on the other hand are fast, but the comparison logic is expensive to implement. Set-associative caches can reduce misses compared to direct-mapped caches, without requiring nearly as much comparison logic as fully associative caches.

Caches are usually designed to treat collections of a small number of adjacent main-memory addresses as one indivisible *block*, also known as a *line*, typically consisting of about eight addresses.

## Cache-Replacement Policy

The cache replacement policy is the technique for choosing which cache block to replace when a fully associative cache is full, or when a set-associative cache's line is full. Note that there is no choice in a direct-mapped cache; a main memory address always maps to the same cache address and thus replaces whatever block is already there. There are three common replacement policies. A *random* replacement policy chooses the block to replace randomly. While simple to implement, this policy does nothing to prevent replacing a block that is likely to be used again soon. A *least-recently used* (LRU) replacement policy replaces the block that has not been accessed for the longest time, assuming that this means that it is least likely to be accessed in the near future. This policy provides for an excellent hit/miss ratio but requires expensive hardware to keep track of the times blocks are accessed. A *first-in-first-out* (FIFO) replacement policy uses a queue of size $N$, pushing each block address onto the queue when the address is accessed, and then choosing the block to be replaced by popping the queue.

## Cache Write Techniques

When we write to a cache, we must at some point update the main memory. Such update is only an issue for data cache, since instruction cache is read-only. There are two common update techniques, write-through and write-back.

In the *write-through* technique, whenever we write to the cache, we also write to main memory, requiring the processor to wait until the write to main memory completes. Although easy to implement, this technique may result in several unnecessary writes to main memory. For example, suppose a program writes to a block in the cache, then reads it, and then writes it again, with the block staying in the cache during all three accesses. There would have been no need to update the main memory after the first write, since the second write overwrites this first write.

The *write-back* technique reduces the number of writes to main memory by writing a block to main memory only when the block is being replaced, and then only if the block was written to during its stay in the cache. This technique requires that we associate an extra bit, called a dirty bit, with each block. We set this bit whenever we write to the block in the cache, and we then check it when replacing the block to determine if we should copy the block to main memory.

## Cache Impact on System Performance

The design and configuration of caches can have a large impact on performance and power consumption of a system. So far, we looked at cache mapping, associativity, write back, and replacement policies. From a performance point of view, the most important parameters in

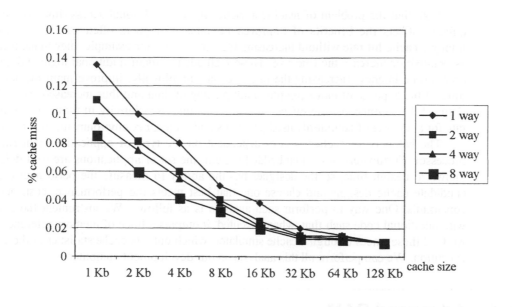

Figure 5.13: Sample cache performance trade-offs.

cache design are the total size of the cache, its degree of associativity, and the data block size, a.k.a., line size, that is read or written during each cache access by the microprocessor.

The total size of the cache is measured as the total number of data bytes that the cache can hold. Notice that a cache stores other information, such as the tags and valid bits, which do not contribute to the size of the cache. So, a 32 Kbyte cache has room for 32,678 bytes of data, plus additional storage for tag and house keeping bits. By making a cache larger, one achieves lower miss rates, which is one of the design goals. However, accessing words within a large cache will be slower than accessing words in a smaller cache. To clarify this, we will give an example. First, let us assume that we are designing a small 2 Kbyte cache for our processor. With this cache, we have measured the miss rate to be 15%, meaning 15 out of every 100 accesses to the cache result in a miss on the average. The cost of going to main memory (i.e., the cost of memory access when there is a miss) is 20 cycles. The cost of going only to the cache (i.e., the cost of memory access when there is a hit) is two cycles. Hence, on the average, the cost of a memory access is $(0.85 * 2) + (0.15 * 20) = 4.7$ cycles. Now let us double the size of the cache, and assume this improves our hit rate to 93.5%, at the expense of slowing the cache down by an extra clock cycle. Now, the average cost of a memory access becomes $(0.935 * 3) + (0.065 * 20) = 4.105$ cycles. This second cache will perform better than our first one. Now, we double the size of our cache one more time, resulting in an additional clock cycle per hit but achieving 94.435% improvement in terms of hit rate. The average cost of memory access, thus, becomes $(0.94435 * 4) + (0.05565 * 20) = 4.8904$ cycles. This larger cache will perform worse than our first two designs.

Note that the problem of making a cache larger is additional access time penalty, which quickly offsets the benefits of improved hit rates. Designers often use other methods to improve cache hit rate without increasing the cache size. For example, they make a cache set associative or increase the line size. These methods too incur additional logic and add to the access time latency. Increasing the line size can, additionally, improve main memory access time, at the expense of more complex multiplexing of data and thus increased access latency. Figure 5.13 summarizes the effects of cache size and associativity in terms of average miss rate for a number of commonly used programs under the Unix environment, such as gcc.

The behavior of caches is very dependent on the type of applications that run on the processor. Fortunately, for an embedded system, the set of applications are well defined and known at design time, so the designer has the ability to measure the performance of some candidate cache designs and choose one that best meets the performance, cost, and power constraints. One way to perform such analysis is as follows. We instrument the executable with additional code such that, when executed, it outputs a trace of memory references. Then, we feed these traces through a cache simulator, which outputs cache statistics at the end of its execution. We can perform all this analysis on our development computer.

## 5.6   Advanced RAM

Earlier we described a DRAM as a type of storage device that uses a single transistor/capacitor pair to store a bit. Because of such architecture and the resulting high capacity and low cost, DRAMs are commonly used as the main memory in processor based embedded systems. In order for DRAMs to keep pace with processor speeds, many variations on the basic DRAM interface has been proposed. In this section, we describe the structure of a basic DRAM as well as some of the more recent and advanced DRAM designs.

### The Basic DRAM

The basic DRAM architecture is depicted in Figure 5.14. The addressing mechanism for a memory read works as follow. The address bus is multiplexed between row and column components. Using the row address select (*ras*) signal, the row component of the address is latched into the row address buffer. Likewise, using the column address select (*cas*) signal, the column component of the address is latched into the column address buffer. (Note that in earlier days, the number of I/O pins were limited, hence manufacturers of DRAMs adopted this multiplexed scheme to reduce the overall I/O requirements. In fact, some DRAM devices used the same I/O pins for multiplexed data as well as multiplexed address signals.) As soon as the row address component is latched into the row address buffer, the row decoder activates an entire row of bits. The length of this bit-row depends on the word size and column address space. Once the column address buffer is latched, the column decoder enables the particular word (referred by the address) in order for it to propagate to the sense amplifier. The sense amplifier's task is to detect the voltage level of the bits (transistor/capacitor pairs) corresponding to the referenced word and amplify them to a high enough level for latching into the output buffers. Once the data is in the output buffers, it can be read by asserting the

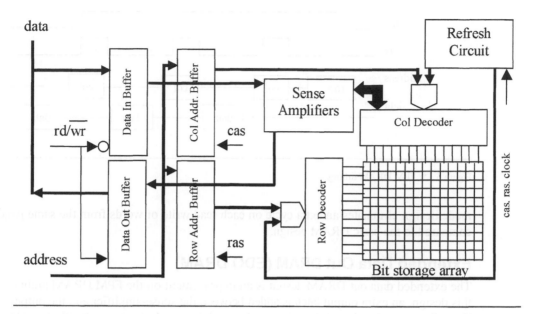

Figure 5.14: Basic DRAM architecture.

data bus read (*rd*) signal. Memory write works in the reverse order. First the word is written to the input buffers using the data bus write (*wr*) signal. Then, the row and column addresses are latched in, sequentially, by strobing the *ras* and *cas* signals, respectively.

Figure 5.14 also depicts the refresh circuitry. As noted earlier in this chapter, due to discharge of the capacitors, the content of a DRAM must be periodically read and written back. This is accomplished by the refresh circuitry (which may be internal or external to the particular DRAM device). An external clock drives the refresh circuitry. Periodically, the refresh circuitry strobes consecutive memory addresses, causing the memory content to be refreshed. (Recall that selecting a row of bits through the row decoder will automatically charge the capacitors in that row.) The refresh circuitry becomes disabled during a memory read or write operation (i.e., when any of the *ras* or *cas* signals are asserted).

## Fast Page Mode DRAM (FPM DRAM)

The fast page mode DRAM design is an improvement on the basic DRAM architecture. In this design, each row of the memory bit-array is viewed as a page. A page contains multiple words. Each word is addressed by a different column address. The sense amplifier in FPM DRAM amplifies the entire page once its address is strobed into the row address latch. Thereafter, each word of that page is read (or written) by strobing the corresponding column address. The timing diagram for FPM DRAM is depicted in Figure 5.15. Here, after selecting a particular page (row), three data words within that page are read consecutively. The page

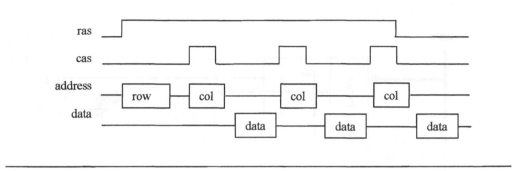

Figure 5.15: FPM DRAM timing.

mode design eliminates an extra cycle on each read/write of words from the same page when compared to the basic DRAM design.

## Extended Data Out DRAM (EDO DRAM)

The extended data out DRAM design is an improvement on the FPM DRAM architecture. In this design, an extra output latch is added between the sense-amplifier and the output buffers. This allows overlapping of the column select and data read operations. In other words, while a previously selected word is being read from the output buffer, a new column address can be strobed by asserting the *cas* signal. The timing diagram for EDO DRAM is depicted in Figure 5.16. The extra overlap reduces the read/write latency by an additional cycle when compared to FPM DRAM.

## Synchronous (S) and Enhanced Synchronous (ES) DRAM

The FPM and EDO RAM architectures described so far are controlled asynchronously by the processor or the memory controller. This means that a transaction takes place when the *ras/cas* and *rd/wr* signals are asserted in appropriate order. An alternative is to make the interface to the DRAM synchronous such that the DRAM latches information to and from the controller on the active edge of the clock signal. A synchronous interface will eliminate a small amount of time (thus latency) that is needed by the DRAM to detect the *ras/cas* and *rd/wr* signals. This architecture is referred to as *synchronous* DRAM, or SDRAM.

In addition to a lower latency I/O, after a proper page and column setup, an SDRAM may store the starting address internally and output new data on each active edge of the clock signal, as long as the requested data are consecutive memory locations. This is accomplished by adding a column address counter to the base DRAM architecture. This counter is seeded with a starting column address strobed in by the processor (or memory controller) and is thereafter incremented internally by the DRAM on each clock cycle. The timing diagram of a SDRAM device is depicted in Figure 5.17. Note that in this timing diagram, we have added the clock signal. The clock signal was not present in Figure 5.15 and Figure 5.16 because those DRAMs were asynchronous.

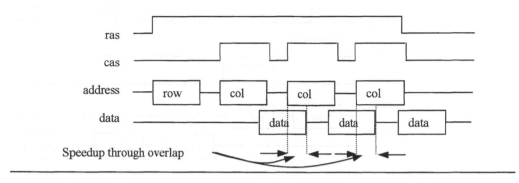

Figure 5.16: EDO DRAM timing.

The enhanced synchronous DRAM, or ESDRAM, is an improvement to the SDRAM design. The improvement is analogous to that made to the FPM DRAM by the EDRAM. In short, caches (buffers) have been added to the sense amplifiers to enable overlapping of the column addressing. This enables faster clocking and lower latency in reading and writing data.

## Rambus DRAM (RDRAM)

Rambus is really more of a bus interface architecture than DRAM architecture. Rambus uses multiplexed address/data lines to connect the memory controller (or processor) to the RDRAM device. The specification for this interface states that the clock runs at 300 MHz. In addition, data is latched on both rising and falling edge of the clock. Using such a bus, theoretically, a transfer rate of 600 million cycles is possible. In addition, each 64-Mbit RDRAM is broken into four banks (parts) each with its own row decoders. So, at any given time, four pages remain open. The RDRAM protocol is packet driven, where address packets are followed by data packets. The smallest transaction requires a minimum of four cycles. Because of its multiple open page schemes and fast bus I/O, RDRAM, when utilized properly, is capable of very high throughput.

## DRAM Integration Problem

So far, we have discussed static and dynamic types of RAMs and brought up the benefits and disadvantages of each type. In this section, we describe the problem of integrating memory and conventional logic (gates) on the same IC. While most static types of RAMs can easily be integrated with other logic on a single chip (e.g., ICs containing a cache and a microprocessor), it is very difficult to integrate DRAMs and conventional logic. The difficulty arises from the different chip making process that is involved when making DRAMs as opposed to conventional logic. When designing conventional logic ICs, the goal of the designers is to minimize the parasitic capacitance in order to reduce signal propagation delays and power consumption. In contrast, when designing DRAMs, the goal of the designers is to

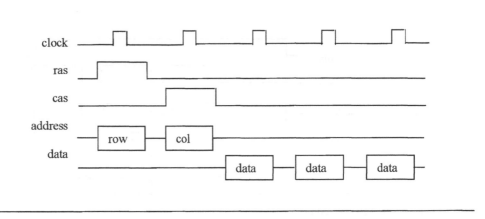

Figure 5.17: SDRAM timing.

create capacitor cells in order to retain stored information. This difference in design goal leads to a design process that is considerably different between DRAM and conventional logic. However, integrated processes are beginning to appear.

### Memory Management Unit (MMU)

We conclude this section by briefly discussing the duties of a MMU. A system that contains DRAM requires some processor that handles tasks such as refresh, DRAM bus interface and arbitration and sharing of a memory among multiple processors. In addition, the MMU translates logical memory addresses, issued by attached processors, to physical memory addresses that make sense to the particular DRAM architecture in use. Modern CPUs often come with a MMU built as part of the processor's core. Otherwise, single-purpose processors can be designed or purchased to handle such memory management tasks.

## 5.7   Summary

Memory stores data for use by processors. We have categorized memory using two characteristics, namely, write ability and storage permanence. ROM typically is only read by an embedded system. It can be programmed during fabrication (mask-programmed) or by the user (programmable ROM, or PROM). PROM may be erasable using UV light (EPROM), or electronically erasable (EEPROM) word by word, or in large blocks (Flash). RAM, on the other hand, is memory that can be read or written by an embedded system. Static RAM uses a flip-flop to store each bit, while dynamic RAM uses a transistor and capacitor, resulting in fewer transistors but the need to refresh the charge on the capacitor and slower performance. Psuedo-static RAM is a dynamic RAM with a built-in refresh controller. Nonvolatile RAM keeps its data even after power is shut off. Designers must not only choose the appropriate type of memories for a given system, but must often compose smaller memory parts into larger memory. Using a memory hierarchy can improve system performance by keeping copies of frequently accessed instructions/data in small, fast memories. Cache is a small and fast memory between a processor and main memory. Several cache design features greatly influence the speed and cost of cache, including mapping techniques, replacement policies, and write techniques. Several advanced DRAMs provide high-speed memory access, like FPM RAM, EDO RAM, and SDRAM. Integrating DRAM with on-chip processors can be difficult due to different IC processes. Thus, choice of memory types and design of a memory architecture is an important part of embedded system design, and can greatly impact performance, power, size, and cost.

# 5.8 References and Further Reading

- http://www.instantweb.com/~foldoc/contents.html, *The Free Online Dictionary of Computing*. Provides definitions of a variety of computer-related terms, including numerous ROM and RAM variations.
- David Patterson and John Hennessy, *Computer Organization and Design*. San Francisco, CA: Morgan Kaufmann Publishers, Inc. Includes discussion of memory hierarchy and cache.

# 5.9 Exercises

5.1 Briefly define each of the following: mask-programmed ROM, PROM, EPROM, EEPROM, flash EEPROM, RAM, SRAM, DRAM, PSRAM, and NVRAM.

5.2 Define the two main characteristics of memories as discussed in this chapter. From the types of memory mentioned in Excercise 5.1, list the worst choice for each characteristic. Explain.

5.3 Sketch the internal design of a $4 \times 3$ ROM.

5.4 Sketch the internal design of a $4 \times 3$ RAM.

5.5 Compose 1K x 8 ROMs into a $1K \times 32$ ROM (Note: 1K actually means 1,024 words).

5.6 Compose 1K x 8 ROMs into an $8K \times 8$ ROM.

5.7 Compose 1K x 8 ROMs into a $2K \times 16$ ROM.

5.8 Show how to use a $1K \times 8$ ROM to implement a $512 \times 6$ ROM.

5.9 Given the following three cache designs, find the one with the best performance by calculating the average cost of access. Show all calculations. (a) 4 Kbyte, 8-way set-associative cache with a 6% miss rate; cache hit costs one cycle, cache miss costs 12 cycles. (b) 8 Kbyte, 4-way set-associative cache with a 4% miss rate; cache hit costs two cycles, cache miss costs 12 cycles. (c) 16 Kbyte, 2-way set-associative cache with a 2% miss rate; cache hit costs three cycles, cache miss costs 12 cycles.

5.10 Given a 2-level cache design where the hit rates are 88% for the smaller cache and 97% for the larger cache, the access costs for a miss are 12 cycles and 20 cycles, respectively, and the access cost for a hit is one cycle, calculate the average cost of access.

5.11 A given design with cache implemented has a main memory access cost of 20 cycles on a miss and two cycles on a hit. The same design without the cache has a main memory access cost of 16 cycles. Calculate the minimum hit rate of the cache to make the cache implementation worthwhile.

5.12 Design your own 8K × 32 PSRAM using an 8K × 32 DRAM, by designing a refresh controller. The refresh controller should guarantee refresh of each word every 15.625 microseconds. Because the PSRAM may be busy refreshing itself when a read or write access request occurs (i.e., the enable input is set), it should have an output signal ack indicating that an access request has been completed. Make use of a timer. Design the system down to complete structure. Indicate at what frequency your clock must operate.

# CHAPTER 6: *Interfacing*

## 6.1   Introduction

As stated in the Chapter 5, we use processors to implement processing, memory to implement storage, and buses to implement communication. The earlier chapters described processors and memory. This chapter describes implementing communication with buses, known as interfacing. Communication is the transfer of data among processors and memories. For example, a general-purpose processor reading or writing a memory is a common form of communication. A general-purpose processor reading or writing a peripheral's register is another common form.

We begin by defining some basic communication concepts. We then introduce several issues relating to the common task of interfacing to a general-purpose processor: addressing, interrupts, and direct memory access. We also describe several schemes for arbitrating among multiple processors attempting to access a single bus or memory simultaneously. We show that many systems may include several hierarchically organized buses. We then discuss some more advanced communication principles and survey several common serial, parallel, and wireless communication protocols.

## 6.2 Communication Basics

### Basic Terminology

We begin by introducing a very basic communication example between a processor and a memory, shown in Figure 6.1. Figure 6.1(a) shows the bus structure, or the wires connecting the processor and the memory. A line *rd'/wr* indicates whether the processor is reading or writing. An *enable* line is used by the processor to carry out the read or write. Twelve address lines *addr* indicate the memory address that the processor wishes to read or write. Eight data lines *data* are set by the processor when writing or set by the memory when the processor is reading. Figure 6.1(b) describes the read protocol over these wires: the processor sets *rd'/wr* to 0, places a valid address on *addr*, and strobes *enable*, after which the memory will place valid data on the *data* lines. Figure 6.1(c) shows a write protocol: the processor sets *rd'/wr* to 1, places a valid address on *addr*, places data on *data*, and strobes *enable*, causing the memory to store the data. This very simple example brings up several points that we now describe.

Wires may be unidirectional, meaning they transmit in only one direction, as did *rd'/wr*, *enable*, and *addr*; or they may be bidirectional, meaning they transmit in two directions, though in only one direction at a time, as did *data*. A set of wires with the same function is typically drawn as a thick line and/or as a line with a small angled line drawn through it, as was the case with *addr* and *data*.

The term *bus* can refer to a set of wires with a single function within a communication. For example, we can refer to the "address bus" and the "data bus" in the above example. The term *bus* can also refer to the entire collection of wires used for the communication (e.g., *rd'/wr*, *enable*, *addr*, and *data*) along with the communication protocol over those wires. Both uses of the term are common and are often used in conjunction with one another. For example, we may say that the processor's bus consists of an address bus and a data bus. A *protocol* describes the rules for communicating over those wires. We deal primarily with low-level hardware protocols in this chapter, while higher-level protocols, like IP (Internet Protocol) can be built on top of these protocols, using a layered approach.

The bus connects to ports of a processor (or memory). A *port* is the actual conducting device, like metal, on the periphery of a processor, through which a signal is input to or output from the processor. A port may refer to a single wire, or to a set of wires with a single function, such as an address port consisting of twelve wires. A related term is *pin*. When a processor is packaged as its own IC, there are actual pins extending from the package, and those pins are often designed to be plugged into a socket on a printed-circuit board. Today, however, a processor commonly coexists on a single IC with other processors and memories. Such a processor does not have any actual pins on its periphery, but rather "pads" of metal in

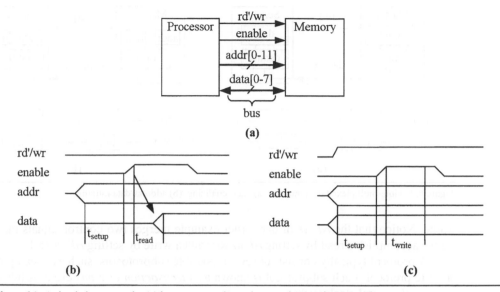

Figure 6.1: A simple bus example: (a) bus structure, (b) read protocol, (c) write protocol.

the IC. In fact, even for a processor packaged in its own IC, alternative packaging-techniques may use something other than pins for connections, such as small metallic balls. However, we can still use the term *pin* to refer to a port on a processor.

The distinction between a bus and a port is similar to the distinction between a street and a driveway — the bus is like the street, which connects various driveways. A processor's port is like a house's driveway, which provides access between the house and the street.

The most common method for describing a hardware protocol is a timing diagram, as was used in Figure 6.1(b) and (c). In the diagram, time proceeds to the right along the x-axis. The diagram shows that the processor must set the *rd'/wr* line low for a read to occur. The diagram also shows, using two vertical lines, that the processor must place the address on *addr* for at least $t_{setup}$ time before setting the *enable* line high. The diagram shows that the high *enable* line triggers the memory to put data on the *data* wires after a time $t_{read}$. Note that a timing diagram represents control lines, like *rd'/wr* and *enable*, as either being high or low, while it represents data lines, like *addr* and *data*, either as being invalid or valid, using a single horizontal line or two horizontal lines, respectively. The actual value of data lines is not normally relevant when describing a protocol, so that value is typically not shown.

In the above protocol, the control line *enable* is active high, meaning that a 1 on the *enable* line triggers the data transfer. In many protocols, control lines are instead active low, meaning that a 0 on the line triggers the transfer. Such a control line's name is typically written with a bar above it, a single quote after it (e.g., *enable'*), a forward slash before it (e.g., */enable*), or the letter L after it (e.g., *enable_l*). To be general, we will use the term *assert* to mean setting a control line to its active value, such as to 1 for an active high line, and to 0 for an active low line. We will use the term *deassert* to mean setting the control line to its inactive

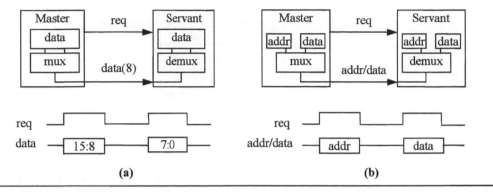

Figure 6.2: Time-multiplexed data transfer: (a) data serializing, (b) address/data muxing.

value. Notice that the *rd'/wr* of our earlier example merges two control signals into one line, so we accomplish a read by setting *rd'/wr* to 0 and a write by setting *rd'/wr* to 1.

A protocol typically consists of several possible subprotocols, such as a read protocol and a write protocol. Each subprotocol is known as a *transaction* or a *bus cycle*. A bus cycle may consist of several clock cycles.

## Basic Protocol Concepts

The processor-memory protocol described above was a simple one. Hardware protocols can be much more complex. However, we can understand them better by defining some basic protocol concepts. These concepts are: actors, data direction, addresses, time-multiplexing, and control methods.

An *actor* is a processor or memory involved in the data transfer. A protocol typically involves two actors: a master and a servant. A master initiates the data transfer. A servant, commonly called a slave, responds to the initiation request. In the example of Figure 6.1, the processor is the master, and the memory is the servant (i.e., the memory cannot initiate a data transfer). The servant could also be another processor. Masters are usually general-purpose processors, and servants are usually peripherals and memories.

*Data direction* denotes the direction that the transferred data moves between the actors. We indicate this direction by denoting each actor as either receiving or sending data. Note that actor types are independent of the direction of the data transfer. In particular, a master may either be the receiver of data, as in Figure 6.1(b), or the sender of data, as shown Figure 6.1(c).

*Addresses* represent a special type of data used to indicate where regular data should go to or come from. A protocol often includes both an address and regular data, as did the memory access protocol in Figure 6.1, where the address specified the location where the data should be read from or written to in the memory. An address is also necessary when a general-purpose processor communicates with multiple peripherals over a single bus; the address not only specifies a particular peripheral, but also may specify a particular register within that peripheral.

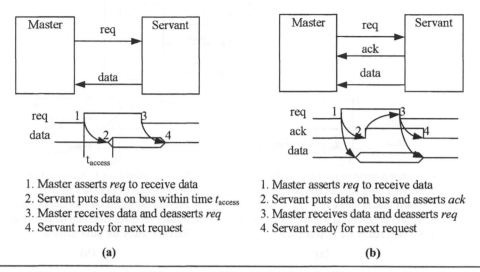

1. Master asserts *req* to receive data
2. Servant puts data on bus within time $t_{access}$
3. Master receives data and deasserts *req*
4. Servant ready for next request

**(a)**

1. Master asserts *req* to receive data
2. Servant puts data on bus and asserts *ack*
3. Master receives data and deasserts *req*
4. Servant ready for next request

**(b)**

Figure 6.3: Two protocol control methods: (a) strobe, (b) handshake. The main differences are underlined.

Another protocol concept is *time multiplexing*. To multiplex means to share a single set of wires for multiple pieces of data. In time multiplexing, the multiple pieces of data are sent one at a time over the shared wires. For example, Figure 6.2(a) shows a master sending 16 bits of data over an 8-bit bus using a strobe protocol and time-multiplexed data. The master first sends the high-order byte and then the low-order byte. The servant must receive the bytes and then demultiplex the data. This serializing of data can be done to any extent, even down to a 1-bit bus, in order to reduce the number of wires. As another example, Figure 6.2(b) shows a master sending both an address and data to a servant, such as a memory. In this case, rather than using separate sets of lines for address and data, as was done in Figure 6.1, we can time multiplex the address and data over a shared set of lines *addr/data*.

*Control methods* are schemes for initiating and ending the transfer. Two of the most common methods are strobe and handshake. In a *strobe* protocol, the master uses one control line, often called the *request* line, to initiate the data transfer, and the transfer is considered to be complete after some fixed time interval after the initiation. For example, Figure 6.3(a) shows a strobe protocol with a master wanting to receive data from a servant. The master first asserts the request line to initiate a transfer. The servant then has time $t_{access}$, to put the data on the data bus. After this time, the master reads the data bus, believing the data to be valid. The master than deasserts the request line, so that the servant can stop putting the data on the data bus, and both actors are then ready for the next transfer. An analogy is a demanding boss who tells an employee "I want that report (the data) on my desk (the data bus) in one hour ($t_{access}$)," and merely expects the report to be on the desk in one hour.

The second common control method is a *handshake* protocol, in which the master uses a request line to initiate the transfer, and the servant uses an *acknowledge* line to inform the master when the data is ready. For example, Figure 6.3(b) shows a handshake protocol with a

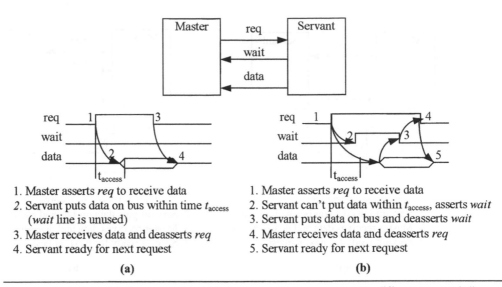

1. Master asserts *req* to receive data
2. Servant puts data on bus within time $t_{access}$ (*wait* line is unused)
3. Master receives data and deasserts *req*
4. Servant ready for next request

**(a)**

1. Master asserts *req* to receive data
2. Servant can't put data within $t_{access}$, asserts *wait*
3. Servant puts data on bus and deasserts *wait*
4. Master receives data and deasserts *req*
5. Servant ready for next request

**(b)**

Figure 6.4: A strobe/handshake compromise: (a) fast-response, (b) slow-response. The differences are underlines.

receiving master. The master first asserts the request line to initiate the transfer. The servant takes as much time as necessary to put the data on the data bus, and then asserts the acknowledge line to inform the master that the data is valid. The master reads the data bus and then deasserts the request line so that the servant can stop putting data on the data bus. The servant deasserts the acknowledge line, and both actors are then ready for the next transfer. In our boss-employee analogy, a handshake protocol corresponds to a more tolerant boss who tells an employee "I want that report on my desk soon; let me know when it's ready." A handshake protocol can adjust to a servant, or servants, with varying response times, unlike a strobe protocol. However, when response time is known, a handshake protocol may be slower than a strobe protocol, since it requires the master to detect the acknowledgment before getting the data, possibly requiring an extra clock cycle if the master is synchronizing the bus control signals. A handshake also requires an extra line for acknowledge.

To achieve both the speed of a strobe protocol and the varying response time tolerance of a handshake protocol, a compromise protocol is often used, as illustrated in Figure 6.4. In this case, when the servant can put the data on the bus within time $t_{access}$, the protocol is identical to a strobe protocol, as shown in Figure 6.4(a). However, if the servant cannot put the data on the bus in time, it instead tells the master to wait longer, by asserting a line we've labeled *wait*. When the servant has finally put the data on the bus, it deasserts the *wait* line, thus informing the master that the data is ready. The master receives the data and deasserts the *request* line. Thus, the handshake only occurs if it is necessary. In our boss-employee analogy, the boss tells the employee "I want that report on my desk in an hour; if you can't finish by then, let me know that and then let me know when it's ready."

Perhaps the most common communication situation in embedded systems is the input and output (I/O) of data to and from a general-purpose processor, as it communicates with its

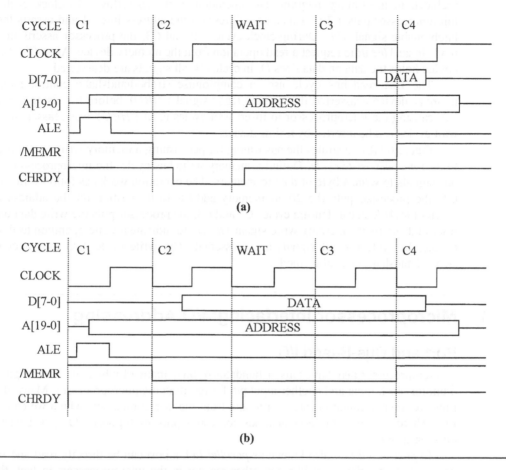

Figure 6.5: ISA bus protocol: (a) read bus timing, (b) write bus timing.

peripherals and memories. I/O is relative to the processor: input means data comes into the processor, while output means data goes out of the processor. In the next three sections, we will discuss three microprocessor-interfacing issues: addressing, interrupts, and direct memory access. We'll use the term *microprocessor* to refer to a general-purpose processor.

## Example: The ISA Bus Protocol — Memory Access

The Industry Standard Architecture (ISA) bus protocol is common in systems using an 80x86 microprocessor. Figure 6.5(a) illustrates the bus timing for performing a memory read operation, referred to as a *memory read cycle*. During a memory read cycle, the microprocessor drives the bus signals to read a byte of data from memory. Note that in Figure 6.5(a), several other control signals that are inactive during a memory read cycle are not included in the timing diagram. The operation works as follows. In clock cycle $C1$, the microprocessor puts a 20-bit memory address on the address lines $A$ and asserts the address latch enable signal $ALE$. During clock cycles $C2$ and $C3$, the processor asserts the memory read signal $MEMR$ to request a read operation from the memory device. After $C3$, the memory device holds the data on data lines $D$. In cycle $C4$, all signals are deasserted.

The ISA read bus cycle uses a compromise strobe/handshake control method. The memory device deasserted the channel ready signal $CHRDY$ before the rising clock edge in $C2$, causing the microprocessor to insert wait cycles until $CHRDY$ was reasserted. Up to six wait cycles can be inserted by a slow device.

Figure 6.5(b) illustrates the bus timing for performing a memory write operation, referred to as a *memory write cycle*. During a memory write bus cycle, the microprocessor drives the bus signals to write a byte of data to memory. The operation works as follows. In clock cycle $C1$, the processor puts the 20-bit memory address to be written on the address lines and asserts the $ALE$ signal. During cycles $C2$ and $C3$, the processor puts the write data on the data lines and asserts the memory write signal $MEMW$ to indicate a write operation to the memory device. In cycle $C4$, all signals are deasserted. The write cycle also uses a compromise strobe/handshake control method.

## 6.3   Microprocessor Interfacing: I/O Addressing

### Port and Bus-Based I/O

A microprocessor may have tens or hundreds of pins, many of which are control pins, such as a pin for clock input and another input pin for resetting the microprocessor. Many of the other pins are used to communicate data to and from the microprocessor, which we call processor I/O. There are two common methods for using pins to support I/O: port-based I/O and bus-based I/O.

In *port-based I/O*, also known as *parallel I/O*, a port can be directly read and written by processor instructions just like any other register in the microprocessor; in fact, the port is usually connected to a dedicated register. For example, consider an 8-bit port named $P0$. A C-language programmer may write to $P0$ using an instruction like: $P0 = 255$, which would set all eight pins to 1s. In this case, the C compiler manual would have defined $P0$ as a special variable that would automatically be mapped to the register $P0$ during compilation. Conversely, the programmer might read the value of a port $P1$ being written by some other device by typing something like $a = P1$. In some microprocessors, each bit of a port can be configured as input or output by writing to a configuration register for the port. For example, $P0$ might have an associated configuration register called $CP0$. To set the high-order four bits to input and the low-order four bits to output, we might say: $CP0 = 15$. This writes 00001111 to the $CP0$ register, where a 0 means input and a 1 means output. Ports are often bit-addressable, meaning that a programmer can read or write specific bits of the port. For example, one might say: $x = P0.2$, giving $x$ the value of the number 2 pin of port $P0$.

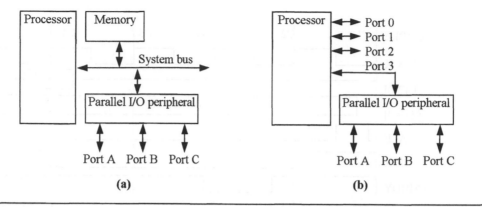

Figure 6.6: Parallel I/O: (a) adding parallel I/O to a bus-based I/O processor, (b) extended parallel I/O.

In *bus-based I/O*, the microprocessor has a set of address, data, and control ports corresponding to bus lines, and uses the bus to access memory as well as peripherals. The microprocessor has the bus protocol built in to its hardware. Specifically, the software does not implement the protocol but merely executes a single instruction that in turn causes the hardware to write or read data over the bus. We normally consider the access to the peripherals as I/O, but don't normally consider the access to memory as I/O, since the memory is considered more as a part of the microprocessor.

A system may require parallel I/O (port-based I/O), but a microprocessor may only support bus-based I/O. In this case, a parallel I/O peripheral may be used, as illustrated in Figure 6.6(a). The peripheral is connected to the system bus on one side, with corresponding address, data, and control lines, and has several ports on the other side, consisting just of a set of data lines. The ports are connected to registers inside the peripheral, and the microprocessor can read and write those registers in order to read and write the ports.

Even when a microprocessor supports port-based I/O, we may require more ports than are available. In this case, a parallel I/O peripheral can again be used, as illustrated in Figure 6.6(b). The microprocessor has four ports in this example, one of which is used to interface with a parallel I/O peripheral, which itself has three ports. Thus, we have extended the number of available ports from four to six. Using such a peripheral in this manner is often referred to as *extended parallel I/O*.

## Memory-Mapped I/O and Standard I/O

In bus-based I/O, there are two methods for a microprocessor to communicate with peripherals, known as memory-mapped I/O and standard I/O.

In *memory-mapped I/O*, peripherals occupy specific addresses in the existing address space. For example, consider a bus with a 16-bit address. The lower 32K addresses may correspond to memory addresses, while the upper 32K may correspond to I/O addresses.

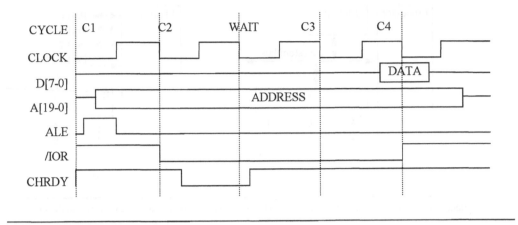

Figure 6.7: ISA bus protocol for standard I/O.

In *standard I/O* (also known as *I/O-mapped I/O*), the bus includes an additional pin, which we label *M/IO*, to indicate whether the access is to memory or to a peripheral (i.e., an I/O device). For example, when *M/IO* is 0, the address on the address bus corresponds to a memory address. When *M/IO* is 1, the address corresponds to a peripheral.

An advantage of memory-mapped I/O is that the microprocessor need not include special instructions for communicating with peripherals. The microprocessor's assembly instructions involving memory, such as MOV or ADD, will also work for peripherals. For example, a microprocessor may have an ADD A, B instruction that adds the data at address B to the data at address A and stores the result in A. A and B may correspond to memory locations, or registers in peripherals. In contrast, if the microprocessor uses standard I/O, the microprocessor requires special instructions for reading and writing peripherals. These instructions are often called IN and OUT. Thus, to perform the same addition of locations A and B corresponding to peripherals, the following instructions would be necessary:

IN R0, A
IN R1, B
ADD R0, R1
OUT A, R0

Advantages of standard I/O include no loss of memory addresses to the use as I/O addresses, and potentially simpler address decoding logic in peripherals. Address decoding logic can be simplified with standard I/O if we know that there will only be a small number of peripherals, because the peripherals can then ignore high-order address bits. For example, a bus may have a 16-bit address, but we may know there will never be more than 256 I/O addresses required. The peripherals can thus safely ignore the high-order 8 address bits, resulting in smaller and/or faster address comparators in each peripheral. Note that we can build a system using both standard and memory-mapped I/O, since peripherals in the memory space act just like memory themselves.

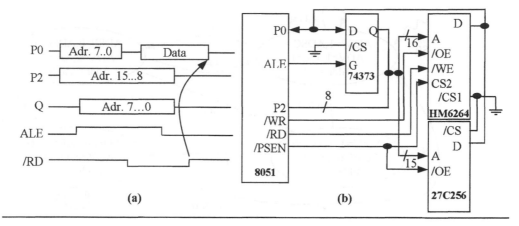

Figure 6.8: A basic memory protocol: (a) timing diagram for a read operation, (b) interface schematic.

## Example: The ISA Bus Protocol — Standard I/O

The ISA bus protocol introduced earlier supports standard I/O. The I/O read bus cycle is depicted in Figure 6.7. During this bus cycle, the microprocessor drives the bus signals to read a byte of data from a peripheral, according to the timing diagram shown. Note that the cycle uses a control line distinct from */MEMR*, namely */IOR*, which is consistent with the standard I/O approach. The I/O device address space is limited to 16 bits, as opposed to 20 bits for memory devices. The I/O write bus cycle is similar to the memory write bus cycle but uses a control signal */IOW* and again limits the address to 16 bits. The I/O read and write bus cycles use the compromise strobe/handshake control method, as did the memory bus cycles.

## Example: A Basic Memory Protocol

In this example, we illustrate how to interface 8K of data and 32K of program code memory to a microcontroller, specifically the Intel 8051. The 8051 uses separate memory address spaces for data and program code. Data or code address space is limited to 64K, hence, addressable with 16 bits through ports *P0* (least significant bits) and *P2* (most significant bits). A separate signal, called *PSEN* (program strobe enable), is used to distinguish between data/code. For the most part, the 8051 generates all of the necessary signals to perform memory I/O, however, since port *P0* is used both for the least significant address bits and for data, an 8-bit latch is required to perform the necessary multiplexing. The timing diagram depicted in Figure 6.8(a) illustrates a memory read operation. A memory write operation is performed in a similar fashion with data flow reversed and *RD* (read) replaced with *WR* (write). The memory read operation proceeds as follows. The microcontroller places the source address (i.e., the memory location to be read) on ports *P2* and *P0*. *P2*, holding the eight most significant address bits, retains its value throughout the read operation. *P0*, holding the eight least-significant address bits, is stored inside an 8-bit latch. The *ALE* signal (address

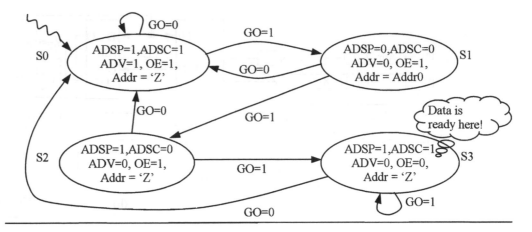

Figure 6.9: A complex memory protocol.

latch enable) is used to trigger the latching of port $P0$. Now, the microcontroller asserts high impedance on $P0$ to allow the memory device to drive it with the requested data. The memory device outputs valid data as long as the $RD$ signal is asserted. Meanwhile, the microcontroller reads the data and deasserts its control and port signals. Figure 6.8(b) illustrates the interface schematic.

### Example: A Complex Memory Protocol

In this example, we will build a finite-state machine (FSM) controller that will generate all the necessary control signals to drive the TC55V2325FF memory chip in burst read mode (i.e., pipelined read operation), as described in Chapter 5. Our specification for this FSM is the timing diagram presented in the earlier example from Chapter 5. The input to our machine is a clock signal ($CLK$), the starting address ($Addr0$) and the enable/disable signal ($GO$). The output of our machine is a set of control signals specific to our memory device. We assume that the chip's *enable* and *WE* signals are asserted. Figure 6.9 gives the FSM description. From the state machine description, we can derive the next-state and output truth tables. From these truth tables, we can compute next-state and output equations. By deriving the next-state transition table, we can solve and optimize the next-state and output equations. These equations can be implemented using logic components. (See Chapter 2 for details.) Any processor that is to be interfaced with one of these memory devices must implement, internally or externally, a state machine similar to the one presented in this example.

## 6.4 Microprocessor Interfacing: Interrupts

Another microprocessor I/O issue is that of interrupt-driven I/O. To introduce this issue, suppose the program running on a microprocessor must, among other tasks, read and process data from a peripheral whenever that peripheral has new data; such processing is called *servicing*. If the peripheral gets new data at unpredictable intervals, how can the program determine when the peripheral has new data? The most straightforward approach is to interleave the microprocessor's other tasks with a routine that checks for new data in the peripheral, perhaps by checking for a 1 in a particular bit in a register of the peripheral. This repeated checking by the microprocessor for data is called *polling*. Polling is simple to implement, but this repeated checking wastes many clock cycles, so it may not be acceptable in many cases, especially when there are numerous peripherals to be checked. We could check at less-frequent intervals, but then we may not process the data quickly enough.

To overcome the limitations of polling, most microprocessors come with a feature called *external interrupt*. A microprocessor with this feature has a pin, say, *Int*. At the end of executing each machine instruction, the processor's controller checks *Int*. If *Int* is asserted, the microprocessor jumps to a particular address at which a subroutine exists that services the interrupt. This subroutine is called an *interrupt service routine*, or ISR. Such I/O is called *interrupt-driven I/O*.

One might wonder if interrupts have really solved the problem with polling, namely of wasting time performing excessive checking, since the interrupt pin is "polled" at the end of every microprocessor instruction. However, in this case, the polling of the pin is built right into the microprocessor's controller hardware, and therefore can be done simultaneously with the execution of an instruction, resulting in no extra clock cycles.

There are two methods by which a microprocessor using interrupts determines the address, known as the *interrupt address vector*, at which the ISR resides. These two methods are *fixed* and *vectored* interrupt. In *fixed interrupt*, the address to which the microprocessor jumps on an interrupt is built into the microprocessor, so it is fixed and cannot be changed. The assembly programmer either puts the ISR at that address, or if not enough bytes are available in that region of memory, merely puts a jump to the real ISR there. For C programmers, the compiler typically reserves a special name for the ISR and then compiles a subroutine having that name into the ISR location, or again just a jump to that subroutine. In microprocessors with fixed ISR addresses, there may be several interrupt pins to support interrupts from multiple peripherals.

Figure 6.10 provides a summary of the flow of actions for an example of interrupt-driven I/O using a fixed ISR address. Figure 6.11 illustrates this flow graphically for the example. In this example, data received by *Peripheral*1 must be read, transformed, and then written to *Peripheral*2. *Peripheral*1 might represent a sensor, and *Peripheral*2, a display. Meanwhile, the microprocessor is running its main program, located in program memory starting at address 100. When *Peripheral*1 receives data, it asserts *Int* to request that the microprocessor service the data. After the microprocessor completes execution of its current instruction, it stores its state and jumps to the ISR located at the fixed program memory location of 16. The ISR reads the data from *Peripheral*1, transforms it, and writes the result to *Peripheral*2. The last ISR instruction is a return from interrupt, causing the microprocessor to restore its state and resume execution of its main program, in this case executing instruction 101.

Other microprocessors use *vectored interrupt* to determine the address at which the ISR resides. This approach is especially common in systems with a system bus, since there may be

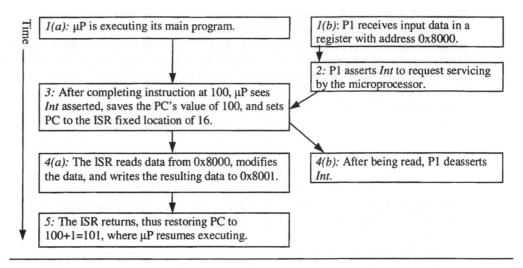

Figure 6.10: Interrupt-driven I/O using fixed ISR location: summary of flow of actions.

numerous peripherals that can request service. In this method, the microprocessor has one interrupt pin, say, *Int*, which any peripheral can assert. After detecting the interrupt, the microprocessor asserts another pin, say, *Inta*, to acknowledge that it has detected the interrupt and to request that the interrupting peripheral provide the address where the relevant ISR resides. The peripheral provides this address on the data bus, and the microprocessor reads the address and jumps to the corresponding ISR. We discuss the situation where multiple peripherals simultaneously request servicing in a later section on arbitration. For now, consider an example of one peripheral using vectored interrupt. The flow of actions is shown in Figure 6.12, which represents an example very similar to the previous one. Figure 6.13 illustrates the example graphically. In contrast to the earlier example, the ISR location is not fixed at 16. Thus, *Peripheral*1 contains an extra register holding the ISR location. After detecting the interrupt and saving its state, the microprocessor asserts *Inta* in order to get *Peripheral*1 to place 16 on the data bus. The microprocessor reads this 16 into the PC and then jumps to the ISR, which executes and completes in the same manner as the earlier example.

As a compromise between the fixed and vectored interrupt methods, we can use an *interrupt address table*. In this method, we still have only one interrupt pin on the processor, but we also create in the processor's memory a table that holds ISR addresses. A typical table might have 256 entries. A peripheral, rather than providing the ISR address, instead provides a number corresponding to an entry in the table. The processor reads this entry number from the bus, and then reads the corresponding table entry to obtain the ISR address. Compared to the entire memory, the table is typically very small, so an entry number's bit encoding is small. This small bit encoding is especially important when the data bus is not wide enough to hold a complete ISR address. Furthermore, this approach allows us to assign each peripheral a

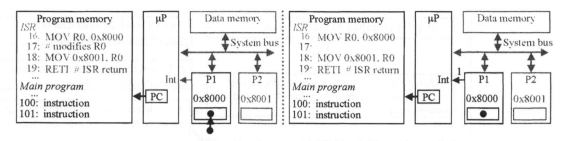

1(a): μP is executing its main program
1(b): P1 receives input data in a register with address 0x8000.

2: P1 asserts *Int* to request servicing by the microprocessor

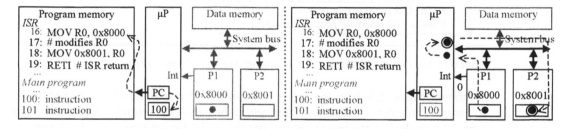

3: After completing instruction at 100, μP sees *Int* asserted, saves the PC's value of 100, and sets PC to the ISR fixed location of 16.

4(a): The ISR reads data from 0x8000, modifies the data, and writes the resulting data to 0x8001.
4(b): After being read, P1 deasserts *Int*.

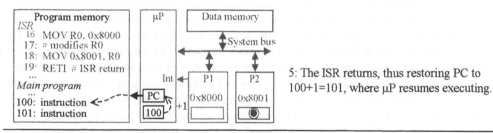

5: The ISR returns, thus restoring PC to 100+1=101, where μP resumes executing.

Figure 6.11: Interrupt-driven I/O using fixed ISR location: flow of actions.

unique number independent of ISR locations, meaning that we could move the ISR location without having to change anything in the peripheral.

External interrupts may be maskable or nonmaskable. In *maskable* interrupt, the programmer may force the microprocessor to ignore the interrupt pin, either by executing a specific instruction to disable the interrupt or by setting bits in an interrupt configuration register. A situation where a programmer might want to mask interrupts is when there exist time-critical regions of code, such as a routine that generates a pulse of a certain duration. The

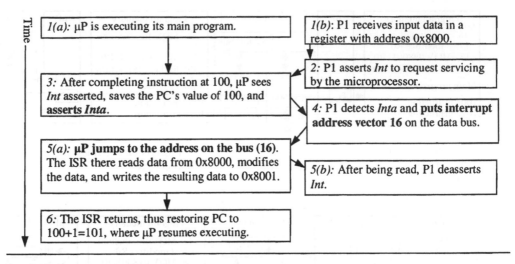

Figure 6.12: Interrupt-driven I/O using vectored interrupt: summary of flow of actions.

programmer may include an instruction that disables interrupts at the beginning of the routine, and another instruction reenabling interrupts at the end of the routine. *Nonmaskable* interrupt cannot be masked by the programmer. It requires a pin distinct from maskable interrupts. It is typically used for very drastic situations, such as power failure. In this case, if power is failing, a nonmaskable interrupt can cause a jump to a subroutine that stores critical data in nonvolatile memory, before power is completely gone.

In some microprocessors, the jump to an ISR is handled just like the jump to any other subroutine, meaning that the state of the microprocessor is stored on a stack, including contents of the program counter, datapath status register, and all other registers. The state is then restored upon completion of the ISR. In other microprocessors, only a few registers are stored, like just the program counter and status registers. The assembly programmer must be aware of what registers have been stored, so as not to overwrite nonstored register data with the ISR. These microprocessors need two types of assembly instructions for subroutine return. A regular return instruction returns from a regular subroutine, which was called using a subroutine call instruction. A return from interrupt instruction returns from an ISR, which was jumped to not by a call instruction but by the hardware itself, and which restores only those registers that were stored at the beginning of the interrupt. The C programmer is freed from having to worry about such considerations, as the C compiler handles them.

The reason we used the term *external interrupt* is to distinguish this type of interrupt from internal interrupts, also called *traps*. An internal interrupt results from an exceptional condition, such as divide-by-0, or execution of an invalid opcode. Internal interrupts, like external ones, result in a jump to an ISR. A third type of interrupt, called *software interrupts*, can be initiated by executing a special assembly instruction.

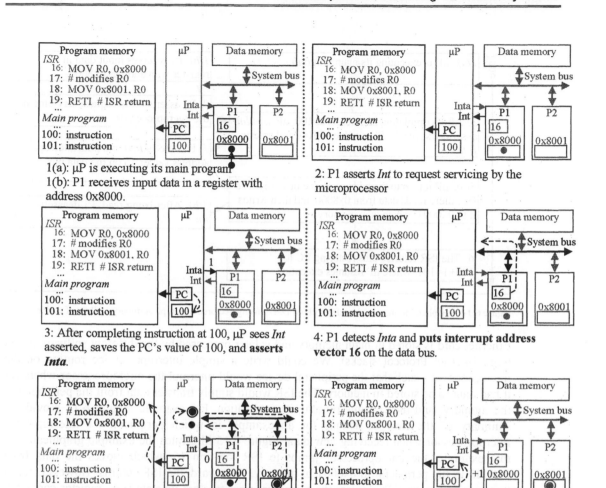

1(a): μP is executing its main program
1(b): P1 receives input data in a register with address 0x8000.

2: P1 asserts *Int* to request servicing by the microprocessor

3: After completing instruction at 100, μP sees *Int* asserted, saves the PC's value of 100, and **asserts Inta**.

4: P1 detects *Inta* and **puts interrupt address vector 16** on the data bus.

5(a): P jumps to the address on the bus (16). The ISR there reads data from 0x8000, modifies the data, and writes the resulting data to 0x80001.
5(b): After being read, P1 deasserts Int.

6: The ISR returns, thus restoring the PC to 100+1=101, where the μP resumes

Figure 6.13: Interrupt-driven I/O using vectored interrupt: flow of actions.

# 6.5 Microprocessor Interfacing: Direct Memory Access

Commonly, the data being accumulated in a peripheral should be first stored in memory before being processed by a program running on the microprocessor. Such temporary storage of data that is awaiting processing is called *buffering*. For example, packet data from an

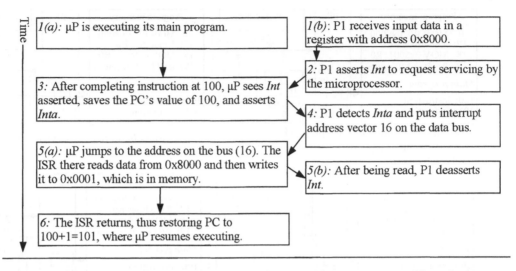

Figure 6.14: Peripheral to memory transfer without DMA, using vectored interrupt: summary of flow of actions.

Ethernet card is stored in main memory and is later processed by the different software layers (e.g., Internet Protocol stacks). We could write a simple interrupt service routine on the microprocessor, such that the peripheral device would interrupt the microprocessor whenever it had data to be stored in memory. The ISR would simply transfer data from the peripheral to the memory, and then resume running its application. For example, Figure 6.14 provides a summary of the flow of actions for an example in which peripheral $P1$ interrupts the microprocessor when receiving new data. Figure 6.15 illustrates the example graphically. In this example, the microprocessor jumps to ISR location 16, which moves the data from 0x8000 in the peripheral to 0x0001 in memory. Afterward, the ISR returns. However, recall that jumping to an ISR requires the microprocessor to store its state (i.e., register contents), and then to restore its state when returning from the ISR. This storing and restoring of the state may consume many clock cycles, and is thus somewhat inefficient. Furthermore, the microprocessor cannot execute its regular program while moving the data, resulting in further inefficiency.

The I/O method of *direct memory access* (DMA) eliminates these inefficiencies. In DMA, we use a separate single-purpose processor, called a *DMA controller*, whose sole purpose is to transfer data between memories and peripherals. Briefly, the peripheral requests servicing from the DMA controller, which then requests control of the system bus from the microprocessor. The microprocessor merely needs to relinquish control of the bus to the DMA controller. The microprocessor does not need to jump to an ISR, and thus the overhead of storing and restoring the microprocessor state is eliminated. Furthermore, the microprocessor can execute its regular program while the DMA controller has bus control, as long as that regular program doesn't require use of the bus (at which point the microprocessor would then have to wait for the DMA to complete).

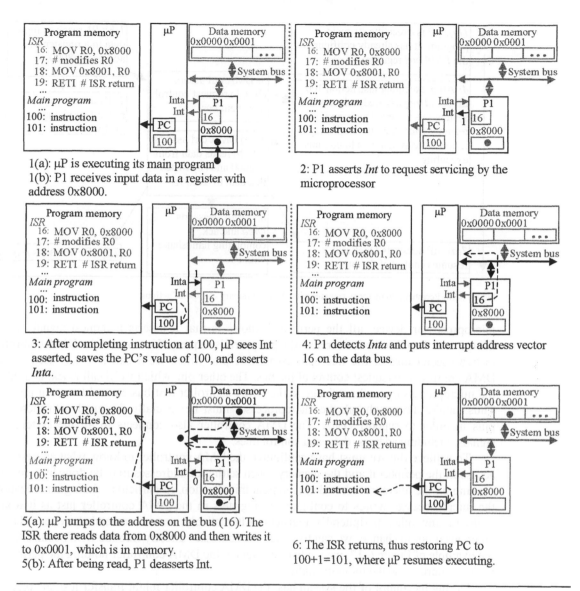

1(a): μP is executing its main program
1(b): P1 receives input data in a register with address 0x8000.

2: P1 asserts *Int* to request servicing by the microprocessor

3: After completing instruction at 100, μP sees Int asserted, saves the PC's value of 100, and asserts *Inta*.

4: P1 detects *Inta* and puts interrupt address vector 16 on the data bus.

5(a): μP jumps to the address on the bus (16). The ISR there reads data from 0x8000 and then writes it to 0x0001, which is in memory.
5(b): After being read, P1 deasserts Int.

6: The ISR returns, thus restoring PC to 100+1=101, where μP resumes executing.

Figure 6.15: Peripheral to memory transfer without DMA, using vectored interrupt: flow of actions.

A system with a separate bus between the microprocessor and cache may be able to execute for some time from the cache while the DMA transfer takes place.

Figure 6.16 summarizes the flow of actions for an example transfer using DMA, and Figure 6.17 depicts the example graphically. As seen in Figure 6.17, we connect the peripheral to the DMA controller rather than the microprocessor. Note that the peripheral does not recognize any difference between being connected to a DMA controller device or a

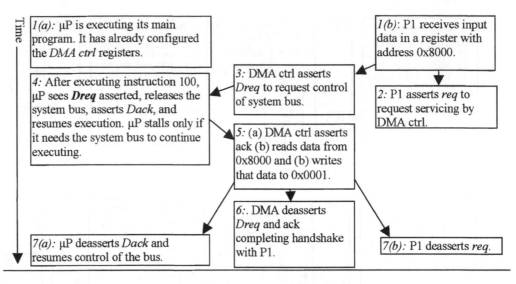

Figure 6.16: Peripheral to memory transfer with DMA: summary of flow of actions.

microprocessor device; all the peripheral knows is that it asserts a request signal on the device, and then that device services the peripheral's request. We connect the DMA controller to two special pins of the microprocessor. One pin, which we'll call *Dreq*, is used by the DMA controller to request control of the bus. The other pin, which we'll call *Dack*, is used by the microprocessor to acknowledge to the DMA controller that bus control has been granted. Thus, unlike the peripheral, the microprocessor must be specially designed with these two pins in order to support DMA. The DMA controller also connects to all the system bus signals, including address, data, and control lines.

To achieve this we must have configured the DMA controller to know what addresses to access in the peripheral and the memory. Such setting of addresses may be done by a routine running on the microprocessor during system initialization. In particular, during initialization, the microprocessor writes to configuration registers in the DMA controller just as it would write to any other peripheral's registers. Alternatively, in an embedded system that is guaranteed not to change, we can hardcode the addresses directly into the DMA controller. In the example of Figure 6.17, we see two registers in the DMA controller holding the peripheral register address and the memory address.

During its control of the system bus, the DMA controller might transfer just one piece of data, but more commonly will transfer numerous pieces of data (called a *block*), one right after other, before relinquishing the bus. This is because many peripherals, such as any peripheral that deals with storage devices (e.g., CD-ROM players or disk controllers) or that deals with network communication, send and receive data in large blocks. For example, a particular disk controller peripheral might read data in blocks of 128 words and store this data in a 128-word internal memory, after which the peripheral requests servicing (i.e., requests that this data be buffered in memory).

Embedded System Design

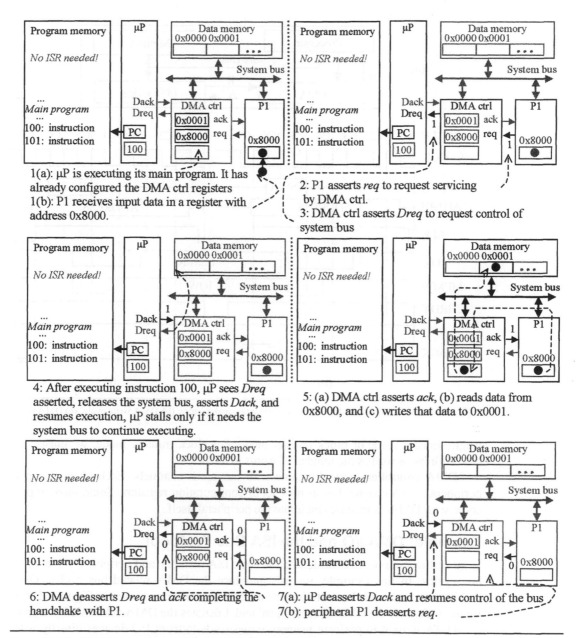

Figure 6.17: Peripheral to memory transfer with DMA: flow of actions.

For the example just given, the DMA controller works as follows. The DMA controller gains control of the bus, makes 128 peripheral reads and memory writes, and only then relinquishes the bus. We must therefore configure the DMA controller to operate in either

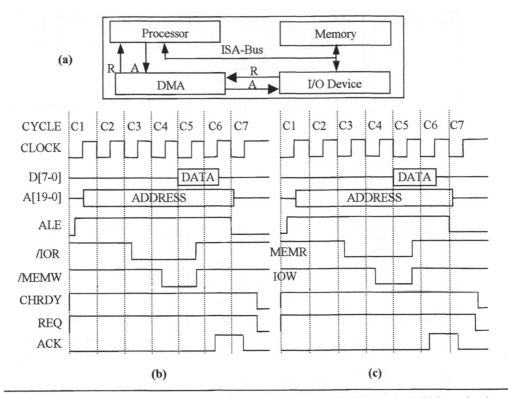

Figure 6.18: DMA using the ISA bus protocol: (a) system architecture, (b) DMA write cycle, (c) DMA read cycle.

single transfer mode or block transfer mode. For block transfer mode, we must configure a base address as well as the number of words in a block.

DMA controllers typically come with numerous channels. Each channel supports one peripheral. Each channel has its own set of configuration registers. Some modern peripherals come with DMA capabilities built into the peripheral itself.

## Example: DMA I/O and the ISA Bus Protocol

In an earlier example, we introduced the basic ISA memory and peripheral I/O read and write bus cycles. In this example, we will introduce the DMA related bus cycles. Our sample architecture is extended now to include a DMA controller as shown in Figure 6.18(a). In this figure, $R$ denotes the DMA request signal and $A$ denotes the DMA acknowledge signal.

DMA is used to perform memory writes/reads to/from I/O devices directly without the intervention of the processor. Let us first look at the DMA memory write bus cycle. A DMA write bus cycle proceeds as follows. First, the processor programs the DMA controller to monitor a particular I/O device for available data. The processor also programs the DMA with the starting memory address where the data item is to be written to. Once the I/O device has available data, it generates a DMA request by asserting its DMA request line ($DRQ$). In

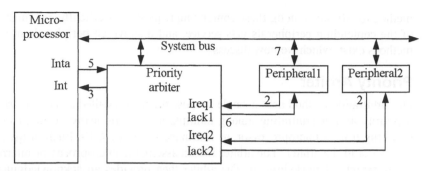

1.  Microprocessor is executing its program.
2.  Peripheral1 needs servicing so asserts *Ireq*1. Peripheral2 also needs servicing so asserts *Ireq*2.
3.  Priority arbiter sees at least one *Ireq* input asserted, so asserts *Int*.
4.  Microprocessor stops executing its program and stores its state.
5.  Microprocessor asserts *Inta*.
6.  Priority arbiter asserts *Iack*1 to acknowledge Peripheral1.
7.  Peripheral1 puts its interrupt address vector on the system bus.
8.  Microprocessor jumps to the address of the ISR read from the data bus, ISR executes and returns (and completes handshake with arbiter).
9.  Microprocessor resumes executing its program.

Figure 6.19: Arbitration using a priority arbiter.

response to this, the DMA controller will assert its *DRQ* to signal the processor. The processor, then, relinquishes the bus control signals and signals to the DMA controller with an acknowledgment (*DACK*). In response, the DMA will acknowledge the I/O device's *DRQ* by asserting its *DACK*. At this point, the actual transfer of data from the device to memory is initiated. Note that the actual DMA signals (*DACK*s and *DRQ*s) are not part of the ISA protocol. The ISA protocol merely provides a scheme for performing an I/O read and a memory write in the same bus cycle. The DMA memory write bus cycle is shown in Figure 6.18(b).

Let us now look at the DMA memory read bus cycle. The DMA memory read bus cycle is almost identical to a DMA memory write bus cycle. The only difference is that *IOW* is replaced with *IOR* and *MEMW* is replaced with *MEMR*. In addition, the order in which the I/O write and memory read signals are asserted is reversed. The DMA memory read bus cycle is shown in Figure 6.18(c).

## 6.6   Arbitration

In our earlier discussions, several situations existed in which multiple peripherals might request service from a single resource. For example, multiple peripherals might share a single microprocessor that services their interrupt requests. As another example, multiple peripherals might share a single DMA controller that services their DMA requests. In such situations, two or more peripherals may request service simultaneously. We therefore must have some method to arbitrate among these contending requests. Specifically, we must decide which one of the contending peripherals gets service, and thus which peripherals need to wait. Several methods exist, which we now discuss.

## Priority Arbiter

One arbitration method uses a single-purpose processor, called a *priority arbiter*. We illustrate a priority arbiter arbitrating among multiple peripherals using vectored interrupt to request servicing from a microprocessor, as illustrated in Figure 6.19. Each of the peripherals makes its request to the arbiter. The arbiter in turn asserts the microprocessor interrupt, and waits for the interrupt acknowledgment. The arbiter then provides an acknowledgment to exactly one peripheral, which permits that peripheral to put its interrupt vector address on the data bus (which, as you'll recall, causes the microprocessor to jump to a subroutine that services that peripheral).

Priority arbiters typically use one of two common schemes to determine priority among peripherals: fixed priority or rotating priority. In *fixed priority* arbitration, each peripheral has a unique rank among all the peripherals. The rank can be represented as a number, so if there are four peripherals, each peripheral is ranked 1, 2, 3, or 4. If two peripherals simultaneously seek servicing, the arbiter chooses the one with the higher rank.

In *rotating priority* arbitration (also called *round-robin*), the arbiter changes priority of peripherals based on the history of servicing of those peripherals. For example, one rotating priority scheme grants service to the least-recently serviced of the contending peripherals. This scheme obviously requires a more complex arbiter.

We prefer fixed priority when there is a clear difference in priority among peripherals. However, in many cases the peripherals are somewhat equal, so arbitrarily ranking them could cause high-ranked peripherals to get much more servicing than low-ranked ones. Rotating priority ensures a more equitable distribution of servicing in this case.

Notice that the priority arbiter is connected to the system bus, since the microprocessor can configure registers within the arbiter to set the priority schemes and/or the relative priorities of the devices. However, once configured, the arbiter does not use the system bus when arbitrating.

Priority arbiters represent another instance of a standard single-purpose processor. They are also often found built into other single-purpose processors like DMA controllers. A common type of priority arbiter arbitrates interrupt requests; this peripheral is referred to as an *interrupt controller*.

## Daisy-Chain Arbitration

The *daisy-chain* arbitration method builds arbitration right into the peripherals. A daisy-chain configuration is shown in Figure 6.20(a), again using vectored interrupt to illustrate the method. Each peripheral has a request output and an acknowledge input, as before. But now each peripheral also has a request input and an acknowledge output. A peripheral asserts its request output if it requires servicing or if its request input is asserted; the latter means that one of the "upstream" devices is requesting servicing. Thus, if any peripheral needs servicing,

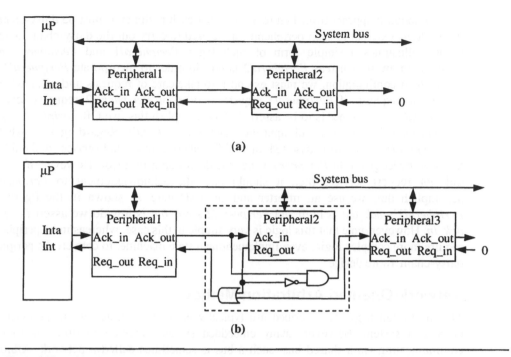

Figure 6.20: Arbitration using a daisy-chain configuration: (a) Daisy-chain aware peripherals, (b) adding logic to make a peripheral daisy-chain aware; more complex logic will typically be necessary, however.

its request will flow through the downstream peripherals and eventually reach the microprocessor. Even if more than one peripheral requests servicing, the microprocessor will see only one request. The microprocessor acknowledge signal connects to the first peripheral. If this peripheral is requesting service, it proceeds to put its interrupt vector address on the system bus. But if it doesn't need service, then it instead passes the acknowledgment upstream to the next peripheral, by asserting its acknowledge output. In the same manner, the next peripheral may either begin being serviced or may instead pass the acknowledgment along. Obviously, the peripheral at the front of the chain, i.e., the one to which the microprocessor acknowledge is connected, has highest priority, and the peripheral at the end of the chain has lowest priority.

We prefer a daisy-chain priority configuration over a priority arbiter when we want to be able to add or remove peripherals from an embedded system without redesigning the system. Although conceptually we could add as many peripherals to a daisy chain as we desired, in reality the servicing response time for peripherals at the end of the chain could become intolerably slow. In contrast to a daisy chain, a priority arbiter has a fixed number of channels; once they are all used, the system needs to be redesigned in order to accommodate more peripherals. However, a daisy chain has the drawback of not supporting more advanced priority schemes, like rotating priority. A second drawback is that if a peripheral in the chain stops working, other peripherals may lose their access to the processor.

Although it appears from Figure 6.20(a) that each peripheral must be daisy-chain aware, in fact logic external to each peripheral can be used to carry out the daisy-chain logic. Figure 6.20(b) illustrates a simple form of such logic. *Peripheral*1 and *Peripheral*3 are both daisy-chain aware, whereas *Peripheral*2 is not. In order to incorporate *Peripheral*2 into the daisy chain configuration, we must extend it to take care of requests and acknowledgments. Regarding requests, if *Peripheral*3 requests service or *Peripheral*2 requests service, then *Peripheral*1's *req_in* needs to be asserted. To accomplish this, we OR *Peripheral*2's *req_out* and *Peripheral*3's *req_out* and input the result to *Peripheral*1. Regarding acknowledgments, if *Peripheral*1's *ack_out* is asserted, then if *Peripheral*2 requested service, it should not pass this acknowledgment to *Peripheral*3, per the daisy-chain protocol. However, if *Peripheral*2 did not request service, then it should pass the acknowledgment to *Peripheral*3. To accomplish this, we use an inverter and an AND gate, as shown in the figure. Only if *Peripheral*1's *ack_out* is high and *Peripheral*2's *req_out* is low do we assert *Peripheral*3's *ack_in*. However, note that this logic is very simple in this case, whereas most peripherals will require more complex logic, even implementing a state machine, to convert the peripheral to a daisy-chain aware device.

## Network-Oriented Arbitration Methods

The arbitration methods described are typically used to arbitrate among peripherals in an embedded system. However, many embedded systems contain multiple microprocessors communicating via a shared bus; such a bus is sometimes called a network. Arbitration in such cases is typically built right into the bus protocol, since the bus serves as the only connection among the microprocessors. A key feature of such a connection is that a processor about to write to the bus has no way of knowing whether another processor is about to simultaneously write to the bus. Because of the relatively long wires and high capacitances of such buses, a processor may write many bits of data before those bits appear at another processor. For example, Ethernet and $I^2C$ use a method in which multiple processors may write to the bus simultaneously, resulting in a collision and causing any data on the bus to be corrupted. The processors detect this collision, stop transmitting their data, wait for some time, and then try transmitting again. The protocols must ensure that the contending processors don't start sending again at the same time, or must at least use statistical methods that make the chances of them sending again at the same time small.

As another example, the CAN bus uses a clever address encoding scheme such that if two addresses are written simultaneously by different processors using the bus, the higher-priority address will override the lower-priority one. Each processor that is writing the bus also checks the bus, and if the address it is writing does not appear, then that processor realizes that a higher-priority transfer is taking place and so that processor stops writing the bus.

## Example: Vectored Interrupt Using an Interrupt table

This is an example of a system using vectored interrupts as well as a vectored interrupt table. We will describe the software programming required to handle the interrupt requests. The relevant portions of the system architecture are shown in Figure 6.21. Here, two peripheral

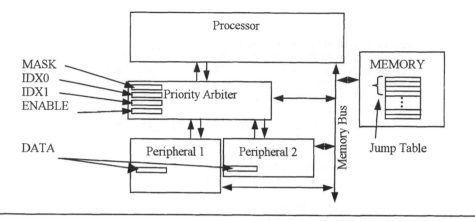

Figure 6.21: Architecture of a system using vectored interrupt and an interrupt table.

devices are connected to a two-channel priority arbiter with fixed priority scheme (i.e., *Peripheral*1 has higher priority than *Peripheral*2). Both the peripherals and the arbiter are connected to the processor's memory bus and communicate with it using memory-mapped I/O. The interrupt table index placed on the memory bus (a.k.a. system bus) by the arbiter is software programmable through two memory-mapped registers. Both peripheral devices receive data from the external environment and raise their interrupt accordingly.

The software to initialize the peripherals and the priority arbiter, and to process the data received by our peripherals, is given in Figure 6.22. Let us now study the code. First, we define a number of variables that correspond to the registers inside the priority arbiter and peripheral devices. However, unlike defining ordinary variables in a program, these variables must refer to specific memory locations, namely, those that are mapped to the peripheral's register. Normally, a compiler will place a variable somewhere in memory where storage for that variable's data is available. By using special keywords, we can force the compiler to place these variables at specific memory locations (e.g., in our compiler the keyword _at_ followed by a memory location is used to accomplish this). The priority arbiter, thus, has four registers located at memory locations 0xfff0 through 0xfff3. Note that our processor has a 16-bit memory address.

Next, we define two procedures, *Peripheral*2_ISR and *Periperhal*2_ISR, that handle the interrupts generated by the peripherals. Since we are using an interrupt jump table, these ISRs can be ordinary C procedures. Each ISR, of course, must perform necessary processing. Often, an ISR merely reads the data from the peripheral, places the data into a buffer, sets a flag indicating to the main program that the buffer was updated.

Finally, we define the procedure *InitializePeripherals*. The procedure first configures the priority arbiter. We can select, in software, which interrupts we are willing to handle. This is done through the mask register. In our case, we set the first two bits of the mask register, indicating that we are to handle interrupts generated by both peripherals. Next, we program the priority arbiter with the indices into the jump table where the location of the ISR is stored. We have chosen to place these in locations 13 and 17, but this choice is arbitrary. The

```
unsigned char ARBITER_MASK_REG                    _at_ 0xfff0;
unsigned char ARBITER_CH0_INDEX_REG               _at_ 0xfff1;
unsigned char ARBITER_CH1_INDEX_REG               _at_ 0xfff2;
unsigned char ARBITER_ENABLE_REG                  _at_ 0xfff3;
unsigned char PERIPHERAL1_DATA_REG                _at_ 0xffe0;
unsigned char PERIPHERAL2_DATA_REG                _at_ 0xffe1;
unsigned void* INTERRUPT_LOOKUP_TABLE[256]   _at_ 0x0100;
void Peripheral1_ISR(void) {
        unsigned char data;
        data = PERIPHERAL1_DATA_REG;
        // do something with the data
}
void Peripheral2_ISR(void) {
        unsigned char data;
        data = PERIPHERAL2_DATA_REG;
        // do something with the data
}
void InitializePeripherals(void) {
        ARBITER_MASK_REG = 0x03; // enable both channels
        ARBITER_CH0_INDEX_REG = 13;
        ARBITER_CH1_INDEX_REG = 17;
        INTERRUPT_LOOKUP_TABLE[13] = (void*)Peripheral1_ISR;
        INTERRUPT_LOOKUP_TABLE[17] = (void*)Peripheral2_ISR;
        ARBITER_ENABLE_REG = 1;
}
void main() {
        InitializePeripherals();
        for(;;) {} // main program goes here
}
```

Figure 6.22: Software for a system using vectored interrupt and an interrupt table.

procedure then places the ISRs into the lookup table at locations 13 and 17, as shown in the code. Last, the procedure enables interrupts by setting the arbiter's interrupt enable register.

## 6.7 Multilevel Bus Architectures

A microprocessor-based embedded system will have numerous types of communications that must take place, varying in their frequencies and speed requirements. The most frequent and high-speed communications will likely be between the microprocessor and its memories. Less frequent communications, requiring less speed, will be between the microprocessor and its peripherals, like a UART. We could try to implement a single high-speed bus for all the communications, but this approach has several disadvantages. First, it requires each peripheral

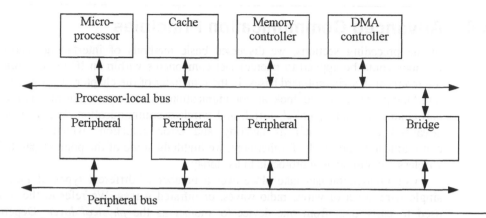

Figure 6.23: A two-level bus architecture.

to have a high-speed bus interface. Since a peripheral may not need such high-speed communication, having such an interface may result in extra gates, power consumption and cost. Second, since a high-speed bus will be very processor-specific, a peripheral with an interface to that bus may not be very portable. Third, having too many peripherals on the bus may result in a slower bus.

Therefore, we often design systems with two levels of buses: a high-speed processor local bus and a lower-speed peripheral bus, as illustrated in Figure 6.23. The *processor local bus* typically connects the microprocessor, cache, memory controllers, and certain high-speed coprocessors, and is processor specific. It is usually wide, as wide as a memory word.

The *peripheral bus* connects those processors that do not have fast processor local bus access as a top priority, but rather emphasize portability, low power, or low gate count. The peripheral bus is typically an industry standard bus, such as ISA or PCI, thus supporting portability of the peripherals. It is often narrower and/or slower than a processor local bus, thus requiring fewer pins, fewer gates and less power for interfacing.

A bridge connects the two buses. A *bridge* is a single-purpose processor that converts communication on one bus to communication on another bus. For example, the microprocessor may generate a read on the processor local bus with an address corresponding to a peripheral. The bridge detects that the address corresponds to a peripheral, and thus it then generates a read on the peripheral bus. After receiving the data, the bridge sends that data to the microprocessor. The microprocessor thus need not even know that a bridge exists — it receives the data, albeit a few cycles later, as if the peripheral were on the processor local bus.

A three-level bus hierarchy is also possible, as proposed by the VSI Alliance. The first level is the processor local bus, the second level a system bus, and the third level a peripheral bus. The system bus would be a high-speed bus, but would offload much of the traffic from the processor local bus. It may be beneficial in complex systems with numerous coprocessors.

## 6.8    Advanced Communication Principles

In the preceding sections, we discussed basic methods of interfacing. Those interfacing methods could be applied to interconnect components within an IC via on-chip buses, or to interconnect ICs via on-board buses. In the remainder of the chapter, we study more advanced interfacing concepts and look at communication from a more abstract point of view. In particular, we study parallel, serial, and wireless communication. We also describe some advanced concepts, such as layering and error detection, which are part of many communication protocols. Furthermore, we highlight some of the popular parallel, serial, and wireless communication protocols in use today.

Communication can take place over a number of different types of media, such as a single wire, a set of wires, radio waves, or infrared waves. We refer to the medium that is used to carry data from one device to another as the *physical layer*. Depending on the protocol, we may refer to an actor as a *device* or *node*. In either case, a device is simply a processor that uses the physical layer to send or receive data to and from another device.

In this section, we provide a general description of serial communication, parallel communication, and wireless communication. In addition, we describe communication principles such as layering, error detection and correction, data security, and plug and play.

### Parallel Communication

*Parallel communication* takes place when the physical layer is capable of carrying multiple bits of data from one device to another. This means that the data bus is composed of multiple data wires, in addition to control and possibly power wires, running in parallel from one device to another. Each wire carries one of the bits. Parallel communication has the advantage of high data throughput, if the length of the bus is short. The length of a parallel bus must be kept short because long parallel wires will result in high capacitance values, and transmitting a bit on a bus with a higher capacitance value will require more time to charge or discharge. In addition, small variations in the length of the individual wires of a parallel bus can cause the received bits of the data word to arrive at different times. Such misalignment of data becomes more of a problem as the length of a parallel bus increases. Another problem with parallel buses is the fact that they are more costly to construct and may be bulky, especially when considering the insulation that must be used to prevent the noise from each wire from interfering with the other wires. For example, a 32-wire cable connecting two devices together will cost much more and be larger than a two-wire cable.

In general, parallel communication is used when connecting devices that reside on the same IC, or devices that reside on the same circuit board. Since the length of such buses is short, the capacitance load, data misalignment and cost problems mentioned earlier do not play an important role.

### Serial Communication

*Serial communication* involves a physical layer that carries one bit of data at a time. This means that the data bus is composed of a single data wire, along with control and possibly power wires, running from one device to another. In serial communication, a word of data is transmitted one bit at a time. Serial buses are capable of higher throughputs than parallel buses when used to connect two physically distant devices. The reason for this is that a serial bus will have less average capacitance, enabling it to send more bits per unit of time. In addition, a serial bus cable is cheaper to build because it has fewer wires. The disadvantage of a serial bus is that the interfacing logic and communication protocol will be more complex. On the sending side, a transmitter must decompose data words into bits and on the receiving side, and the receiver must compose bits into words.

Most serial bus protocols eliminate the need for extra control signals, such as read and write signals, by using the same wire that carries data for this purpose. This is performed as follows. When data is to be sent, the sender first transmits a bit called a *start bit*. A start bit merely signals the receiver to wakeup and start receiving data. The start bit is then followed by $N$ data bits, where $N$ is the size of the word, and a *stop bit*. The stop bit signals to the receiver the end of the transmission. Often, both the transmitter and the receiver agree on the transmission speed used to send and receive data. After sending a start bit, the transmitter sends all $N$ bits at the predetermined transmission speed. Likewise, on seeing a start bit, a receiver simply starts sampling the data at a predetermined frequency until all $N$ bits are assembled. Another common synchronization technique is to use an additional wire for clocking purposes (see the $I^2C$ bus protocol). Here, the transmitter and receiver devices use this clock line to determine when to send or sample the data.

## Wireless Communication

Wireless communication eliminates the need for devices to be physically connected in order to communicate. The physical layer used in wireless communication is typically either an infrared (IR) channel or a radio frequency (RF) channel.

*Infrared* uses electromagnetic wave frequencies that are just below the visible light spectrum, thus undetectable by the human eye. These waves can be generated by using an infrared diode and detected by using an infrared transistor. An infrared diode is similar to a red or green diode except that it emits infrared light. An infrared transistor is a transistor that conducts (i.e., allows current to flow from its source to its drain), when exposed to infrared light. A simple transmitter can send 1s by turning on its infrared diode and can send 0s by turning off its infrared diode. Correspondingly, a receiver will detect 1s when current flows through its infrared transistor and 0s otherwise. The advantage of using infrared communication is that it is relatively cheap to build transmitters and receivers. The disadvantage of using infrared is the need for line of sight between the transmitter and receiver, resulting in a very restricted communication range.

*Radio frequency* (RF) uses electromagnetic wave frequencies in the radio spectrum. A transmitter here will need to use analog circuitry and an antenna to transmit data. Likewise, a receiver will need to use an antenna and analog circuitry to receive data. One advantage of using RF is that, generally, a line of sight is not necessary and thus longer distance communication is possible. The range of communication is, of course, dependent on the transmission power used by the transmitter.

Typically, RF transmitters and receivers must agree on a specific frequency in order to send and receive data. Using *frequency hopping*, it is possible for the transmitter and receiver to communicate while constantly changing the transmission frequency. Of course, both devices must have a common understanding of the sequence for frequency hops. Frequency hopping allows more devices to share a fixed set of frequencies and is commonly used in wireless communication protocols designed for networks of computers and other electronic devices.

## Layering

*Layering* is a hierarchical organization of a communication protocol where lower levels of the protocol provide services to the higher levels. We have already discussed the physical layer. The physical layer provides the basic service of sending and receiving bits or words of data. The next higher-level protocol uses the physical layer to send and receive packets of data, where a packet of data is composed of possibly multiple bytes. The next higher level uses the packet transmission service of its lower level to perhaps send different type of data such as acknowledgments, special requests, and so on. Typically, the lowest level consists of the physical layer and the highest level consists of the application layer. The application layer provides abstract services to the application such as ftp or http.

Layering is a way to break the complexity of a communication protocol into independent pieces, thus making it easier to design and understand, much like a programmer abstracting away complexities of a program by creating objects or libraries of routines. In communication and networking, the concept of layering is very fundamental.

## Error Detection and Correction

*Error detection* is the ability of a receiver to detect errors that may occur during the transmission of a data word or packet. The most common types of errors are bit errors and burst of bit errors. A *bit error* occurs when a single bit in a word or data packet is received as its inverted value. A *burst of bit error* occurs when consecutive bits of a word or data packet are received incorrectly. Given that an error is detected, *error correction* is the ability of a receiver and transmitter to cooperate in order to correct the problem. The ability to detect and correct errors is often part of a bus protocol. We will next discuss parity and checksum error detection algorithms, which are commonly used in bus protocols.

*Parity* is a single bit of information that is sent along with a word of data by the transmitter to give the receiver some additional knowledge about the data word. This additional knowledge is used by the receiver to detect, to some degree, a bit or burst of bit error in receiving a word. Common types of parity are odd or even. Odd parity is a bit that if set indicates to the receiver that the data word bits plus parity bit contain an odd number of 1s. Even parity is a bit that if set indicates to the receiver that the data word bits plus parity bit contain an even number of 1s. Prior to sending a word of data, the transmitter will compute the parity and send that along with the data word to the receiver. On reception of the data word and parity bit, the receiver will compute the parity of the data and make sure that it agrees with the parity bit received from the transmitter. If a parity check fails, it indicates with certainty that there was at least one transmission error. Parity checks will always detect a single bit error. However, burst bit errors may or may not be detected by parity checking — an even number of errors, for example, will not be detected.

As an example of parity-based error checking, consider wanting to transmit the following 7-bit word: 0101010. Assuming even parity, we would actually transmit the 8-bit word: 01010101, where the least-significant bit is the parity bit. Now, suppose during transmission, a bit gets flipped, so that a receiver receives the following 8-bit word: 11010101. The receiver detects that this word has odd parity; knowing that the word was supposed to have even parity, the receiver determines that this word has an error. Instead, suppose the receiver receives: 11110101. This word has even parity, and so the receiver thinks the word is correct, even though it contains two errors.

*Checksum* is a stronger form of error checking that is applied to a packet of data. A packet of data will contain multiple words of data. Using parity checking, we used one extra bit per word to help us detect errors. Using checksum, we use an extra word per packet for the same purpose. For example, we may compute the XOR sum of all the data words in a packet and send this value along with the data packet. Upon receiving the data packet words and the checksum word, the receiver will compute the XOR sum of all the data words it received. If the computed checksum word equals the received checksum word, the data packet is assumed to be correct. Otherwise, it is assumed to be incorrect. Again, not all error combinations can be detected. We can of course use both parity and checksum for stronger error checking.

As an example, suppose a packet consists of four words: 0000000, 0101010, 1010101, and 0000000. The XOR checksum of these four words is 1111111. A transmitter can thus send that checksum word at the end of the packet. Now, suppose the receiver receives 1000001, 0101010, 1010101, and 0000000. Note that two bits have switched in the first word, and that parity-based error checking would not detect this error. The receiver computes the checksum of this packet and obtains 0111110. This differs from the received checksum of 1111111, and thus the receiver determines that an error has occurred.

Note that errors can also occur in the parity bit or the checksum word itself.

When using parity or checksum error detection, error correction is typically done by a retransmission and acknowledgment protocol. Here, the transmitter sends a data packet and expects to receive an acknowledgment from the receiver indicating that the data packet was received correctly. If an acknowledgment is not received, the transmitter retransmits the data packet and waits for a second acknowledgment.

# 6.9 Serial Protocols

In this section, we describe four popular serial protocols, namely the $I^2C$ protocol, the CAN protocol, the FireWire protocol, and the USB protocol.

## $I^2C$

Philips Semiconductors developed the *Inter-IC*, or $I^2C$, bus nearly 20 years ago. $I^2C$ is a two-wire serial bus protocol. This protocol enables peripheral ICs in electronic systems to

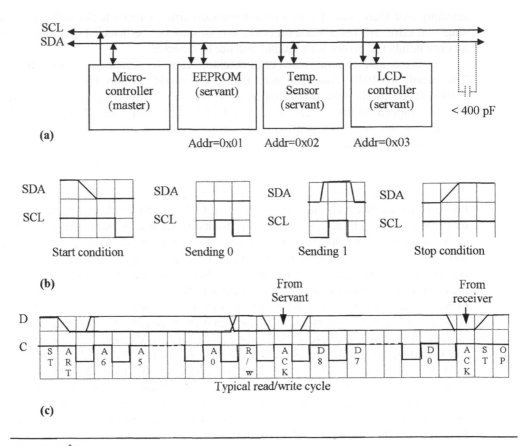

Figure 6.24: I²C bus structure.

communicate with each other using simple communication hardware. Based on the original specification of the I²C, data transfer rates of up to 100 kbits/s and 7-bit addressing are possible. Seven-bit addressing allows a total of 128 devices to communicate over a shared I²C bus. With increased data transfer rate requirements, the I²C specification has been recently enhanced to include fast-mode, 3.4 Mbits/s, with 10-bit addressing. Common devices capable of interfacing to an I²C bus include EPROMs, Flash and some RAM memory devices, real-time clocks, watchdog timers, and microcontrollers.

A sample I²C network is depicted in Figure 6.24(a). The bus consists of two wires; a data wire called serial-data-line (*SDA*) and a clock wire called serial-clock-line (*SCL*). The I²C specification does not limit the length of the bus wires, as long as the total capacitance of the bus remains under 400 pF. In this example, there are four devices attached to the bus. One of these devices, the microcontroller, is a master. The other three devices, a temperature sensor, an EEPROM, and a LCD-controller, are servants. Each of these servant devices is assigned a unique address, as shown in Figure 6.24(a). Only master devices can initiate a data transfer on an I$^2$C bus. The protocol does not limit the number of master devices on an I$^2$C bus, but typically, in a microcontroller-based system, the microcontroller serves as the master. Both master and servant devices can be senders or receivers of data. This will depend on the function of the device. In our example, the microcontroller and EEPROM send and receive data, while the temperature sensor sends data and the LCD-controller receives data. In Figure 6.24(a), arrows connecting the devices to the I$^2$C bus wires depict the data movement direction. Normally, all servant devices residing on an I$^2$C assert high-impedance on the bus while the master device maintains logic high, signaling an idle condition.

All data transfers on an I$^2$C bus are initiated by a start condition. A start condition is shown in Figure 6.24(b). A high to low transition of the *SDA* line while the *SCL* signal is held high signals a start condition. All data transfers on an I$^2$C bus are terminated by a stop condition. A stop condition is shown in Figure 6.24(b). A low to high transition of the *SDA* line while the *SCL* signal is held high signals a stop condition. Actual data is transferred in between start and stop conditions. A typical I$^2$C byte write cycle works as follows. The master device initiates the transfer by a start condition. Then, the address of the device that the byte is being written to is sent starting with the most significant down to the least significant bit. Ones and zeros are sent as shown in Figure 6.24(b). Here, the bit value is placed on the *SDA* line by the master device while the *SCL* line is low and maintained stable until after a clock pulse on *SCL*. If performing a write, right after sending the address of the receiving device, the master sends a zero. The receiving device in return acknowledges the transmission by holding the *SDA* line low during the first *ACK* clock cycle. Following the acknowledgment, the master device transmits a byte of data starting with the most significant down to the least significant bit. The receiving device, in this case the servant, acknowledges the reception of data by holding the *SDA* line low during the second *ACK* clock cycle. If performing a read operation, the master initiates the transfer by a start condition, sends the address of the device that is being read, sends a one (logic high on *SDA* line) requesting a read and waits to receive an acknowledgment. Then, the sender sends a byte of data. The receiver, master device in this case, acknowledges the reception of data and terminates the transfer by generating a stop condition. The timing diagram of a typical read/write cycle is depicted in Figure 6.24(c).

## CAN

The *controller area network* (CAN) bus is a serial communication protocol for real-time applications, possibly carried over a twisted pair of wires. This protocol was developed by Robert Bosch GmbH to enable communication among various electronic components of cars as an alternative to expensive and cumbersome wiring harnesses. The robustness of the protocol has expanded its use to many other automation and industrial applications. Some characteristics of the CAN protocol include high-integrity serial data communications, real-time support, data rates of up to 1 Mbit/s, 11-bit addressing, error detection, and confinement capabilities. The CAN protocol is documented in ISO 11898 (for high-speed applications) and ISO 11519-2 (for lower speed applications). Common applications, other than automobiles, using CAN include elevator controllers, copiers, telescopes, production-line control systems, and medical instruments. Among devices that incorporate a CAN interface are the 8051-compatible 8592 processor, and a variety of standalone CAN controllers, such as the 80C200, from Philips.

The CAN specification does not specify the actual layout and structure of the physical bus itself. Instead, it requires that a device connected to the CAN bus is able to transmit, or detect, on the physical bus, one of two signals called dominant or recessive. For example, a dominant signal may be represented as logic '0' and recessive as logic '1' on a single data wire. Furthermore, the physical CAN bus must guarantee that if one of two devices asserts a dominant signal and another device simultaneously a recessive signal, the dominant signal prevails. Given a physical CAN bus with the above-mentioned properties, the protocol defines data packet format and transmission rules to prioritize messages, guarantee latency times, allow for multiple masters, handles transmission errors, retransmit corrupted messages, and distinguish between a permanent failure of a node versus temporary errors.

## FireWire

The *FireWire* (a.k.a. *I-Link* or *Lynx*) is a high-performance serial bus developed by Apple Computer Inc. Because the specification of the FireWire protocol is given by the 1394 IEEE designation, many refer to it as the IEEE 1394, or simply 1394. The need for FireWire is driven by the rapidly growing need for mass information transfer. Typical local or wide area networks (LANs/WANs) are incapable of providing cost-effective connection capabilities and do not guarantee bandwidth for real-time applications. Some characteristics of the FireWire protocol include transfer rates of 12.5 to 400 Mbits/s, 64-bit addressing, real-time connection/disconnect and address assignment (a.k.a., plug-and-play capabilities), and packet-based layered design structure.

While $I^2C$ and CAN bus protocols are designed mostly for interfacing ICs, FireWire is designed for interfacing among independent electronic devices (e.g., a desktop computer and a digital scanner). Moreover, FireWire is capable of supporting an entire local-area network similar to one based on Ethernet. The 64-bit wide address space of FireWire is partitioned as 10 bits for network identifiers, 6 bits for node identifiers, and 48 bits for memory address. A local-area network based on FireWire can consist of 1,023 subnetworks, each consisting of 63 nodes, with each node, in turn, addressable by 281 terabytes of distinct locations! FireWire is feasible for applications such as disk drives, printers, scanners, cameras, and many other consumer electronics devices.

## USB

The *Universal Serial Bus* (USB) protocol is designed to make it easier for PC users to connect monitors, printers, digital speakers, modems and input devices like scanners, digital cameras, joysticks, and multimedia game equipment. USB has two data rates, 12 Mbps for devices requiring increased bandwidth, and 1.5 Mbps for lower-speed devices like joysticks and game pads. USB uses a tiered star topology, which means that some USB devices, called USB hubs, can serve as connection ports for other USB peripherals. Only one device needs to be plugged into the PC. Other devices can then be plugged into the hub. USB hubs may be embedded in such devices as monitors, printers and keyboards. Standalone hubs could also be made available, providing a handful of convenient USB ports right on the desktop. Hubs feature an upstream connection (pointed toward the PC) as well as multiple downstream ports to allow the connection of additional peripheral devices. Up to 127 USB devices can be connected together in this way.

USB host controllers manage and control the driver software and bandwidth required by each peripheral connected to the bus. Users don't need to do a thing, because all the configuration steps happen automatically. The USB host controller even allocates electrical power to the USB devices. Like USB host controllers, USB hubs can detect attachments and detachments of peripherals occurring downstream and supply appropriate levels of power to downstream devices. Since power is distributed through USB cables, with a maximum length of 5 meters, you no longer need a clunky AC power supply box for many devices.

# 6.10 Parallel Protocols

In this section, we briefly describe two popular parallel protocols, namely the PCI bus protocol and the ARM Bus protocol.

## PCI Bus

The *Peripheral Component Interconnect* (PCI) bus is a high-performance bus for interconnecting chips, expansion boards (e.g., a video card that plugs into a main board like a Pentium mother board), and processor memory subsystems. The PCI bus originated at Intel in the early 1990s, was then adopted by the industry as a standard and administered by the PCI Special Interest Group (PCISIG), and was first used in personal computers in 1994 along with Intel 486 processors. The PCI bus has since largely replaced the earlier bus architectures such as the ISA/EISA bus described earlier, and Micro Channel bus protocols. Some characteristics of the PCI bus protocol include transfer rates of 127.2 to 508.6 Mbits/s, 32-bit addressing, synchronous bus architecture (i.e., all transfers take place with respect to a clock signal), and multiplexed 32-bit data/address lines. It must be noted that later additions to the specification of the PCI bus extend the protocol to allow 64-bit data and addressing while maintaining compatibility with the 32-bit schemes.

## ARM Bus

While PCI is a widely used industry standards, many other bus protocols are predominantly designed and used internally by various IC design companies. One such bus is the ARM bus designed by the ARM Corporation and documented in ARM's application note 18v. This bus is designed to interface with the ARM line of processors. The ARM bus supports 32-bit data transfer and 32-bit addressing and, similar to PCI, is implemented using synchronous data transfer architecture. The transfer rate on an ARM bus is not specified and instead is a function of the clock speed used in a particular application. More specifically, if the clock speed of the ARM bus is denoted as $X$, then the transfer rate is $16 \times X$ bits/s.

## 6.11 Wireless Protocols

In this section, we briefly introduce three new and emerging wireless protocols, namely IrDA, Bluetooth, and the IEEE 802.11.

### IrDA

The Infrared Data Association (IrDA) is an international organization that creates and promotes interoperable, low-cost, infrared data interconnection standards that support a walk-up, point-to-point user model. Their protocol suite, also commonly referred to as IrDA, is designed to support transmission of data between two devices over short-range point-to-point infrared at speeds between 9.6 kbps and 4 Mbps. IrDA is that small, semitransparent, red window that you may have wondered about on your notebook computer. Over the last several years, IrDA hardware has been deployed in notebook computers, printers, personal digital assistants, digital cameras, public phones, and even cell phones. One of the reasons for this has been the simplicity and low cost of IrDA hardware. Unfortunately, until recently, the hardware has not been available for applications programmers to use because of a lack of suitable protocol drivers.

Microsoft Windows CE 1.0 was the first Windows operating system to provide built-in IrDA support. Windows 2000 and Windows 98 now also include support for the same IrDA programming APIs that have enabled file sharing applications and games on Windows CE. IrDA implementations are becoming available on several popular embedded operating systems.

### Bluetooth

*Bluetooth* is a new and global standard for wireless connectivity. This protocol is based on a low-cost, short-range radio link. The radio frequency used by Bluetooth is globally available. When two Bluetooth-equipped devices come within 10 meters of each other, they can establish a connection. Because Bluetooth uses a radio-based link, it doesn't require a line-of-sight connection in order to communicate. For example, your laptop could send information to a printer in the next room, or your microwave oven could send a message to your cordless phone telling you that your meal is ready. In the future, Bluetooth is likely to be standard in tens of millions of mobile phones, PCs, laptops and a whole range of other electronic devices.

### IEEE 802.11

*IEEE 802.11* is an IEEE-proposed standard for wireless local area networks (LANs). There are two different ways to configure a network: ad-hoc and infrastructure. In the ad-hoc network, computers are brought together to form a network on the fly, Here, there is no structure to the network, there are no fixed points, and usually every node is able to communicate with every other node. Although it seems that order would be difficult to maintain in this type of network, special algorithms have been designed to elect one machine as the master station of the network with the others being servants. Another algorithm in ad-hoc network architectures uses a broadcast and flooding method to all other nodes to establish who's who. The second type of network structure used in wireless LANs is the infrastructure. This architecture uses fixed network access points with which mobile nodes can communicate. These network access points are sometime connected to landlines to widen the LAN's capability by bridging wireless nodes to other wired nodes. If service areas overlap, handoffs can occur. This structure is very similar to the present day cellular networks around the world.

The IEEE 802.11 protocol places specifications on the parameters of both the physical PHY and medium access control MAC layers of the network. The PHY layer, which actually handles the transmission of data between nodes, can use direct sequence spread spectrum, frequency-hopping spread spectrum, or infrared pulse position modulation. IEEE 802.11 makes provisions for data rates of either 1 Mbps or 2 Mbps, and calls for operation in the 2.4 to 2.4835 GHz frequency band, which is an unlicensed band for industrial, scientific, and medical applications, and 300 to 428,000 GHz for IR transmission. Infrared is generally considered to be more secure to eavesdropping, because IR transmissions require absolute line-of-sight links (no transmission is possible outside any simply connected space or around corners), as opposed to radio frequency transmissions, which can penetrate walls and be intercepted by third parties unknowingly. However, infrared transmissions can be adversely affected by sunlight, and the spread-spectrum protocol of IEEE 802.11 does provide some rudimentary security for typical data transfers.

The MAC layer is a set of protocols, which is responsible for maintaining order in the use of a shared medium. The IEEE 802.11 standard specifies a carrier sense multiple access with collision avoidance CSMA/CA protocol. In this protocol, when a node receives a packet to be transmitted, it first listens to ensure no other node is transmitting. If the channel is clear, it then transmits the packet. Otherwise, it chooses a random backoff-factor, which determines the amount of time the node must wait, until it is allowed to transmit its packet. During periods in which the channel is clear, the transmitting node decrements its backoff counter. When the backoff counter reaches zero, the node transmits the packet. Since the probability that two nodes will choose the same backoff factor is small, collisions between packets are minimized. Collision detection, as is employed in Ethernet, cannot be used for the radio frequency transmissions of IEEE 802.11. The reason for this is that when a node is transmitting it cannot hear any other node in the system, which may be transmitting, since its own signal will drown out any others arriving at the node.

Whenever a packet is to be transmitted, the transmitting node first sends out a short ready-to-send RTS packet containing information on the length of the packet. If the receiving node hears the RTS, it responds with a short clear-to-send CTS packet. After this exchange, the transmitting node sends its packet. When the packet is received successfully, as determined by a cyclic redundancy check, the receiving node transmits an acknowledgment ACK packet.

## 6.12 Summary

Interfacing processors and memory represents a challenging design task. Timing diagrams provide a basic means for us to describe interface protocols. Thousands of protocols exist, but they can be better understood by understanding basic protocol concepts like actors, data direction, addresses, time multiplexing, and control methods. A general-purpose processor typically has either a bus-based I/O structure or a port-based I/O structure for interfacing. Interfacing with a general-purpose processor is the most common interfacing task and involves three key concepts. The first is the processor's approach for addressing external data locations, known as its I/O addressing approach, which may be memory-mapped I/O or standard I/O. The second is the processor's approach for handling requests for servicing by peripherals, known as its interrupt handling approach, which may be fixed or vectored. The third is the ability of peripherals to directly access memory, known as direct memory access. Interfacing also leads to the common problem of more than one processor simultaneously seeking access to a shared resource such as a bus, requiring arbitration. Arbitration may be carried out using a priority arbiter or using daisy chain arbitration. A system often has a hierarchy of buses, such as a high-speed processor local bus and a lower-speed peripheral bus. Communication protocols may carry out parallel or serial communication, and may use wires, infrared, or radio frequencies as the transmission medium. Communication protocols may include extra bits for error detection and correction, and typically involve layering as an abstraction mechanism. Popular serial protocols include I$^2$C, CAN, FireWire, and USB. Popular parallel protocols include PCI and ARM. Popular serial wireless protocols include IrDA, Bluetooth, and IEEE 802.11.

## 6.13 References and Further Reading

- VSI Alliance, On-Chip Bus Development Working Group, Specification 1 version 1.0, "On-Chip Bus Attributes," August 1998, http://www.vsi.org.
- L. Eggebrecht. *Interfacing to the IBM Personal Computer.* Indianapolis, IN: SAMS, Macmillan Computer Publishing, 1990.
- Peter W. Gofton. *Mastering Serial Communications.* Alameda, CA: SYBEX Inc., 1994.
- Bob O'Hara and Al Petrick. *IEEE 802.11 Handbook — A Designer's Companion.* Piscataway, NJ: Standards Information Network, IEEE Press, 1999.
- John Hyde. *USB Design by Example.* New York: John Wiley & Sons, Inc., 1999.

## 6.14 Exercises

6.1   Draw the timing diagram for a bus protocol that is handshaked, nonaddressed, and transfers 8 bits of data over a 4-bit data bus.

6.2   Explain the difference between port-based I/O and bus-based I/O.

6.3 Show how to extend the number of ports on a 4-port 8051 to 8 by using extended parallel I/O. (a) Using block diagrams for the 8051 and the extended parallel I/O device, draw and label all interconnections and I/O ports. Clearly indicate the names and widths of all connections. (b) Give C code for a function that could be used to write to the extended ports.

6.4 Discuss the advantages and disadvantages of using memory-mapped I/O versus standard I/O.

6.5 Explain the benefits that an interrupt address table has over fixed and vectored interrupt methods.

6.6 Draw a block diagram of a processor, memory, and peripheral connected with a system bus, in which the peripheral gets serviced using vectored interrupt. Assume servicing moves data from the peripheral to the memory. Show all relevant control and data lines of the bus, and label component inputs/outputs clearly. Use symbolic values for addresses. Provide a timing diagram illustrating what happens over the system bus during the interrupt.

6.7 Draw a block diagram of a processor, memory, peripheral, and DMA controller connected with a system bus, in which the peripheral transfers 100 bytes of data to the memory using DMA. Show all relevant control and data lines of the bus, and label component inputs/outputs clearly. Draw a timing diagram showing what happens during the transfer; skip the 2nd through 99th bytes.

6.8 Repeat problem 6.7 for a daisy-chain configuration.

6.9 Design a parallel I/O peripheral for the ISA bus. Provide: (a) a state-machine description and (b) a structural description.

6.10 Design an extended parallel I/O peripheral. Provide: (a) a state-machine description and (b) a structural description.

6.11 List the three main transmission mediums described in the chapter. Give two common applications for each.

6.12 Assume an 8051 is used as a master device on an I2C bus with pin P1.0 corresponding to I2C_Data and pin P1.1 corresponding to I2C_Clock. Write a set of C routines that encapsulate the details of the I2C protocol. Specifically, write the routines called StartI2C/StopI2C, that send the appropriate start/stop signal to slave devices. Likewise, write the routines ReadByte and WriteByte, each taking a device Id as input and performing the appropriate I/O actions.

6.13 Select one of the following serial bus protocols, then, perform an internet search for information on transfer rate, addressing, error correction (if applicable), and plug-and-play capability (if applicable). Then give timing diagrams for a typical transfer of data (e.g., a write operation). The protocols are USB, I2O, Fibre Channel, SMBus, IrDA, or any other serial bus in use by the industry and not described in this book.

6.14 Select one of the following parallel bus protocols, then, perform an Internet search for information on transfer rate, addressing , DMA and interrupt control (if applicable), and plug-and-play capability (if applicable). Then give timing diagrams for a typical transfer of data (e.g., a write operation). The protocols are STD 32, VME, SCSI, ATAPI, Micro Channel, or any other parallel bus in use by the industry and not described in this book.

# CHAPTER 7: *Digital Camera Example*

## 7.1    Introduction

In the previous chapters, we introduced general-purpose processors, custom single-purpose processors, standard single-purpose processors, memory, and techniques for interfacing processors and memory. In this chapter, we apply this knowledge to design a simple digital camera. In particular, we will examine the trade-offs of using general-purpose versus single-purpose processors to implement the necessary camera functionality. We will see that choosing a good partitioning of functionality among the different processor types is essential to building a good design. This in turn requires a unified view of different processor types, as this book has thus far stressed.

We begin with a general introduction to digital cameras and their inner workings. We then develop the camera's specifications, which describe the desired behavior as well as constraints on design metrics like performance, size, and power. We explore several alternative implementations of the digital camera and compare their design metrics.

## 7.2    Introduction to a Simple Digital Camera

A digital camera is a popular consumer electronic device that can capture images, or "take pictures," and store them in a digital format. A digital camera does not contain film, but rather one or more ICs possessing processors and memories. Digital cameras were not possible over a decade ago, because small-enough ICs could not process fast enough or store enough bits to be feasible. The advent of systems-on-a-chip and high-capacity flash memory has made such cameras possible.

## User's Perspective

From a user's point of view, a simple digital camera works as follows. The user turns on the digital camera, points the camera lens to the scene to be photographed, and clicks the "shutter" button. The user can repeat these steps until up to $N$ images are stored internally in the camera. Here, $N$ is a constant that depends on the model of the camera, which in turn depends on the amount of memory in the camera and the number of bits used per image. The user may also attach the digital camera to a PC, say, by using a serial cable, to download the photos to a hard disk for permanent storage.

## Designer's Perspective

From a designer's point of view, a simple digital camera performs two key tasks. The first task is that of processing images and storing them in internal memory. The second task is that of uploading the images serially to an attached PC.

The task of processing and storing images is initiated when the user presses the shutter button. At this point, the image is captured and converted to digital form by a *charge-coupled device* (CCD). Then, the image is processed and stored in internal memory. The task of uploading the image is initiated when the user attaches the digital camera to a PC and uses special software to command the digital camera to transmit the archived images serially. Let us look at these actions in more detail.

A CCD is a special sensor that captures an image. A CCD is a light-sensitive silicon solid-state device composed of many small cells. The light falling on a cell is converted into a small amount of electric charge, which is then measured by the CCD electronics and stored as a number. The number usually ranges from 0, meaning no light, to 256 or 65,535, meaning very intense light per pixel. Figure 7.1 illustrates the internals of a CCD. On the periphery, a CCD is composed of a mechanical shutter. This is a screen that normally blocks the light from falling on the light sensitive surface. When activated, the screen opens momentarily and allows light to hit the light sensitive surface, charging the cells with electrical energy that is proportional to the amount of light passed in. The screen typically sits behind an optical lens that focuses the scene observed through the viewfinder onto the light sensitive surface of the CCD. A CCD also has internal circuitry that measures the electric charge of each cell, converts it to a digital value, and provides an interface for outputting the data.

Due to manufacturing errors, the light-sensitive cells of a CCD may always measure the light intensity to be slightly above or below the actual value. This error, called the zero-bias error, is typically the same across columns but different across rows. For this reason, some of the left most columns of a CCD's light-sensitive cells are blocked by a strip of black paint. The actual intensity registered by these blocked cells should be zero. Therefore, a reading of other than zero would indicate the zero-bias error for that row. Figure 7.1 shows the covered cells. This becomes clearer as we give an example in the next paragraphs.

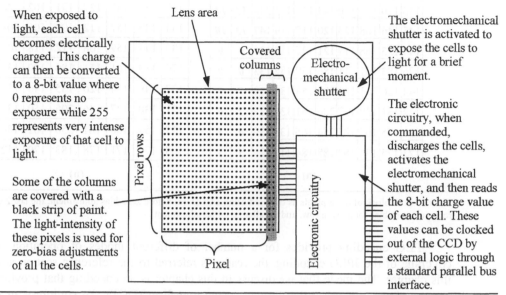

When exposed to light, each cell becomes electrically charged. This charge can then be converted to a 8-bit value where 0 represents no exposure while 255 represents very intense exposure of that cell to light.

Some of the columns are covered with a black strip of paint. The light-intensity of these pixels is used for zero-bias adjustments of all the cells.

Lens area

Covered columns

Electro-mechanical shutter

Pixel rows

Electronic circuitry

Pixel

The electromechanical shutter is activated to expose the cells to light for a brief moment.

The electronic circuitry, when commanded, discharges the cells, activates the electromechanical shutter, and then reads the 8-bit charge value of each cell. These values can be clocked out of the CCD by external logic through a standard parallel bus interface.

Figure 7.1: Internals of a charge-coupled device (CCD).

A digital camera uses a CCD to capture an image. Once the image is captured, it must be corrected to eliminate the zero bias error. Then, the image must be encoded using the JPEG encoding scheme. The task of bias adjustment is described next.

Figure 7.2 shows a raw image block of size $8 \times 8$ pixels that is captured using a CCD of that size. Normally, the CCD would be of much greater resolution, say $640 \times 480$ pixels, but we use a small one to be able to illustrate the various operations of a digital camera in this chapter. Notice in Figure 7.2(a) that there are 10 columns. As mentioned earlier, the last two columns are extra and are used to detect zero-bias. Recall that these two columns are covered and should normally read a value of zero. Looking at the last two columns of the first row, we see that the measured light intensity is on the average 13 units larger than the actual light intensity. We obtain 13 by averaging the last two columns $((12 + 14) / 2) = 13$). We can thus correct the error for this row by subtracting 13 from each element of the first row. We can repeat this process for each row to obtain a block of $8 \times 8$ pixels that has been corrected for zero bias errors. The corrected block is given in Figure 7.2(b).

The next step is to compress the image, which reduces the number of bits needed to store the image in memory. Compression allows us to store more images in limited amount of memory. Compressed images can also be transmitted to a PC in less time. We'll perform JPEG encoding of the image. JPEG is a popular standard format for representing digital images in a compressed form. JPEG, pronounced "jay-peg," is short for Joint Photographic Experts Group. The word *joint* refers to the group's status as a committee working on both ISO and ITU-T standards. Their best-known standard is for still-image compression.

| 136 | 170 | 155 | 140 | 144 | 115 | 112 | 248 | *12* | *14* |
|-----|-----|-----|-----|-----|-----|-----|-----|------|------|
| 145 | 146 | 168 | 123 | 120 | 117 | 119 | 147 | *12* | *10* |
| 144 | 153 | 168 | 117 | 121 | 127 | 118 | 135 | *9* | *9* |
| 176 | 183 | 161 | 111 | 186 | 130 | 132 | 133 | *0* | *0* |
| 144 | 156 | 161 | 133 | 192 | 153 | 138 | 139 | *7* | *7* |
| 122 | 131 | 128 | 147 | 206 | 151 | 131 | 127 | *2* | *0* |
| 121 | 155 | 164 | 185 | 254 | 165 | 138 | 129 | *4* | *4* |
| 173 | 175 | 176 | 183 | 188 | 184 | 117 | 129 | *5* | *5* |

(a)

| 123 | 157 | 142 | 127 | 131 | 102 | 99 | 235 |
|-----|-----|-----|-----|-----|-----|-----|-----|
| 134 | 135 | 157 | 112 | 109 | 106 | 108 | 136 |
| 135 | 144 | 159 | 108 | 112 | 118 | 109 | 126 |
| 176 | 183 | 161 | 111 | 186 | 130 | 132 | 133 |
| 137 | 149 | 154 | 126 | 185 | 146 | 131 | 132 |
| 121 | 130 | 127 | 146 | 205 | 150 | 130 | 126 |
| 117 | 151 | 160 | 181 | 250 | 161 | 134 | 125 |
| 168 | 170 | 171 | 178 | 183 | 179 | 112 | 124 |

(b)

Figure 7.2: A block of 8 × 8 pixels as captured using a CCD: (a) before zero-bias adjustment; the last 2 columns help represent zero bias for a given row, and (b) after zero-bias adjustment.

JPEG encoding provides for a number of different modes of operation. For a full coverage of the JPEG encoding, the reader is referred to the reference section at the end of this chapter. The mode that we discuss in this chapter is an encoding that provides for high compression ratios using the discrete cosine transform (DCT). To compress an image, the image data is divided into blocks of 8 × 8 pixels each. Each block is then processed in three steps. The first step performs the DCT, the second step performs quantization, and the last step performs Huffman encoding.

The DCT step transforms our original 8 × 8 pixel block into a cosine-frequency domain. Once in this form, the upper-left corner values of the transformed data represent more of the essence of the image while the lower-right corner values represent finer details. We can, therefore reduce the precision of these lower-right corner values to facilitate compression while retaining reasonable overall image quality. The actual DCT operation is given in this formula:

$$C(h) = \text{if ( h == 0 ) then } 1/\text{sqrt}(2) \text{ else } 1.0$$

$$F(u,v) = 1/4 \times C(u) \times C(v) \sum_{x=0..7} \sum_{y=0..7} D_{xy} \times \cos(\pi(2x + 1)u / 16) \times \cos(\pi(2y + 1)v / 16)$$

Here, $C(h)$ is simply an auxiliary function used in the main equation, namely, $F(u,v)$. The function $F(u,v)$ gives the encoded pixel at row $u$, column $v$. $D_{xy}$ is the original pixel value at row $x$, column $y$. Of course, it would be useless to have a DCT transform if we are unable to reverse the process and obtain the original. Below is the inverse DCT (IDCT), although it is not necessary in the implementation of our simple digital camera:

$$C(h) = \text{if ( h == 0 ) then } 1/\text{sqrt}(2) \text{ else } 1.0$$

$$f(x,y) = 1/4 \sum_{u=0..7} \sum_{v=0..7} C(u) \times C(v) \times E_{uv} \times \cos(\pi(2u + 1)x / 16) \times \cos(\pi(2v + 1)y / 16)$$

Again, $C(h)$ is simply an auxiliary function used in the main equation, namely, $f(x,y)$. The function $f(x,y)$ gives the original pixel at row $x$, column $y$. $E_{uv}$ is the DCT-encoded pixel value,

| 1150 | 39 | −43 | −10 | 26 | −83 | 11 | 41 |
|------|-----|-----|-----|-----|-----|-----|-----|
| −81 | −3 | 115 | −73 | −6 | −2 | 22 | −5 |
| 14 | −11 | 1 | −42 | 26 | −3 | 17 | −38 |
| 2 | −61 | −13 | −12 | 36 | −23 | −18 | 5 |
| 44 | 13 | 37 | −4 | 10 | −21 | 7 | −8 |
| 36 | −11 | −9 | −4 | 20 | −28 | −21 | 14 |
| −19 | −7 | 21 | −6 | 3 | 3 | 12 | −21 |
| −5 | −13 | −11 | −17 | −4 | −1 | 7 | −4 |

(a)

| 144 | 5 | −5 | −1 | 3 | −10 | 1 | 5 |
|------|-----|-----|-----|-----|-----|-----|-----|
| −10 | 0 | 14 | −9 | −1 | 0 | 3 | −1 |
| 2 | −1 | 0 | −5 | 3 | 0 | 2 | −5 |
| 0 | −8 | −2 | −2 | 5 | −3 | −2 | 1 |
| 6 | 2 | 5 | −1 | 1 | −3 | 1 | −1 |
| 5 | −1 | −1 | −1 | 3 | −4 | −3 | 2 |
| −2 | −1 | 3 | −1 | 0 | 0 | 2 | −3 |
| −1 | −2 | −1 | −2 | −1 | 0 | 1 | −1 |

(b)

Figure 7.3: A block of 8 × 8 pixel as captured using a CCD, zero bias corrected: (a) after being encoded using DCT, (b) then after quantization.

using the previous equation, for row $u$ and column $v$. Figure 7.3(a) shows the DCT-encoded values for our sample block of 8 × 8 pixels. The inverse process will obtain the block in Figure 7.2(b) from that in Figure 7.3(a).

The DCT is sometimes distinguished from the ICDT by referring to the DCT as the forward DCT, or FDCT.

The next processing step is to reduce the quality, of the encoded DCT image, which helps us compress the image. We do this by reducing the bit precision of the encoded data. Note that if we represent the pixels with less precision, we will need fewer bits to encode them, thus achieving compression. For example, we can divide all the values by some factor of 2 (since division by a factor of 2 is achieved simply by right shifts), such as 8. This is the step where we actually loose image quality in order to achieve high compression ratios. This process is referred to as *quantization*. To decompress, we would perform a dequantization. In other words, we would multiply each pixel by the same factor of 2 (i.e., 8 in our example). Figure 7.3(b) illustrates the quantization applied to the block of 8 × 8 shown in Figure 7.3(a).

The last step of the JPEG compression is the encoding of data. Here, the block of 8 × 8 pixels is first serialized. Specifically, the values are converted into a single list according to a zigzag pattern, as shown in Figure 7.4. Then, the values are Huffman encoded. *Huffman encoding* is a minimal variable-length encoding based on the frequency of each pixel. In other words, the frequently occurring pixels will be assigned a short binary code while those that don't occur as frequently will be assigned a longer code. Let us explain that with an example. In Figure 7.5(a), we have given the frequency of pixel occurrence of the encoded and quantized 8 × 8 block shown in Figure 7.3(b). Here, as shown, the encoded pixel value −1 occurs fifteen times while the encoded pixel value 14 occurs only one time.

From this information, we construct a Huffman tree as illustrated in Figure 7.5(b). With each node in such a tree, we associate a value that is computed as follows. For an internal node, the value is the sum of the values of the children of that node. For a leaf node, the value is the frequency of occurrence of the pixel being represented by that leaf node. The tree is constructed from the bottom up (i.e., starting from leafs and working up toward the root).

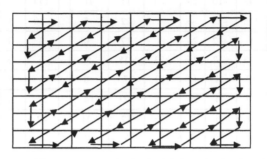

Figure 7.4: Data encoding sequence of a block of 8 × 8 pixel.

Initially, we create a leaf node for each of the pixels and initialize the values of these nodes according to the pixel's frequency. Then we create an internal node by joining any two nodes that will result in the minimum value. We repeat this process until we have a complete binary tree.

Once the Huffman tree is constructed, we can obtain a binary code for each of the pixel values by traversing the tree starting at the root down to the leaf labeled with that pixel. While traversing the tree, we construct a binary string. Each time we traverse down past a right child we append a "1" to our binary string, whereas each time we traverse down a left child we append a "0" to our binary string. For example, in order to obtain the binary code for the pixel value –3 in Figure 7.5(b), we would make four right traversals and a left traversal, thus obtaining the binary string "11110". Figure 7.5(c) gives the Huffman codes for the remaining pixel values.

Given these Huffman codes, we encode our block of 8 × 8 pixels by creating a long string of 0s and 1s. Here we take the sequence of pixels generated by the zigzag ordering shown in Figure 7.4, and for each pixel we output the Huffman binary code. In our example of Figure 7.4, we would obtain the binary string "111111011001110...."

As stated earlier, Huffman encoding achieves compression by assigning a short binary code to the most frequently appearing pixel values, while leaving longer binary codes for the least frequently appearing pixels. Of course, this process is reversible since Huffman encoding also ensures that no two codes are a prefix of each other.

Our next processing step is to archive our image. This step is rather easy. We simply record the starting address and size of each image. We can use a linked list data structure to record this information. If we know beforehand that the camera will hold at most $N$ images, we can set aside a portion of memory for our $N$ addresses and $N$ image-size variables. In addition, we would need to keep a counter that tells us the location of the next available address in memory. For example, initially, all $N$ addresses and image-size variables might be set to 0. Our global memory address will be set to $N \times 4$, assuming that the address and image-size variables occupy the initial $N \times 4$ bytes in memory. Then, the first image will be archived in memory starting at location $N \times 4$. Assuming the image was of size 1024, then we will update our global memory address to $N \times 4 + 1024$, and so on. Of course, there are other

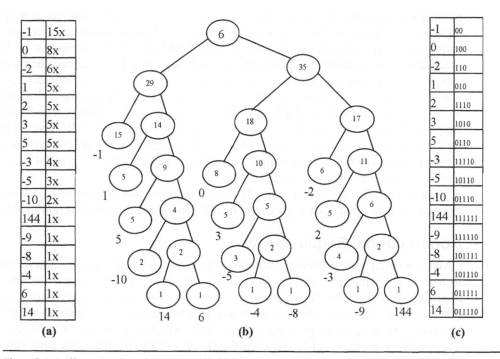

Figure 7.5: Huffman encoding of the block of 8 × 8 pixels shown in Figure 7.3(b): (a) the pixel values and associated frequencies, (b) the resulting Huffman tree, (c) and the Huffman codes.

ways to perform such archiving. In any event, our memory requirement will be based on $N$, the image size and the average compression ratio that we can obtain using JPEG encoding.

Finally, the only processing task that remains is to upload the images and free the space in memory when a PC is connected to the camera and an upload command is received. To accomplish this, we use a UART. As you'll recall, a UART transmits data serially over a single data wire. Our processing task will be to read the images from memory and transmit them using the UART. As we transmit images, we reset the pointers, image-size variables and the global memory pointer accordingly.

It must be noted again that our description of a digital camera is very simple. A real digital camera will enable you to take pictures of varied sizes, display images on an LCD, allow image deletion, perform advanced image processing such as digitally stretching, zooming in and out, and many other things.

# 7.3 Requirements Specification

Our digital camera product's life begins with a requirements specification. A specification describes what a particular system should do, namely the system's requirements. Specifications include both functional and nonfunctional requirements. Functional requirements describe the system's behavior, meaning the system's outputs as a function of inputs (e.g., "output X should equal input Y times 2"). Nonfunctional requirements describe constraints on design metrics (e.g., "the system should use 0.001 watt or less"). The initial specification of a system may be very general and may come from our company's marketing department. The initial specification for our camera might be a short document detailing the market need for "a very basic low-end digital camera capable of capturing and storing at least 50 low-resolution images and uploading such images to a PC, costing around $100, with a single medium-sized IC costing less than $25, including amortized NRE costs. Battery life should be as long as possible. Expected sales volume is 200,000 if market entry is earlier than 6 months, and 100,000 if market entry is between 6 to 12 months. Beyond 12 months, this product will not sell in significant quantities."

Let us begin by discussing the nonfunctional requirements in more detail, followed by an informal high-level functional specification, and then a more detailed description of behavior.

## Nonfunctional Requirements

Given our initial requirements specification, we might want to pay attention to several design metrics in particular: performance, size, power, and energy. Performance is the time required to process an image. Size is the number of elementary logic gates (such as a two input NAND gate) in our IC. Power is a measure of the average electrical energy consumed by the IC while processing an image. Energy is power times time, which directly relates to battery lifetime. Some of these metrics will be constrained metrics — those metrics must have values below (or in some cases above) a certain threshold. Some metrics may be optimization metrics — those metrics should be improved as much as possible, since this optimization improves the product. A metric can be both a constrained and optimization metric.

Regarding performance, our design must process images fast enough to be useful. We might determine that a reasonable timing constraint is 1 second per image. Note that the terms timing and performance are often used interchangeably. More time than 1 second would probably be quite annoying from a camera user's perspective. Imagine having to wait 10 seconds after pressing the shutter button before you could press the button again. A typical soccer parent would probably not buy such a camera, for fear of missing a great goal! On the other hand, since we are aiming for the low-end of the digital camera market, our performance doesn't need to be much better than 1 second. Thus, performance is a constrained metric but not an optimization metric — anything less than 1 second is equally good.

Regarding size, our design must use an IC that fits in a reasonably sized camera. Suppose that, based on current technology, we determine that our IC has a size constraint of 200,000 gates. In addition to being a constrained metric, size is also an optimization metric, since smaller ICs are generally cheaper. They are cheaper because we can either get higher yield from a current technology or use an older and hence cheaper technology.

Finally, power is a constrained metric because the IC must operate below a certain temperature. Note that our digital camera cannot use a fan to cool the IC, so low power operation is crucial. Let's assume we determine the power constraint to be 200 milliwatt. Energy will be an optimization metric because we want the battery to last as long as possible. Notice that reducing power or time each reduces energy.

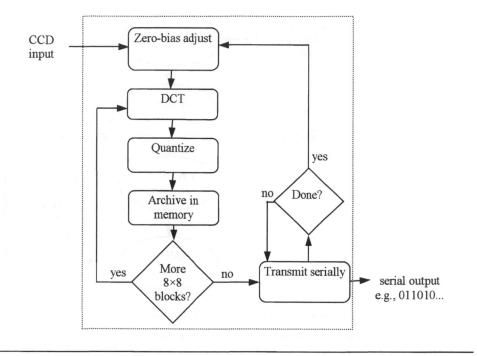

Figure 7.6: Functional block-diagram specification of a digital camera.

## Informal Functional Specification

We can describe the high-level functionality of the digital camera by using the flowchart in Figure 7.6. We see the major functions involved in image capture, namely zero-bias adjust, DCT, quantize and archive in memory. We also see the function transmit serially. We could then describe each function's details in English; we omit such descriptions here since they were included earlier in the chapter. We'll assume a very low-quality image with a $64 \times 64$ resolution, meaning the CCD has 64 rows and 64 columns.

Note that Figure 7.6 does not dictate that each of the blocks be mapped onto a distinct processor. Instead, the description only aids in capturing the functionality of the digital camera by breaking that functionality down into simpler functions. The functions could be implemented on any combination of single-purpose and general-purpose processors.

## Refined Functional Specification

We can now concentrate on refining the informal functional specification into one that can actually be executed. This typically consists of a C or C++ program describing the functionality. In our case, we could write C or C++ code to describe each function in Figure 7.6. Such a software prototype of the system is often referred to as a system-level model, a

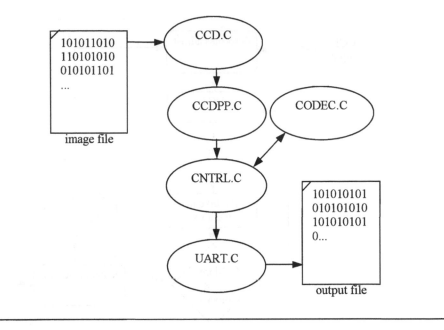

Figure 7.7: Block-diagram of the executable model of the digital camera.

prototype, or simply a model, though the prototype is also a first implementation. Keep in mind that one person's specification may be another person's implementation.

The software prototype can be executed on our development computer to verify its correctness. It can also provide insight into the operations of our system. For example, in our digital camera, we can profile our executable specification as it is running, in order to find the computationally intensive functions. Recall that a profiling tool is a tool that watches a program under execution and records the number of times a particular procedure or function call was made, or a variable was written or read. We can also use the prototype to obtain sample output that is later used to verify the correctness of our final implementation. For example, we can run an image through our executable specification and obtain the serially encoded output and store that in a file. Later, when we are testing our final IC chip, we can feed it the same image and check that the output matches the expected output.

Figure 7.7 gives the block-diagram of our high-level model of the digital camera. Our executable model is composed of five modules. We start with the CCD module and its corresponding C file called CCD.C, as shown in Figure 7.8. This module is responsible for simulating a real CCD (i.e., it is designed to mimic the operations of an actual CCD). It does that by simply reading the pixels of an image directly from a file that we specify. This module exports three procedures, *CcdInitialize*, *CcdCapture*, and *CcdPopPixel*.

```
#include <stdio.h>
#define SZ_ROW      64
#define SZ_COL      (64 + 2)
static FILE *imageFileHandle;
static char buffer[SZ_ROW][SZ_COL];
static unsigned rowIndex, colIndex;
void CcdInitialize(const char *imageFileName) {
    imageFileHandle = fopen(imageFileName, "r");
    rowIndex = -1;
    colIndex = -1;
}
void CcdCapture(void) {
    int pixel;
    rewind(imageFileHandle);
    for(rowIndex=0; rowIndex<SZ_ROW; rowIndex++) {
        for(colIndex=0; colIndex<SZ_COL; colIndex++) {
            if( fscanf(imageFileHandle, "%i", &pixel) == 1 ) {
                buffer[rowIndex][colIndex] = (char)pixel;
            }
        }
    }
    rowIndex = 0;
    colIndex = 0;
}
char CcdPopPixel(void) {
    char pixel;
    pixel = buffer[rowIndex][colIndex];
    if( ++colIndex == SZ_COL ) {
        colIndex = 0;
        if( ++rowIndex == SZ_ROW ) {
            colIndex = -1;
            rowIndex = -1;
        }
    }
    return pixel;
}
```

Figure 7.8: High-level implementation of the CCD module.

The *CcdInitialize* procedure is called to initialize our model just prior to execution. It takes as a parameter the name of the image file that is used to obtain the pixel data. The *CcdCapture* procedure is called to actually capture an image, in this case, read it from a file. The *CcdPopPixel* procedure is called to get the pixels out of the CCD, one at a time. At this point, you should have noted that in our executable specification, our modules communicate using procedure calls and parameter passing.

Our next module is called, rather cryptically, CCDPP, and its corresponding C file is called CCDPP.C, as shown in Figure 7.9. The PP stands for preprocessing. This module

```
#define SZ_ROW      64
#define SZ_COL      64
static char buffer[SZ_ROW][SZ_COL];
static unsigned rowIndex, colIndex;
void CcdppInitialize() {
    rowIndex = -1;
    colIndex = -1;
}
void CcdppCapture(void) {
    char bias;
    CcdCapture();
    for(rowIndex=0; rowIndex<SZ_ROW; rowIndex++) {
        for(colIndex=0; colIndex<SZ_COL; colIndex++) {
            buffer[rowIndex][colIndex] = CcdPopPixel();
        }
        bias = (CcdPopPixel() + CcdPopPixel()) / 2;
        for(colIndex=0; colIndex<SZ_COL; colIndex++) {
            buffer[rowIndex][colIndex] -= bias;
        }
    }
    rowIndex = 0;
    colIndex = 0;
}

char CcdppPopPixel(void) {
    char pixel;
    pixel = buffer[rowIndex][colIndex];
    if( ++colIndex == SZ_COL ) {
        colIndex = 0;
        if( ++rowIndex == SZ_ROW ) {
            colIndex = -1;
            rowIndex = -1;
        }
    }
    return pixel;
}
```

Figure 7.9: High-level implementation of the CCDPP module.

performs the zero-bias adjustment processing, shown in Figure 7.9 and described at the beginning of this chapter.

This module also exports three procedures called *CcdppInitialize*, *CcdppCapture*, and *CcdppPopPixel*. The *CcdppInitialize* procedure performs any necessary initializations. The *CcdppCapture* procedure is called to actually capture an image. Note that this procedure calls on the *CcdCapture* and *CcdPopPixel* procedures of the CCD module to obtain an image. As it is obtaining the image pixels, it also performs the zero-bias adjustments. The *CcdppPopPixel* procedure is called to get the pixels out of the CCDPP. Note that the interface to the CCDPP

```
#include <stdio.h>
static FILE *outputFileHandle;
void UartInitialize(const char *outputFileName) {
    outputFileHandle = fopen(outputFileName, "w");
}
void UartSend(char d) {
    fprintf(outputFileHandle, "%i\n", (int)d);
}
```

Figure 7.10: High-level implementation of the UART module.

module is identical to that of the CCD module. We can think of the CCDPP as a CCD that performs the zero-bias adjustments internally

Let us now look at the UART module and its corresponding C file called UART.C, as shown in Figure 7.10. This is really a model of a half UART (i.e., one that only transmits, but does not receive). As with the other modules, the UART module exports an initialization procedure, called *UartInitialize*. This procedure takes a file name, were the transmitted data is written to. The other procedure, *UartSend*, is called when the digital camera is transmitting a byte. The procedure simply writes the transmitted byte to the output file.

Our next module is called CODEC and its corresponding C file is called CODEC.C, as shown in Figure 7.11. This file models the forward DCT encoding that was described earlier in this chapter. The CODEC module exports the procedures *CodecInitialize*, *CodecPushPixel*, *CodecPopPixel*, and *CodecDoFdct*. The *CodecInitialize* procedure resets an index that is used by the push and pop procedures for traversing two buffers, described next. The *CodecPushPixel* is called 64 times to fill an input buffer, called *ibuffer*, which holds the original block of 8 × 8 pixels that is to be encoded. The *CodecPopPixel* is called 64 times to retrieve pixels from the output buffer, called *obuffer*, which holds the encoded block of 8 × 8 pixels. Once a block is placed in the input buffer, *CodedDoFdct* is called to actually perform the transform. Therefore, to encode a block of 8 × 8 pixels, we call *CodecPushPixel* 64 times, and *CodecDoFdct* once followed by 64 calls to *CodecPopPixel*. Let us now discuss the actual implementation of this module. The module simply implements the FDCT equation given earlier and presented here again:

$$C(h) = \text{if } ( h == 0 ) \text{ then } 1/\text{sqrt}(2) \text{ else } 1.0$$

$$F(u,v) = 1/4 \times C(u) \times C(v) \sum_{x=0..7} \sum_{y=0..7} D_{xy} \times \cos(\pi(2x + 1)u / 16) \times \cos(\pi(2y + 1)v / 16)$$

The first thing that you may note after studying the code is the large table called *COS_TABLE*. If you look at the above equation, you'll notice that the argument to the cosine function is always one of 64 possible values, because the only variables in the cosine argument expression are the integers $x$ and $u$ (or $y$ and $v$) and each of these variables can take one of 8 values, from 0 to 7. Thus, for performance purposes, we have decided to precompute the cosine value for all these 64 possibilities and store them in a table. Actually, we have done more than that. Instead of storing the floating-point values, we have converted these to an integer representation.

```
static const short COS_TABLE[8][8] = {
    { 32768,  32138,  30273,  27245,  23170,  18204,  12539,   6392 },
    { 32768,  27245,  12539,  -6392, -23170, -32138, -30273, -18204 },
    { 32768,  18204, -12539, -32138, -23170,   6392,  30273,  27245 },
    { 32768,   6392, -30273, -18204,  23170,  27245, -12539, -32138 },
    { 32768,  -6392, -30273,  18204,  23170, -27245, -12539,  32138 },
    { 32768, -18204, -12539,  32138, -23170,  -6392,  30273, -27245 },
    { 32768, -27245,  12539,   6392, -23170,  32138, -30273,  18204 },
    { 32768, -32138,  30273, -27245,  23170, -18204,  12539,  -6392 }
};
static short ONE_OVER_SQRT_TWO = 23170, ibuffer[8][8], obuffer[8][8], idx;
static double COS(int xy, int uv) {  return COS_TABLE[xy][uv] / 32768.0; }
static double C(int h) { return h ? 1.0 : ONE_OVER_SQRT_TWO / 32768.0; }
static int FDCT(int u, int v, short img[8][8]) {
    double s[8], r = 0; int x;
    for(x=0; x<8; x++) {
      s[x] = img[x][0] * COS(0, v) + img[x][1]*COS(1, v) + img[x][2] * COS(2, v) +
             img[x][3] * COS(3, v) + img[x][4]*COS(4, v) + img[x][5] * COS(5, v) +
             img[x][6] * COS(6, v) + img[x][7]*COS(7, v);
    }
    for(x=0; x<8; x++) r += s[x] * COS(x, u);
    return (short)(r * .25 * C(u) * C(v));
}
void CodecInitialize(void) { idx = 0; }
void CodecPushPixel(short p) {
    if( idx == 64 ) idx = 0;
    ibuffer[idx / 8][idx % 8] = p; idx++;
}
short CodecPopPixel(void) {
    short p;
    if( idx == 64 ) idx = 0;
    p = obuffer[idx / 8][idx % 8]; idx++;
    return p;
}
void CodecDoFdct(void) {
    int x, y;
    for(x=0; x<8; x++) {
        for(y=0; y<8; y++) obuffer[x][y] = FDCT(x, y, ibuffer);
    }
    idx = 0;
}
```

Figure 7.11: High-level implementation of the CODEC module.

More specifically, we have multiplied the 64 cosine values by 32,678 and rounded the result to the nearest integer. The value 32,678 is chosen to allow us to store each value in 2 bytes of memory. To convert these integers back to floating point, we need to divide the stored values by 32,678.0. This is accomplished in the procedure called COS. This is a form

```
#define SZ_ROW           64
#define SZ_COL           64
#define NUM_ROW_BLOCKS   (SZ_ROW / 8)
#define NUM_COL_BLOCKS   (SZ_COL / 8)
static short buffer[SZ_ROW][SZ_COL], i, j, k, l, temp;
void CntrlInitialize(void) {}
void CntrlCaptureImage(void) {
    CodppCapture();
    for(i=0; i<SZ_ROW; i++)
        for(j=0; j<SZ_COL; j++)
            buffer[i][j] = CodppPopPixel();
}
void CntrlCompressImage(void) {
    for(i=0; i<NUM_ROW_BLOCKS; i++)
        for(j=0; j<NUM_COL_BLOCKS; j++) {
            for(k=0; k<8; k++)
                for(l=0; l<8; l++)
                    CodecPushPixel((char)buffer[i * 8 + k][j * 8 + l]);
            CodecDoFdct();                          /* part 1 - FDCT */
            for(k=0; k<8; k++)
                for(l=0; l<8; l++) {
                    buffer[i * 8 + k][j * 8 + l] = CodecPopPixel();
                    buffer[i*8+k][j*8+l] >>= 6;   /* part 2 - quantization */
                }
        }
}
void CntrlSendImage(void) {
    for(i=0; i<SZ_ROW; i++)
        for(j=0; j<SZ_COL; j++) {
            temp = buffer[i][j];
            UartSend(((char*)&temp)[0]);    /* send upper byte */
            UartSend(((char*)&temp)[1]);    /* send lower byte */
        }
}
```

Figure 7.12: High-level implementation of the CNTRL module.

of fixed-point representation, which is described later in this chapter. Thus the COS procedure handles the portions of the above equation involving the cosine and its arguments.

We have also implemented a procedure called $C$ that simply corresponds to the function $C(h)$ given above. All that remains now is the implementation of the nested summations. These summations are performed in the FDCT procedure. The inner summation is simply unrolled (i.e., we have expanded it into eight terms that are added together). The outer summation is implemented as two consecutive for loops. This choice of implementation, of course, is not unique. There are many ways to perform FDCT and the reader is encouraged, as an exercise, to implement these DCT functions with performance in mind.

```
int main(int argc, char *argv[]) {
    char *uartOutputFileName = argc > 1 ? argv[1] : "uart_out.txt";
    char *imageFileName = argc > 2 ? argv[2] : "image.txt";
    /* initialize the modules */
    UartInitialize(uartOutputFileName);
    CcdInitialize(imageFileName);
    CcdppInitialize();
    CodecInitialize();
    CntrlInitialize();
    /* simulate functionality */
    CntrlCaputreImage();
    CntrlCompressImage();
    CntrlSendImage();
}
```

Figure 7.13: Putting it all together is the main module.

The last module that we need in order to complete the implementation of our digital camera is the heart of the system, or what we have called the CNTRL, short for controller. The corresponding C file of the CNTRL module is called CNTRL.C and is shown in Figure 7.12. This module exports three procedures named *CntrlInitialize*, *CntrlCompressImage*, and *CntrlSendImage*. The *CntrlInitialize* procedure does nothing and is provided for consistency purposes only. The *CntrlCompressImage* procedure uses the other modules that we have described so far, namely the CCDPP and the CODEC to capture and perform FDCT and quantization on an image. Part of what this procedure has to do is to break the image into windows, or what we have referred to as blocks of $8 \times 8$ pixels. Once a block is FDCT encoded, it is quantized and stored in memory. The *CntrlSendImage* procedure simply transmits the encoded image, serially, using the UART module.

Putting all this together is our main program, shown in Figure 7.13, that simply initializes all the modules and calls on the controller to capture, compress and transmit one image.

We now have a system-level model (executable specification) of our digital camera. We can experiment with this extensively. Note that any bugs we find here will be orders of magnitude easier to correct than if found at a later design stage.

# 7.4   Design

Design consists primarily of determining the system's architecture, and mapping the functionality to that architecture. The architecture consists of a set of processors, memories and buses. Processors may be any combination of single-purpose (custom or standard) or general-purpose processors. Multiple functions may be mapped to a single processor, and a function may be mapped to multiple processors. We'll say that an implementation is a particular architecture and mapping. The set of possible implementations defines the solution space. Note that the solution space is usually enormous. So where do we begin?

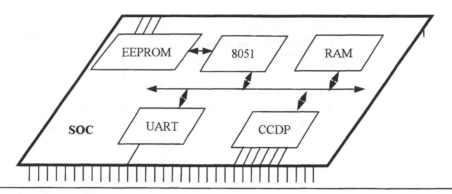

Figure 7.14: Block-diagram of our first implementation.

We might begin by examining a low-end general-purpose processor connected to flash memory, and trying to map all functionality to software running on that microprocessor. Such an implementation is often a good starting point for embedded system design, since the implementation will usually satisfy our power, size, and time-to-market constraints. If it also satisfies performance, then design is nearly complete. If this design doesn't satisfy constraints, then we could try a faster processor, we could use single-purpose processors for time-critical functions, or we could even rewrite the functional specification. We'll now start with such an implementation and then speed it up using different approaches.

## Implementation 1: Microcontroller Alone

Suppose we choose an Intel 8051 microcontroller (or similar such device) as our low-end processor. We determine that total IC cost (including NRE) would be about $5, power well below 200 mW, and time-to-market only about three months. However, a rough analysis shows that there is no way an 8051 alone will satisfy our performance requirement of one image per second. Suppose the particular microcontroller we choose runs at 12 MHz and requires 12 cycles per instruction, meaning it executes one million instructions per second. Suppose we noticed during the execution of our earlier system-level model that CCD preprocessing consumed a lot of the computation time. Figure 7.9 shows the original code for the CCD preprocessor. The *CcdppCapture* function has a pair of nested loops that result in 64 × 64 = 4,096 iterations per image. Looking at the code, we might estimate that each iteration will require about 100 assembly instructions during execution. Thus, this function alone will require 4,096 × 100 = 409,600 instructions per image. This is nearly half of our budget of one million instructions per second, just to read the image alone, and not even considering the other more compute-intensive tasks of DCT and Huffman coding. Clearly, performance will be much worse than one image per second. We'll have to speed things up somehow.

## Implementation 2: Microcontroller and CCDPP

One method for improving performance is to implement a function using a custom single-purpose processor. Normally, we resist designing custom single-purpose processors

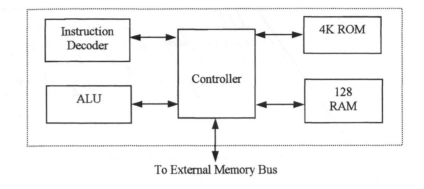

Figure 7.15: Block-diagram of the Intel 8051 processor core.

because they can increase NRE cost and time to market. However, the CCDPP function is a prime candidate for such implementation — not only is it taking up many microcontroller cycles, but it looks simple to implement as a single-purpose processor. There is no complicated arithmetic, so the datapath will be very simple, and the controller doesn't look like it will have many states either, since most of the cycles come from the 64 × 64 loop iterations — these will likely translate to a couple of simple counters.

Thus, we decide to use an 8051 microcontroller coupled with a CCDPP single-purpose processor. Let's also implement a simple UART for the transmit-serially function. We'll also add an EEPROM for program memory and a RAM for data memory. Note that the CCDPP and UART processors could be implemented by finding standard components for each, but they are straightforward components, so let's implement them as custom instead. The CCDPP implements the zero-bias operations and interacts with the actual CCD chip, which resides external to our system-on-a-chip IC.[2] The rest of the functionality will be implemented in software on the microcontroller.

Let us briefly describe the three main processors depicted in Figure 7.14 in more detail. We begin with the microcontroller. A synthesizable implementation of this microcontroller, captured at the register transfer level (RTL) and written in VHDL, is available to us for integration into the rest of the system. A block-diagram of the main components of the 8051 is given in Figure 7.15. The controller fetches instructions from its read-only program memory and decodes them using the decoder component. The ALU component is used to actually execute arithmetic operations such as addition, multiplication, and division among many others. The source and destination of these operations are registers that reside in the internal RAM of the processor. Special data movement instructions are used to load and store data from external memory through the external memory bus. A C compiler/linker is used to

---

[2] We assume that the CCD chip resides external to our system-on-a-chip since given today's mainstream technology, and mostly due to fabrication process differences, combining a CCD with ordinary logic is not feasible.

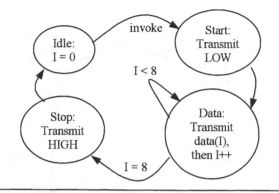

Figure 7.16: The UART single-purpose processor as an FSMD.

compile C programs for execution on our processor. The ROM is generated using a special program that reads the output of the C compiler/linker and outputs a VHDL description of the ROM.

The UART is a simple single-purpose processor. Its behavior is depicted in Figure 7.16 as a finite-state machine with data (FSMD). Normally, the UART is in its idle state. When invoked, it transitions into the start state, where it transmits a 0 indicating the start of a byte transmission. Then, it transitions into the data state, where it sends the 8 bits of the byte being sent. Then, it transitions into the stop state, where it transmits a 1 indicating the stop of the byte transmission. Finally, it transitions back into the idle state, ready to repeat the processes, when summoned again. Since the UART is memory mapped to the processor's memory address space, it is invoked when the processor executes a store instruction with the UART's enable register as its target memory location. Of course, the UART is constantly monitoring the address-bus, and when it detects the enable register's address, it captures the data on the data-bus and starts the transmission processes as just described. Note that we will use memory-mapped I/O for communication between the 8051 processor and any other single-purpose processor in our system. Since the 8051 processor's address space is 16 bits wide, we use lower memory address, those starting at 0 and going up, for RAM and upper memory address, and we use those starting at 65,535 and going down for memory-mapped I/O devices.

The CCDPP is one of the single-purpose processors that has been implemented in hardware. The FSMD of the CCDPP is depicted in Figure 7.17. Internally, the CCDPP single-purpose processor has a buffer, labeled $B$, and three variables called $R$, $C$, and $Bias$. The variables $R$ and $C$ are used as row and column indices. The variable $Bias$ holds the zero-bias error for each of the rows as the rows are processed. The FSMD works as follows. Once invoked, it transitions into the $GetRow$ state where it reads from the actual CCD a complete row including the last two blacked-out pixels. (For details, refer to the description of a CCD given at the beginning of this chapter.) Then, the FSMD transitions into the $ComputeBias$ state where it computes the bias of the current row and stores it into the $Bias$ variable. In the next state, called $FixBias$, the FSMD iterates over the same row subtracting away the bias from each element in that row. In the next state, called $NextRow$, the row index is incremented

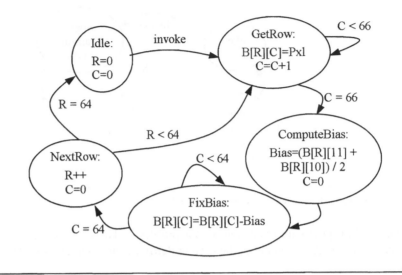

Figure 7.17: The CCDPP single-purpose processor as a FSMD.

and the process either repeats, reading the next row, or stops when the entire image is processed. We assume that, as with the UART, this single-purpose processor is connected to the 8051 processor's memory bus with the content of the internal buffer mapped to upper memory addresses of the processor.

We now have all the components of our system-on-a-chip and are ready to connect things together making up our digital camera. This is accomplished through the 8051's memory bus, as stated before. The 8051 memory bus uses a simple read and write protocol and is composed of an 8-bit data-bus, a 16-bit address-bus, a read control signal and a write-control-signal. A memory read works as follows. The processor places the memory address on the address-bus, then asserts the read control signal for exactly one clock-cycle and reads the data from the data-bus one clock-cycle later. The device that is being read, either the RAM or one of our memory mapped single-purpose processors, when detecting that the read control signal is asserted, and after checking the content of the address-bus, places and holds the requested data on the data-bus for exactly one clock cycle. A write operation works in a similar fashion. The processor places the memory and the data on the address and data-bus, respectively. Then, it asserts the write control signal for exactly one clock cycle. The device that is being written, when detecting that the write control signal is asserted, and after checking the content of the address-bus, reads and stores the data from the data-bus.

Now that we have the hardware portion of our design implemented, we need to write the software to complete the project. Fortunately, our executable specification will provide the majority of the code that we need. In fact, we will maintain the same structure of the code (i.e., we will keep the same module hierarchy, procedure names, and main program). The only thing that needs to be done is to design the UART and CCDPP custom single-purpose processors. This is rather easy to do. All that we need to do is replace the code in these

Embedded System Design

```
static unsigned char xdata U_TX_REG _at_ 65535;
static unsigned char xdata U_STAT_REG _at_ 65534;
void UARTInitialize(void) {}
void UARTSend(unsigned char d) {
    while( U_STAT_REG == 1 ) {
        /* busy wait */
    }
    U_TX_REG = d;
}
```

Figure 7.18: Rewriting the UART module to utilize the hardware UART.

procedures with memory assignments to the respective hardware devices. Let us show this with the UART example. The code for this module is given in Figure 7.18. Here we have defined two variables, called U_TX_REG, and U_STAT_REG. There are two keywords used in defining these two variables that you may not recognize. The first one, called *xdata*, instructs our compiler to place these variables in the external memory; in other words, the compiler will generate code that will load and store these variables over the external memory bus of the processor. The second keyword, called *_at_* instructs our compiler to place these variables at the specified memory address. These two keywords allow us to declare a variable such that when read or written will cause appropriate read or write operations to be performed on the bus. Now, all we have to do to send a byte using our UART single-purpose processor is write the byte to be sent to the U_TX_REG causing it to be invoked. But since our processor may be much faster than the UART, we need to first make sure that the UART is in its idle state. This is accomplished by the while loop. Having designed our UART such that we can check weather its busy or not, we can busy-wait until it becomes idle before sending the next data byte. The implementation of the CCDPP module is similarly modified to utilize the CCDPP single-purpose processor. The rest of the modules are untouched.

Now we can compile and link all our software modules and obtain the final program executable. This program executable is then translated into the VHDL representation of the ROM using a ROM generator. All that remains is to test our entire system-on-a-chip. This is done using a VHDL simulator program. A VHDL simulator takes as input the VDHL files, making up our system, and functionally simulates the execution of the final IC by interpreting the descriptions. By simulating, we are able to learn weather our design is functionally correct. Moreover, we can also measure the amount of time, or clock-cycles, that it takes to process a single image. This is our first metric of interest, namely, performance. Figure 7.19(a) shows how after simulating the VHDL models, we obtain the execution time. Figure 7.19(b) shows how we synthesize the high-level VHDL models and obtain the gate-level description of the corresponding circuits. Then, we simulate the gate-level models to obtain the intermediate data necessary to compute the power consumption of the circuit. Figure 7.19(c) shows how by adding the number of gates, we obtain the total area of the chip.

Once we are satisfied that our design functions correctly, we can use our synthesis tool to translate the VHDL files down to an interconnection of logic gates. A synthesis tool is like a

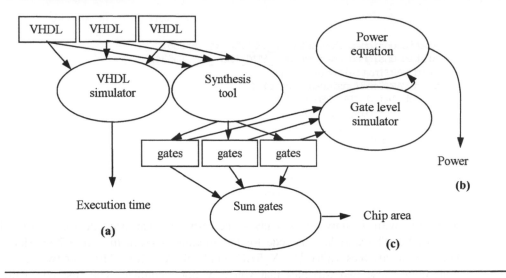

Figure 7.19: Obtaining design metrics of interest; (a) performance, (b) power, (c) area.

compiler for single-purpose processors. It reads a VHDL file and translates it to a corresponding gate-level description. You'll learn more about this process in a later chapter of this book. At this stage, these gates can be sent to an IC fabrication company to make our IC chip. But what we are interested in is counting the total number of gates to get an idea of how big our design is. This will tell us how big of an area we need to implement the digital camera, or the third metric of interest. To obtain the power consumption, our second metric of interest, we simulate the gate-level description of the digital camera and keep track of the number of times these gates switch from zero to one and from one to zero. Recall that we can estimate power consumption if we know the amount of switching that takes place in a circuit.

We can now analyze our first implementation using the approach outlined in Figure 7.19. Using simulation, we have measured the total execution time for processing a single image to be 9.1 seconds. The power consumption is measured to be 0.033 watt. The energy consumption is 9.1 s × 0.033 watt = 0.30 joule. The area is measured to be 98,000 gates.

## Implementation 3: Microcontroller and CCDPP/Fixed-Point DCT

The previous implementation does not achieve 1-image-per-second processing. Looking at the execution of the previous implementation, we see that most of the microcontroller computer cycles are spent performing the DCT operation. Thus, we could consider pulling this compute-intensive function out from software to custom hardware, as we did for the CCD preprocessor. However, unlike the CCD preprocessor, the DCT functionality is fairly complex and thus will likely require more design effort. We can instead speed up the DCT functionality by modifying its behavior.

Recall that each DCT operation involves numerous floating-point operations. Actually, for each pixel that is transformed, about 260 floating-point operations are performed. There are 64 × 64 = 4,096 pixels that are encoded, for a total of about one million floating-point operations. To make matters worse, our processor is an 8-bit processor with no floating-point support; thus, the compiler needs to emulate each of these floating-point operations. Floating-point emulation is performed as follows. The compiler generates procedures for each of the floating-point operations, such as multiplication and addition. These procedures may execute tens of integer instructions in order to perform a single floating-point operation. Then, when the compiler encounters floating-point operations in the source file, it places a call to these compiler-generated procedures. Consequently, our one million floating-point operations will require ten million or more integer operations. In addition, our program will be larger, since it has to accommodate the compiler-generated procedures.

We can thus consider speeding up the CODEC module to use fixed-point arithmetic. We hope to reduce the total number of integer instructions required to encode each pixel. Our implementation is shown in Figure 7.20. Let us first describe how fixed-point arithmetic works. In fixed-point arithmetic, we use an integer to represent real numbers. The bits within this integer are interpreted as follows. We use a constant and known number of these bits to represent the portion of a real number after the decimal and the rest of the bits to represent the portion of the real number before the decimal point.

In our implementation of the CODEC, we have chosen to use 6 bits to represent the fractional part of all arithmetic operations. The choice here has to do with the accuracy that we desire. The more bits we use for the portion after the decimal, the more accurately we can represent a real number. However, this will leave us fewer bits to represent the portion of the real number before the decimal point (i.e., the magnitude of the real number).

Once we have chosen the number of bits to represent the portion after the decimal point, a.k.a. the fractional part, we can translate any constant to the fixed-point representation. For example, imagine that we are using 8-bit integers. Let us use 4 bits to represent the fractional part. The fixed-point representation of the real value 3.14 would be 50, or 00110010. We obtain 50 by multiplying the real value, 3.14, by 2 raised to the number of bits we are using for the fractional part, $2^4 = 16$, and rounding it to the nearest integer, $3.14 \times 16 = 50.24 \approx 50$. Note that the 4 least significant bits equal 2. Since there are a total of 16 possibilities, each would represent .0625. Given that we have 2, we get $2 \times 0.0625 = 0.125$. The four most significant bits encode the value 3, which when added to our fractional part, gives 3.125. Of course, our representation is not exact but close. We can improve this by using more bits for the fractional part. In fact, the cosine table in Figure 7.20 gives the fixed-point representation of the cosine values, using 8-bit integers.

Now that we know how to represent a real number using integers, we have to define the two operations that are used in our calculations, namely addition and multiplication. Addition is straightforward. All that we have to do is add the integers. For example, assume that we have 3.14 encoded as 50, or 00110010 and 2.71 as 43, or 00101011. To add these two together, we add the integers 50 and 43 to obtain 93, or 01011101. Converting this back to a real, we get $5 + 13 \times 0.625 = 5.8125$. This number is close to the actual value, which is 5.85, but not exact, as expected.

Similarly, with multiplication, we can multiply the two fixed-point values to obtain our result. But, at this point we need to perform an additional operation. Let us multiply the value 3.14 encoded as 50, or 00110010 and 2.71 as 43, or 00101011. From this we obtain 2,150, or

```
static const char code COS_TABLE[8][8] = {
    {   64,   62,   59,   53,   45,   35,   24,   12 },
    {   64,   53,   24,  -12,  -45,  -62,  -59,  -35 },
    {   64,   35,  -24,  -62,  -45,   12,   59,   53 },
    {   64,   12,  -59,  -35,   45,   53,  -24,  -62 },
    {   64,  -12,  -59,   35,   45,  -53,  -24,   62 },
    {   64,  -35,  -24,   62,  -45,  -12,   59,  -53 },
    {   64,  -53,   24,   12,  -45,   62,  -59,   35 },
    {   64,  -62,   59,  -53,   45,  -35,   24,  -12 }
};
static const char ONE_OVER_SQRT_TWO = 5;
static short xdata inBuffer[8][8], outBuffer[8][8], idx;
static unsigned char C(int h) { return h ? 64 : ONE_OVER_SQRT_TWO; }
static int F(int u, int v, short img[8][8]) {
    long s[8], r = 0;
    unsigned char x, j;
    for(x=0; x<8; x++) {
        s[x] = 0;
        for(j=0; j<8; j++) s[x] += (img[x][j] * COS_TABLE[j][v] ) >> 6;
    }
    for(x=0; x<8; x++) r += (s[x] * COS_TABLE[x][u]) >> 6;
    return (short)(((((r * (((16 * C(u)) >> 6) * C(v)) >> 6)) >> 6) >> 6);
}
void CodecInitialize(void) { idx = 0; }
void CodecPushPixel(short p) {
    if( idx == 64 ) idx = 0;
    inBuffer[idx / 8][idx % 8] = p << 6; idx++;
}
void CodecDoFdct(void) {
    unsigned short x, y;
    for(x=0; x<8; x++)
        for(y=0; y<8; y++)
            outBuffer[x][y] = F(x, y, inBuffer);
    idx = 0;
}
```

Figure 7.20: Fixed-point implementation of the CODEC module.

100001100110. Note that, when multiplying two 8-bit integers, we can expect the result to be 16 bits wide. What we have to do to obtain our final result is to discard the lower 6 bits of our 16-bit result, obtaining 10000110. Converting this back to a real, we get, $8 + 6 \times 0.0625 = 8.375$. The number is close to the correct value, which is 8.5094, but not exact, as expected.

The biggest difficulty with fixed-point arithmetic is to ensure that the resulting values, after performing addition and multiplication operations, do not exceed the bit-width of the integers that are being used. Therefore, it is important to consider the intervals, or range, of the real values that are being operated on. We have applied the fixed-point arithmetic scheme presented here in recoding the CODEC. This time our CODEC uses integer operations only and we expect it to execute faster than our first implementation.

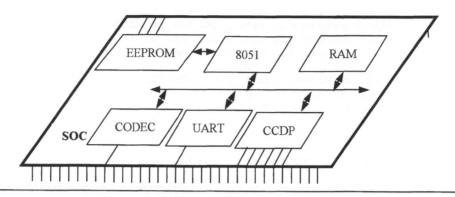

Figure 7.21: Block-diagram of our fourth implementation.

We can now analyze our second implementation using the approach outlined in Figure 7.19. Using simulation, we have measured the total execution time for processing a single image to be 1.5 seconds. The power consumption is measured to be 0.033 watt, the same as before. The energy consumption of this design is 1.5 s × 0.033 watt = 0.050 joule. This is means that our batteries will last six times longer when compared to the previous design! The area is measured to be 90,000 gates. We have improved performance by a factor of six and reduced the chip area by about 8,000 gates over the previous design. The gate reduction is because our program no longer needs to emulate the complex floating-point operations, thus requiring less memory for storing the corresponding code.

## Implementation 4: Microcontroller and CCDPP/DCT

Our third implementation's performance is close to that required by our specification, achieving 1.5 seconds per image. Let us try to improve performance further to obtain 1 second per image. In our next implementation, we will resort to implementing the CODEC in hardware. That means that we will design a single-purpose processor that performs the DCT operation on a block of 8 × 8 pixels. The block-diagram of our new system-on-a-chip is given in Figure 7.21. Designing the processor for the CODEC may take some time to get correct.

To use this CODEC, we will need to make some changes to our software. Specifically, we will need to change the CODEC module, as we did the UART and the CCDPP modules. The code is presented in Figure 7.22. We have designed our hardware CODEC to have four memory-mapped registers. Two of these registers, called $C\_DATAI\_REG$ and $C\_DATAO\_REG$, are used to push and pop a block of 8 × 8 pixels into and out of the CODEC. Another register, called $C\_CMND\_REG$, is used to command the CODEC. Specifically, writing a one to this register will invoke the CODEC. The last register, called $C\_STAT\_REG$, can be polled in software to tell when our CODEC is done encoding a block of pixels. The actual implementation of the CODEC is a direct translation of our fixed-point version of the CODEC written in C, and used in our second implementation, into VHDL. Using a single-purpose processor for encoding data, we expect to improve our execution time, and thus satisfy our timing constraints.

```
static unsigned char xdata C_STAT_REG _at_ 65527;
static unsigned char xdata C_CMND_REG _at_ 65528;
static unsigned char xdata C_DATAI_REG _at_ 65529;
static unsigned char xdata C_DATAO_REG _at_ 65530;
void CodecInitialize(void) {}
void CodecPushPixel(short p) { C_DATAO_REG = (char)p; }
short CodecPopPixel(void) {
    return ((C_DATAI_REG << 8) | C_DATAI_REG);
}
void CodecDoFdct(void) {
    C_CMND_REG = 1;
    while( C_STAT_REG == 1 ) { /* busy wait */ }
}
```

Figure 7.22: Rewriting the CODEC module to utilize the hardware CODEC.

We can now analyze our final implementation using the approach outlined in Figure 7.19. Using simulation, we have measured the total execution time for processing a single image to be 0.099 seconds. The power consumption is measured to be 0.040 watt. Notice that the power consumption increased, because our chip is now doing more (i.e., there are multiple processors working). The energy consumption of this design is 0.099 s × 0.040 watt ≈ .00040 joule. This means that our batteries will last 12 times longer than the previous design. The area is measured to be 128,000 gates. We are now well under 1 second, processing one image in about 1/10th of a second (approaching video camera speed now). However, we have increased the IC size significantly. This implementation certainly meets our timing requirements. More importantly, if we design the DCT ourselves, we will likely increase our NRE cost and time-to-market. If we purchase an existing DCT, we may increase our IC cost.

We have summarized our results in Figure 7.23. In designing an embedded system, many other metrics need to be considered. As with any other commercial product, in addition to engineering issues, a careful cost analysis of a system must be made.

Implementation 3 is close in terms of performance but a little slow, and consumes more energy, but is likely much cheaper and will be built in less time. Implementation 4 meets the performance (by a lot) and consumes much less energy (by a lot), but will be more expensive and may result in missing our time-to-market cutoff. Which is better? It's a choice that our company will have to make. As mentioned in Chapter 1, a key challenge facing the embedded system designer is to construct an implementation that simultaneously optimizes numerous design metrics. We can't always get what we want!

|  | Implementation 2 | Implementation 3 | Implementation 4 |
|---|---|---|---|
| Performance (second) | 9.1 | 1.5 | 0.099 |
| Power (watt) | 0.033 | 0.033 | 0.040 |
| Size (gate) | 98,000 | 90,000 | 128,000 |
| Energy (joule) | 0.30 | 0.050 | 0.0040 |

Figure 7.23:: Summary of design metrics.

# 7.5 Summary

We have introduced a digital camera and have described its various components. These components capture, digitize, process, and store images, among other things. As part of our presentation, we have described JPEG encoding, to a limited extent. We have specified our design project in an informal format using English as well as an executable specification. We have described three design metrics of interest, namely, performance, power consumption, and chip area. For each of these metrics, we have suggested optimization techniques. In the second part of the chapter, we have described several successively improved implementations. The first implementation we considered used a single microcontroller, but would have been far too slow. Our second implementation used a coprocessor to speed things up a bit, but we were still much too slow. Our third implementation gave up some accuracy during compression by using fixed instead of floating-point numbers. It came close to our performance constraint, but was a still a bit slow. Our last implementation involved another coprocessor for compression, meeting performance easily but costing more and taking more design time. The better of these last two implementations is not clear.

The executable specification and the three latter implementations are available in source code format on this book's Web page.

# 7.6 References and Further Reading

- C. Wayne Brown and Barry J. Shepherd. *Graphics File Formats — Reference and Guide*. Connecticut: Manning Publications Company, 1995.
- P. van der Wolf, P. Lieverse, M. Goel, D.L. Hei, and K. Vissers. An MPEG 2 Decoder Case Study as a Driver for a System-level Design Methodology. International Workshop on Hardware/Software Co-Design, March 1999.

# 7.7 Exercises

7.1 Using any programming language of choice, (a) implement the FDCT and IDCT equations presented in section 7.2 using double precision and floating-point arithmetic. (b) Use the block of 8 × 8 pixel given in Figure 7.2(b) as input to your FDCT and obtain the encoded block. (c) Use the output of part (b) as input to your IDCT to obtain the original block. (e) Compute the percent error between your decoder's output and the original block.

7.2 Assuming 8 bits per each pixel value, calculate the length, in bits, of the block given in Figure 7.3(b).

7.3 Using the Huffman codes given in Figure 7.5, encode the block given in Figure 7.3(b). (a) What is the length, in bits? (b) How much compression did we achieve be using Huffman encoding? Use the results of the last question to calculate this.

7.4 Convert 1.0, 1.1, 1.2, 1.3, 1.4, 1.5, 1.6, 1.7, 1.8, and 1.9 to fixed-point representation using (a) two bits for the fractional part, (b) three bits for the fractional part, and (c) three bits for the fractional part.

7.5 Write two C routines that, each, take as input two 32-bit fixed-point numbers and perform addition and multiplication using 4 bits for the fractional part and the remaining bits for the whole part.

7.6 Using any programming language of choice to (a) implement the FDCT and IDCT equations presented in Section 7.2 using fixed-point arithmetic with 4 bits used for the fractional part and the remaining bits used for the whole part, (b) use the block of $8 \times 8$ pixels given in Figure 7.2(b) as input to your FDCT and obtain the encoded block, (c) use the output of part (b) as input to your IDCT to obtain the original block, and (d) compute the percent error between your decoder's output and the original block.

7.7 List the modifications made in implementations 2 and 3 and discuss why each was beneficial in terms of performance.

# CHAPTER 8: *State Machine and Concurrent Process Models*

## 8.1   Introduction

We implement a system's processing behavior with processors. But to accomplish this, we must have first described that processing behavior. One method we've discussed for describing processing behavior uses assembly language. Another more powerful method uses a high-level programming language like C. Both methods use what is known as a sequential program computation model, in which a set of instructions executes sequentially. A high-level programming language provides more advanced constructs for sequencing among the instructions than does an assembly language, and the instructions are more powerful, but nevertheless, the sequential execution model (one statement at a time) is the same.

However, the increasing complexity of embedded system functionality requires more advanced computation models. The increasing complexity results from increasing IC capacity: The more we can put on an IC, the more functionality we want to put into our embedded system. Thus, while embedded systems previously encompassed simple applications like washing machines and small games, requiring perhaps hundreds of lines of code, today they also cover sophisticated applications like television set-top boxes and cellular telephones, requiring perhaps hundreds of thousands of lines of code.

Trying to describe the behavior of such systems can be extremely difficult. The desired behavior is often not even fully understood initially. Therefore, designers must spend much time and effort simply understanding and describing the desired behavior of a system, and they often make mistakes at this stage, before a single line of code has been written. Some studies have found that many system bugs come from mistakes made describing the desired behavior rather than from mistakes in implementing that behavior. The common method today of using an English (or some other natural language) description of desired behavior provides a reasonable first step, but it is not nearly sufficient because English is not precise. Trying to describe a system precisely in English can be an arduous and often futile endeavor — many long and hard-to-read legal documents serve as examples of what happens when attempting to be precise and complete in a natural language.

A computation model assists the designer to understand and describe the behavior by providing a means to compose the behavior from simpler objects. A computation model provides a set of objects, rules for composing those objects, and execution semantics of the composed objects. Several models are commonly used for describing embedded systems. These include:

- The *sequential program model*, which provides a set of statements, rules for putting statements one after another, and semantics stating how the statements are executed one at a time.
- The *communicating process model*, which supports description of multiple sequential programs running concurrently.
- The *state machine model*, used commonly for control-dominated systems. A *control-dominated* system is one whose behavior consists mostly of monitoring control inputs and reacting by setting control outputs.
- The *dataflow model*, used commonly for data-dominated systems. A *data-dominated* system's behavior consists mostly of transforming streams of input data into streams of output data.
- The *object-oriented model*, which provides an elegant means for breaking complex software into simpler, well-defined pieces.

In fact, a system may be described using a combination of models. We will describe several models in this chapter.

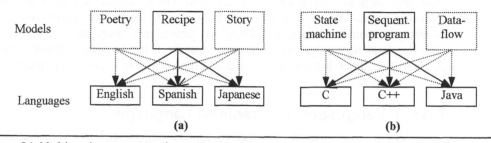

Figure 8.1: Models vs. languages: (a) recipes vs. English, (b) sequential programs vs. C.

## 8.2  Models vs. Languages, Text vs. Graphics

A common point of confusion is the difference between a computation model and a language. Another is the difference between a textual language and a graphical language. Thus, we will explicitly state the differences here.

### Models vs. Languages

A *computation model* describes desired system behavior, while a *language* captures models. A model is a conceptual notion, while a language captures that concept in a concrete form. A model can be captured in a variety of languages, while a language can capture a variety of models, as illustrated in Figure 8.1.

Let us consider an analogy involving cooking recipes. A recipe is like a model, a conceptual notion, consisting of a set of instructions for cooking something, and a notion of how to sequence among those instructions. For example, a particular recipe may include a requirement of first putting flour in a bowl and then mixing in two eggs. English is a language capable of capturing a recipe. This simple example illustrates three important points. First, a recipe can be captured faithfully in various languages, such as English, Spanish, or Japanese. In fact, a recipe exists independent of its capture in a particular language — some recipes are never written down! Second, a particular language can capture many different conceptual notions other than recipes, such as poetry or stories. Third, certain languages may be better at capturing recipes than others — while English works fine, a primitive language without words for "boil" or "simmer" may be cumbersome to use for capturing recipes.

Returning now from cooking to computing, consider sequential programs. A *sequential program* is a model, a conceptual notion, consisting of a set of program instructions for computing something, and a notion of how to sequence among those instructions. For example, a particular sequential program may include a requirement of first initializing a variable to 10, and then adding 2 to that variable. C is a language capable of capturing a sequential program. As in our analogy above, there are three important points to remember. First, a sequential program can be captured in any of various languages, such as C, C++, or Java. Second, a particular language can capture many different models other than sequential programs, such as state machines or dataflow. Third, certain languages may be better at capturing sequential programs than others — while C works fine, a primitive language like assembly without constructs for "loops" or "procedures" may be cumbersome to use for capturing sequential programs. As another example, C can be used to capture state machines, as we will see later, but a language intended specifically to capture state machines might be more convenient.

### Textual Languages vs. Graphical Languages

Languages may use a variety of methods to capture models, such as text or graphics. Defining a graphical language equivalent to a textual one is fairly straightforward, and vice versa. The choice of a textual language versus a graphical language is entirely independent of the choice of a computation model.

Let us return to our analogy involving recipes. We could choose to capture a particular recipe in the English textual language. On the other hand, we could choose to capture the recipe using a graphical recipe language, which might include icons of objects like eggs and bowls, as well as icons for tasks like "mix" or "simmer."

Likewise, we could choose to capture a particular sequential program in the C textual language. On the other hand, we could choose to capture the sequential program using a graphical sequential programming language, which might include icons of objects like variables and constants, as well as icons for tasks like "assign" or "loop." Graphical sequential programming languages were commonly proposed in the 1980s, but have not become very popular. The state machine model is often captured in textual languages, but it is also commonly captured in graphical languages found in numerous commercial products.

## 8.3 An Introductory Example

Here, we introduce an example system that we'll use in the chapter, and we'll use the sequential program model, introduced in an earlier chapter, to describe part of the system. Consider the simple elevator controller system in Figure 8.2(a). It has several control inputs corresponding to the floor buttons inside the elevator and corresponding to the up and down buttons on each of the $N$ floors at which the elevator stops. It also has a data input representing the current floor of the elevator. It has three control outputs that make the elevator move up or down, and open the elevator door. A partial English description of the system's desired behavior is shown in Figure 8.2(b).

We decide that this system is best described as two blocks. *RequestResolver* resolves the various floor requests into a single requested floor. *UnitControl* actually moves the elevator unit to this requested floor, as shown in Figure 8.2. Figure 8.2(c) shows a sequential program description for the *UnitControl* process. Note that this process is more precise than the English description. It firsts opens the elevator door and then enters an infinite loop. In this loop, it first waits until the requested and current floors differ. It then closes the door and moves the elevator up or down. It then waits until the current floor equals the requested floor, stops moving the elevator, and opens the door for 10 seconds (assuming there's a routine

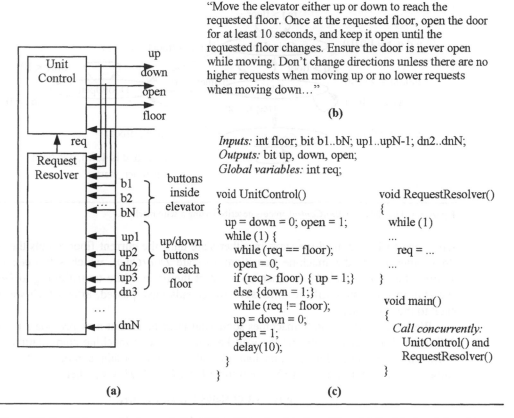

"Move the elevator either up or down to reach the requested floor. Once at the requested floor, open the door for at least 10 seconds, and keep it open until the requested floor changes. Ensure the door is never open while moving. Don't change directions unless there are no higher requests when moving up or no lower requests when moving down..."

**(b)**

*Inputs:* int floor; bit b1..bN; up1..upN-1; dn2..dnN;
*Outputs:* bit up, down, open;
*Global variables:* int req;

```
void UnitControl()
{
    up = down = 0; open = 1;
    while (1) {
        while (req == floor);
        open = 0;
        if (req > floor) { up = 1;}
        else {down = 1;}
        while (req != floor);
        up = down = 0;
        open = 1;
        delay(10);
    }
}
```

```
void RequestResolver()
{
    while (1)
    ...
        req = ...
    ...
}

void main()
{
    Call concurrently:
        UnitControl() and
        RequestResolver()
}
```

**(a)**                                                         **(c)**

Figure 8.2: Specifying an elevator controller system: (a) system interface, (b) partial English description, (c) more precise description using a sequential program model.

called delay). It then goes back to the beginning of the infinite loop. The *RequestResolver* would be written similarly.

## 8.4 A Basic State Machine Model: Finite-State Machines

In a *finite-state machine* (FSM) model, we describe system behavior as a set of possible states; the system can only be in one of these states at a given time. We also describe the possible transitions from one state to another depending on input values. Finally, we describe the actions that occur when in a state or when transitioning between states.

For example, Figure 8.3 shows a state machine description of the *UnitControl* part of our elevator example. The initial state, *Idle*, sets *up* and *down* to 0 and *open* to 1. The state machine stays in state *Idle* until the requested floor differs from the current floor. If the requested floor is greater, then the machine transitions to state *GoingUp*, which sets *up* to 1, whereas if the requested floor is less, then the machine transitions to state *GoingDown*, which

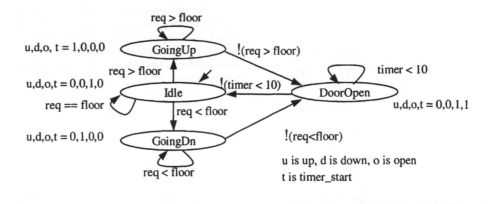

Figure 8.3: The elevator's *UnitControl* process described using a state machine.

sets *down* to 1. The machine stays in either state until the current floor equals the requested floor, after which the machine transitions to state *DoorOpen*, which sets *open* to 1. We assume the system includes a timer, so we start the timer while transitioning to *DoorOpen*. We stay in this state until the timer says 10 seconds have passed, after which we transition back to the *Idle* state.

We have described state machines somewhat informally, but now provide a more formal definition. We start by defining the well-known finite-state machine computation model, or FSM, and then we'll define extensions to that model to obtain a more useful model for embedded system design. An FSM is a 6-tuple $F<S, I, O, F, H, s_0>$, where

$S$ is a set of states $\{s_0, s_1, \ldots, s_l\}$,

$I$ is a set of inputs $\{i_0, i_1, \ldots, i_m\}$,

$O$ is a set of outputs $\{o_0, o_1, \ldots, o_n\}$,

$F$ is a next-state function (i.e., transitions), mapping states and inputs to states $(S \times I \rightarrow S)$,

$H$ is an output function, mapping current states to outputs $(S \rightarrow O)$,

$s_0$ is an initial state.

The above is a *Moore*-type FSM, which associates outputs with states. A second type of FSM is a *Mealy*-type FSM, which associates outputs with transitions (i.e., $H$ maps $S \times I \rightarrow O$). You might remember that Moore outputs are associated with states by noting that the name Moore has two o's in it, which look like states in a state diagram. Many tools that support FSMs support combinations of the two types, meaning we can associate outputs with states, transitions, or both.

We can use some shorthand notations to simplify FSM descriptions. First, there may be many system outputs, so rather than explicitly assigning every output in every state, we can say that any outputs not assigned in a state are implicitly assigned 0. Second, we often use an FSM to describe a single-purpose processor (i.e., hardware). Most hardware is synchronous,

Embedded System Design

meaning that register updates are synchronized to clock pulses (e.g., registers are updated only on the rising (or falling) edge of a clock). Such an FSM would have every transition condition ANDed with the clock edge (e.g., clock'rising and $x = y$). To avoid having to add this clock edge to every transition condition, we can simply say that the FSM is synchronous, meaning that every transition condition is implicitly ANDed with the clock edge.

# 8.5 Finite-State Machine with Datapath Model: FSMD

When using an FSM for embedded system design, the inputs and outputs represent Boolean data types, and the functions therefore represent Boolean functions with Boolean operations. This model may be sufficient for many purely control systems that do not input or output data. However, when we must deal with data, two new features would be helpful: more complex data types (such as integers or floating point numbers) and variables to store data. Gajski (see Chapter 2) refers to an FSM model extended to support more complex data types and variables as an FSM with datapath, or FSMD. Most authors refer to this model as an extended FSM, but there are many kinds of extensions and therefore we prefer the more precise name of FSMD. One possible FSMD model definition as a 7-tuple is $<S, I, O, V, F, H, s_0>$, where:

$S$ is a set of states $\{s_0, s_1, \dots, s_l\}$,

$I$ is a set of inputs $\{i_0, i_1, \dots, i_m\}$,

$O$ is a set of outputs $\{o_0, o_1, \dots, o_n\}$,

$V$ is a set of variables $\{v_0, v_1, \dots, v_n\}$,

$F$ is a next-state function, mapping states and inputs and variables to states ($S \times I \times V \rightarrow S$),

$H$ is an action function, mapping current states to outputs and variables ($S \rightarrow O + V$),

$s_0$ is an initial state.

In an FSMD, the inputs, outputs and variables may represent various data types perhaps as complex as the data types allowed in a typical programming language. Furthermore, the functions $F$ and $H$ may include arithmetic operations, such as addition, rather than just Boolean operations as in an FSM. We now call $H$ an action function rather than an output function, since it describes not just outputs, but also variable updates. Note that the above definition is for a Moore-type FSMD, and it could easily be modified for a Mealy type or a combination of the two types. During execution of the model, the complete system state consists not only of the current state $s_i$, but also the values of all variables. Our earlier state machine description of *UnitControl* was an FSMD, since its input data types were integers, and it had arithmetic operations, like magnitude comparisons, in its transition conditions.

# 8.6 Using State Machines

Having introduced the basic FSM and FSMD models, we now discuss several issues related to using those models to describe desired system behavior.

## Describing a System as a State Machine

Describing a system's behavior as a state machine, in particular as an FSMD, consists of several steps:

1. List all possible states, giving each a descriptive name.
2. Declare all variables.
3. For each state, list the possible transitions, with associated conditions, to other states.
4. For each state and/or transition, list the associated actions.
5. For each state, ensure that exiting transition conditions are exclusive, meaning that no two conditions could be true simultaneously, and complete, meaning that one of the conditions is true at any time.

If the transitions leaving a state are not exclusive, then we have a nondeterministic state machine. When the machine executes and reaches a state with more than one transition that could be taken, then one of those transitions is taken, but we don't know which one that would be. The nondeterminism prevents having to over-specify behavior in some cases, and may result in don't-cares that may reduce hardware size, but we won't focus on nondeterministic state machines in this book.

If the transitions leaving a state are not complete, then that usually means that we stay in that state until one of the conditions becomes true. This way of reducing the number of explicit transitions should probably be avoided when first learning to use state machines.

## Comparing State Machine and Sequential Program Models

Many would agree that the state machine model excels over the sequential program model for describing a control-based system like the elevator controller. The state machine model is designed such that it encourages a designer to think of all possible states of the system, and to think of all possible transitions among states based on possible input conditions. The sequential program model, in contrast, is designed to transform data through a series of instructions that may be iterated and conditionally executed. Each model encourages a different way of thinking of a system's behavior.

A common point of confusion is the distinction between state machine and sequential program models versus the distinction between graphical and textual languages. In particular, a state machine description excels in many cases, not because of its graphical representation, but rather because it provides a more natural means of computing for those cases; it can be captured textually and still provide the same advantage. For example, while in Figure 8.3 we described the elevator's *UnitControl* as a state machine captured in a graphical state-machine language, called a *state diagram*, we could have instead captured the state machine in a textual state-machine language. One textual language would be a *state table*, in which we list each state as an entry in a table. Each state's row would list the state's actions. Each row would also list all possible input conditions, and the next state for each such condition. Conversely, while in Figure 8.2 we described the elevator's *UnitControl* as a sequential program captured using a textual sequential programming language, in this case C, we could have instead captured the sequential program using a graphical sequential programming language, such as a flowchart.

```
#define IDLE        0
#define GOINGUP     1
#define GOINGDN     2
#define DOOROPEN    3
void UnitControl() {
  int state = IDLE;
  while (1) {
    switch (state) {
      IDLE:    up=0; down=0; open=1; timer_start=0;
        if  (req==floor)   {state = IDLE;}
        if  (req > floor)  {state = GOINGUP;}
        if  (req < floor)  {state = GOINGDN;}
        break;
      GOINGUP: up=1; down=0; open=0; timer_start=0;
        if  (req > floor)  {state = GOINGUP;}
        if  (!(req>floor)) {state = DOOROPEN;}
        break;
      GOINGDN: up=1; down=0; open=0; timer_start=0;
        if  (req < floor)  {state = GOINGDN;}
        if  (!(req<floor)) {state = DOOROPEN;}
        break;
      DOOROPEN: up=0; down=0; open=1; timer_start=1;
        if (timer < 10) {state = DOOROPEN;}
        if (!(timer<10)){state = IDLE;}
        break;
    }
  }
}
```

Figure 8.4: Capturing the elevator's *UnitControl* state machine in a sequential programming language.

## Capturing State Machines in Sequential Programming Language

As elegant as the state machine model is for describing control-dominated systems, the fact remains that the most popular embedded system development tools use sequential programming languages like C, C++, Java, Ada, VHDL, or Verilog. Such tools are typically complex and expensive, supporting tasks like compilation, synthesis, simulation, interactive debugging, and/or in-circuit emulation. Thus, although sequential programming languages do not directly support the capture of state machines (i.e., they don't possess specific constructs corresponding to states or transitions) we still want to use the popular embedded system development tools to protect our financial and educational investments in them. Fortunately, we can still describe our system using a state machine model while capturing the model in a sequential program language, by using one of two approaches.

In a *front-end tool* approach, we install an additional tool that supports a state machine language. These tools typically define graphical and perhaps textual state machine languages, and include nice graphic interfaces for drawing and displaying states as circles and transitions as directed arcs. They may support graphical simulation of the state machine, highlighting the

```
#define S0            0
#define S1            1
...
#define SN            N
void StateMachine() {
   int state = S0; // or whatever is the initial state.
   while (1) {
      switch (state) {
         S0:
            // Insert S0's actions here & Insert transitions Ti leaving S0:
            if( T0's condition is true ) {state = T0's next state; /*actions*/ }
            if( T1's condition is true ) {state = T1's next state; /*actions*/ }
            ...
            if( Tm's condition is true ) {state = Tm's next state; /*actions*/ }
            break;
         S1:
            // Insert S1's actions here
            // Insert transitions Ti leaving S1
            break;
         ...
         SN:
            // Insert SN's actions here
            // Insert transitions Ti leaving SN
            break;
      }
   }
}
```

Figure 8.5: General template for capturing a state machine in a sequential programming language.

current state and active transition. Such tools automatically generate code in a sequential program language (e.g., C code) with the same functionality as the state machine. This sequential program code can then be input to our main development tool. In many cases, the front-end tool is designed to interface directly with our main development tool, so that we can control and observe simulations occurring in the development tool directly from the front-end tool. The drawback of this approach is that we must support yet another tool, which includes additional licensing costs, version upgrades, training, integration problems with our development environment, and so on.

In contrast, we can use a language subset approach. In this approach, we directly capture our state machine model in a sequential program language, by following a strict set of rules for capturing each state machine construct in an equivalent set of sequential program constructs. This approach is by far the most common approach for capturing state machines, both in software languages like C as well as hardware languages like VHDL and Verilog. We now describe how to capture a state machine model in a sequential program language.

We start by capturing our *UnitControl* state machine in the sequential programming language C, illustrated in Figure 8.4. We enumerate all states, in this case using the #define C

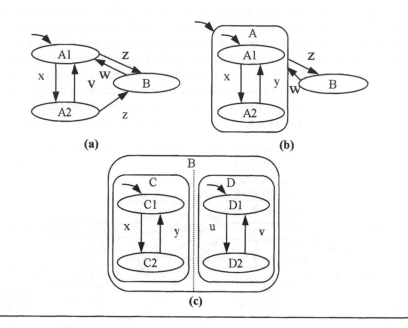

Figure 8.6: Adding hierarchy and concurrency to the state machine model: (a) three-state example without hierarchy, (b) same example with hierarchy, (c) concurrency.

construct. We capture the state machine as a subroutine, in which we declare a state variable initialized to the initial state. We then create an infinite loop, containing a single switch statement that branches to the case corresponding to the value of the state variable. Each state's case starts with the actions in that state, and then the transitions from that state. Each transition is captured as an *if* statement that checks if the transition's condition is true and then sets the next state. Figure 8.5 shows a general template for capturing a state machine in C.

To be safer, we could replace the sequence of *if* statements representing a state's transitions by an *if-then-else* statement. This would ensure that if the transition conditions were mistakenly nonexclusive, the code would merely execute the first transition whose condition was true, rather than executing all such transitions.

# 8.7    HCFSM and the Statecharts Language

*Hiererarchical/concurrent state machine models* (HCFSM) are extensions to the state machine model. Harel proposed extensions to the state machine model to support hierarchy and concurrency, and developed *Statecharts*, a graphical state machine language designed to capture that model. We refer to the model as a hierarchical/concurrent FSM, or HCFSM.

The *hierarchy* extension in HCFSMs allows us to decompose a state into another state machine, or conversely stated, to group several states into a new hierarchical state. For example, consider the state machine in Figure 8.6(a), having three states $A1$, $A2$, and $B$. $A1$ is the initial state. Whenever we are in either $A1$ or $A2$ and event $z$ occurs, we transition to state $B$. We can simplify this state machine by grouping $A1$ and $A2$ into a hierarchical state $A$, as shown in Figure 8.6(b). State $A$ is the initial state, which in turn has an initial state $A1$. We draw the transition to $B$ on event $z$ as originating from state $A$, not $A1$ or $A2$. The meaning is that regardless of whether we are in $A1$ or $A2$, event $z$ causes a transition to state $B$.

As another hierarchy example, consider our earlier elevator example, and suppose that we want to add a control input fire, along with new behavior that immediately moves the elevator

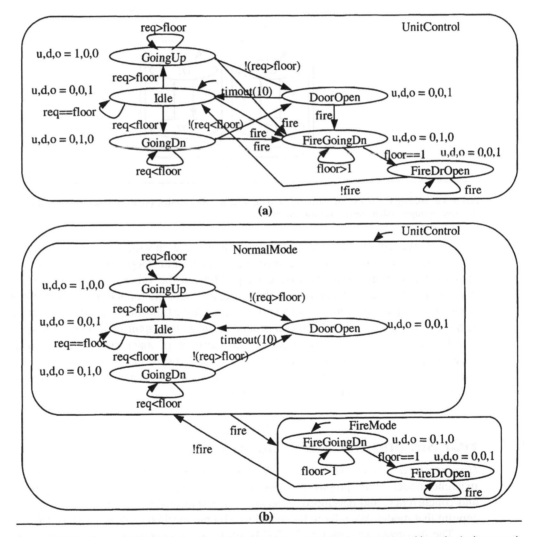

Figure 8.7: The elevator's UnitControl with new behavior for a new input *fire*: (a) without hierarchy (quite a mess), (b) with hierarchy.

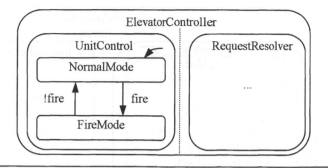

Figure 8.8: Using concurrency in an HCFSM to describe both processes of the *ElevatorController*.

down to the first floor and opens the door when fire is true. As shown in Figure 8.7(a), we can capture this behavior by adding a transition from every state originally in *UnitControl* to a new state called *FireGoingDn*, which moves the elevator to the first floor, followed by a state *FireDrOpen*, which holds the door open on the first floor. When fire becomes false, we go to the *Idle* state. While this new state machine captures the desired behavior, the state machine is becoming more complex due to many more transitions, and harder to comprehend due to more states. We can use hierarchy to reduce the number of transitions and enhance understandability. As shown in Figure 8.7(b), we can group the original state machine into a hierarchical state called *NormalMode*, and group the fire-related states into a state called *FireMode*. This grouping reduces the number of transitions, since instead of four transitions from each original state to the fire-related states, we now need only one transition, in this case from *NormalMode* to *FireMode*. This grouping also enhances understandability, since it clearly represents two main operating modes, one normal and one in case of fire.

The second extension that HCFSMs possess, *concurrency*, allows us to use hierarchy to decompose a state into two concurrent states, or conversely stated, to group two concurrent states into a new hierarchical state. For example, Figure 8.6 (c), shows a state *B* decomposed into two concurrent states *C* and *D*. *C* happens to be decomposed into another state machine, as does *D*. Figure 8.8 shows the entire *ElevatorController* behavior captured as a HCFSM with two concurrent states.

Therefore, we see that there are two methods for using hierarchy to decompose a state into substates. OR-decomposition decomposes a state into sequential states, in which only one state is active at a time — either the first state OR the second state OR the third state, etc. AND-decomposition decomposes a state into concurrent states, all of which are active at a time — the first state AND the second state AND the third state, etc.

The Statecharts language includes numerous additional constructs to improve state machine capture. A *timeout* is a transition with a time limit as its condition. The transition is automatically taken if the transition source state is active for an amount of time equal to the limit. Note that we used a timeout to simplify the *UnitControl* state machine in Figure 8.7; rather than starting and checking an external timer in state *DoorOpen*, we instead created a transition from *DoorOpen* to *Idle* with the condition timeout(10). History is a mechanism for remembering the last substate that an OR-decomposed state *A* was in before transitioning to

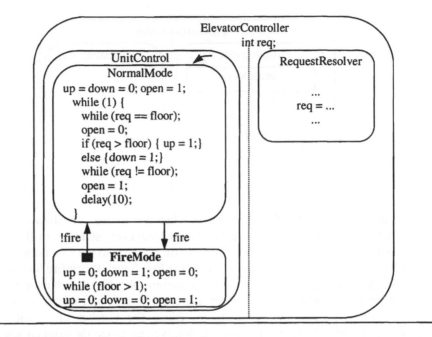

Figure 8.9: Using PSM to describe the *ElevatorController*.

another state *B*. Upon reentering state *A*, we can start with the remembered substate rather than *A*'s initial state. Thus, the transition leaving *A* is treated much like an interrupt and *B* as an interrupt service routine.

## 8.8 Program-State Machine Model (PSM)

The *program-state machine* (PSM) model extends state machines to allow use of sequential program code to define a state's actions, including extensions for complex data types and variables. PSM also includes the hierarchy and concurrency extensions of HCFSM. Thus, PSM is a merger of the HCFSM and sequential program models, subsuming both models. A PSM having only one state, called a program-state in PSM terminology, where that state's actions are defined using a sequential program, is equivalent to a sequential program. A PSM having many states, whose actions are all just assignment statements, is equivalent to an HCFSM. Lying between these two extremes are various combinations of the two models.

For example, Figure 8.9 shows a PSM description of the *ElevatorController* behavior, which we AND-decompose into two concurrent program-states *UnitControl* and *RequestResolver*, as in the earlier HCFSM example. Furthermore, we OR-decompose *UnitControl* into two sequential program-states, *NormalMode* and *FireMode*, again as in the HCFSM example. However, unlike the HCFSM example, we describe *NormalMode* as a sequential program, identical to that of Figure 8.2(c), rather than a state machine. Likewise, we describe *FireMode* as a sequential program. We didn't have to use sequential programs for those program-states, and could have used state machines for one or both — the point is that PSM allows the designer to choose whichever model is most appropriate.

PSM enforces a stricter hierarchy than the HCFSM model used in Statecharts. In Statecharts, transitions may point not just between states at the same level of hierarchy, but may cross hierarchical levels also. An example is the transition in Figure 8.7(b) pointing from the *FireDrOpen* substate of the *FireMode* state to the *NormalMode* state. Having this transition start from *FireDrOpen* rather than *FireMode* causes the elevator to always go all the way down to the first floor when the fire input becomes true, even if the input is true just momentarily. PSM, on the other hand, allows transitions only between sibling states (i.e., between states with the same parent state). PSM's model of hierarchy is the same as in sequential program languages that use subroutines for hierarchy; namely, we always enter the subroutine from one point, and when we exit the subroutine we do not specify to where we are exiting.

As in the sequential programming model, but unlike the HCFSM model, PSM includes the notion of a program-state *completing*. If the program-state is a sequential program, then reaching the end of the code means the program-state is complete. If the program-state is OR-decomposed into substates, then a special *complete* substate may be added. Transitions may occur from a substate to the complete substate, but no transitions may leave the complete substate. Transitioning to the complete substate means that the program-state is complete. Consequently, PSM introduces two types of transitions. A *transition-immediately* (TI) transition is taken immediately if its condition becomes true, regardless of the status of the source program-state — this is the same as the transition type in an HCFSM. A second, new type of transition, *transition-on-completion* (TOC), is taken only if the condition is true AND the source program-state is complete. Graphically, a TOC transition is drawn originating from a filled square inside a state, rather than from the state's perimeter. We used a TOC transition in Figure 8.9 to transition from *FireMode* to *NormalMode* only after *FireMode* completed, where such completion meant that the elevator had reached the first floor. By supporting both types of transitions, PSM elegantly merges the reactive nature of HCFSM models, using TI transitions, with the transformational nature of sequential program models, using TOC transitions.

The *SpecCharts* language was the first language designed to easily capture the PSM model. Actually, two languages were defined, one graphical and the other textual. SpecCharts was designed as an extension of VHDL, using VHDL's syntax and semantics for all variable declarations and sequential program statements. More recently, the *SpecC* language was developed to capture PSM, but uses an extension of C rather than VHDL.

## 8.9   The Role of an Appropriate Model and Language

Specifying embedded system functionality can be a hard task, but an appropriate computation model can help. The model shapes the way we think of the system. The language should capture the model easily.

Consider how models shaped the way we thought about the elevator controller example's *UnitControl* behavior. In order to create the sequential program that we captured in Figure 8.2(c), we were thinking in terms of a *sequence of actions*. First, we wait for the requested floor to differ from the target floor, then we close the door, then we move up or down to the desired floor, then we open the door, and then we repeat this sequence. In contrast, in order to create the state machine that we captured in Figure 8.3, we were thinking in terms of possible system states and the transitions among those states. Many individuals say that, for this example, the state machine model feels more natural than the sequential program model. When a system must react to a variety of changing inputs, a state machine model may be a good choice. Furthermore, notice that the HCFSM model was able to describe the fire behavior nicely, while the FSM or FSMD models would have become somewhat complex.

The language should capture our chosen model easily. Ideally, the language would have constructs that directly capture features of the model — a language for capturing state machines should have constructs for capturing states and transitions, for example. However, such a model/language match is not always the case. As you may have already ascertained, the most common situation of a model/language mismatch in embedded systems is that of having a language designed to support the sequential program model, but wanting to capture a system using a state machine model. In this case, we can use structured techniques for capturing the state machine model in the sequential program language, as shown earlier. To see the benefit of using the best model, think of how the fire behavior would have been incorporated into the sequential program of Figure 8.2(c). We would have had to insert checks for the signal throughout the code, making the code very complex.

The moral of the story here is that often we cannot choose the language used to capture embedded system functionality — that choice is often dictated by other factors. But we need not be limited to using the model directly supported by that language. We can use a different model if that model provides an advantage, and then capture the model in the language using structured techniques.

## 8.10 Concurrent Process Model

Thus far in this chapter, we have looked at computational models such as finite-state machines and drawn an important distinction between computational models and languages. As defined in the previous chapter, a computation model provides a set of objects and rules operating on those object that help a designer describe a system's functionality. A system's functionality, in fact, may be described using multiple computational models. A language, on the other hand, provides semantics and constructs that enable a designer to capture a computational model. Some languages, in fact, capture more than one computational model. In this chapter, we present a new computational model called concurrent process. In addition, we extend our distinction between computational models and languages to include implementation.

```
ConcurrentProcessExample() {
  x = ReadX()
  y = ReadY()
  Call concurrently:
    PrintHelloWorld(x) and
    PrintHowAreYou(y)
}
PrintHelloWorld(x) {
  while( 1 ) {
    print "Hello world."
    delay(x);
  }
}
PrintHowAreYou(x) {
  while( 1 ) {
    print "How are you?"
    delay(y);
  }
}
```

ReadX → ReadY → PrintHelloWorld
                PrintHowAreYou

time

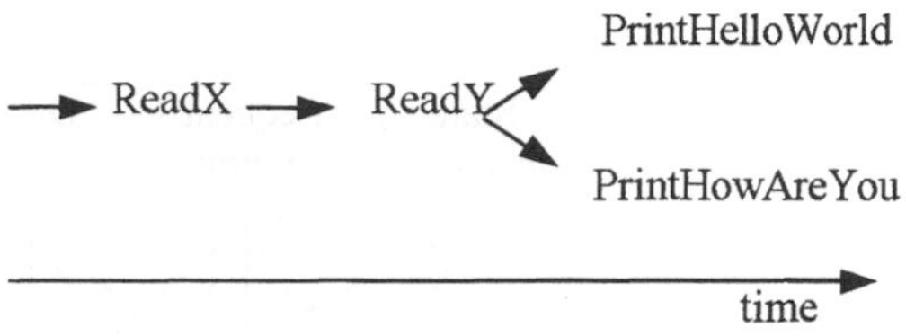

**(b)**

```
Enter X: 1
Enter Y: 2
Hello world.     (Time = 1 s)
Hello world.     (Time = 2 s)
How are you?     (Time = 2 s)
Hello world.     (Time = 3 s)
How are you?     (Time = 4 s)
Hello world.     (Time = 4 s)
...
```

**(a)**                                             **(c)**

Figure 8.10: A simple concurrent process example: (a) pseudo-code, (b) subroutine execution over time, (c) sample input and output.

The concurrent process model is a model that allows us to describe the functionality of a system in terms of two or more concurrently executing subtasks. Many systems are easier to describe as a set of concurrently executing tasks because they are inherently multitasking. For instance, imagine this variation on the Hello World example. This system allows a user to provide two numbers $X$ and $Y$. We then want to write "Hello World" to a display every $X$ seconds, and "How are you" to the display every $Y$ seconds. A very simple way to describe this system using concurrent tasks is shown in Figure 8.10(a). After reading in $X$ and $Y$, we call two subroutines, each describing one of the tasks, concurrently. One subroutine prints "Hello World" every $X$ seconds, the other prints "How are you" every $Y$ seconds. (Note that you cannot call two subroutines concurrently in a pure sequential program model, such as the model supported by the basic version of the C language). As shown in Figure 8.10(b), these two subroutines execute simultaneously. Sample output for $X = 1$ and $Y = 2$ is shown in Figure 8.10(c). To see why concurrent processes are helpful, try describing the same system using a finite-state machine or Pascal program. You will find yourself exerting effort figuring out how to schedule the two subroutines into one sequential program. Since this example is a trivial one, this extra effort is not a serious problem, but for a complex system, this extra effort can be significant and can detract from the time you have to focus on the desired system behavior. In general, the concurrent process model is useful when describing systems that are inherently multitasking. That is to say that the function of these systems can best be described in terms of a number of subtasks each executing concurrently to one another.

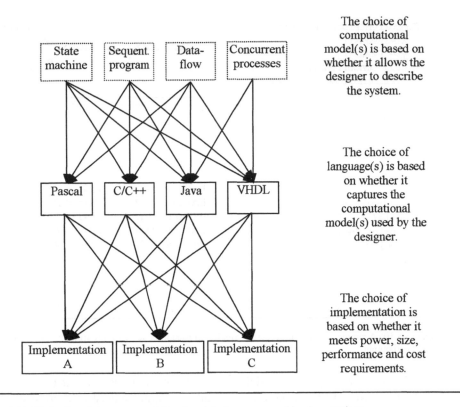

Figure 8.11: Distinctions between computational models, languages, and implementations.

To describe a system as a set of concurrently executing tasks, we use a language that captures the concurrent process model. An implementation is then derived from such a description. An implementation is a mapping of a system's functionality, captured using a computational model (or models) and written in some language (or languages), onto hardware processors. This relationship is shown in Figure 8.11. The choice of the programming language is independent of the implementation. A particular language may be used because it captures the computational model used to describe our system. A particular implementation may be used because it meets all power, timing, performance, and cost requirements of the system. Once a final implementation is obtained, a designer can execute the system and observe the behavior, measure design metrics of interest, and decide if the implementation is feasible. A final implementation also serves as a blueprint or prototype for mass manufacturing of the final product.

In this chapter, we describe the concurrent process model and related implementation issues. In addition, we introduce real-time systems as systems that are inherently composed of multiple processes. However, processes of a real-time system have stringent timing requirements.

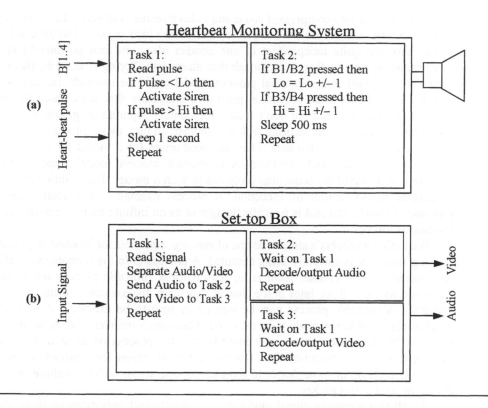

Figure 8.12: Typical examples of embedded system: (a) Heartbeat monitoring system (b) Set-top box system.

# 8.11 Concurrent Processes

We are familiar with describing a system's desired behavior using a sequential program model, captured perhaps in the C language. A sequential program model consists of a set of statements, and its execution consists of executing each statement one at a time. However, some systems have behavior that really consists of several somewhat independent subbehaviors. For example, a heartbeat monitoring system's behavior, shown in Figure 8.12(a), can be decomposed into two parts. The first part, once a second, samples the input pulse and computes the heartbeat of the patient, making sure that it does not exceed or drop below thresholds called *Hi* and *Lo*. The second part, twice a second, checks to see if one of the four buttons labeled *B*1 through *B*4 is pressed and if so, increments or decrements the corresponding *Lo* or *Hi* threshold. These two subparts are quite independent from each other and can be thought of as executing concurrently, even though they share access to common data (*Hi, Lo*). In another example, a set-top box system's behavior, shown in Figure 8.12(b), may consist of three parts. The first part would receive a digital broadcast from the antenna

---

and decompose it into compressed audio and video streams. The second and third parts of the system, in turn, will decode the compressed audio and video signals. The three subparts in the set-top box are quite independent of one another also, and can be thought of executing concurrently to one another, even though they share data. Trying to describe them as a single sequential program in a sequential program model could be difficult. Instead, we'd like to describe them using three sequential programs, indicating that these three programs could execute concurrently. But we don't want three entirely separate programs, since those three programs do need to communicate with one another. In fact, these three programs share large volumes of audio and video data. Thus, the need arises for a model for describing multiple communicating sequential programs. A concurrent process model achieves this goal. A *process* is just one of the sequential programs in such a model. The traditional definition of a process is simply a unit of execution. A process executes concurrently with the other processes in the model and is typically thought of as an infinite loop, executing its sequential statements forever.

We define a process's state to be one of *running*, *runnable*, or *blocked*. A process is in the running state if it is currently being executed. A process is in the runnable state if it is ready and executable. Of course, there is no reason for a runnable process not to be running. However, as we will see later in the chapter, when we discuss implementation of concurrent processes, a runnable process may be waiting its turn to be executed. A process is in the blocked state if it is not ready to be executed. There are a number of reasons for a process to be in the blocked state. One reason could be that the process needs to wait for some other process to finish its execution first. Another common reason for a process to be blocked is when it is waiting for some device to complete an operation, such as, waiting for the network device to send a data packet.

Recall that a computational model defines objects and operations on those objects. In a concurrent process model, a process becomes the fundamental object encapsulating some portion of a system's functionality. The basic operations defined by the concurrent process model on processes are *create*, *terminate*, *suspend*, *resume*, and *join*, which we now describe.

## Process Create and Terminate

Create creates a new process, initializes any associated data and starts execution of that process. In our Hello World example, shown in Figure 8.10(a), we created two processes by executing concurrently two procedures called *PrintHelloWorld(x)* and *PrintHowAreYou(y)*. Each of these procedures described the sequential execution of one of the processes of our example. Conceptually, one can think of a create operation as an asynchronous procedure call. In a sequential programming model, a procedure call blocks the calling procedure and starts executing the called procedure. Once the called procedure terminates, control is transferred back to the calling procedure, and it is allowed to resume execution. In our analogy, a procedure acts like a process and the procedure call behaves like creating another process. In contrast, in the concurrent process model, an asynchronous procedure call does not block the calling procedure (process). Instead both the calling procedure (process) and the called procedure (new process), start executing concurrently. Either one of these processes can further create other processes and so on. Again, keep in mind that in this discussion the term procedure and process are used interchangeably.

Terminate terminates an already executing process and destroys all data associated with that process. Terminate is an operation that is performed by one process on another. If a process does not implement an infinite loop, it is terminated automatically when it reaches the end of its execution (i.e., right after executing its last instruction). The need for terminating a process may arise when handling exceptional events. For instance, in an assembly-line monitoring system composed of multiple processes, if one process detects an error condition, it may terminate other processes, such as those controlling the conveyer belt driver motor and guide arms.

## Process Suspend and Resume

Suspend suspends the execution of an already created process. Once a process, say, $X$, has started to execute, another process may need to stop it without terminating it. That means that the state of $X$ (i.e., all the intermediate data values that have been computed by that process) and the location of the currently executing instruction or the program counter need to be saved. A suspended process can, at some later point, be allowed to execute again by restoring its state and allowing it to execute. This operation is called Resume.

## Process Join

Once a process, say, $X$, has started to execute, another process, typically the one that created $X$, may need to wait until $X$ finishes execution and terminates. That means that the process invoking the join operation is suspended until the to-be-joined process has reached the end of its executing. This operation is called Join. Join is an important operation that is uses for synchronization of processes and their execution. We will discuss process synchronization in detail later in this chapter.

# 8.12 Communication among Processes

When a system's functionality is divided into two or more concurrently executing processes, it is essential to provide means for communication among these processes. Two common methods for communication among processes are *shared memory* and *message passing*. In shared memory, processes can read and write the same memory locations. In message passing, processes explicitly send or receive data to and from each other.

## Shared Memory

Using shared memory, multiple processes communicate by reading and writing the same memory locations or common variables. This form of communication is very efficient and easy to implement. An example of using shared memory is shown in Figure 8.13. In this particular example, we have two processes that share the same memory address space. In particular, they shared an array of $N$ data items called buffer and a variable that holds the

```
01: data_type buffer[N];
02: int count = 0;
03: void processA() {
04:    int i;
05:    while( 1 ) {
06:       produce(&data);
07:       while( count == N );/*loop*/
08:       buffer[i] = data;
09:       i = (i + 1) % N;
10:       count = count + 1;
11:    }
12: }
13: void processB() {
14:    int i;
15:    while( 1 ) {
16:       while( count == 0 );/*loop*/
17:       data = buffer[i];
18:       i = (i + 1) % N;
19:       count = count - 1;
20:       consume(&data);
21:    }
22: }
23: void main() {
24:    create_process(processA); create_process(processB);
26: }
```

Figure 8.13: An incorrect solution to the consumer-producer problem.

number of valid data items in the array called count. One of the processes, named $A$, produces as part of its computation data elements that are consumed by the other process, named $B$. (For example, the producer process is decoding video packets while the consumer process displays the decoded packets on a LCD display.) When process $A$ has a new data element ready, it waits (line 7) for a location in the array to become available. Then, it puts the data element in the array and increments count. Likewise, process $B$ waits (line 16) until at least one packet becomes available in the array. Then, process $B$ removes that element, decrements count, and consumes the data. This example is known as the *consumer-producer* problem.

Although the code in Figure 8.13 is very simple and appears to be correct, it will not function correctly. To illustrate the problem, consider the case where count holds the value 3 and both processes $A$ and $B$ are about to update it concurrently (lines 9 and 19). The following execution sequence will results in an incorrect final value stored into the count variable:

- $A$: loads count from memory into CPU register $R1(R1 = 3)$,
- $A$: increments value in register $R1$ ($R1 = 4$),
- $B$: loads count from memory into CPU register $R2$ ($R2 = 3$),
- $B$: decrements value in register $R2$ ($R2 = 2$),
- $A$: stores $R1$ back to memory location of count (*count* = 4),
- $B$: stores $R2$ back to memory location of count (*count* = 2).

```
01: data_type buffer[N];
02: int count = 0;
03: mutex count_mutex;
04: void processA() {
05:   int i;
06:   while( 1 ) {
07:     produce(&data);
08:     while( count == N );/*loop*/
09:     buffer[i] = data;
10:     i = (i + 1) % N;
11:     count_mutex.lock();
12:     count = count + 1;
13:     count_mutex.unlock();
14:   }
15: }
16: void processB() {
17:   int i;
18:   while( 1 ) {
19:     while( count == 0 );/*loop*/
20:     data = buffer[i];
21:     i = (i + 1) % N;
22:     count_mutex.lock();
23:     count = count - 1;
24:     count_mutex.unlock();
25:     consume(&data);
26:   }
27: }
28: void main() {
29:   create_process(processA); create_process(processB);
31: }
```

Figure 8.14: A correct solution to the consumer-producer problem.

After the above execution sequence, the value of *count* will be incorrectly set to 2. The problem is that the execution of lines 9 and 19 should never be performed concurrently. Instead they should execute in *mutual exclusion* of each other. We can consider the code segments that update the memory location of count as a *critical section*. A critical section is a possibly noncontiguous section of code where simultaneous updates, by multiple processes to a shared memory location, can occur. In order to guarantee such mutual exclusion, it is necessary to introduce primitives that enable us to lock a section of code allowing only one processes to be executing in that section at a time.

A *mutex* is a primitive that allows us to do just that. A mutex itself is a shared object with two operations, *lock* and *unlock*. A mutex is typically associated with a segment of shared data and serves as a guard, disallowing multiple read/write access to the shared memory it is guarding. Two or more processes can simultaneously perform the lock operation, but only one of the processes will actually acquire the lock, and others will be put in the blocked state

```
01: mutex mutex1, mutex2;
02: void processA() {
03:   while( 1 ) {
04:     ...
05:     mutex1.lock();
06:     /* critical section 1 */
07:     mutex2.lock();
08:     /* critical section 2 */
09:     mutex2.unlock();
10:     /* critical section 1 */
11:     mutex1.unlock();
12:   }
13: }
14: void processB() {
15:   while( 1 ) {
16:     ...
17:     mutex2.lock();
18:     /* critical section 2 */
19:     mutex1.lock();
20:     /* critical section 1 */
21:     mutex1.unlock();
22:     /* critical section 2 */
23:     mutex2.unlock();
24:   }
```

Figure 8.15: Deadlock among processes.

unable to enter the critical section of the code. When the process holding the lock exits the critical section of the code, it performs an unlock operation allowing the blocked processes to be put back in the runable state where they can compete to acquire the lock. Using a mutex, we have corrected our consumer and producer implementation as shown in Figure 8.14. Let us once again assume that the *count* variable currently holds the value 3 and processes *A* and *B* are about to update it simultaneously using the following execution sequence:

- *A/B*: execute *lock* operation on *count_mutex* (say *B* acquires the lock, *A* is blocked and unable to execute),
- *B*: loads *count* from memory into CPU register $R2$ ($R2 = 3$),
- *B*: decrements value in register $R2$ ($R2 = 2$),
- *B*: stores $R2$ back to memory location of *count* (*count* = 2),
- *B*: executes *unlock* operation on *count_mutex* (*A* is made runnable again),
- *A*: loads *count* from memory into CPU register $R1$ ($R1 = 2$),
- *A*: increments value in register $R1$ ($R1 = 3$),
- *A*: stores $R1$ back to memory location of *count* (*count* = 3).

This time the value of *count* is correctly set to 3.

```
void processA() {                    void processB() {
  while( 1 ) {                         while( 1 ) {
    produce(&data)                       receive(A, &data);
    send(B, &data);                      transform(&data)
    /* region 1 */                       send(A, &data);
    receive(B, &data);                   /* region 2 */
    consume(&data);                    }
  }                                  }
}
```

Figure 8.16: Communication among processes using send and receive.

Locking sections of code is necessary to correctly implement shared memory based communication among processes. However, using locks may lead to a deadlock, causing a system to hang. Therefore care must be taken in using locks. A *deadlock* is a name given to a condition where two or more processes are blocked waiting for each other to unlock critical sections of code. Since both are waiting, neither can proceed and hence they will wait forever. As an example, consider the code segment in Figure 8.15. Here we have two processes, $A$ and $B$, that may execute two different critical sections of code simultaneously. Therefore, two locks are used to disallow simultaneous access to these regions of code. The following sequence of execution will illustrate the deadlock problem:

- $A$: executes *lock* operation on *mutex*1 ($A$ acquires the lock on *mutex*1),
- $B$: executes *lock* operation on *mutex*2 ($B$ acquires the lock on *mutex*2),
- $A/B$: they are both executing in critical sections 1 and 2, respectively,
- $A$: executes *lock* operation on *mutex*2 ($A$ is blocked until B unlocks *mutex*2),
- $B$: executes *lock* operation on *mutex*1 ($B$ is blocked until A unlocks *mutex*1).

At this point, both processes are waiting for the other to unlock *mutex*1 or *mutex*2. A deadlock has occurred and the two processes will wait indefinitely.

One protocol for eliminating deadlocks is to only allow locking of mutexes in increasing order. That means that mutexes need to be numbered in an increasing order. In addition to this requirement, we must further impose the restriction that once a process unlocks a mutex, it does not acquire anymore mutexes until it unlocks all the mutexes that it currently holds the lock to. In essence, a process will undergo an initial phase where it is acquiring locks of increasing order and a second phase where it is releasing locks it has acquired in the first phase. This form of locking is known as *two-phase locking* (2PL). It is left as an assignment to show why it is important to have a two-phase locking in addition to our initial requirement of locking mutexes in increasing order.

## Message Passing

Using message passing, data is exchanged between two processes in an explicit fashion. That means that when a process wants to send data to another process it performs a special operation, called *send*. Likewise, a processes must explicitly perform a special operation, called *receive*, in order to receive data from another process. The send and receive operations both require an identifier that specifies what process data is to be sent to or received from.

The identifier uniquely identifies one of the processes that are currently executing in the system. An example of message passing is illustrated in Figure 8.16. Here process $A$, after producing a data packet, sends it to process $B$. Meanwhile, process $B$ receives the packet, performs some transformation on the data and sends it back to $A$. Process $A$, after receiving the data packet, consumes it and the cycle repeats. Regions of code labeled 1 and 2 are segments that perform auxiliary functions in each process.

Note that receive operations are always blocking. That means the once a process executes a receive operation, it is blocked until another process executes the corresponding send operation. The send operations, on the other hand, may or may not be blocking. One reason for having nonblocking send operations is to allow a process that just performed a send operation to continue with its execution. In our example, the regions of code labeled 1 and 2 are executed immediately after a send operation, even though the receiving process may not have received the data item.

## 8.13  Synchronization among Processes

In order for two or more concurrent processes to accomplish a common task, they must at times synchronize their execution. Synchronization among processes means that one process must wait for another process to compute some value, reach a known point in its execution, or signal some condition, before it (the waiting process) proceeds. To clarify this concept, consider the consumer-producer example shown in Figure 8.14. Recall that on lines 8 and 19 processes $A$ and $B$ looped waiting for some condition to become untrue. The condition for the consumer process $A$ was that the value of *count* becomes less than $N$, meaning that buffer contained at least one empty slot. The condition for the producer process $B$ was that the value of *count* becomes greater than zero, meaning that buffer contained at least one new data item. This form of waiting on a condition is called *busy-waiting*. It is called busy-waiting because the waiting process is simply executing noops, instead of being blocked until the condition is met, hence making the CPU available for useful computation. In this section, we will introduce constructs that are more efficient to use in place of busy-waiting. Note that we have discussed the join operation and blocking send and receive primitives earlier in this chapter, which are both forms of synchronization primitives.

The join operation that we discussed earlier is a limited form of synchronization among two processes. Recall that here, one process performed a join operation on another process, indicating that it should be blocked until that other process terminates. The blocking send and receive protocols, a.k.a. synchronous send and receive, discussed in the previous section, also serve to synchronize processes. When one process performs a send or receive operation, it is blocked until the other process reaches its receive or send point, respectively, before the blocked process is allowed to continue. We will next describe *condition variables* and *monitors* as synchronization mechanisms.

## Condition Variables

One way to achieve synchronization among concurrently executing processes is to use a special construct called a *condition variable*. A condition variable is an object that permits two kinds of operations, called *signal* and *wait*, to be performed on it. When wait is performed on a condition variable, the process that performed the wait operation is blocked until another process performs a signal operation on the same condition variable. The semantics of a wait operation is in fact a bit more complex. When a process, say, $A$, executes a wait operation, it passes it a mutex variable that it has already acquired the lock for. The wait operation will then cause the mutex to be unlocked such that another process, say, $B$, may be able to enter a critical section and compute some value or make some condition become true. Once the

```
01: data_type buffer[N];
02: int count = 0;
03: mutex cs_mutex;
04: condition buffer_empty, buffer_full;
06: void processA() {
07:   int i;
08:   while( 1 ) {
09:     produce(&data);
10:     cs_mutex.lock();
11:     if( count == N ) buffer_empty.wait(cs_mutex);
13:     buffer[i] = data;
14:     i = (i + 1) % N;
15:     count = count + 1;
16:     cs_mutex.unlock();
17:     buffer_full.signal();
18:   }
19: }
20: void processB() {
21:   int i;
22:   while( 1 ) {
23:     cs_mutex.lock();
24:     if( count == 0 ) buffer_full.wait(cs_mutex);
26:     data = buffer[i];
27:     i = (i + 1) % N;
28:     count = count - 1;
29:     cs_mutex.unlock();
30:     buffer_empty.signal();
31:     consume(&data);
32:   }
33: }
34: void main() {
35:   create_process(processA); create_process(processB);
37: }
```

Figure 8.17: Synchronized consumer-producer problem using condition variables.

condition becomes true, process *B* will signal the condition variable causing process *A* to become runnable and implicitly reacquire the mutex lock.

To clarify, we will implement our consumer-producer problem using condition variables, as in Figure 8.17. We have chosen two condition variables, one that signals whether there is at least one free location available in our buffer, called *buffer_empty*, and another that signals weather there is at least one valid data item in our buffer, called *buffer_full*. The two processes execute as follows. Once the producer process *A* has produced valid data, it acquires the lock to the critical section. It then checks the value of *count*. If the value is *N*, the buffer is full, so it executes a wait operation on the *buffer_empty* condition variable, thus waiting until the buffer becomes empty. Meanwhile, by executing the wait operation, it releases the lock to the critical section such that the producer process is able to enter and execute that region of code. (Otherwise, the consumer process will never be able to enter the critical section and consume data; therefore, the system will be deadlocked!) If the value of *count* is less than *N*, the consumer process simply inserts the data into buffer, increments *count*, releases the lock, and signals to the producer process (possibly making it runnable

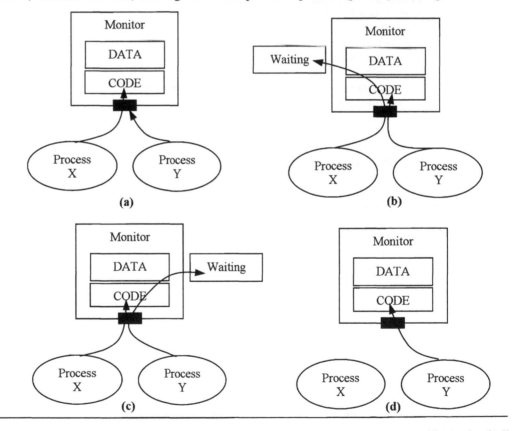

Figure 8.18: Producer-consumer example with monitors: (a) *X* is allowed to enter the monitor while *Y* waits, (b) *X* executes a *wait* on a condition and is blocked, *Y* is allowed to enter the monitor, (c) *Y* signals the condition that *X* is waiting on and thus is blocked allowing *X* to finish and exit the monitor, (d) *Y* is allowed to finish its execution.

```
01: Monitor {
02:    data_type buffer[N];
03:    int count = 0;
04:    condition buffer_full, condition buffer_empty;
06:    void processA() {
07:       int i;
08:       while( 1 ) {
09:          produce(&data);
10:          if( count == N ) buffer_empty.wait();
12:          buffer[i] = data;
13:          i = (i + 1) % N;
14:          count = count + 1;
15:          buffer_full.signal();
16:       }
17:    }
18:    void processB() {
19:       int i;
20:       while( 1 ) {
21:          if( count == 0 ) buffer_full.wait();
23:          data = buffer[i];
24:          i = (i + 1) % N;
25:          count = count - 1;
26:          buffer_empty.signal();
27:          consume(&data);
28:          buffer_full.signal();
29:       }
30:    }
31: }   /* end monitor */
32: void main() {
33:    create_process(processA); create_process(processB);
35: }
```

Figure 8.19: Synchronized consumer-producer problem using monitors.

again) that there is now at least one new data item available. The consumer process *B* works in reverse order. It too attempts to acquire the lock to the critical section, then it checks whether *count* is zero or not. If *count* is zero, it waits on *buffer_full* condition variable, otherwise, it removes a data item from buffer, decrements *count*, releases the lock and signal to the producer process.

## Monitors

Another way to achieve synchronization among concurrently executing processes is to use a special construct called a monitor. A *monitor* is a collection of data and methods or subroutines that operate on this data similar to an object in an object-oriented paradigm. A special guarding property of a monitor guarantees that only one process is allowed to execute inside the monitor at a given time. In other words, one and only one of the methods of a monitor can be active at any given time. A process, say, $X$, is allowed to enter a monitor if there are no other processes executing in that monitor. This is shown in Figure 8.18(a). Once in a monitor, $X$ has exclusive access to the data inside the monitor. If, and when, $X$ executes a wait operation on a condition variable, also defined inside the monitor, it will be blocked waiting as shown in Figure 8.18 (b). At this point, another process, say $Y$, is allowed to enter the monitor. If $Y$ signals the condition that $X$ is currently waiting on, $Y$ will be blocked and $X$ will be allowed to reenter the monitor. This is shown in Figure 8.18 (c). Then, once X terminates, or waits on a condition, $Y$ is allowed to reenter and finish its execution as shown in Figure 8.18 (d).

To clarify this a bit more, we have implemented the consumer-producer problem using monitors as shown in Figure 8.19. A single monitor is used to encapsulate the sequential programs of the consumer and producer processes. The shared buffer is also encapsulated in the monitor. Initially, one of the consumer or producer processes will be allowed to execute. Let us assume that the consumer process $A$ will be allowed to execute first. Once the consumer checks the buffer size and discovers that there are no data items produced, it will wait on the *buffer_full* condition variable and thus allow the producer process $A$ to enter the monitor and produce a data item. Once the producer process $A$ signals the *buffer_full* condition, the producer process will be allowed to reenter and execute. This behavior will repeat and the two processes will take turn producing and consuming data items. Here, it is left as an exercise to show that, the size of the buffer will never exceed 1.

# 8.14 Implementation

So far we have discussed numerous operations permitted by the concurrent process model. Here we will discuss how these operations are implemented using single or general-purpose processors.

## Creating and Terminating Processes

One way to implement multiple processes in a system is to use multiple processors, each executing one process. Each of these processors may be a general-purpose processor, in which case we can use a programming language like C to describe the function of the process and compile it down to the instructions of that processor. Or, we can build a custom single-purpose processor that implements the function of the process. In both cases, when using processors to implement multiple processes, we can achieve true multitasking (i.e., each process will execute in parallel to other processes in the system). Implementing each process on its own processor is common when each process is to be implemented using a single-purpose processor. However, we often decide that several processes should be implemented using general-purpose processors. While we could conceptually use one general-purpose processor per process, this would likely be very expensive and in most cases is not necessary. It is not necessary because the processes likely do not require 100% of the processor's processing time; instead, many processes may share a single processor's time and

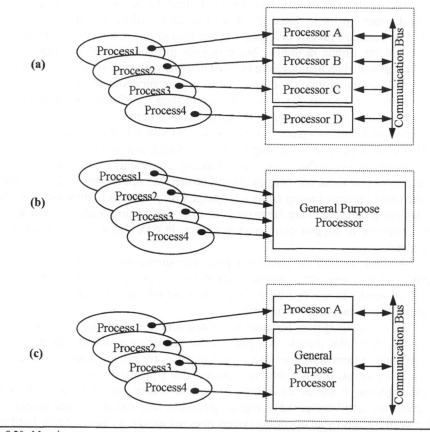

Figure 8.20: Mapping processes on processors: (a) processes mapped on multiple single-purpose processors, (b) processes mapped on one general-purpose processor, (c) processes mapped to a combination of single and general purpose processors.

still execute at the necessary rates. Different ways to map processes to processors are illustrated in Figure 8.20.

One method for sharing a processor among multiple processes is to manually rewrite the processes as a single sequential program. For example, consider our Hello World program from earlier. We could rewrite the concurrent process model as a sequential one by replacing the concurrent running of the *PrintHelloWorld* and *PrintHowAreYou* routines by the following:

```
I = 1; T = 0;
while (1) {
    Delay(I); T = T + I
    if X modulo T is 0 then call PrintHelloWorld
    if Y modulo T is 0 then call PrintHowAreYou
}
```

We would also modify each routine to have no parameter, no loop and no delay; each would merely print its message. If we wanted to reduce iterations, we could set $I$ to the greatest common divisor of $X$ and $Y$ rather than to one. Manually rewriting a model may be practical for simple examples, but extremely difficult for more complex examples. While some automated techniques have evolved to assist with such rewriting of concurrent processes into a sequential program, these techniques are not very commonly used.

Instead, a second, far more common method for sharing a processor among multiple processes is to rely on a multitasking operating system. An operating system is a low-level program that runs on a processor, responsible for scheduling processes, allocating storage, and interfacing to peripherals, among many other things. A *real-time operating system* (RTOS) is an operating system that allows one to specify constraints on the rate of processes, and that guarantees that these rate constraints will be met. In such an approach, we would describe our concurrent processes using either a language with processes built-in (such as Ada or Java), or a sequential programming language (like C or C++) using a library of routines that extends the language to support concurrent processes. POSIX threads were developed for the latter purpose.

A third method for sharing a processor among multiple processes is to convert the processes to a sequential program that includes a process scheduler right in the code. This method results in less overhead since it does not rely on an operating system but also yields code that may be harder to maintain.

In operating system terminology, a distinction is made between regular processes and threads. A regular process is a process that has its own virtual address space (stack, data, code) and system resources (e.g., open files). A thread, in contrast, is really a subprocess within a process. It is a lightweight process that typically has only a program counter, stack, and registers; it shares its address space and system resources with other threads. Since threads are small compared to regular processes, they can be created quickly, and switching between threads by an operating system does not incur very heavy costs. Furthermore, threads can share resources and variables so they can communicate quickly and efficiently. Throughout this chapter, we use the term *process* to denote a heavyweight process or lightweight thread.

## Suspending and Resuming Processes

If multiple processes are implemented using single-purpose processors, suspending or resuming them must be built as part of the processor's implementation. For example, the processors may be designed having an extra input. When this input is asserted, the processor is suspended, otherwise it is executing. If multiple processors are implemented using a single general-purpose processor, than suspending or resuming the processes must be built into the programming language or multitasking library that is used to describe the processes. In both cases, the programming language or library may rely on the underlying operating system to handle these operations.

## Joining a Process

If multiple processes are implemented using single-purpose processors, than for one process $X$ to join another process $Y$ would require building additional logic that will determine when $Y$ has reached its completion point and in response resume $X$. Therefore, in addition to having input signals that signal when a processor should suspend, each processor must have output signals that indicate when that processor is done executing its task. If multiple processors are implemented using a single general-purpose processors, join must be built into the language or multitasking library that is used to describe the processes. In both cases, the programming language or library may rely on the underlying operating system to handle this operation.

## Scheduling Processes

When multiple processes are implemented on a single general-purpose processor, the manner in which these processes are executed on a single shared processor plays an important role in meeting each process's timing requirements. This task of deciding when and for how long a processor executes a particular process is know as *process scheduling*. A *scheduler* is a special process that performs process scheduling. A scheduler can either be implemented as a *nonpreemptive scheduler* or *preemptive scheduler*. A nonpreemptive scheduler only decides on what process to select for execution, on the processor, once the currently executing process completes its execution. A preemptive scheduler is a scheduler that only allows a process to executed for a predetermined amount of time, called a *time quantum*, before preempting in order to allow another process to execute on the processor. This time quantum may be 10 to 100s of milliseconds long. The length of this time quantum greatly determines the response time of a system.

We have already defined a process state as being one of running, runnable, and blocked. We further assign to each process an integer valued *priority*. Without loss of generality, we assume that the process with highest priority is always selected first by the scheduler to be executed on the processor. A process's priority is often statically determined during the creation of the process and may be dynamically changed during execution.

A very simple scheduler is one that employs a *first in first out* FIFO scheduler. Using a FIFO scheduler, processes are added to the FIFO as they are created or become runnable, and processes are removed from the FIFO to be executed on the general-purpose processor whenever the time quantum of the currently executing process ends or the process is blocked.

Another type of a simple scheduler maintains a *priority queue* of processes that are in the runnable state. When the scheduler is ready to select a new process for execution, it simply selects the process with highest priority for execution. When a blocked process becomes runnable, it is added to the priority queue of the scheduler to be selected for execution at some later point. When multiple processes have equal priority, the scheduler uses a first-come first-served basis to select among the processes with equal priorities. When nonpreemptive scheduling is being used, this form of scheduling is called *priority scheduling*. When preemption is used, this form of scheduling is called *round-robin scheduling*.

Of course, the real question is how to assign priorities to processes. Before we do this, we have to have an understanding of how often each of the processes in our system need to

| Process | Period | Priority | Process | Deadline | Priority |
|---------|--------|----------|---------|----------|----------|
| A | 25 ms | 5 | G | 17 ms | 5 |
| B | 50 ms | 3 | H | 50 ms | 2 |
| C | 12 ms | 6 | I | 32 ms | 3 |
| D | 100 ms | 1 | J | 10 ms | 6 |
| E | 40 ms | 4 | K | 140 ms | 1 |
| F | 75 ms | 2 | L | 32 ms | 4 |
|   | **(a)** |   |   | **(b)** |   |

Figure 8.21: Priority assignment; (a) rate monotonic, (b) deadline monotonic priority assignment.

execute. Let us define the *period* of a process to be a repeating time interval during which that processes has to execute once. For example, if we assign to process *A* a period of 100 ms, then, process *A* must execute once every 100 ms. The period of a process is often obtained from the description of a system (e.g., a processes responsible for refreshing the screen on a display device must run 27 times per second, which equals a period of 37 ms). This notion of period is similar to the period of a sound wave. In *rate monotonic scheduling*, processes are assigned priorities such that those with shorter periods are given higher priorities. We have given an example of rate monotonic priority assignment in Figure 8.21(a). Here there are six processes, labeled *A* through *F*, with the corresponding periods given in the next column. We can assign priorities to these processes, as follows. We assign the to the process with the largest period, *D*, the smallest priority, one. Then we assign to the next process with the largest period, *F*, the next smallest priority, two, and so on.

In the previous discussion, we have assumed that the *execution deadline* of a process is equal to its period. The deadline of a process is defined as the time before which a process must run to completion. For example, if a process has a deadline of 20 ms, than it must complete 20 ms after it starts. Note that the actual execution time of a process is equal or less than its deadline. For example, process *A* may have an execution time of 5 ms, and a deadline of 20 ms. This means that once A is started, it can execute for 4 ms, than sleep for 14 ms, and resumed to execute for the additional 1 ms. Thus, the total time since that process started would be 4 + 14 + 1 = 19 ms, which is less than the deadline, therefore such scheduling would be valid. If we know that a deadline of a process, being scheduled, is less than its period, we can use *deadline monotonic priority assignment*. As in rate monotonic priority assignment, instead of the period, we use the deadline to assign priorities. In deadline monotonic scheduling, processes are assigned priorities such that those with shorter deadlines are given higher priorities. We have given an example of deadline monotonic priority assignment in Figure 8.21(b). Here there are six processes, labeled *G* through *L*, with the corresponding deadlines given in the next column. We can assign priorities to these processes, as follows. We assign the to the process with the largest deadline, *K*, the smallest priority, one. Then we assign to the next process with the largest period, *H*, the next smallest priority, two, and so on.

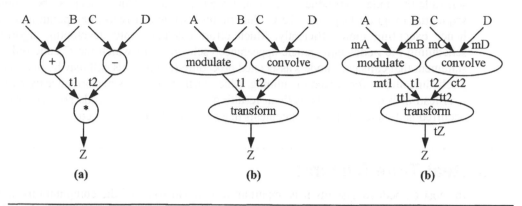

Figure 8.22: Simple dataflow models: (a) nodes representing arithmetic transformations, (b) nodes representing more complex transformations, (c) synchronous dataflow.

## 8.15 Dataflow Model

A derivative of the concurrent process model is the *dataflow model*. In a dataflow model, we describe system behavior as a set of nodes representing transformations, and a set of directed edges representing the flow of data from one node to another. Each node consumes data from its input edges, performs its transformation, and produces data on its output edge. All nodes may execute concurrently. For example, Figure 8.22(a) shows a dataflow model of the computation $Z = (A + B) * (C - D)$. Figure 8.22 (b) shows another dataflow model having more complex node transformations. Each edge may or not have data. Data present on an edge is called a token. When all input edges to a node have at least on token, the node may fire. When a node fires, it consumes one token from each input edge, executes its data transformation on the consumed token, and generates a token on its output edge. Note that multiple nodes may fire simultaneously, depending only on the presence of tokens.

Several commercial tools support graphical languages for the capture of dataflow models. These tools can automatically translate the model to a concurrent process model for implementation on a microprocessor. We can translate a dataflow model to a concurrent process model by converting each node to a process, and each edge to a channel. This concurrent process model can be implemented either by using a real-time operating system or by mapping the concurrent processes to a sequential program.

We observe that in many digital signal-processing systems, data flows into and out of the system at a fixed rate, and that a node may consume and produce many tokens per firing. We therefore created a variation of dataflow called synchronous dataflow. In this model, we annotate each input and output edge of a node with the number of tokens that node consumes and produces, respectively, during one firing. The advantage of this model is that, rather than translating to a concurrent process model for implementation, we can instead statically schedule the nodes to produce a sequential program model. This model can be captured in a sequential program language like C, thus running without a real-time operating system and hence executing more efficiently. Much effort has gone into developing algorithms for scheduling the nodes into "single-appearance" schedules, in which the C code only has one statement that calls each node's associated procedure (though this call may be in a loop). Such a schedule allows for procedure inlining, which further improves performance by reducing the overhead of procedure calls, without resulting in an explosion of code size that would have occurred had there been many statements that called each node's procedure.

## 8.16 Real-Time Systems

In most embedded systems it is important to perform some of the computations in a timely manner. For example, in the set-top box example, shown in Figure 8.12(b), at least 20 video frames need to be decoded within each second for the output to appear continues. Likewise, a digital cell phone decodes audio packets, converts digital signals to analog, and reproduces the voice in the speaker. All this takes place during strictly defined time periods, or else the sound of the remote speaker would appear to be delayed to the listener. Other systems that have stringent timing requirements include navigation and process control systems, assembly line monitoring systems, multimedia systems, and network systems, to name a few. Real-time systems are systems that are fundamentally composed of two or more concurrent processes that execute with stringent timing requirements and cooperate with each other in order to accomplish a common goal. In order for these concurrent processes to work together, it is essential to provide means for communication and synchronization among them. The concurrent process model addresses most of these requirements and is best suited for use in describing real-time systems. Thus, a system described using the concurrent process model with the additional stringent execution-timing requirement imposed on each process, is a real-time system. The additional timing requirement of real-time systems is met by adapting scheduling algorithms that guarantee timely execution of each process in the system as described earlier in this chapter.

We will discuss some operating systems that are designed to support real-time systems. Note that the term real-time system refers to a class of applications or embedded systems that exhibit the real-time characteristics and requirements mentioned above. Real-time operating systems, on the other hand, refer to underlying implementations or systems that supports real-time systems. In other words, real-time operating systems provide mechanisms, primitives, and guidelines for building embedded systems that are real-time in nature.

### Windows CE

Windows CE was built specifically for the embedded system and the appliance market providing a scalable real-time 32-bit platform that can be used in a wide variety of embedded systems and products. One of the benefits of using Windows CE as an RTOS that supports the Windows application-programming interface API, which has gained great popularity. This operating system provides a set of Internet browsing and serving services that make it suitable for systems that are designed to interface to the Internet. The Windows CE kernel allows for 256 priority levels per processes and implements preemptive priority scheduling. The size of the Windows CE kernel is 400 Kbytes.

## QNX

The QNX RTOS architecture consists of a real-time micro-kernel surrounded by a collection of optional processes (called resource managers) that provide POSIX and UNIX compatible system services. A micro-kernel is a name given to a kernel that only supports the most basic services and operations that typical operating system's provide. However, by including or excluding resource manager processes the developer can scale QNX down for ROM-based embedded systems, or scale it up to encompass hundreds of processors connected by various networking and communication technologies. Resource manager processes are modules that can be added or removed from the basic micro-kernel to best fit the functionality provided by the operating system to that needed by the application. The micro-kernel of QNX occupies less than 10 Kbytes and complies with POSIX real-time standard. QNX supports up to 32 priority levels per process and implements preemptive process scheduling using either FIFO, round robin, adaptive, or priority-driven scheduling.

# 8.17 Summary

We have introduced the concurrent process model as a well suitable model for describing a large class of embedded systems. Since much of an embedded system's behavior can be described as two or more concurrently executing tasks, the concurrent process model is well suited for describing them. The concurrent process model provides operations to create, terminate, suspend, resume, and join processes. The concurrent process model provides for communication and synchronization of processes, since both of these are essential for correctly implementing a system in terms of multiple processes. Processes must be able to share data and synchronize their execution in order to achieve a common goal. We have described communication protocols that use shared memory and send/receive primitives. In the shared memory scheme, two processes communicate by reading and writing variables that are visible to both. A mutex is used to lock for a period of time a region of shared data and only allow one process to update it. Synchronization primitives such as condition variable and monitors are also used to allow processes to signal various events to each other. We have looked at the implementation of concurrent processes as single- and general-purpose processes. We have defined a real-time system as a system composed of multiple concurrently executing processes each having stringent timing requirements. We have looked at two real-time operating systems and their features, namely the Windows CE and the QNX RTOS.

## 8.18 References and Further Reading

- Abraham Silberschatz and Peter B. Galvin. *Operating System Concepts*. Reading, MA: Addison-Wesley, 1995. Describes concepts in operating systems.
- Jean Bacon. *Concurrent Systems*. New York: Addison-Wesley, 1993. Describes concurrent systems including real-time, database, and distributed systems.
- Mukesh Singhal and Niranjan G. Shivaratri. *Advanced Concepts in Operating Systems*. New York: McGraw-Hill, 1994. Describes advanced concepts in operating systems and multitasking environments.
- Gary Cornell and Cay S. Horstmann. *Core Java*. Englewood Cliffs, NJ: Prentice Hall, 1997. This book describes the Java programming language, including the multithreaded programming.

## 8.19 Exercises

8.1 Define the following terms: finite-state machines, concurrent processes, real-time systems, and real-time operating system.

8.2 Briefly describe three computation models commonly used to describe embedded systems and/or their peripherals. For each model list two languages that can be used to capture it.

8.3 Describe the elevator UnitControl state machine in Figure 8.4 using the FSMD model definition <S, I, O, V, F, H, s0> given in this chapter. In other words, list the set of states (S), set of inputs (I), and so on.

8.4 Show how using the process create and join semantics one can emulate the procedure call semantics of a sequential programming model.

8.5 List three requirements of real-time systems and briefly describe each. Give examples of actual real-time systems to support your arguments.

8.6 Show why, in addition to ordered locking, two-phase locking is necessary in order to avoid deadlocks. Give an example and execution trace that results in deadlock if two-phase locking is not used.

8.7 Give pseudo-code for a pair of functions implementing the send and receive communication constructs. You may assume that mutex and condition variables are provided.

8.8 Show that the buffer size in the consumer-producer problem implemented in Figure 8.9 will never exceed one. Re-implement this problem, using monitors, to allow the size of the buffer to reach its maximum.

8.9 Given the processes A through F in Figure 8.21(a) where their deadline equals their period, determine whether they can be scheduled on time using a non-preemptive scheduler. Assume all processes begin at the same time and their execution times are as follows: A: 8 ms, B: 25 ms, C: 6 ms, D: 25 ms, E: 10 ms, F: 25 ms. Explain your answer by showing that each process either meets or misses its deadline.

# CHAPTER 9: *Control Systems*[3]

## 9.1    Introduction

*Control systems* represent a very common class of embedded systems. A control system seeks to make a physical system's output track a desired reference input, by setting physical system inputs. Perhaps the best-known example is an automobile cruise controller, which seeks to make a car's speed track a desired speed, by setting the car's throttle and brake inputs. Another example is a thermostat controller, which seeks to force a building's temperature to a desired temperature, by turning on the heater or air conditioner and adjusting the fan speed. More examples include controlling the speed of a spinning disk drive by varying the applied motor voltage, and maintaining the altitude of an aircraft by adjustment of the aileron and elevator positions. In contrast, digital cameras, video games, and cell phones are not examples of control systems, as they do not seek to track a reference input. Figure 9.1 illustrates the idea of tracking in a control system.

Designing control systems is not easy. Think of a car's cruise controller. It should never let the car speed deviate significantly from the reference speed specified by the driver. It must adjust to external factors like wind speed, road grade, tire pressure, brake conditions, and

---

[3] This chapter was contributed mainly by Jay Farrell of the University of California, Riverside.

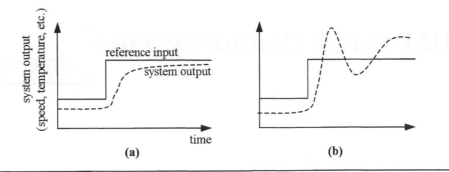

Figure 9.1: The goal of a control system is to force a physical system's output to track a reference input: (a) good tracking, (b) not-as-good tracking.

engine performance. It must correctly handle any situation presented to it, like accelerating from 20 mph to 50 mph while going down a steep hill. It should control the car in a way that is comfortable to the car's passengers, avoiding extremely fast acceleration or deceleration, and avoiding speed oscillations.

Control systems have been widely studied, and a rich theory for control system design exists. This chapter does not describe that theory in detail, since that requires a book in itself as well as a strong background in differential equations. Instead, we will introduce the basic concepts of control systems using a greatly simplified example. This introduction will lead up to PID controllers, which are extremely common. One of the goals of the chapter is to enable the reader to detect when an embedded system is an instance of a control system, so that the reader knows to turn to control theory (or to someone trained in control theory), rather than using ad hoc techniques, in those cases. However, in some cases, PID controllers can be used without extensive knowledge of control theory, and thus we will introduce some commonly used PID tuning techniques.

## 9.2   Open-Loop and Closed-Loop Control Systems

### Overview

Control systems minimally consist of several parts, illustrated in Figure 9.2:

1. The *plant*, also known as the process, is the physical system to be controlled. An automobile is an example of a plant, as in Figure 9.2(a).
2. The *output* is the particular physical system aspect that we are interested in controlling. The speed of an automobile is an example of an output.
3. The *reference* input is the desired value that we want to see for the output. The desired speed set by an automobile's driver is an example of a reference input.

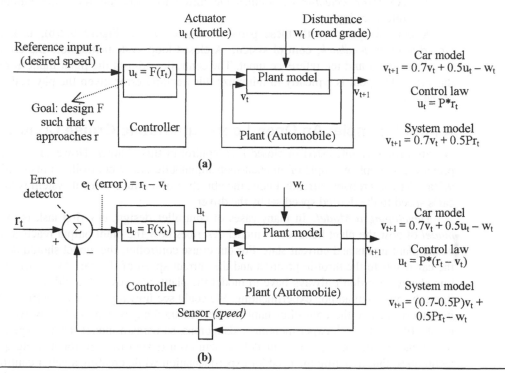

Figure 9.2: Control systems and automobile cruise controller example: (a) open-loop control, (b) closed-loop control.

4. The *actuator* is the device that we use to control the input to the plant. A stepper motor controlling a car's throttle position is an example of an actuator.
5. The *controller* is the system that we use to compute the input to the plant such that we achieve the desired output from the plant.
6. A *disturbance* is an additional undesirable input to the plant imposed by the environment that may cause the plant output to differ from what we would have expected based on the plant input. Wind and road grade are examples of disturbances that can alter the speed of an automobile.

A control system with these components, configured as in Figure 9.2(a), is referred to as an *open-loop*, or *feed-forward*, control system. The controller reads the reference input, and then computes a setting for the actuator. The actuator modifies the input to the plant, which, along with any disturbance, results some time later in a change in the plant output. In an open-loop system, the controller does not measure how well the plant output matches the reference input. Thus, open-loop control is best suited to situations where the plant output responds very predictably to the plant input (i.e., the model is accurate and disturbance effects are minimal).

Many control systems possess some additional parts, as illustrated in Figure 9.2(b):

1. A *sensor* measures the plant output.

2. An *error detector* determines the difference between the plant output and the reference input.

A control system with these parts, configured as in Figure 9.2(b), is known as a *closed-loop*, or *feedback*, control system. A closed-loop system monitors the error between the plant output and the reference input. The controller adjusts the plant input in response to this error. The goal is typically to minimize this tracking error given the physical constraints of the system.

## A First Example: An Open-Loop Automobile Cruise Controller

We are primarily interested in closed-loop control in this chapter. However, let us begin by providing a simple example of an open-loop automobile cruise controller, illustrated in Figure 9.2(a). As you probably already know, the objective of a cruise-control system is to match the car's speed to the desired speed set by the driver.

*Developing a Model:* In many cases of controller design, our first task is to develop a *model* of how the plant behaves. A model describes how the plant output reacts as a function of the plant inputs and current state. For our cruise controller, the model should describe how the car reacts to the throttle position and the current speed of the car. As we will see later in this chapter, we don't always have to model the plant, and instead could design a controller through somewhat ad hoc experimenting. We could see how a particular controller works and iteratively modify the controller until the desired tracking is achieved. However, for many plants, like a car, such experimenting is dangerous, so using a model for the experimenting is preferable. Furthermore, with a model, we can even design the controller using quantitative techniques, thus avoiding the need for experimentation while creating a better controller.

The car has a throttle input whose position u can vary from 0 to 45 degrees. We decide to begin by test-driving the car on a flat road and taking measurements. Suppose that with the car traveling steadily at 50 mph and the throttle set at 30 degrees, we quickly change the throttle to 40 degrees, and measure the car's speed every second thereafter, until the car's speed finally becomes constant. Based on the measured speed data, suppose we determine that the following equation describes the car's speed as a function of the current speed and throttle position:

$$v_{t+1} = 0.7v_t + 0.5u_t$$

Here, $v_t$ is the car's current speed, $u_t$ is the throttle position, and $v_{t+1}$ is the car's speed one second later. For example, $v_2 = 0.7v_1 + 0.5u_1 = 0.7 * 50 + 0.5 * 40 = 55$. Suppose further that we try a variety of other speeds and throttle positions, and we find that the above equation holds for all those other situations. Therefore, we decide that the above equation is a suitable first model for the car over the range of speed that is of interest. Please note that this is not actually a reasonable model of a car, and is instead used for illustrative purposes only.

*Developing a Controller:* Now let's turn our attention away from modeling the car and toward designing the cruise controller for the car. Suppose the only input to the controller is the desired speed $r_t$, as shown in Figure 9.2(a). The controller's behavior is a function $F$ of the commanded speed, so that the throttle position is $u_t = F(r_t)$. The control designer can choose

$F$ to be as simple or as complex a function as desired. Let's start by assuming that $F$ is a simple linear function of the form:

$$u_t = F(r_t)$$

$$u_t = P * r_t$$

Here, $P$ is a constant that the designer must specify. This linear proportional controller makes intuitive sense since it increases the throttle angle as the desired speed increases. In other words, the throttle angle is proportional to the desired speed.

Given this proportional control function, we can now write an equation that models the combined controller and plant, which will help us determine what value to use for $P$:

$$v_{t+1} = 0.7v_t + 0.5u_t$$

$$u_t = P * r_t$$

$$v_{t+1} = 0.7v_t + 0.5P * r_t$$

The design goal for the cruise controller is to keep the actual speed of the car $v$ equal to the desired speed $r$ at all times. Of course, it is impossible to keep these two values equal *at all times*, since the car will require some time to react to any changes the controller makes to the throttle angle. For example, the car cannot accelerate from 0 to 50 mph instantaneously. Rather, from the moment the controller sets the throttle, a car will take several seconds to accelerate to its final speed. Therefore, the design goal can be relaxed to that of forcing the car's actual speed $v$ to be equal to the desired speed $r$ in *steady state*. Steady state means that if the controller sets the throttle to a constant value, and nothing else changes, then at some time in the future, $v$ will also not change. So in steady state, $v_{t+1} = v_t$. Let's refer to this steady-state velocity as $v_{ss}$. Substituting $v_{ss}$ for both $v_{t+1}$ and $v_t$ above, we get:

$$v_{t+1} = 0.7v_t + 0.5P * r_t$$

$$let, v_{t+1} = v_t = v_{ss}$$

$$v_{ss} = 0.7v_{ss} + 0.5P * r_t$$

$$v_{ss} - 0.7v_{ss} = 0.5P * r$$

$$v_{ss} = 1.67P * r_t$$

So, if we want $v_{ss} = r_t$, we merely need to set $P = 1/1.67 = 0.6$. We have now designed our first controller:

$$u_t = F(r_t)$$

$$u_t = P * r_t$$

$$u_t = 0.6r_t$$

The controller merely multiplies the desired speed $r_t$ by $0.6P$ to determine the desired throttle angle.

| Time (t) | $v_t$ | $v_t$ for w = +5 | $v_t$ for w = –5 |
|---|---|---|---|
| 0 | 20.00 | 20.00 | 20.00 |
| 1 | 29.00 | 24.00 | 34.00 |
| 2 | 35.30 | 26.80 | 43.80 |
| 3 | 39.71 | 28.76 | 50.66 |
| 4 | 42.80 | 30.13 | 55.46 |
| 5 | 44.96 | 31.09 | 58.82 |
| 6 | 46.47 | 31.76 | 61.18 |
| 7 | 47.53 | 32.24 | 62.82 |
| 8 | 48.27 | 32.56 | 63.98 |
| 9 | 48.79 | 32.80 | 64.78 |
| 10 | 49.15 | 32.96 | 65.35 |
| 11 | 49.41 | 33.07 | 65.74 |
| 12 | 49.58 | 33.15 | 66.02 |
| (a) | (b) | | (c) |

Figure 9.3: Open-loop cruise controller trying to accelerate the car from 20 mph to 50 mph, when the grade is: (a) 0%, (b) +5%, (c) –5%.

***Analyzing Our First Controller:*** Let's analyze how well this controller achieves its goal. Two issues are of interest: (1) what is the transient behavior when *r* changes; and (2) what effects do disturbances have on the system? The equation representing the entire system is:

$$v_{t+1} = 0.7v_t + 0.5*0.6r_t$$

$$v_{t+1} = 0.7v_t + 0.3r_t$$

To see how the system behaves, suppose a car is traveling steadily at 20 mph at time $t = 0$, at which time the desired speed $r_0$ is set to 50. Given the form of our controller above, we see that the controller will set the throttle position to 0.6 * 50 = 30 degrees, and hold it there until $r_t$ changes again. We can "simulate" the system by evaluating the above equation for various time values (a spreadsheet program makes this task easy).[4] Figure 9.3(a) illustrates the car's speed over time. We see that (in the absence of disturbances) the controller does well, approaching the desired speed of 50 mph to within 0.3% in 10 seconds.

***Considering Disturbances:*** Suppose now that additional testing of the car is performed on roads with grades w varying from –5 degrees, corresponding to downhill roads, to +5

---

[4] Note that the simulation evaluates the controller performance relative to a model. For the simulation results to accurately predict the results of the future control experiments with the actual hardware, the model must be accurate. However, since there is expense involved with developing the model, there is always a trade off and art to determining when the model is sufficiently accurate to complete the analytic portion of the design. Tuning of the design typically occurs during the initial hardware experiments to accommodate differences between the model and hardware.

Embedded System Design

degrees, corresponding to uphill roads. The car goes faster downhill and slower uphill. Suppose road grade is incorporated into the earlier model for the car alone as follows:

$$v_{t+1} = 0.7v_t + 0.5u_t - w_t$$

Since the open-loop controller has no means of sensing the road grade or its effect on the speed, this disturbance will obviously result in speed error when driving downhill or uphill. Figure 9.3(b) displays the behavior of the car with the open loop controller when driving up a +5% grade, and Figure 9.3(c) when driving down a –5% grade. The speed error at time $t = 12$ is about $50 - 33 = 17$ mph in the uphill case, and about $50 - 66 = -16$ mph in the downhill case. This error is quite bad! Closed-loop control systems, which will be discussed shortly, can help reduce errors caused by disturbances.

*Determining Performance Parameters:* Using the model of the system created earlier, a designer can quickly determine various important performance parameters. Assume that the initial speed is $v_0$, the desired speed is $r_0$, and the disturbance is $w_0$, then we can develop an equation for $v_t$ as follows:

$$v_1 = 0.7v_0 + 0.5P * r_0 - w_0$$

$$v_2 = 0.7 * (0.7v_0 + 0.5P * r_0 - w_0) + 0.5P * r_0 - w_0$$

$$v_2 = 0.7 * 0.7v_0 + (0.7 + 1.0) * 0.5P * r_0 - (0.7 + 1.0) * w_0$$

$$v_t = 0.7^t * v_0 + (0.7^{t-1} + 0.7^{t-2} + \ldots + 0.7 + 1.0)(0.5P * r_0 - w_0)$$

The last equation shows three important points. First, in the model $v_{t+1} = 0.7v_t + 0.5u_t - w_t$, let's refer to the coefficient of $v_t$ as $\alpha$; in this case $\alpha = 0.7$. Looking at the last equation, we see that $\alpha$ determines the *rate of decay of the effect of the initial speed*. In other words, a bigger $\alpha$ will result in the car taking longer to reach its desired speed. Notice that, in open loop control, the controller gain $P$ has no effect on this rate of decay. In closed-loop control, it will.

Also note that if $|\alpha| > 1$, then $v_t$ would grow without bound as time increased, since $\alpha$ is being raised to the power of $t$. Furthermore, note that a negative $\alpha$ will result in an oscillating speed. Again, in closed-loop control, we will be able to change $\alpha$.

Second, the sensitivity of the speed to the *disturbance* is not altered by the open loop controller.

Third, if our assumed model were not correct, then this model error would cause the steady state speed, that results from the open loop controller $u = P_r$, to not equal the desired speed.

## A Second Example: A Closed-Loop Automobile Cruise Controller

We can reduce the speed error caused by disturbances, like grade or wind, by enabling the controller to detect speed errors and correct for them. To detect speed errors, we introduce a speed sensor into the system, as shown in Figure 9.2(b), to measure the car's speed. We also introduce a device that outputs the difference between the desired speed $r_t$ and the actual speed $v_t$. This difference is the speed error $e_t = r_t - v_t$. Note that the penalties for this closed-loop approach are the cost of the sensor, added controller complexity, and the addition of sensor noise. The benefits will be the ability to change the rate of response, reduction of sensitivity to disturbances, and reduction of sensitivity to model error. If we select the form of the controller to be linear and proportional as before, namely $u_t = P * (r_t - v_t)$, then:

$$v_{t+1} = 0.7v_t + 0.5u_t - w,$$

$$v_{t+1} = 0.7v_t + 0.5P * (r_t - v_t) - w_t$$

$$v_{t+1} = (0.7 - 0.5P) * v_t + 0.5P * r_t - w_t$$

Note that the closed-loop controller results in $\alpha = 0.7 - 0.5P$, and remember that $\alpha$ determines the rate of decay of the effect of the initial speed. Therefore, by choice of the parameter $P$, the control system designer can alter the rate of convergence of the closed-loop system. However, we cannot make $P$ arbitrarily large, because if the designer selects a value of $P$ such that $|0.7 - 0.5P| > 1.0$, then the speed will not converge to the commanded speed, but instead grow without bound. The constraint $|0.7 - 0.5P| < 1.0$ is necessary for the system to be stable. This stability constraint translates to the following:

$$0.7 - 0.5P < 1.0$$

$$0.7 - 0.5P > -1.0$$

$$-0.5P < 0.3$$

$$-0.5P > -1.7$$

$$P > -0.6$$

$$P < 3.4$$

$$\text{so, } -0.6 < P < 3.4$$

We could set $P$ close to 3.4 to obtain the fastest decay of the initial condition. However, remember that a negative $\alpha$ will cause oscillation, which is something we'd usually like to avoid. To keep $\alpha$ positive, we need:

$$0.7 - 0.5P >= 0$$

$$-0.5P >= -0.7$$

$$P <= 1.4$$

So the fastest rate of convergence to steady state without oscillation, known as deadbeat control, occurs when $P = 1.4$.

A control design goal is to achieve $v$ equal to $r$ in steady state, meaning $v_{t+1} = v_t = v_{ss} = r$. To analyze the steady-state response, we again assume the commanded speed and disturbance have the constant values $r_0$ and $w_0$. Substituting into the earlier system equation yields:

$$v_{ss} = (0.7 - 0.5P) * v_{ss} + 0.5P * r_0 - w_0$$

$$(1 - 0.7 + 0.5P) * v_{ss} = 0.5P * r_0 - w_0$$

Embedded System Design

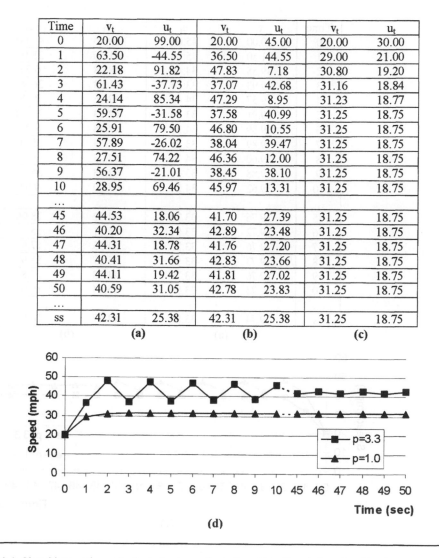

| Time | $v_t$ | $u_t$ | $v_t$ | $u_t$ | $v_t$ | $u_t$ |
|---|---|---|---|---|---|---|
| 0 | 20.00 | 99.00 | 20.00 | 45.00 | 20.00 | 30.00 |
| 1 | 63.50 | -44.55 | 36.50 | 44.55 | 29.00 | 21.00 |
| 2 | 22.18 | 91.82 | 47.83 | 7.18 | 30.80 | 19.20 |
| 3 | 61.43 | -37.73 | 37.07 | 42.68 | 31.16 | 18.84 |
| 4 | 24.14 | 85.34 | 47.29 | 8.95 | 31.23 | 18.77 |
| 5 | 59.57 | -31.58 | 37.58 | 40.99 | 31.25 | 18.75 |
| 6 | 25.91 | 79.50 | 46.80 | 10.55 | 31.25 | 18.75 |
| 7 | 57.89 | -26.02 | 38.04 | 39.47 | 31.25 | 18.75 |
| 8 | 27.51 | 74.22 | 46.36 | 12.00 | 31.25 | 18.75 |
| 9 | 56.37 | -21.01 | 38.45 | 38.10 | 31.25 | 18.75 |
| 10 | 28.95 | 69.46 | 45.97 | 13.31 | 31.25 | 18.75 |
| ... | | | | | | |
| 45 | 44.53 | 18.06 | 41.70 | 27.39 | 31.25 | 18.75 |
| 46 | 40.20 | 32.34 | 42.89 | 23.48 | 31.25 | 18.75 |
| 47 | 44.31 | 18.78 | 41.76 | 27.20 | 31.25 | 18.75 |
| 48 | 40.41 | 31.66 | 42.83 | 23.66 | 31.25 | 18.75 |
| 49 | 44.11 | 19.42 | 41.81 | 27.02 | 31.25 | 18.75 |
| 50 | 40.59 | 31.05 | 42.78 | 23.83 | 31.25 | 18.75 |
| ... | | | | | | |
| ss | 42.31 | 25.38 | 42.31 | 25.38 | 31.25 | 18.75 |
| | **(a)** | | **(b)** | | **(c)** | |

**(d)**

Figure 9.4: Closed-loop cruise controller trying to accelerate from 20 to 50 mph, ignoring disturbance, where $v$ is car speed and $u$ is throttle position: (a) invalid data when throttle saturation is ignored, (b) valid data for $P = 3.3$, (c) valid data for $P = 1.0$, (d) plot for $P = 3.3$ and $P = 1.0$.

$$v_{ss} = (0.5P / (0.3 + 0.5P)) * r_0 - (1.0 / (0.3 + 0.5P)) * w_0$$

From this equation, we see that we can reduce the effect of the disturbance $w_0$ by making the coefficient $(1.0 / (0.3 + 0.5P))$ less than 1, meaning that $P > 1.4$. But, remember that $P > 1.4$ will cause oscillation!

| Time | $v_t$ | $u_t$ | $v_t$ | $u_t$ |
|------|-------|-------|-------|-------|
| 0 | 20.00 | 45.00 | 20.00 | 45.00 |
| 1 | 31.50 | 45.00 | 41.50 | 28.05 |
| 2 | 39.55 | 34.49 | 48.08 | 6.35 |
| 3 | 39.93 | 33.24 | 41.83 | 26.97 |
| 4 | 39.57 | 34.42 | 47.76 | 7.38 |
| 5 | 39.91 | 33.30 | 42.13 | 25.99 |
| 6 | 39.59 | 34.37 | 47.48 | 8.31 |
| 7 | 39.89 | 33.35 | 42.39 | 25.10 |
| 8 | 39.60 | 34.32 | 47.23 | 9.15 |
| 9 | 39.88 | 33.40 | 42.63 | 24.30 |
| 10 | 39.62 | 34.27 | 47.00 | 9.91 |
| ... | | | | |
| 45 | 39.76 | 33.78 | 44.52 | 18.09 |
| 46 | 39.72 | 33.91 | 45.21 | 15.82 |
| 47 | 39.76 | 33.78 | 44.55 | 17.97 |
| 48 | 39.73 | 33.91 | 45.17 | 15.92 |
| 49 | 39.76 | 33.79 | 44.58 | 17.87 |
| 50 | 39.73 | 33.90 | 45.14 | 16.02 |
| ... | | | | |
| ss | 39.74 | 33.85 | 44.87 | 16.92 |
| **(a)** | | | **(b)** | |

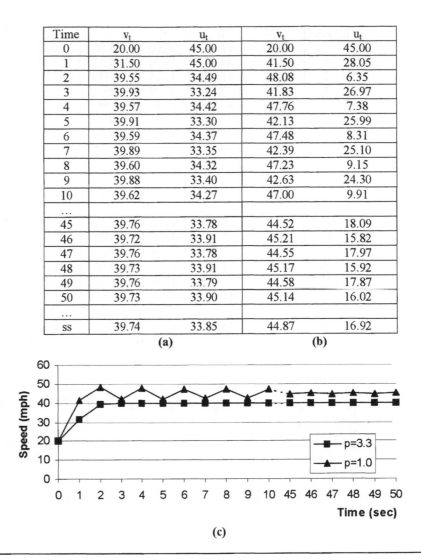

(c)

Figure 9.5: The same closed-loop cruise controller, trying to accelerate from 20 to 50 mph, this time in the presence of a disturbance of a grade equal to: (a) +5%, (b) –5%, (c) graphical illustration of (a) and (b).

Also, if we want $v_{ss}$ to be approximately equal to $r_0$, then we need to select $P$ as large as possible, so that the term multiplying $r_0$, namely, $(0.5P / (0.3 + 0.5P))$, is approximately equal to 1. There is no value of $P$ in the range $-0.6 < P < 3.4$ for which this coefficient equals 1, so perfect steady state tracking is not achievable by proportional control for this example. The best we can do to minimize steady-state error, therefore, is to set $P$ reasonably close to 3.4. Note that the designer must select $P$ to balance the trade-offs between the conflicting constraints of convergence rate, disturbance rejection, and steady-state tracking accuracy. To continue, assuming that steady-state tracking is of primary performance, let $P = 3.3$.

We have now designed our second controller. The controller sets its output, the throttle angle $u_t$, to 3.3 times its input, as follows:

$$u_t = 3.3 * (r_t - v_t)$$

This controller will result in oscillation, but that's the price we pay to achieve the smallest steady-state error. Notice that the input to our second controller is the speed error, in contrast to our first controller, whose input was the desired speed. Let's analyze how well this second controller achieves its input-tracking goal by "simulating" the system, namely, by iterating the closed-loop equation over the time range of interest (again, a spreadsheet helps with such simulation). Initially, assume an initial speed of 20 mph, a grade $w$ of 0, and then a desired speed setting of 50 mph. Figure 9.4(a) shows the speed $v_t$ and the throttle position $u_t$ from time 0 to 50 seconds. Notice that the controller generates throttle angle commands outside of the range of possible throttle positions of 0 to 45 degrees. Thus, the data in Figure 9.4(a) is not valid. Instead, we must treat any value less then 0 as 0, and greater than 45 as 45. The throttle is said to saturate at 0 and 45.

Figure 9.4(b) shows the speed and throttle position when we include this saturation in the model. Figure 9.4(d) shows the speed versus time graphically. Notice that, for $P = 3.3$ ($a = 0.7$ $-0.5P = -0.95$), the speed oscillates for many seconds until it finally reaches a steady-state speed of 42.31 mph. Recall that a negative a causes such oscillation. Intuitively, this oscillation means the cruise controller is accelerating too hard when the current speed is less than the desired speed, thus overshooting the desired speed. Also notice that the steady-state speed is not 50 mph, but rather 42.31 mph, representing an error of about 8 mph. The simulated responses in Figure 9.4(b) and (d) thus confirm our earlier analysis of oscillation and steady-state error.

Since oscillation of the car speed could be uncomfortable to the car's passengers, we would like to reduce or eliminate the oscillation. We can reduce the oscillation by decreasing the constant $P$ in the controller. For example, Figure 9.4(c) shows the speed and throttle positions for $P = 1.0$. Figure 9.4(b) shows the speed graphically. The result of the smaller $P$ is that oscillation is eliminated and convergence time is reduced; however, the steady-state speed is only 31.25 mph, representing a large error of nearly 19 mph.

We have learned an important lesson of control, namely, that system-performance objectives, such as reducing oscillation, obtaining fast convergence, and reducing steady-state error, often compete with one another.

Recall that a motivation for using closed-loop control was to reduce the speed error caused by disturbances like grade. Figure 9.5(a) and (b) show the effects of +5% and –5% grades, respectively, using $P = 3.3$ in the controller. Figure 9.5(c) shows the results for both situations graphically. Notice that steady-state errors of about 10 mph and 5 mph are not too much different than the 7 mph error with a 0% grade, but are much improved over the 17 mph and –16 mph errors that resulted from the open-loop controller in Figure 9.3(b) and (c). Thus, the goal of reducing the sensitivity to disturbances has been achieved, involving a trade-off of

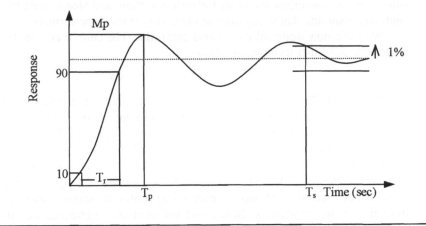

Figure 9.6: Control system response performance metrics.

having introduced additional steady-state error when there is no disturbance, and of having introduced oscillation.

To allow more control objectives to be satisfied with fewer trade-offs, the complexity of the controller will have to increase, as will be described subsequently.

## 9.3 General Control Systems and PID Controllers

Having seen the above examples, we can now discuss control systems more generally. This section discusses objectives of control design, modeling real physical systems, and the PID approach to controller design.

### Control Objectives

The objective of control system design is to make a physical system behave in a useful fashion, in particular, by causing its output to track a desired reference input even in the presence of measurement noise, model error, and disturbances. Satisfaction of this objective can be evaluated through several metrics specified relative to a step change in the control systems input:

1. *Stability*: The main idea of stability is that all variables in the control system remain bounded. Preferably, the error variables, like desired output minus plant output, would converge to zero. Stability is of primary importance, since without stability, all of the other objectives are immaterial.

2. *Performance*: Assuming stability, performance describes how well the output tracks a change in the reference input. Performance has several aspects, illustrated in Figure 9.6.

a) *Rise time $T_r$* is the time required for the response to change from 10% to 90% of the distance from the initial value to the final value, for the first time. Different percentages may be of interest in different applications.

b) *Peak time $T_p$* is the time required to reach the first peak of the response.

c) *Overshoot $M_p$* is the percentage amount by which the peak of the response exceeds the final value.

d) *Settling time $T_s$* is the time required for the system to settle down to within 1% of its final value. A different percentage may be of interest in different applications.

3. *Disturbance rejection*: Disturbances are undesired effects on the system behavior caused by the environment. A designer cannot eliminate disturbances, but can reduce their impact on system behavior.

4. *Robustness*: The plant model is a simplification of a physical system, and is never perfect. Robustness requires that the stability and performance of the controlled system should not be significantly affected by the presence of model errors.

## Modeling Real Physical Systems

An essential prelude to control system design is accurate modeling of the behavior of the plant. The controller will be designed based on this plant model. If the plant model is inaccurate, then the controller will be controlling the wrong plant. There are two key features that real systems display that our earlier example did not consider.

The first feature of real physical systems is that they typically respond as continuous variables and as continuous functions of time. In the cruise-controller example, we assumed that the car's speed would change exactly one second after a change in the throttle. Obviously, cars do not synchronize their reactions to the discrete time intervals, but instead they are continuously reacting. Therefore, the plant dynamic model is usually a differential equation. There are methods for determining a discrete time model that is equivalent — only at the sampling instants — to the plant differential equation. Between the sampling instants, the discrete time model tells the designer nothing about the continuous time response. Therefore, the sampling period must be selected much smaller than the system's reaction time so that the system cannot change significantly between sampling instants. The 1 second sample time used in the earlier examples of this chapter is not meant to be realistic. See also the subsequent discussion of aliasing.

The second feature of real physical systems is that they are typically much more complex than any model we create. The model will not include all nonlinear effects, all system states, or all state interactions. For example, the response of the speed of a car to a change in throttle depends on spark advance, manifold pressure, engine speed, and additional variables. Therefore, any model is a simplified abstraction. Modeling and control design is an iterative process, where the model of the actual plant is improved at each iteration to include key features identified during the prior iteration. Then the controller is improved to properly address the improved model. Linear models usually suffice when the variables of the model have a small operating range.

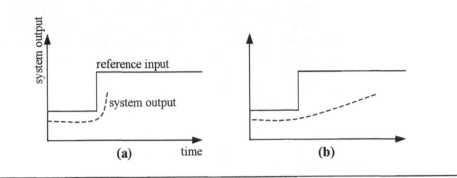

Figure 9.7: A better controller could be designed if it could predict the future. Both controllers have forced the output halfway to the desired value. But the controller for (a) should start to reduce the plant input, while the controller for (b) should have increased the input earlier. Derivative control seeks to satisfy this prediction goal.

## Controller Design

The earlier closed loop example showed that increasing $P$ caused the steady state speed $v_{ss}$ to better match the desired speed $r$, and to resist tracking error caused by disturbances. A controller that multiplies the tracking error by a constant is known as using *proportional control*. To summarize, when proportional control is applied to a first order plant, the resulting closed loop model is similar to our particular cruise-controller model of:

$$v_{t+1} = (0.7 - 0.5P) * v_t + 0.5P * r_t - w_t$$

Therefore, the controller parameter $P$ affects transient response, steady state tracking error, and disturbance rejection. However, we saw that adjusting $P$ resulted in trade-offs among these control objectives. We could reduce oscillation and improve convergence, but at the expense of worse steady-state error, and vice versa.

*PD Control:* More degrees of freedom must be introduced into the controller design to allow greater flexibility in the optimization of the trade-offs involved in the closed loop performance. We can achieve this by using a proportional plus derivative controller. In proportional plus derivative control (*PD control*), the form of the control law is:

$$u_t = P * e_t + D * (e_t - e_{t-1})$$

Here, $e_t = r_t - v_t$ is the measured speed error, and $e_t - e_{t-1}$ is the derivative of the error (meaning the change in error over time). $P$ is the proportional constant, and $D$ is the derivative constant.

Intuitively, the derivative term is being used to predict the future. Consider Figure 9.7. The two plots show two different responses. In (a), we as humans can see that the system output is approaching the reference input quickly, and so we should probably reduce the plant input to prevent overshoot. In (b), we can see that the output is increasing very slowly, so we

Embedded System Design

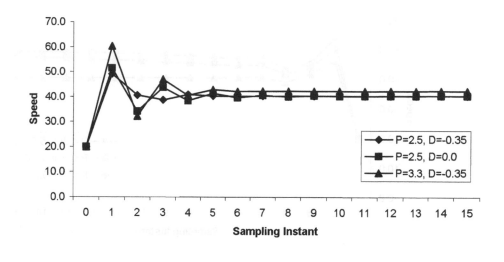

Figure 9.8: PD step response.

probably should increase the plant input, and actually should have increased it earlier. We see these things because we predict the system's future behavior will be similar to its past behavior, a good assumption when dealing with physical systems. The derivative term, which looks at the difference in the output between two successive time instances, can be used to achieve similar prediction, and thus can cause the controller to react accordingly. In the language of control systems, this is referred to as *adding lead*.

PD control implies a more complex controller, since the controller must keep track of the error derivative. However, PD control will give us more flexibility in achieving our control objectives. We can see this by deriving the equation for the complete cruise-controller system using PD control, just as we did for the simpler P controller:

$$v_{t+1} = 0.7v_t + 0.5u_t - w_t$$

$$let\ u_t = P * e_t + D * (e_t - e_{t-1})$$

$$and\ e_t = r_t - v_t$$

$$v_{t+1} = 0.7v_t + 0.5 * (P * (r_t - v_t) + D * ((r_t - v_t) - (r_{t-1} - v_{t-1}))) - w_t$$

$$...$$

$$v_{t+1} = (0.7 - 0.5 * (P + D)) * v_t + 0.5D * v_{t-1} + 0.5 * (P + D) * r_t - 0.5D * r_{t-1} - w_t$$

When the reference input and disturbance are constant, the steady-state speed is again:

$$v_{ss} = (0.5P / (1 - 0.7 + 0.5P)) * r$$

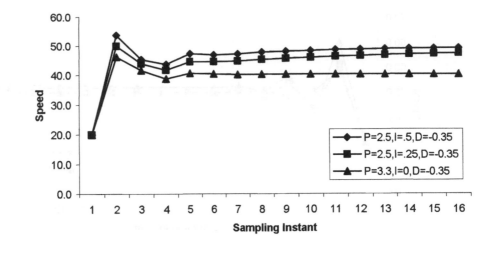

Figure 9.9: PID step response.

This is the same as for proportional control, since in steady state the effect of the derivative term is zero.

The characteristics of convergence of the tracking error e to its steady-state value is determined by the roots of the polynomial: $z^2 - (0.7 - 0.5 * (P + D)) * z - 0.5D = 0$, under the assumption that the magnitude of the roots (they may be complex) is less than 1. Therefore, adding the derivative term allows the transient response to be modified without affecting the steady state tracking or disturbance rejection characteristics. Figure 9.8 plots step responses for various values of $P$ and $D$. Note that the steady state value of the response is affected by $P$, not $D$. The parameter $D$ does significantly affect the character of the transient response, in other words, the rate of convergence and the oscillation. The dashed-dotted line should be compared with the response in Figure 9.4, for which $P = 3.3$ and for which we can treat $D = 0$. In summary, by building a slightly more complex controller, namely, a PD controller, which considers not just the error input but also the derivative of the error input, we can adjust the transient response and the steady-state error independently by adjusting $D$ and $P$.

***PI and PID Control:*** In proportional plus integral control (*PI control*), the form of the control law is:

$$u_t = P * e_t + I * (e_0 + e_1 + \ldots + e_t)$$

The integral term sums up the error over time. Let's consider this term intuitively. Look at Figure 9.4(d) again. Notice that both controllers achieve a steady-state value that is below the desired value of 50 mph. As humans, we can see that we should just increase the plant input again until this error goes to zero. In other words, as long as there's error, we shouldn't rest! The integral term achieves this goal by summing the error over time, we ensure that the

Embedded System Design

error will eventually go to zero, since otherwise the controller output would increase forever. In other words, with integral control, the steady state will not even exist unless $e_{ss} = 0$, since otherwise the integral term would be increasing. Therefore, if values of $P$ and $I$ are found such that the system is stable, then for a constant input the steady state tracking error is zero.

We can combine proportional, integral, and derivative control as follows:

$$u_t = P * e_t + I * (e_0 + e_1 + \ldots + e_t) + D * ((e_1 - e_0) + (e_2 - e_1) + \ldots + (e_t - e_{t-1}))$$

This is known as *PID control*. The controller design goal is then to select the PID gains to achieve the desired stable transient behavior. Figure 9.9 plots step responses for three different values of PID. The main effect of varying $I$ is that as $I$ is increased, the rate at which the response converges to its desired value increases; however, the $I$ term does also affect the nature of the transient. If $I$ is increased too much, then the response can become oscillatory or even unstable.

PID controllers are extremely common in embedded control systems. Several tools exist to help a designer choose the appropriate PID values for a given plant model. Off-the-shelf IC and cores with settable $P$, $I$, and $D$ values, called PID controllers, are available to accomplish PID control.

## 9.4 Software Coding of a PID Controller

A PID controller can be implemented quite easily in software. Consider writing a program in C to implement a PID controller. It might consist of a main function with the following loop:

```
void main()
{
    double sensor_value, actuator_value, error_current;
    PID_DATA pid_data;
    PidInitialize(&pid_data);
    while (1) {
        sensor_value = SensorGetValue();
        reference_value = ReferenceGetValue();
        actuator_value =
         PidUpdate(&pid_data,sensor_value,reference_value);
        ActuatorSetValue(actuator_value);
    }
}
```

We create the main function to loop forever. During each iteration, we first read the plant output sensor, read the current desired reference input value, and pass this information to function *PidUpdate*. *PidUpdate* determines the value of the plant actuator, which we then use to set the actuator. Note that reading the sensor will typically involve an analog-to-digital converter, and setting the actuator will involve a digital-to-analog converter; the details of these functions are omitted.

Our *PID_DATA* data structure has the following form:

```
typedef struct PID_DATA {
    double Pgain, Dgain, Igain;
    double sensor_value_previous; // find the derivative
    double error_sum; // cumulative error
}
```

So *PID_DATA* holds the three gain constants, which we assume are set in the *PidInitialize* function. It also holds the previous sensor value, which will be used for the derivative term. Finally, it holds the cumulative sum of error values, used for the integral term.

We can now define our *PidUpdate* function as follows:

```
double PidUpdate(PID_DATA *pid_data, double sensor_value,
                 double reference_value)
{
    double Pterm, Iterm, Dterm;
    double error, difference;

    error = reference_value - sensor_value;
    Pterm = pid_data->Pgain * error; /* proportional term*/
    pid_data->error_sum += error; /* current + cumulative*/
    // the integral term
    Iterm = pid_data->Igain * pid_data->error_sum;
    difference = pid_data->sensor_value_previous -
                 sensor_value;
    // update for next iteration
    pid_data->sensor_value_previous = sensor_value;
    // the derivative term
    Dterm = pid_data->Dgain * difference;
    return (Pterm + Iterm + Dterm);
}
```

There are some modifications that are typically made to the basic code above to improve PID controller performance. For example, the *error_sum* is typically constrained to stay within a particular range, to reduce oscillation, and to avoid having the variable reach its upper limit and hence roll over to 0. Also, the integration of the error is typically stopped both when the tracking error is large and during periods of actuator saturation.

## 9.5  PID Tuning

Until now, we have discussed controller design based on a model of the plant. $P$, $I$, and $D$ values could therefore be determined through quantitative analysis. In many cases, however, quantitatively determining the $P$, $I$, and $D$ values is not necessary. In particular, in cases where safety is not a concern, and the cost of using the plant is not a major concern either, we can select the PID values through a somewhat ad hoc tuning process. This has two advantages. First, our model of the plant may be too complex for us to work with quantitatively. Second, we may not even have a model of the plant, perhaps because we don't have the time or knowledge to create such a model. The tuning process we'll discuss has been shown to result in PID values that are reasonably close to the values that would have been obtained through quantitative analysis.

One tuning approach is to start by setting the $P$ gain to some small value, and the $D$ and $I$ gains to 0. We then increase the $D$ gain, usually starting about 100 times greater than $P$, until we see oscillation, at which point we reduce $D$ by a factor of 2 to 4. At this point, the system will probably be responding slowly. Next, we begin increasing the $P$ gain until we see oscillation or excessive overshoot, and then we reduce $P$ by a factor of 2 to 4. Finally, we begin increasing the $I$ gain, starting perhaps between 0.0001 and 0.01, and again backing off when we see oscillation or excessive overshoot. These three steps can be repeated until either satisfactory performance is achieved or performance cannot be further improved. There are many more detailed tuning approaches, but the one introduced here should give an idea of the basic approach.

## 9.6    Practical Issues Related to Computer-Based Control

### Quantization and Overflow Effects

*Quantization* occurs when a signal or machine number must be altered to fit the constraints of the computer memory. For example, if the number 0.36 were to be stored as a 4-bit fraction, then it would have to quantized to one of the following machine numbers: 0.75, 0.50, 0.25, 0.00, −0.25, −0.50, −0.75, −1.00. The closed machine number is 0.25, which would result in a quantization error of 0.11. Quantization occurs for two reasons.

First, machine arithmetic can generate results requiring more precision that the original values. A simple example is the product of two 4-bit machine numbers:

$$0.50 * 0.25 = 0.125$$

This product cannot be stored as a signed four bit machine number. To limit the effects of quantization effects due to machine arithmetic, many digital processors will store intermediate results with higher precision than the final result. In such applications, arithmetic quanitzation only occurs when the final result of an operation is stored in a memory location. It is up to the designer to optimize the software implementation to take full advantage of such processor design features.

Second, the analog signals available from the sensors are real valued. These analog signals are quantized into machine numbers through the analog-to-digital conversion process. Accuracy and expense increase as the number of bits in the digital representation increase.

Overflow results when a machine operation outputs a number with magnitude too large to be represented by the numeric processor. In the 4-bit example above, $0.75 + 0.50 = 1.25$ is too

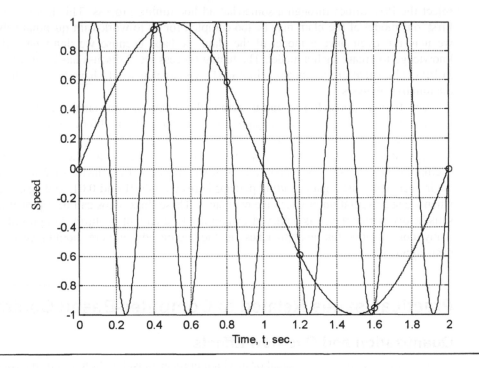

Figure 9.10: Illustration of aliasing. The sampling frequency is 2.5 Hz.

large to be represented as a machine number. The results of overflow are dependent on the method that the numeric processor uses to implement the binary representation of machine numbers.

The designer has a few design choices to address the affects of quantization and overflow. The first is fixed versus floating point representation of machine numbers. Fixed-point implementations are less expensive from the hardware perspective, but require the designer to carefully analyze and design the system to accommodate both quantization and overflow effects. The hardware for floating point implementations is typically more expensive, but the floating-point implementation may result in a faster time to market.

## Aliasing

Physical systems typically evolve in continuous time, but discrete time control signals operate on samples of the evolving process. These simple facts can lead to counter intuitive behavior, if the sampling processes are not properly designed.

Figure 9.10 illustrates a process referred to as aliasing. The circles every 0.4 s represent the discrete time samples. The sampling frequency is 2.5 Hz. The actual signal is $y(t) = 1.0 *$ $\sin(6\pi t)$, which is periodic with frequency 3.0 Hz. The figure shows that based on the samples available to it from the sampling process, the actual signal is indistinguishable from $v(t) = 1.0$ * $\sin(\pi t)$. In fact, any of the sinusoids given by $z(t) = 1.0 * \sin((2\pi)(0.5 + 2.5n) * t)$ for any integer $n$ would result in these same samples.

Aliasing is an artifact of the sampling process. When the sampling frequency is $f_s$ based on the sample record, the computer can only resolve frequencies in a range of $f_s$ Hz. In most applications, the system is designed so that this range is $f \in [-f_N, f_N]$, where $f_N = f_s / 2$ is the *Nyquist* frequency. When the actual signal has frequency content above the *Nyquist* frequency, it will appear to the computer as being within $[-f_N, f_N]$. For example, in Figure 9.10, the actual signal had a frequency of 3 Hz, which is above the *Nyquist* frequency of $f_N = 1.25$ Hz for that example. The computer treats the measured signal as if it has a frequency of $3.0 - f_S = 0.5$ Hz. Therefore, due to aliasing, the computer control system would be trying to compensate for a signal at the wrong frequency. The consequences of aliasing can be significant. For example, based on the sampling process above, the signal $\cos((2\pi / 0.4) * t)$ would be interpreted by the numeric processor as a unit amplitude constant signal.

This section has not addressed the theory of the aliasing phenomenon (see one of the references on discrete time control or signal processing). Instead, the objective of this section is to ensure that the reader understands that this phenomenon exists. Aliasing places two constraints on the design. First, the designer must understand the application well enough to judiciously specify the sampling frequency. Too large of a sampling frequency will result in unnecessary increases in the cost of the final product. Too small of a sampling frequency will either result in aliasing effects that can be very difficult to debug or too low of a system bandwidth. Second, analog anti-aliasing filters must be designed and used at the interface of each analog signal to the analog to digital converter. The purpose of the anti-aliasing filter is to attenuate frequency content above $f_N$ so that the effect of aliasing is negligible.

### Computation Delay

Time lags are of critical importance in control systems. Intuitively, delay results in the control signal being applied later than desired. Obviously, too much delay will result in performance degradation. The effect of delay can be accurately analyzed. For the designer of embedded control systems there are two important conclusions. First, analyze at an early stage in the design process, the hardware platform and processor speed relative to the phase lag that can be tolerated. Second, organize the software so that only the necessary computations occur between the time the sensor signals are sampled and the time that the control signal is output. Move all possible computations to outside of this time critical path.

## 9.7 Benefits of Computer-Based Control Implementations

Control systems can be implemented by either continuous time (analog component) or digital time (computer based) approaches. Since most processes that we are interested in controlling evolve as continuous variables in continuous time, and computer-based control approaches add additional complications such as quantization, overflow, aliasing, and computation delay, it is important to consider briefly the benefits obtained through embedded computer control.

### Repeatability, Reproducability, and Stability

The analog components in a control system are affected by aging, temperature, and manufacturing tolerance effects. Alternatively, digital systems are inherently repeatable. If two processors are loaded with the same program and data, they will compute identical results. They are also more stable than analog implementations in the presence of aging.

### Programmability

Programmability allows advanced features to be easily included in computer implementations that would be very complex in analog implementations. Examples of such advanced features include: control mode and gain switching, on-line performance evaluation, data storage, performance parameter estimation, and adaptive behavior. In addition to being programmable, computer-based control systems are easily reprogrammable. Therefore, it is straightforward to periodically upgrade and enhance the system characteristics.

## 9.8 Summary

This chapter introduced control systems. A control system has several components and signals, including the actuator, controller, plant, sensor, output, reference input, and disturbance. We developed increasingly complex controllers, specifically a proportional open-loop controller, a proportional closed-loop controller, a proportional-derivative (PD) closed-loop controller, and a proportional-integral-derivative (PID) closed-loop controller. There are numerous control objectives, including stability, and performance objectives such as rise time, peak time, overshoot, and settling time. These objectives may compete with one another. The more complex controllers assist us to achieve various objectives with less restrictive trade-offs between objectives. Several additional issues must be considered when using computers to implement a controller, including quantization and overflow effects, aliasing, and computation delay.

## 9.9 References and Further Reading

- Astrom, Karl J. and Bjorn Wittermark. *Computer Controlled Systems: Theory and Design*, Englewood Cliffs, NJ: Prentice-Hall, 1984.
- Franklin, Gene F., J. David Powell, and Abbas Emami-Naeini. *Feedback Control of Dynamic Systems, 3rd Ed.*, Reading, MA: Addison-Wesley, 1994.
- Marven, Craig and Gillian Ewers. *A Simple Approach to Digital Signal Processing*, Texas Instruments, 1994.
- Wescott, Tim. *PID without a PhD*, Embedded Systems Programming, Vol. 13, No. 11, October 2000.

# 9.10 Exercises

9.1    Explain the difference between open-looped and closed-looped control systems. Why are we more concerned with closed-looped systems?

9.2    List and describe the eight parts of the closed-loop system. Give a real-life example of each (other than those mentioned in the book).

9.3    Using a spreadsheet program, create a simulation of the cruise-control systems given in this chapter, using PI control only. Show simulations (graphs and data tables) for the following $P$ and $I$ values. Remember to include throttle saturation in your equations. You can ignore disturbance. (a) $P = 3.3$, $I = 0$. (b) $P = 4.0$, $I = 0$ (How do the results differ from part (a)? Explain!) (c) $P = 3.3$, $I = X$. (d) $P = 3.3$, $I = Y$. (Choose $X$ and $Y$ to achieve a meaningful trade-off. Explain that trade-off.

9.4    Write a generic PID controller in C.

# CHAPTER 10: *IC Technology*

10.1    Introduction
10.2    Full-Custom (VLSI) IC Technology
10.3    Semi-Custom (ASIC) IC Technology
10.4    Programmable Logic Device (PLD) IC Technology
10.5    Summary
10.6    References and Further Reading
10.7    Exercises

## 10.1  Introduction

In Chapter 1, we introduced the idea that embedded system design includes the use of three classes of technologies: processor technology, IC technology and design technology. Chapters 2–7 have focused mostly on processor technology, since one should understand how to build a processing system first, before learning what IC technologies are available to implement such a system, and before learning what design technologies are available to help build the system more rapidly. In this chapter, we provide an overview of three key IC technologies.

Several earlier chapters focused on an embedded system's structure. A system's structural representation describes the numbers and types of processors, memories, and buses, with which we implement the system's functionality. In this chapter, we focus on mapping that structure to a physical implementation. A system's physical implementation describes the mapping of the structure to actual chips, known as integrated circuits (ICs). A given structure can be mapped to one of several alternative physical implementations, each representing different design trade-offs. In fact, different parts of a structure may be mapped to different physical implementations. We might think of the structural representation as food menu for a banquet meal, and the physical implementation as the meal itself. A wedding banquet might call for a menu of chicken and vegetables, whereas a sports team banquet might call for spaghetti. Thus, we see trade-offs made in choosing the structure. Each meal itself can be prepared in different ways (e.g., the vegetables could be fresh or frozen). Thus, we see further trade-offs in choosing the physical implementation.

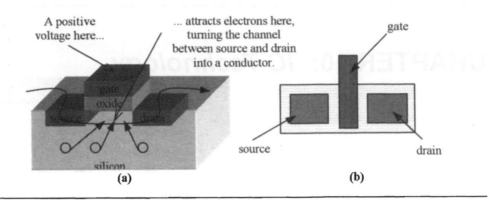

Figure 10.1: (a) a CMOS transistor (nMOS), (b) top-down view.

We will consider three major categories of physical implementations, or IC technologies: custom, semi-custom and programmable. We should mention that the term "technology" in the context of ICs is often used to instead refer to a particular manufacturing process technology, describing the type and generation of manufacturing equipment being used to build the IC. For example, a chip may be manufactured using a CMOS 0.3-micron process technology. Our use of the term *IC technology* here refers instead to different categories of ICs; each category can be implemented using any manufacturing process.

One should recall from Chapter 1 that processor technologies and IC technologies are independent of one another. Any type of processor can be mapped to any type of IC. Furthermore, a single IC may implement part of a processor, an entire processor, or as is commonly the case today, multiple processors.

Let us begin our discussion of IC technology by again examining a basic transistor. A simplified version of a complementary metal-oxide-semiconductor (CMOS) transistor is shown in Figure 10.1(a). It consists of three terminals: the source, drain, and gate. The source and drain regions lie within the silicon itself, created by implanting ions into those regions. The gate, made from polysilicon, sits between the source and drain but above the silicon, separated from the silicon by a thin layer of insulator, silicon dioxide. The voltage at the gate controls whether current can flow between the source and the drain, while the insulator prevents current from flowing through the gate itself. For an nMOS transistor, if a high enough voltage is applied to the gate, electrons are attracted from throughout the silicon substrate into the channel between the source and the drain, creating a field that allows current conduction between source and drain. On the other hand, if 0 V is applied to the gate, then the channel cannot conduct.

Notice that the transistor has three layers. The source and drain regions lie within the silicon substrate; these regions are known as p-diffusion or n-diffusion, depending on whether we are building an nMOS or pMOS transistor. The silicon dioxide insulating layer lies on top of the substrate, and is typically referred to as oxide. The gate region lies on top of the silicon dioxide, and is made from a substance known as polysilicon.

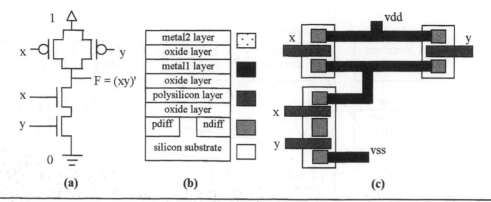

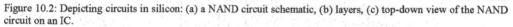

Figure 10.2: Depicting circuits in silicon: (a) a NAND circuit schematic, (b) layers, (c) top-down view of the NAND circuit on an IC.

When drawing tens or hundreds of transistors, the three-dimensional view of Figure 10.1(a) quickly becomes cumbersome to create and is really unnecessary. Instead, we can use a top-down two-dimensional view, wherein we first assign a unique pattern to represent each layer. Thus, the transistor of Figure 10.1(a) could be represented using the top-down view shown in Figure 10.1(b). The oxide layer is implicit, since it must always exist below the polysilicon.

Transistors are not very useful unless they are connected with one another, and so we'll need to introduce at least two layers of metal, which we'll call metal 1 and metal 2, to serve as connections. These layers will need to be insulated from each other and from the polysilicon, requiring two more oxide layers. Figure 10.2(b) depicts the ordering of the various layers we've introduced so far. This figure only depicts the ordering of layers, and doesn't show the connections that must also exist between higher and lower layers.

Note that we always need at least two layers of metal, since otherwise we will be unable to implement all but the most trivial of circuits. Think of trying to build a system of freeways without being allowed to build any bridges and without being able to cross roads going to different places, and you'll understand why at least two metal levels are necessary. Manufacturing processes that use even more than two levels of metal are common.

Now that we have layers for representing transistors and their connections, we can build a simple circuit on an IC. Suppose that we want to build the simple NAND circuit that was introduced in Chapter 2, and is redrawn in Figure 10.2(a) for convenience, consisting of two nMOS and two pMOS transistors. We'll use a top-down view, and use the patterns shown in Figure 10.2(b) for each layer. Figure 10.2(c) shows the top-down view of the NAND circuit, with black representing metal1. Take some time to see if you can see the correspondence between (a) and (c).

Let's consider how a circuit on an IC is actually manufactured. We'll begin by revisiting the simple transistor of Figure 10.1 and considering how this transistor would actually be manufactured. Since the transistor consists of three layers, we might mistakenly assume that we could manufacture this transistor in three steps. In such an idealized manufacturing

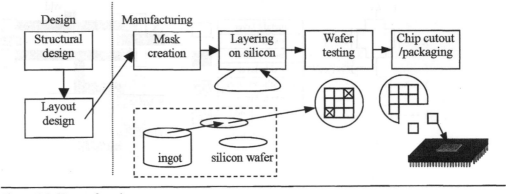

Figure 10.3: IC manufacturing steps.

process, we would first inject into the substrate the ions necessary to create the source and drain regions. Second, we would lay the silicon dioxide over the channel. Third, we would place the gate's polysilicon on top of the silicon dioxide.

Unfortunately, IC manufacturing is not quite so simple. Many steps are necessary to create each layer. For example, in a common manufacturing process, creating the silicon dioxide layer under the gate actually consists of several steps. First, we grow silicon dioxide on top of the entire IC by exposing the IC to extreme heat and gas, akin to growing rust on metal. Second, we cover the silicon dioxide with a substance called *photoresist*, which becomes soluble when exposed to ultraviolet light. Third, we pass ultraviolet light through a mask, which is designed to cast a shadow on the photoresist wherever we want silicon dioxide to stay; the remaining photoresist will be exposed to light and thus become soluble. This process is called *photolithography*. Fourth, we wash away the soluble photoresist with a solvent, thus exposing regions of silicon dioxide. Fifth, we etch away the exposed silicon dioxide with chemicals. Sixth, we remove the remaining photoresist to expose the regions of silicon dioxide that we wanted in the first place.

A similar process is repeated for each layer of the IC. An IC may have about 20 layers. So we see that there may be hundreds of steps, involving hundreds of masks, required to manufacture an IC.

Fortunately, embedded system designers need not worry too much about the details of the IC manufacturing process. Instead, they may only have to provide the input to the IC manufacturing process, which is a layout. A *layout* specifies the placement of every transistor and every wire connecting those transistors on the desired IC. The top-down view that we used for depicting a circuit on an IC was in fact a layout. A layout is akin to a map showing the placement of every city and every highway connecting those cities. From a layout, an IC manufacturer can derive the appropriate set of masks and thus manufacture the IC.

Figure 10.3 illustrates IC manufacturing steps. During the design phase, a designer creates a structural design and then generates a layout for that design. The design phase may take many months. Once fully satisfied, the designer provides the layout to an IC manufacturer, also known as a fabrication plant, "fab," or foundry. Because the layout is often provided to the manufacturer on a magnetic tape commonly used for storing large quantities of digital data, providing the layout to a manufacturer is commonly referred to as "tape-out." Because part of the manufacturing process involves spinning molten silicon, generating ICs is also referred to as a "silicon spin." IC manufacturing may take months.

Manufacturing consists of several main steps. The first step is to create a set of masks corresponding to the layout. Hundreds of masks may be required. The second step is to use each of these masks to create the various layers on the silicon surface, consisting of several substeps per mask. We point out that this layering process doesn't just create a single IC, but rather numerous ICs at once. The reason is that ICs are built on a silicon wafer. A silicon wafer is a thin polished circle, sliced from a cylinder of silicon, like a pepperoni slice intended for a pizza is sliced from a cylinder of sausage. A silicon wafer may be tens of centimeters in diameter, whereas an IC is usually less than one centimeter on a side, thus meaning that a wafer can hold tens of ICs (perhaps 100). Thus, the masks actually contain tens of identical regions, so that tens of ICs are being created simultaneously on a silicon wafer, as shown in the figure. Think of this the next time that you watch a movie where everyone is trying to get their hands on some "prototype chip" that must be found lest the world be destroyed; if there's one chip, there's probably 50 or 100 more that were made on the same wafer, lying around somewhere! (Never mind — just enjoy the movie).

The third step is to test the ICs on the wafer. ICs determined to be bad are marked, literally, so that they will be thrown away later. The machines that perform such testing are known appropriately as *testers*. They use probes that contact the pads, or input and output ports, of a particular IC on the wafer. They then apply streams of input sequences and look for the appropriate output sequences. These testers are very expensive devices, and their cost per IC pin has actually increased. Unfortunately, with all the steps required to build an IC and because of the extremely small sizes of the transistors and wires involved, bad ICs are quite common. Yield is a measure of the percentage of good ICs versus bad ICs containing errors.

Finally, the last step is to cut out each IC and mount the good ones in an IC package, which of course gets tested again.

Now that we have a better idea of how ICs implement circuits and how ICs are manufactured, we can survey the three main IC technologies: full-custom, semi-custom, and programmable logic device IC technology. Figure 10.4 provides an overview of the designer's tasks for each of the technologies. Full-custom provides the best size and performance but is costly to design and manufacture, while programmable-logic devices involve the simplest design process at the expense of size and performance. Semi-custom represents a compromise between these two extremes.

## 10.2 Full-Custom (VLSI) IC Technology

In a full-custom IC technology, the designer creates the complete layout — a task often called *physical design* or *VLSI design* (where VLSI stands for very large scale integrated circuit). The designer must design or obtain a transistor-level circuit for every processor and memory. After this point, there are several key physical design tasks necessary to obtain a good layout:

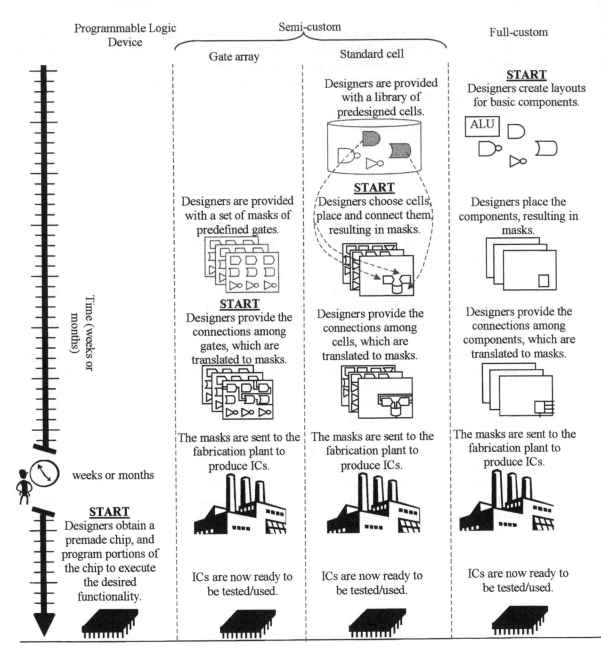

Figure 10.4: The three IC technologies.

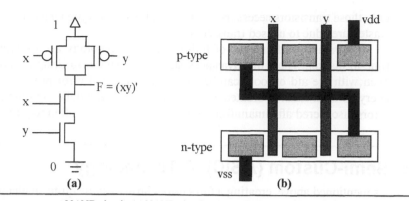

Figure 10.5: A more compact NAND circuit: (a) NAND circuit schematic, (b) compacted layout.

- *Placement*: the task of placing and orienting every transistor somewhere on the IC.
- *Routing*: the task of running wires between the transistors, without intersecting other wires or transistors.
- *Sizing*: the task of deciding how big each wire and transistor will be. Larger wires and transistors provide better performance but consume more power and require more silicon area.

A good layout is typically defined by characteristics like speed and size. Speed is the longest path from input to output, or from register to register, typically measured in nanoseconds. Size is the total silicon area necessary to implement the complete circuit. Both of these features are usually improved when the circuit is highly compacted, namely, when transistors that are connected are placed close together and hence their connecting wires are shorter. Consider for example the NAND layout of Figure 10.2(c). In that example, we did not pay attention to creating a compact layout. Figure 10.5(b) shows a compacted version of the NAND circuit. Notice how much less area is wasted in this compacted version. However, such compaction must obey certain *design rules*. For example, two transistors must be spaced apart a minimum distance lest they electrically interfere with one another.

In the past, many transistor circuits were converted by hand into compact layouts. Such *circuit design* was a common job. However, ICs can now hold so many transistors, numbering in the hundreds of millions, that laying out complete ICs by hand would require an absurd amount of time. Thus, hand layout is usually used only for relatively small, critical components, like the ALU of a microprocessor, or for basic components like logic gates that will be heavily reused.

Instead of hand layout, most layout today is done using automated layout tools, known as *physical design* tools. These tools typically include powerful optimization algorithms that run for hours or days seeking to improve the speed and size of a layout.

The advantages of full-custom IC technology include its excellent efficiency with respect to power, performance, and size. Interconnected transistors can be placed near each other and thus be connected by very short wires, yielding good performance and power. Furthermore, only those transistors necessary for the circuit being designed appear on the IC, resulting in no wasted area due to unused transistors.

The main disadvantages of full-custom IC technology are its high NRE cost and long time-to-market. These disadvantages stem from having to design a complete layout, which even with the aid of tools can be time-consuming and error-prone. Furthermore, masks for every IC layer must be created, increasing NRE cost and delaying time-to-market. In addition, errors discovered after manufacturing the IC are common, often requiring several respins.

## 10.3 Semi-Custom (ASIC) IC Technology

As mentioned above, creating a full-custom layout can be quite challenging. A designer using a semi-custom IC technology has this burden partially relieved, since rather than creating a full-custom layout, the designer connects pre-layed-out building blocks. The common name for such a semi-custom IC is an *application specific integrated circuit* (ASIC). The term *application specific* was likely chosen to contrast with general-purpose processor ICs, since for many years a processor was implemented as its own IC. ASICs in contrast implemented a circuit specific to a particular application (i.e., a single-purpose processor). Today, however, a single ASIC may implement a combination of general-purpose and single-purpose processors. Needless to say, there is much confusion related to use of the term *ASIC* today. Thus, we prefer the term *semi-custom IC*.

The two main types of semi-custom IC technologies are gate array and standard cell. With either type, the main advantages versus full-custom are reduced NRE cost and faster time-to-market, since less layout and mask creation must be performed. The main disadvantage is reduced performance, power, and size efficiency. However, relative to programmable IC technology (yet to be discussed), semi-custom is extremely efficient in terms of performance, power, and size. Because of its good efficiency coupled with reduced NRE costs, semi-custom is the most popular IC technology today.

### Gate Array Semi-Custom IC Technology

In a gate array IC technology, all of the logic gates of the IC have already been layed out with their placement on the IC known, leaving the designer with the task of connecting the gates (routing) in a manner implementing the desired circuit. Note that gate here refers to a logic gate (e.g., AND, OR) rather than a terminal of a CMOS transistor. A simplified gate array layout is shown Figure 10.6(a).

Because the IC's gates are placed beforehand, many of them may go unused, since we may not need all instances of each type of gate in our particular circuit. Furthermore, routing wires between gates may be quite long since the gate placement was decided before knowing what connections would be made.

### Standard Cell Semi-Custom IC Technology

In standard cell IC technology, common logic functions, or *cells*, have already been

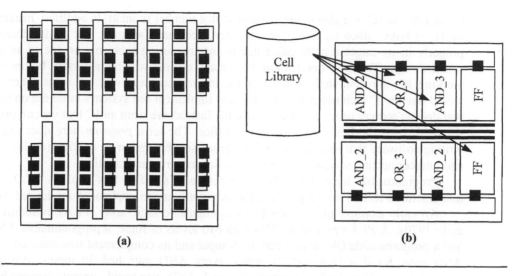

Figure 10.6: Semi-custom IC technology: (a) gate array, (b) standard cell.

compactly layed out. Examples of cells include a NAND gate, a NOR gate, a $2 \times 1$ multiplexor, and a combination of AND-OR-INVERT gates. The transistors within a cell are already layed out, but the placement of cells has not been determined. A designer thus must decide which cells to use, where to place them, and how to route among them. A standard cell layout is shown in Figure 10.6(b).

Standard cell therefore requires more NRE cost and longer time-to-market than gate array, since there is more layout remaining to be performed and all masks must still be made. However, NRE and time-to-market is still much less than full-custom, since the intricate layout within each cell is already completed. In addition, efficiency is very good compared to gate array, since only those cells needed are actually used, and their placement can be made so as to reduce interconnect. Furthermore, each cell may implement more complex functions than in gate arrays, leading to more compact designs.

A compromise between gate array and standard cell semi-custom ICs is known as a *cell array*, or cell-based array. A cell array is pretty much what we'd expect it to be based on its name. Cells, which you'll remember can be more complex than gates, have already been layed out, and have also already been placed. Thus, the designer need only connect the cells together.

## 10.4 Programmable Logic Device (PLD) IC Technology

The time required to manufacture an IC is measured in months, typically two to three months. While we may accept this time once we're ready to manufacture our final system, we probably can't wait so long to obtain a prototype of our system. Furthermore, the NRE cost to manufacture an IC (i.e., creating a layout and masks) may be too expensive to amortize over the number of ICs we plan to manufacture if that number is small. In addition, manufacturing an IC is risky, since we may discover after such manufacturing that an IC doesn't work properly in its target system, either due to manufacturing problems or due to an incorrect initial design. Thus, we never know how many respins will be necessary before we get a working IC; a recent study stated that the industry average was 3.5 spins. Therefore, we would like an IC technology that allows us to implement our system's structure on an IC, but that doesn't require us to manufacture that IC. Instead, we want an IC that we can program in the field, with the field being our lab or office. The term *program* here does not refer to writing software that executes on a microprocessor, but rather to configuring logic circuits and interconnection switches to implement a desired structural circuit.

Programmable logic device (PLD) technology satisfies this goal. A *PLD* is a pre-manufactured IC that we can purchase and then configure to implement our desired circuit.

An early example of a PLD was a programmable logic array (PLA), introduced in the early 1970s. A *PLA* was a small PLD with two levels of logic, a programmable AND array and a programmable OR array. Every PLA input and its complement was connected to every AND gate. So if a PLA had 10 inputs, every AND gate had 20 inputs. Any of these connections could be broken, meaning that each AND gate could generate any product term. Likewise, each OR gate could generate any sum of AND gate outputs. A PAL (programmable array logic) is another PLD type that eliminates the programmability of the OR array to reduce size and delay. PLAs and PALs are often referred to as simple PLDs, or *SPLD*s.

As IC capacity grew over the years, SPLDs could not simply be extended by adding more inputs, since the number of required connections to the AND array inputs would grow too high. Thus, the new capacity was taken advantage of instead by integrating numerous SPLDs on a single chip and adding programmable interconnect between them, resulting in what is known as a complex PLD, or *CPLD*. CPLDs often contain latches to enable implementation of sequential circuits also. Figure 10.7 illustrates a sample architecture for a CPLD. The top half of the figure is an SPLD that can implement any function of the chip's input signals as well as any SPLD output signal. The bottom half represents another identical SPLD. The array on the left consists of vertical lines that can be programmed to connect with any of the horizontal lines, so that any signal's true or complemented value can be fed into any gate. The output of each SPLD feeds into an IO cell. The IO cell can be programmed to pass the latched or unlatched, true or complemented, output to the CPLD's external output, and/or to the programmable array on the left as input to SPLDs.

While able to implement more complex circuits than SPLDs, CPLDs suffer from the problem of not scaling well as their sizes increase. For example, supposed the CPLD architecture of Figure 10.7 had 4 inputs and 2 outputs. Then there would be 6 signals in the programmable array, plus 6 more for those signals' complements, thus requiring 12-input AND gates. Likewise, suppose there were 12 inputs and 6 outputs. Then there would be 18 + 18 signals, requiring 36-input AND gates. Notice such an architecture doesn't scale well.

The logical solution is to build devices that are more modular in nature. In particular, there is no need to connect every input signal and every output signal to every AND gate. A more flexible approach can be used in which a subset of inputs and outputs are input to each SPLD. This more modular, more scalable approach to PLD design resulted in architectures

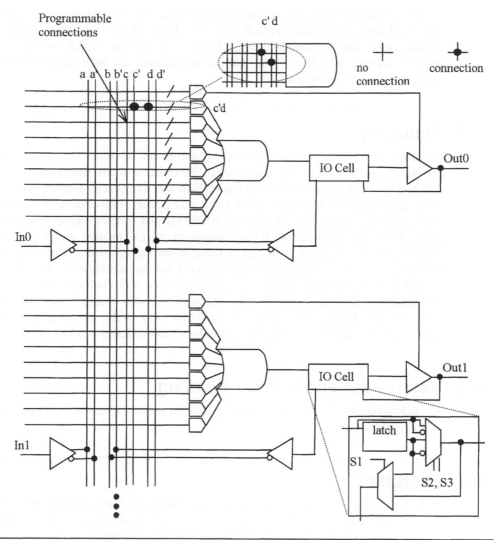

Figure 10.7: A CPLD architecture.

known as field-programmable gate arrays (FPGAs). An *FPGA* consists of arrays of programmable logic blocks connected by programmable interconnect blocks.

The name FPGA was intended to contrast these devices with traditional gate arrays, which need masks to create the interconnections between the already layed-out gates. FPGAs, in contrast, have their interconnections, as well as logic blocks, programmed in the field, meaning in the designer's lab. However, most FPGA architectures do not have arrays of gates anywhere to be found, and thus the name FPGA can be somewhat misleading.

Programming is done by setting bits within the logic or interconnect blocks. Those bits are stored using nonvolatile (EPROM, EEPROM) or volatile (SRAM) memory technology. Another nonvolatile technique used in PLDs is an antifuse, which, as the name implies, behaves opposite to a fuse — an antifuse is originally an open circuit but takes on low resistance when programmed.

## 10.5 Summary

Creating an IC circuit layout and manufacturing an IC from this layout are complex, expensive, and time-consuming processes. Embedded systems designers can choose from different IC technologies, in order to reduce NRE cost and time-to-market by trading off with other design metrics, like size, performance, and power. Full-custom IC technology is the most expensive technology in terms of NRE cost and time-to-market but yields the most efficient circuits. Semi-custom IC technology, or ASICs, involve use of predesigned basic components, thus reducing NRE cost and time-to-market, but still providing good efficiency. Programmable logic devices are premanufactured and thus eliminate the need for the designer to go through the manufacturing stage, greatly reducing NRE cost and time-to-market, but are significantly inferior to custom or semi-custom IC in terms of size, power, performance, and unit cost. The designer may choose to use PLDs early in the design process, switching to ASICs and even full-custom later in the process when the design has stabilized.

## 10.6 References and Further Reading

- Sebastian Smith, M.J. *Application-Specific Integrated Circuits*. Reading, MA: Addison Wesley, 1997.

## 10.7 Exercises

10.1 Using the NAND gate (shown in figure Figure 10.1) as building block, (a) draw the circuit schematic for the function $F = xz + yz'$, and (b) draw the top-down view of the circuit on an IC (make your layout as compact as possible.)

10.2 Draw (a) the transistor-level circuit schematic for a two-input multiplexor, and (b) the top-down view of the circuit on an IC (make your layout as compact as possible.)

10.3 Implement the function $F = xz + yz'$ using the gate array structure given in Figure 10.6(a).

# CHAPTER 11: *Design Technology*

11.1    Introduction
11.2    Automation: Synthesis
11.3    Verification: Hardware/Software Co-Simulation
11.4    Reuse: Intellectual Property Cores
11.5    Design Process Models
11.6    Summary
11.7    Book Summary
11.8    References and Further Reading
11.9    Exercises

## 11.1 Introduction

We have described how to design embedded systems from processors, memories, and interfaces, and in Chapter 10 we described the various IC technologies available for implementing such systems. Recall that in Chapter 1, we pointed out that IC transistor capacity is growing faster than the ability of designers to produce transistors in their designs. This difference in growth rate has resulted in the well-known productivity gap. Thus, there has been tremendous interest over the past few decades in developing design technologies that will enable designers to produce transistors more rapidly. These technologies have been developed for both software and for hardware, but the recent developments in hardware design technology deserves special attention since they've brought us to a new era in embedded system design.

Design is the task of defining a system's functionality and converting that functionality into a physical implementation, while satisfying certain constrained design metrics and optimizing other design metrics. Design is hard. Just getting the functionality right is tricky because embedded system functionality can be very complex, with millions of possible environment scenarios that must be responded to properly. For example, consider an elevator controller, and in particular the many possible combinations of buttons being pressed, the elevator moving, the doors being open, and so on. Not only is getting the functionality right

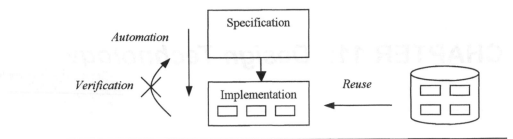

Figure 11.1: Productivity improvers.

hard, but creating a physical implementation that satisfies constraints is also very difficult because there are so many competing, tightly constrained metrics.

These difficulties slow designer productivity. Embedded system designer productivity can be measured by software lines of code produced per month or hardware transistors produced per month. Productivity numbers are surprisingly low, with some studies showing just tens of lines of code or just hundreds of transistors produced per designer-day. In response to low production rates, the design community has focused much effort and resources to developing design technologies that improve productivity. We can classify many of those technologies into three general techniques, illustrated in Figure 11.1:

1. *Automation* is the task of using a computer program to replace manual design effort.
2. *Reuse* is the process of using predesigned components (whether designed by humans or computers) rather than designing those components oneself.
3. *Verification* is the task of ensuring the correctness and completeness of each design step.

Providing thorough coverage of the advances in these productivity-improving techniques for embedded systems over the past couple of decades would require an entire book itself. Instead, we will focus in this chapter on a few advances that have enabled the unified view of hardware and software design. First, we will discuss the automation technique of synthesis, which has made hardware design look like software design. Second, we will discuss the reuse of cores in the hardware domain, which has enabled the coexistence of general-purpose processors (software) and single-purpose processors (hardware) on a single IC. Third, we will describe the verification of hardware-software co-simulation, which has enabled designers to verify complete hardware/software systems before they are implemented.

## 11.2 Automation: Synthesis

### "Going up": The Parallel Evolution of Compilation and Synthesis

When processors were first being designed in the late 1940s and early 1950s, designing a computer system consisted mostly of hardware design; software, if it was used, was fairly simple. However, as the idea of the general-purpose processor began to take hold, software

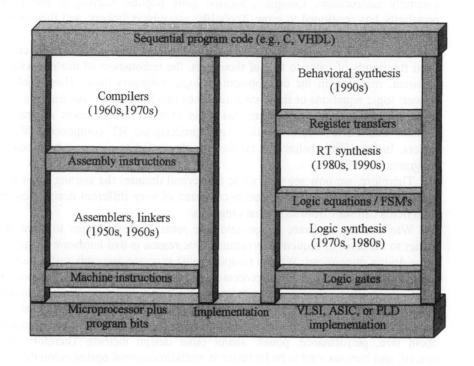

Figure 11.2: The codesign ladder.

complexity began to grow. Because of the different techniques used to design software and hardware, a division between the fields of hardware design and software design occurred. As illustrated in Figure 11.2, design tools simultaneously evolved in both fields, albeit at different rates, to allow behavior description at progressively more abstract levels, in order to manage increasing design complexity. This simultaneous evolution has brought us to a point today where both fields use the sequential program model to describe behavior, thus a rejoining of the two fields into one field seems imminent.

As shown in Figure 11.2, early software consisted of *machine instructions*, coded as sequences of 0s and 1s, necessary to carry out the desired system behavior on a general-purpose processor. A collection of machine instructions was called a program. As program sizes grew from hundreds of instructions to thousands of instructions, the tediousness of dealing with 0s and 1s became evident, resulting in use of assemblers and linkers. These tools automatically translate assembly instructions, consisting of instructions written using letters and numbers to represent symbols, into equivalent machine instructions. Soon, the limitations of assembly instructions became evident for programs consisting of tens of thousands of instructions, resulting in the development of compilers. Compilers automatically translate sequential programs, written in a high-level language like C, into equivalent assembly instructions. Compilers became quite popular starting in the 1960s, and their popularity has continued to grow. Tools like assemblers/linkers, and then compilers, helped software designers climb to higher abstraction levels.

Early hardware consisted of circuits of interconnected logic gates. As circuit sizes grew from thousands of gates to tens of thousands, the tediousness of dealing with gates became apparent, resulting in the development of *logic synthesis* tools. These tools automatically convert logic equations or finite-state machines into logic gates. As circuit sizes continued to grow, register–transfer (RT) synthesis tools evolved. These tools automatically convert FSMDs into FSMs, logic equations, and predesigned RT components like registers and adders. In the 1990s, behavioral synthesis tools started to appear, which convert sequential programs into FSMDs.

Therefore, we now see that, while for several decades the starting point for the fields of hardware design and software design consisted of very different design descriptions, today both fields can start from sequential programs.

Why did the hardware design field take some 30 years longer to climb the abstraction ladder to the level of sequential programs? One reason is that hardware design involves many more design dimensions. While a compiler must generate assembly instructions to implement a sequential program on a given processor, a synthesis tool must actually design the processor itself. Extensive research and more powerful computers have enabled synthesis tools to address the problem adequately. A second reason is that the very fact that one chooses to implement behavior in hardware rather than software implies that one is extremely concerned about size, performance, power, and/or other design metrics. Therefore, optimization is crucial, and humans tend to be far better at multidimensional optimization than are computers, as long as the problem size is not too large and enough design time is available. Just look, for example, at how many decades it has taken for computers to be able to seriously challenge the world's best chess players. If the game of chess had evolved such that players only had 10 seconds to think of each move, and the playing board was the size of a football field with tens of thousands of pieces, then we'd have a situation more like that of IC design, in which automation today is clearly better.

We see above that, like an elevator going up, both hardware and software design fields have continued to focus design effort on increasingly higher abstraction levels. Starting design from a higher abstraction level has two advantages. First, descriptions at higher levels tend to be smaller and easier to capture. For example, one line of sequential program code might translate to one thousand logic gates. Second, as Figure 11.3(a) illustrates, a description at a higher abstraction level has many more possible implementations than those at lower levels. One can think of holding a flashlight higher above the ground — the higher we go, the more ground we illuminate. For example, a sequential program description may have possible implementations whose performance and transistor counts differ by orders of magnitude. However, a logic-level description may have transistor implementations varying in performance and size by only a factor of two or so.

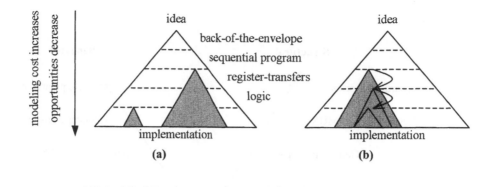

Figure 11.3: The abstraction pyramid: (a) a model at a higher abstraction level has more potential implementations; (b) the design process proceeds to lower abstraction levels, narrowing in on a single implementation.

## Synthesis Levels

In the following sections, we provide brief overviews of the details of synthesis at different abstraction levels. Unlike compiler users, synthesis tool users must have a fair amount of knowledge about synthesis. Compilers tend to be fairly inexpensive and easy-to-use tools. Synthesis tools, on the other hand, range from costing hundreds of dollars to tens of thousands of dollars. The user must control perhaps hundreds of synthesis options. Furthermore, synthesis tools may take many hours to run, and their output occasionally needs to be modified. This complexity associated with synthesis stems from the fact that optimization is absolutely crucial when synthesizing hardware, and each user will have different optimization criteria. If optimization wasn't so crucial, one would simply implement one's system as software rather than as hardware.

We now provide a brief overview of the various levels of synthesis. A standard definition for *synthesize* is "forming a complex whole by combining parts." In the context of digital hardware design, however, the term has taken on the meaning of "automatically converting a system's behavioral description into a structural implementation," where that implementation is a complex whole formed by parts. The structural implementation must optimize some set of design metrics, such as performance, size, and power.

To better understand the meaning of converting from a behavioral description to a structural implementation, Gajski developed the Y-chart, shown in Figure 11.4. The chart consists of three axes, behavioral, structural, and physical, each representing a type of a description of a digital system, as follows:

- A *behavioral* description defines outputs as a function of inputs. It describes the algorithms we'll use to obtain those outputs, but does not say how we'll implement those algorithms.
- A *structural* description implements that behavior by connecting components with known behavior.

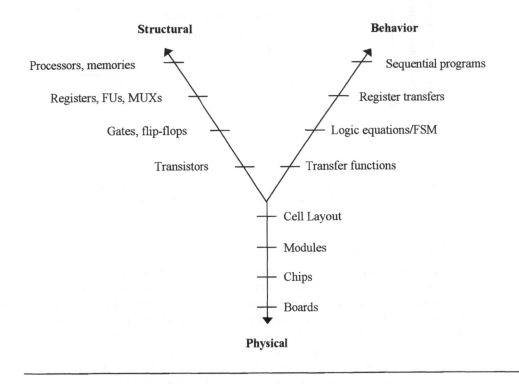

**Structural**

Processors, memories

Registers, FUs, MUXs

Gates, flip-flops

Transistors

**Behavior**

Sequential programs

Register transfers

Logic equations/FSM

Transfer functions

Cell Layout

Modules

Chips

Boards

**Physical**

Figure 11.4: Gajski's Y-chart.

- A *physical* description tells us the sizes and locations on a chip or board of a system's components and their interconnecting wires.

For example, addition is a behavior, while a carry-ripple adder is a structure. Likewise, a sequential program that sequences through an array to find the array's largest-valued element is a behavior, while a controller and datapath implementing that algorithm is a structure.

The chart also shows that each description can exist at one of various levels of abstraction. For example, at the gate-level of abstraction, a behavioral description consists of logic equations, a structural description consists of a connection of gates, and a physical description consists of a placement of gates/cells and a routing among them. As another example, at the system level of abstraction, a behavioral description may consist of communicating sequential programs (processes), a structural description of a connection of processors and memories, and a physical description of a placement of processor/memory cores and buses on an IC or a board.

Synthesis can generally be thought of as converting a behavioral description at a particular abstraction level to a structural description. That structural description may be at the same level or a lower one, but not a higher one. We now describe synthesis techniques at several different abstraction levels.

## Logic Synthesis

Logic synthesis automatically converts a logic-level behavior, consisting of logic equations and/or an FSM, into a structural implementation, consisting of connected gates. Let us divide logic synthesis into combinational-logic synthesis and FSM synthesis. Combinational logic synthesis can be further subdivided into two-level minimization and multilevel minimization.

*Two-level logic minimization*: We can represent any logic function as a sum of products (or a product of sums). We can implement this function directly using a level consisting of AND gates, one for each product term, and a second level consisting of a single OR gate. Thus, we have two levels, plus inverters necessary to complement some inputs to the AND gates. The longest possible path from an input signal to an output signal passes through at most two gates, not counting inverters. We cannot in general obtain faster performance. For example, the function $F = abc'd' + a'cd + ab'cd$ would be implemented with three AND gates followed by one OR gate, as shown in Figure 11.5(b).

Since performance is already the best possible, the main goal of two-level logic minimization is to minimize size. We can set a goal of minimizing the number of AND gates in a sum of products implementation. We can state this goal more formally as that of finding a minimum cover of a logic expression, or function. We will now provide several definitions that lead us to the definition of a minimum cover. We are given a set of variables (inputs to the function), such as: $\{a, b, c, d\}$.

- A *literal* is the appearance of a variable or its complement in a function. For example, the above function has 11 literals: $a, b, c', d', a', c, d, a, b', c, d$.
- A *minterm* is a product of literals in which each variable or its complement appears exactly once. For example, in the previous function, $abc'd'$ is a minterm, but $a'cd$ is not, because $b$ does not appear. Any logic function can be expressed as a sum of minterms; note that each minterm corresponds to a row in a truth table. For example, F could be expressed as $abc'd' + ab'cd + a'bcd + a'b'cd$.
- An *implicant* is a product of literals in which each variable or its complement appears no more than once, rather than exactly once as for minterms. In the earlier function, $ab'cd$ and $a'cd$ are examples of implicants. An implicant covers one or more minterms; for example, $a'cd$ covers minterms $a'bcd$ and $a'b'cd$.
- A *cover* of a logic function is a set of implicants that covers all of the function's minterms.
- Finally, a *minimum cover* is a cover having the minimum possible number of implicants.

Since each implicant corresponds to an AND gate, by finding a minimum cover, we have achieved our goal of minimizing the number of AND gates.

We can extend our goal by not only minimizing the number of AND gates but also minimizing the number of inputs to each AND gate. We can state this goal formally as finding a minimum cover that is prime. A prime cover's implicants are all prime implicants. A prime implicant of a logic function is an implicant that is not covered by any other implicant of the

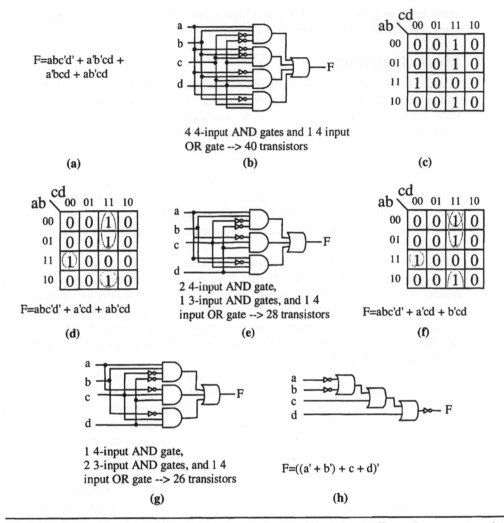

F=abc'd' + a'b'cd +
a'bcd + ab'cd

**(a)**

4 4-input AND gates and 1 4 input
OR gate --> 40 transistors

**(b)**

**(c)**

F=abc'd' + a'cd + ab'cd

**(d)**

2 4-input AND gate,
1 3-input AND gates, and 1 4
input OR gate --> 28 transistors

**(e)**

F=abc'd' + a'cd + b'cd

**(f)**

1 4-input AND gate,
2 3-input AND gates, and 1 4
input OR gate --> 26 transistors

**(g)**

F=((a' + b') + c + d)'

**(h)**

Figure 11.5: Logic minimization: (a) original function, (b) direct implementation, (c) Karnaugh-map representation, (d) minimum cover and its (e) implementation, (f) minimum cover that is prime and its (g) implementation, (h) multilevel implementation using three levels but fewer transistors.

function. For example, in the earlier function, *abc'd'*, *b'cd*, and *a'cd* are all prime implicants, but *a'b'cd* is not, because even though it is an implicant of the function, it is covered by *a'cd*, as well as by *b'cd*.

We can optimally solve the two-level logic minimization problem of finding a minimum cover that is prime. One popular pencil-and-paper approach uses Karnaugh maps (K-maps), illustrated in Figure 11.5(c) and (d). While we won't describe it in detail here, we note for those familiar with K-maps that the 1s in the chart correspond to minterms, and drawing the minimal number of maximum-sized circles covering the 1s corresponds to finding the minimum number of prime implicants, where each maximum-sized circle represents one prime implicant. Figure 11.5(d) illustrates a minimum cover, and Figure 11.5(e) illustrates the corresponding logic circuit. Note that this circuit has fewer gates and wires than the unoptimized circuit of Figure 11.5(b). Figure 11.5(f) and (g) show a minimum cover that is prime (all circles are maximum size) and the corresponding circuit, having a smaller gate and fewer wires than the minimum cover that was not prime. This circuit represents the optimum two-level circuit.

However, the K-map approach becomes too complicating for functions with more than 5 or 6 inputs. Another popular, computer-based, optimal approach uses an algorithm based on a two-step tabular method. The first step finds all of a function's prime implicants, and the second step finds a minimum number of these implicants that covers the function. Unfortunately, the first step requires that we first list all the minterms of a function, but there may be a prohibitively large number of minterms. In particular, if there are $n$ inputs, there may be up to $2^n$ minterms. For a function with 8 inputs, there may be 256 minterms, which is reasonable. For a function with 32 inputs, there may be over 4 billion minterms, which would exceed the memory limits of most computers. Larger sized examples, which are extremely common, would require trillions of years on the fastest computers just to enumerate the minterms. This phenomenon is called exponential complexity, and it limits the tabular method to systems with relatively few inputs. Adding to the problem is the fact that the second step of finding a minimum cover also has exponential complexity.

Because solving the two-level logic minimization problem optimally is very hard for examples with even a moderate number of inputs, most logic synthesis tools include inexact approaches using heuristics. A heuristic is a solution technique that is not guaranteed to result in the optimal solution but hopefully will come close. A popular heuristic approach is iterative improvement. In this approach, we start with an initial solution, such as the original logic equation, and we repeatedly (iteratively) make modifications to that solution to bring us toward a better solution. For example, suppose we are given the function F = $a'b'cde + a'bcde + defghij + klmnopqrstuv$. We might try to improve this by trying to merge pairs of implicants into a single implicant that covers the pair. For example, we could merge the first two implicants into the single implicant $a'cde$, which is obviously an improvement. Note that we didn't have to enumerate all the minterms to find this improvement.

There are several common modifications used in heuristic two-level logic synthesis. *Expand* replaces each nonprime implicant by a prime implicant that covers it, deleting all other implicants covered by the new prime implicant. *Reduce* does basically the opposite of expand. *Reshape* expands one implicant while reducing another, thus maintaining the same total number of implicants. *Irredundant* selects a minimum number of implicants from the existing ones while still covering the function. Logic synthesis tools differ by which of these modifications they use and the order in which they apply these modifications.

*Multilevel Logic Minimization*: The previous paragraphs dealt with minimizing the AND gates and their sizes in a two-level sum-of-products implementation. We noted that a two-level implementation has excellent performance, with the longest path being only two gates. However, perhaps we don't need such great performance. Rather, perhaps we are willing to

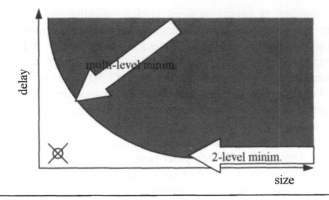

Figure 11.6: Trading off size and performance.

sacrifice some performance if such a sacrifice would decrease the circuit size further than even the best two-level implementation. We can achieve such a trade-off by using multiple levels of logic.

As a simple example, consider the function $F = adef + bdef + cdef + gh$. The function can not be minimized further in two levels, and would require five gates (four AND gates and one OR gate) if implemented. However, we could easily reduce the number of gates by factoring out the $def$ term from the first three implicants, resulting in $F = (a + b + c)def + gh$. This function requires only four gates (two AND gates and two OR gates). Furthermore, note that the number of inputs per gate is reduced too. If each gate input requires two transistors, then we've reduced the number of transistors from $18 * 2 = 36$ down to $11 * 2 = 22$. The trade-off is that this implementation has slower performance, since it now has three levels rather than two, due to inputs $a$, $b$, and $c$ passing through three gates before reaching the output.

We illustrate this trade-off of size and performance in Figure 11.6. The filled gray area represents the set of all possible circuit implementations of a particular logic expression. The $x$-axis represents circuit size, and the $y$-axis represents circuit delay. Ideally, we'd like to minimize both, but generally no such circuit exists, as illustrated by the hypothetical point in the lower left of the figure with an X through it. Two-level logic has minimum delay, and thus two-level logic minimization seeks to find the smallest-sized two-level implementation, as illustrated. Further size reduction requires an increase in delay (i.e., more than two logic levels). Multilevel logic minimization seeks to find the Pareto-optimal solution (one on the lower-left curved boundary of the filled area) for a given delay or size.

As another example, consider the earlier two-level logic function: $F = abc'd' + b'cd + a'cd$. Simple algebraic manipulation yields the equivalent function: $F = abc'd' + (a' + b')cd$. We now have three levels, but fewer transistors. We can simplify even further by noting that $abc'd' = (abc'd')'' = (a' + b' + c + d)' = ((a' + b') + c + d)'$. So now the original function is: $F = ((a' + b') + c + d)' (a' + b')cd$. So we can reuse the $(a' + b')$ term to further reduce transistors down to only 20, as shown in Figure 11.5(f).

But how did we come up with this new function using fewer transistors? You can probably see that it is not easy. There are many different ways to manipulate the equations.

Multilevel logic minimization is thus an even harder problem than two-level minimization. Therefore, heuristics are again used by logic synthesis tools addressing this problem. Iterative improvement heuristics drawing from a suite of equation modifications are again the prevailing approach.

*FSM Synthesis:* Synthesizing an FSM to gates consists of two main tasks, state minimization and state encoding. *State minimization* reduces the number of FSM states by identifying and merging equivalent states. Reducing the number of states may result in a smaller state register and fewer gates. Two states are equivalent if their outputs and next states are equivalent for all possible inputs. We can use an algorithm based on a tabular method to solve this problem exactly. We start with a table showing each possible pair of states as a cell in the table. We step through the cells, marking each cell as not equivalent, equivalent, or dependent on other pairs of states being equivalent, which we list in the cell. "Not equivalent" means the cell's two states either have different outputs or have a next state pair whose cell is marked as not equivalent. "Equivalent" means the cell's two states have the same outputs, and next state pairs that are all known to be equivalent. We step through the cells several times until all cells are either marked equivalent or not equivalent.

The drawback of the above algorithm is that the table size is $n^2$, where $n$ is the number of states in the original FSM. Although $n^2$ is not nearly as bad as $2^n$, it still grows quickly for larger $n$, requiring much computer memory and computations. An example with perhaps 500 states would require a table of size 250,000. Thus, many tools resort to heuristics.

*State encoding* encodes each state as a unique bit sequence, such that some design metric like size is optimized. Given $n$ states, we require a minimum of $\log_2(n)$ bits to represent $n$ unique encodings. There are $n!$ possible assignments of $n$ states to $n$ encodings (the first state has $n$ possible encodings, the second state has $n - 1$ since the first state already used one encoding, the third state has $n - 2$, and so on). We can't possibly try all possible assignments of states to encodings for moderate size examples, because $n!$ grows so quickly. Heuristics are again common.

*Technology Mapping:* We must specify the library of gates available for use in an implementation. For example, as a trivial extreme, we may have only simple two-input AND and OR gates available in our library. At the other extreme, we may have numerous sizes of AND, OR, NAND, NOR, XOR, and XNOR gates, plus efficiently implemented meta-gates (called *cells* or *macros*) such as multiplexors, decoders, and combinations of gates (like AND-OR-INVERT). Thus, logic synthesis must generate final structure consisting of only the available library components and should use cells and macros as much as possible to improve the overall design efficiency. This task is called *technology mapping*. Technology mapping is again a complex problem, requiring use of heuristics. Furthermore, a tool that integrates technology mapping with logic minimization, while making the synthesis problem harder, will likely result in a more efficient circuit.

*The Impact of Complexity on Logic Synthesis User:* In the previous paragraphs, we described the basic subproblems that together make up the logic synthesis problem. We saw that each problem had a number of possible solutions that was enormous for moderate-sized problems, such that enumerating all possible solutions and choosing the best resulted in prohibitive space and/or time complexity. In most cases, no algorithm of reasonable complexity exists to optimally solve those problems. Therefore, most tools resort to heuristics having a far lower complexity in order to solve the problems using a reasonable amount of memory and computation time.

The impact of complexity and of the use of heuristics on logic synthesis users is significant. Logic synthesis tools differ tremendously according to the heuristics they use. Some tools use computationally expensive heuristics, thus requiring long run times measured in hours or even days, and requiring huge amounts of memory typically found only on expensive computer servers or engineering workstations. In contrast, other tools use fast heuristics, requiring run times measured in minutes and requiring only small amounts of memory typically found on PCs. Users should not expect the same quality of results from these different tools. Furthermore, the tools with expensive heuristics usually allow a user to control the optimization effort that the tool will apply. When just trying to develop prototypes, the user therefore should select low optimization to get fast synthesis run times, while the near-final product should use high optimization. Additionally, these tools may allow the designer to indicate the relative importance of various design metrics, like performance, size, and power, so the designer must indicate this information.

To achieve decent results, nearly all tools use super-linear-time heuristics. A linear-time heuristic requires roughly $n$ computations (times some constant factor) for a problem of size $n$. A super-linear-time heuristic (usually just called nonlinear, though that could refer to sublinear, too), in contrast grows more quickly than that, for example, requiring $n^3$ computations. This nonlinear growth means that a large problem may require much longer run time than two problems each half the size of the large problem. For example, $100^3$ is more than $50^3 + 50^3$ (i.e., 1,000,000 > 250,000). Furthermore, $100^3$ is much more than $25^3 + 25^3 + 25^3 + 25^3$ (i.e., 1,000,000 >> 62,500). Likewise, memory usage may grow nonlinearly. Thus, a logic synthesis tool user must often partition a system into several smaller systems having equivalent behavior, in order to achieve acceptable synthesis tool run times and memory usage.

*Integrating Logic Synthesis and Physical Design*: In the past, transistors, and hence logic gates, had a very large time delay compared with wires. Thus, it made sense to create synthesis tools that evaluated performance in terms of the number of levels of gates from input to output. As the industry moves to IC manufacturing processes that involve smaller and smaller feature sizes, transistors shrink not only in their size, but also in their delay. That's the good news.

Now for the bad news. While transistor delays shrink with reduced feature sizes, wire delays have actually begun to increase! This phenomenon is illustrated in Figure 11.7. Therefore, in the past, it made sense to think of circuits as transistors connected by wires. However, in the future, it appears that we'll have to start thinking of circuits as wires connected by transistors!

This change in the ratio of transistor delay and wire delay impacts logic synthesis tremendously. To understand the delay of a given logic expression, a synthesis tool can no longer just count the number of logic gates from input to output. Instead, the tool must measure the length of the wires connecting those gates. But in order to know those lengths, the tool must know how the transistors are placed on an IC. Placing transistors was previously

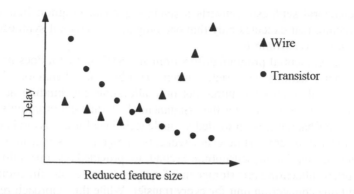

Figure 11.7: The changing values transistor delay and wire delay. Source: International Technology Roadmap for Semiconductors, 1999.

the domain of physical design. Thus, we see that the clean separation of logic synthesis and physical design is no longer possible. Instead, we must perform logic synthesis and physical design simultaneously if we are really to design efficient circuits.

## Register–Transfer Synthesis

Logic synthesis allowed us to describe our system as boolean equations, or as an FSM. However, many systems are too complex to initially describe at this logic level of abstraction. Instead, we often describe our system using a more abstract (and hence powerful) computation model, such as an FSMD.

Recall that an FSMD allows variable declarations of complex data types, and allows arithmetic actions and conditions. Clearly, more work is necessary to convert an FSMD to gates than to convert an FSM to gates, and this extra work is performed by register–transfer synthesis. Register–transfer (RT) synthesis takes an FSMD and converts it to a custom single-purpose processor, consisting of a datapath and an FSM controller. In particular, it generates a complete datapath, consisting of register units to store variables, functional units to implement arithmetic operations, and connection units (buses and multiplexors) to connect these other units. It also generates an FSM that controls this datapath.

Creating the datapath requires solving two key subproblems: allocation and binding. Allocation is the problem of instantiating storage units, functional units, and connection units. Binding is the problem of mapping FSMD operations to specific units.

As in logic synthesis, both of these RT synthesis problems are hard to solve optimally.

## Behavioral Synthesis

In RT synthesis, we describe the actions that occur on every clock cycle of the system, using an FSMD. However, for many systems, we are only interested in having the output be a correct function of the inputs, and we don't care how that function is broken down into clock cycles. Therefore, we may want to describe such a system using a sequential program.

Behavioral synthesis converts a single sequential program into a single-purpose processor structure that executes only that one program. Behavioral synthesis has also been referred to as *high-level synthesis*.

A sequential program differs from an FSMD in that it does not require us to schedule the system's actions into states when describing the behavior. Therefore, implementing a sequential program requires not only allocation and binding as in RT synthesis, but also scheduling. Scheduling is the assignment of a sequential program's operations to states.

In Chapter 2, we provided a simple technique for behavioral synthesis. First, we provided templates for converting every sequential program construct into an equivalent set of states, thus accomplishing scheduling. Second, we provided a simple allocation and binding method, namely, allocating one storage unit for every variable, one functional unit for every operation, and one connection unit for every transfer. While this approach results in a correct processor circuit, the circuit is clearly not optimized. Thus, behavioral synthesis tools use advanced techniques to carry out the tasks of scheduling, allocation, and binding in order to optimize a circuit. They also typically include standard compiler optimizations that are applied before those tasks, such as constant propagation, dead-code elimination, and loop unrolling.

## System Synthesis and Hardware/Software Codesign

Behavioral synthesis converts a single sequential program (behavior) to a single-purpose processor (structure). However, complex embedded systems may require more than this. In particular, using multiple processors may provide better performance or power. Furthermore, the original behavior may be better described using multiple concurrently executing sequential programs, known as *processes*. *System synthesis* converts multiple processes into multiple processors. The term *system* here refers to a collection of processors.

Given one or more processes, system synthesis involves several tasks. *Transformation* is the task of rewriting the processes to be more amenable to synthesis. For example, a designer may have described some behavior using two processes, but analysis might show that those two processes are really exclusive to one another and thus could be merged into one process. Likewise, a large process might actually consist of two independent operations that could be done concurrently, so that process could be divided into two processes. Other common transformations include procedure inlining and loop unrolling.

*Allocation* is the task of selecting the numbers and types of processors to use to implement the processes. A designer might choose to use an 8-bit general-purpose processor along with a single-purpose processor. Alternatively, the designer might use a 32-bit general-purpose processor, an 8-bit general-purpose processor, and multiple single-purpose processors. Allocation actually includes selecting processors, memories, and buses. Allocation is essentially the design of the system architecture.

*Partitioning* is the task of mapping the processes to processors. One process can be implemented on multiple processors, and multiple processes can be implemented on a single processor. Likewise, variables must be partitioned among memories; and communications, among buses.

*Scheduling* is the task of determining when each of the multiple processes on a single processor will have its chance to execute on the processor. Likewise, memory accesses and bus communications must be scheduled.

These tasks may be performed in a variety of orders, and iteration among the tasks is common.

System synthesis, like all forms of synthesis, is driven by constraints. A typical set of constraints dictates that certain performance requirements must be met at minimum cost. In such a situation, system synthesis might seek to allocate as much behavior as possible to a general-purpose processor, since a GPP may provide for low-cost, flexible implementation. A minimum number of single-purpose processors might be used to meet the performance requirements.

System synthesis for general-purpose processors only (software) has been around for a few decades, but hasn't been called system synthesis. Names like multiprocessing, parallel processing, and real-time scheduling have been more common. The maturation of behavioral synthesis in the 1990s has enabled the consideration of single-purpose processors (hardware) during the allocation and partitioning tasks of system synthesis. This joint consideration of general-purpose and single-purpose processors by the same automatic tools was in stark contrast to the prior art. Thus, the term *hardware/software codesign* has been used extensively in the research community, to highlight research that focuses on the unique requirements of such simultaneous consideration of both hardware and software during synthesis. However, this term may be temporary in nature, as the distinction between GPPs and SPPs continues to blur.

## Temporal and Spatial Thinking

As we discussed earlier, the evolution of synthesis to higher abstraction levels has had the effect of enabling a unified view of hardware and software design, since implementing functionality on general-purpose or single-purpose processors can be seen to have the same design starting point of sequential programs. In fact, some researchers think that synthesis has fundamentally changed to the nature of the skills needed to build hardware.

Before synthesis, designers of hardware worked primarily in the structural domain. They connected simpler components, each having a well-defined functionality, to build more complex systems. For example, a designer might have spent most of his/her time connecting logic gates to build a controller, or connecting registers, multiplexors and ALUs to build a datapath. Gajski referred to this era as the "capture-and-simulate" era of hardware design, since designers would capture these systems using computer-aided design tools, and then simulate the system to verify correctness, before fabricating a chip.

With the advent of synthesis, designers of hardware work primarily in the behavioral domain. They describe FSMDs or sequential programs, and they then synthesize these items automatically into structural connections of components. Gajski refers to this era as the "describe-and-synthesize" era.

This paradigm shift from working in the structural domain to the behavioral domain has not only increased productivity but also had the effect of dramatically changing the skills necessary to be a good hardware designer. During the capture-and-simulate era, strong spatial reasoning skills were needed to connect components. Structural diagrams were the main method for communicating system design information, supplemented with English descriptions of how the system worked. For example, recall that in Chapter 4, we mentioned that timers were typically described in datasheets using a diagram of the internal structure of the timer. However, during the describe-and-synthesize era, designers must have very strong temporal reasoning skills, since they aren't working so much with components as they are with things like FSMDs. FSMDs (and sequential programs) are created by composing states (or statements) that have relationships with one another over time. Although designers always had to have some temporal reasoning skills, those skills have now become extremely important to create good hardware. These skills are often associated with people who are strong programmers.

At the same time, the structure of the implementations output by today's synthesis tools is heavily influenced by the style with which a designer describes the behavior. Thus, the design must still have a strong understanding hardware structure and know how to write behavior that will synthesize into an efficient implementation.

## 11.3 Verification: Hardware/Software Co-Simulation

### Formal Verification and Simulation

Verification is the task of ensuring that a design is correct and complete. Correctness means that the design implements its specification accurately. Completeness means that the design's specification described appropriate output responses to all relevant input sequences.

The two main approaches to verification are known as *formal verification* and *simulation*. Formal verification is an approach to verification that analyzes a design to prove or disprove certain properties. We might seek to formally verify correctness of a particular design step, such as verifying that a particular structural description correctly implements a particular behavioral description, by proving the equivalence of the two descriptions. For example, we might describe an ALU behaviorally and then create a structural implementation using gates. We can prove the correctness of the structure by deriving a Boolean equation for the outputs, creating a truth table for those equations, and showing that this truth table is identical to the table created from the original behavior. Alternatively, we might seek to formally verify completeness of a behavioral description, be proving formally that certain situations always or never occur. For example, we might prove that for an elevator controller, the elevator door can never be open while the elevator is moving by deriving the conditions for the door being open and showing that these conditions conflict with those for the elevator moving.

The more common approach to verification is simulation. Formal verification is a very hard problem, and as such has been limited in practice to either small designs or to verifying only certain key properties. Instead, by far the most common approach to verification in practice is simulation. Simulation is an approach in which we create a model of the design that can be executed on a computer. We provide sample input values to this model, and check that the output values generated by the model match our expectations. For example, we can verify the correctness of an ALU by providing all possible input combinations, and checking the ALU outputs for correct results, which we of course have to compute using other means. Likewise, we can verify that an elevator controller won't have the door open while the elevator is moving, by simulating the controller for all possible input sequences and checking that the door is always closed when the elevator is moving.

Unfortunately, simulating "all possible inputs" or "all possible input sequences" is impossible for all but the simplest of systems. Notice that simulating all possible inputs of a 32-bit ALU requires simulating $2^{32} * 2^{32}$, or $2^{64}$, possible input combinations. Even if we could simulate one million combinations per second, simulating that number of combinations would require over half-a-million years. Furthermore, an ALU is only a combinational circuit; for a sequential circuit, like an elevator controller, we must simulate not only all possible input combinations but also all possible sequences of such combinations. Instead of simulating all possible inputs or input sequences, designers can only simulate a tiny subset of possible inputs. This subset usually includes typical values, plus known boundary conditions. Boundary conditions for an ALU might include one case where both operands are 0s and another where both operands are all 1s. Thus, simulation increases our confidence that a design is correct and complete, but doesn't prove anything.

Compared with a physical implementation, simulation has several advantages with respect to testing and debugging a system. The two most important advantages are excellent *controllability* and *observability*. Controllability is the ability to control the execution of the system. A designer can control time as well as data values. As for time, a designer can stop or start a simulation whenever desired. As for data values, a designer can set a system's inputs, or even a system's internal values, to any desired quantities. Observability is the ability to examine system values. A designer can stop a simulation and examine any system or environment values. With excellent controllability and observability, simulation allows a designer to perform debugging that would have been nearly impossible on a physical implementation. A designer can, for example, stop a simulation after, say, 2 seconds of simulated time, observe internal system values, and modify system or environment values before restarting the simulation. The designer could also step through small intervals, say, 500 nanoseconds, observing values at each step.

Simulation has some other advantages. Setting up a simulation of a system may require less time than setting up a physical implementation. For example, setting up a simulation of a behavioral description may take hours or days, versus weeks or months to obtain a physical implementation. Furthermore, simulation is safe, so if the system doesn't work properly, no property damage or threat to lives occurs. For example, we would most certainly want to simulate an automobile cruise-controller before testing one in an automobile.

Unfortunately, simulation also has several disadvantages compared with a physical implementation:

- Setting up simulation could take much time for systems with complex external environments. A designer may spend more time modeling the external environment than the system itself.

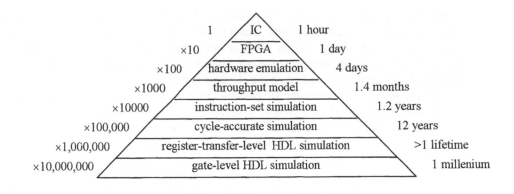

Figure 11.8: Sample relative speeds of different types of simulation/emulation compared with real-time execution. These numbers depend on the system size. Source: VLSI and Philips product literature.

- The models of the environment will likely be somewhat incomplete, so may not model complex environment behavior correctly, especially when that behavior is undocumented.
- Simulation speed can be quite slow compared to execution of a physical implementation.

Techniques for overcoming these problems, especially the speed problem, will be discussed in the next few sections.

## Simulation Speed

Perhaps the most significant disadvantage of simulation is that simulation is very slow compared to execution on a physical implementation. For example, while a physical implementation of a microprocessor may execute 100 million instructions per second, a simulation of a gate-level model of that microprocessor may only execute 10 instructions per second, meaning that the gate-level simulation is 10 million times slower than actual execution. Figure 11.8 illustrates this difference with a pyramid, using sample numbers representative of an SOC with perhaps hundreds of millions of transistors. One hour of actual execution of an SOC would require about 10 million hours of gate-level simulation, equivalent to about 1,000 years. One hour of simulation is quite a reasonable duration to want to simulate. For example, consider an automobile cruise-controller as an example. Given the wide variety of possible speeds, road grades, and wind velocities, we might certainly want to investigate about an hour's worth of environment scenarios and cruise-controller responses.

Simulation is slow for several reasons. One reason is because we are sequentializing a parallel design. Suppose there are 1,000,000 logic gates in a design. When implemented as an IC, all 1,000,000 gates operate in parallel. However, in simulation, we essentially have to analyze the inputs and generate the output of each gate one at a time.

A second reason simulation is slow is because we are adding several programs in between the system being simulated and real hardware. For example, suppose we want to simulate a simple operation like $A = B + C$. A simulator has to read and understand this operation, determine the current values of $B$ and $C$, compute $A$, and send the results somewhere. Thus, this single operation might require 10 to 100 simulator operations. The simulator is actually running under an operating system, so each simulator operation may actually require perhaps 10 to 100 operating system operations. Finally, each operating system operation may translate to 10 hardware operations. So each operation we wish to simulate may require 1,000 to 100,000 actual hardware operations.

To overcome this problem of long simulation time, we have some options. One option is to reduce the amount of real time that we simulate. So rather than simulating 1 hour of execution, we might just simulate 1 millisecond of execution, requiring 10,000,000 * 0.001 = 10,000 seconds, or about 3 hours. However, simulating 1 milisecond of execution does give us much confidence in the correctness and completeness of our system. For example, 1 millisecond of execution of a cruise-controller tells us very little about how the controller responds in a variety of scenarios. Nevertheless, because of the slow speed of simulation, many embedded systems are only simulated for perhaps a few seconds of real-time before they are first implemented physically.

Another way to overcome this problem is to use a faster simulator. There are two common ways that simulators can be made faster. One way is to build or use special hardware for simulation purposes. These devices are known as emulators, which we'll discuss in an upcoming section. Another way is to use a simulator that is less precise or accurate. In other words, we can reduce controllability and observability in exchange for speed.

As an example of reducing precision or accuracy to gain speed, consider the earlier example where we used a gate-level microprocessor model as our simulation model. When testing the cruise control program for correctness and completeness, we probably don't care about what's happening at the inputs and outputs of every logic gate in the microprocessor. Simulating at the gate level of detail is costing us tremendously in terms of speed, since the microprocessor may have hundreds of thousands of gates. Instead, we might replace the gate-level model by a model made up of register–transfer level components, which might execute 10 times faster than the gate-level model, as illustrated in Figure 11.8. An even faster simulation approach is known as cycle-based simulation, in which we design a simulator that is only accurate at clock cycle boundaries, and does not provide any information of signal changes in between cycles. As shown in the figure, this may gain us another factor of 10 speed improvement. Going for more speed, we may not need to model the structural components inside the microprocessor at all, and instead we might just use an instruction-set simulator, which may gain yet another factor of 10. An instruction-set simulation may thus be 10,0000 times slower than real execution, so now simulating our desired 1 hour requires 10,000 hours, or just over 1 year. Such faster simulation is often coupled with the above-mentioned reduction of the real time being simulated. So if we are willing to simulate for 10 hours, we could simulate $10 \times 1 / 10,000 = 0.001$ hour of real time, or 3.6 seconds of real time.

## Hardware-Software Co-Simulation

More generally, a variety of simulation approaches exist, varying in their simulation speed and precision/accuracy. For a given processor, whether general-purpose or single-purpose, simulation can vary from very detailed, like a gate-level model, to very abstract, like an instruction-level model. An instruction-level model of a general-purpose processor is known as an instruction-set simulator (ISS). An instruction-level model of a single-purpose processor is simply known as a system-level model. Lower-level simulations of either type of processor is usually done by creating a behavior, RT, or gate-level model in a hardware description language (HDL) environment. Because of the past separation of software design and hardware design, the simulation tools for each domain have evolved quite independently. The emphasis in software simulation has been on ISSs. The emphasis of hardware simulation has been models in hardware description languages (HDLs).

The integration of general-purpose and single-purpose processors onto a single IC has increased the need for an integrated method for simultaneously simulating these different types of processors. Thus, there is much interest in merging previously distinct software and hardware simulation tools.

One simple but naive form of integration is to create an HDL model of the microprocessor that will run the software of a system, and then integrate that model with the HDL models of the remaining single-purpose processors. While straightforward to implement, simulating a microprocessor in an HDL has two key disadvantages. First, this approach will be much slower than an ISS, since the HDL simulator represents an extra layer of software that must be executed. Second, such an approach ignores the fact that ISSs have excellent controllability and observability features that designers have become accustomed to.

Another approach to integrating general-purpose and single-purpose processor simulations is to create communication between an ISS and HDL simulator. Thus, each simulator runs independently of the other, except when data needs to be transferred between a general-purpose processor and single-purpose processor. A simulator that is designed to hide the details of the integration of an ISS and HDL simulator is known as a hardware-software co-simulator. While faster than HDL-only simulation and while capitalizing and the popularity of ISSs, co-simulators can still be quite slow if the general-purpose and single-purpose processors must communicate with one another frequently.

As it turns out, in many embedded systems, those processors do have frequent communication. Therefore, modern hardware-software co-simulators do more than just integrate two simulators. They also seek to minimize the communication between those simulators. Consider, for example, a system having one microprocessor, one single-purpose processor representing a coprocessor, and one memory, all connected using a single shared bus. Suppose the microprocessor's program is stored in this memory, and that the coprocessor uses the memory extensively also. We can simulate the microprocessor using an ISS and the coprocessor using an HDL. But where should the shared memory be modeled, in the ISS or the HDL? If in the HDL, then on every instruction, the ISS will need to stall in order to communicate with the HDL simulator to fetch the next instruction from memory. If in the ISS, then the HDL simulator will need to stall in order interrupt the ISS for access to the memory. However, note that most of these stalls are probably not necessary. For example, the ISS accesses of its instructions in memory are really irrelevant to the coprocessor. Likewise, the coprocessor's manipulation of data in memory is not relevant to the microprocessor, except in cases where that data is being transferred between the processors using the memory.

In order to minimize this communication, we can model the memory in both the ISS and the HDL simulator. Each simulator can use its own copy of the memory without bothering the other simulator most of the time. The co-simulator must ensure that the memories remain consistent and that shared data does get communicated properly. Co-simulators using this speedup technique exhibit much faster performance, with some reports indicating a factor of 100 or more.

## Emulators

Emulators were created to help solve the problems associated with simulation listed earlier, namely, expensive environment setup, incomplete environment models, and slow simulation speed. An emulator is a general physical device onto which a system can be mapped relatively quickly, perhaps in hours or days, and which usually can be placed into the system's real eventual environment. A microprocessor emulator typically consists of a microprocessor IC with some monitoring and control circuitry. An emulator for single-purpose processors typically consists of tens or hundreds of FPGAs. Both types of emulators usually support designer debug tasks, like stopping execution and viewing internal values.

Emulation has several advantages over simulation. The environment setup needed with simulation is not necessary, and obviously the incomplete environment problem is not a problem since we aren't modeling the environment. Furthermore, because the emulator is a physical implementation, it is typically much faster than simulation.

However, emulators have some disadvantages, too. First, they are still not as fast as real implementations, which could lead to timing problems in the real environment. For example, an emulated cruise-controller system may not respond quickly enough to keep control of the car it controls. Second, mapping a system to an emulator can still be time-consuming. For example, mapping a complex SOC description to 10 FPGAs requires partitioning the system into 10 parts, a task which itself could take weeks. Third, emulators can be very expensive. For example, a top-of-the-line FPGA-based emulator can cost between $100,000 to $1,000,000. Not only is the cost a problem in itself, but it can also lead to a resource bottleneck. Specifically, a company may only purchase one emulator that must be shared by several different design groups, requiring one group to wait days or weeks until another group finishes.

# 11.4 Reuse: Intellectual Property Cores

Designers have always had at their disposal commercial off-the-shelf (COTS) components, which they could purchase and use in building a given system. Using such predesigned and prepackaged ICs, each implementing general-purpose or single-purpose processors, greatly reduced design and debug time, as compared to building all system components from scratch.

As discussed in Chapter 1, the trend of growing IC capacities is leading to all the components of a system being implemented on a single chip, known as a system-on-a-chip (SOC). This trend, therefore, is leading to a major change in the distribution of such off-the-shelf components. Rather than being sold as ICs, such components are increasingly being sold in the form of intellectual property, or IP. Specifically, they are sold as behavioral, structural or physical descriptions, rather than actual ICs. A designer can integrate those descriptions with other descriptions to form one large SOC description that can then be fabricated into a new IC.

Processor-level components that are available in the form of IP are known as *cores*. Initially, the term core referred only to microprocessors, but now is used for nearly any general-purpose or single-purpose processor IP component.

## Hard, soft and firm cores

Cores come in three forms:

- A *soft core* is a synthesizable behavioral description of a component, typically written in a hardware description language (HDL) like VHDL or Verilog.
- A *firm core* is a structural description of a component, again typically provided in an HDL.
- A *hard core* is physical description, provided in any of a variety of physical layout file formats.

Note that the three forms of cores, namely, soft, firm, and hard, correspond to the three axes in Gajski's Y-chart in Figure 11.4.

A hard core has the advantages of ease of use and predictability. Since the core developer has already designed and tested the core, the core can be used right away and can be expected to work correctly. Furthermore, the size, power and performance of the core can be predicted quite accurately. However, a hard core is specific to a particular IC process, and thus cannot be easily mapped to a different process. For example, a hard core $A$ may be available for IC vendor $X$'s 0.25 micrometer CMOS process. If a designer wishes to use vendor $X$'s 0.18 micrometer process, or wishes to use vendor $Y$, then the hard core $A$ cannot be used.

On the other hard, a soft core has the advantages of retargeting and optimization potential. A hard core must be designed using a particular IC technology, and thus can't be used in a different technology. In contrast, a soft core can be synthesized (targeted) to nearly any technology, as long as the user has access to the synthesis and physical design tools for the desired technology. Furthermore, a designer can modify the behavior to be optimized for a particular use — for example, deleting unused functions of the core — resulting in lower-power and smaller designs. But, soft cores obviously require more design effort, and may not work properly in a technology for which it has never been tested. Furthermore, a soft core will likely not be as optimized as a hard core for the same processor, since hard cores typically have been given much more design attention.

Firm cores are a compromise between soft and hard cores, providing some retargetability and some limited optimization, but also providing better predictability and ease of use.

## New Challenges Posed by Cores to Processor Providers

The advent of cores has dramatically changed the business model of vendors of general-purpose processors and standard single-purpose processors. Two key areas that have changed significantly are pricing models and IP protection.

Pricing models have proliferated. In the past, vendors could provide their products to designers in the form of an IC. Designers could not (economically) copy these ICs, so if they wanted more copies, they had to buy more ICs. The more ICs the designer purchased, the more money the vendor earned. Today, the vendors provide their products to designers in the form of IP, transmitted via an electronic format like the World Wide Web or CD-ROM. The designer incorporates this IP into an SOC and then produces as many copies as he/she needs. The vendor can now choose whether to sell the IP to the designer using different pricing models. One pricing model follows that of ICs, namely, the designer must pay a certain amount for each copy he or she creates. This is known as a royalty-based model. A very different model is that of a fixed price, namely, the designer pays for the right to use the IP and then creates as many copies as desired. Many companies now give out cores for free when their products are purchased, such as synthesis tools or an FPGAs. Countless variations and combinations of these models exist in today's IP licensing arrangements. Each pricing model comes with accompanying challenges of enforcing those models. A royalty-based model requires, for example, that the IP vendor be aware of how many products incorporating its IP are being sold. Extensive contracts must often be created to enforce these licensing arrangements.

IP protection has become a key concern of core providers. In the past, illegally copying an IC would have required a tremendous amount of deliberate effort reverse engineering effort. "Accidental" copying of an IC was not even possible. Today, cores are sold in an electronic format, and so deliberate and even accidental unauthorized copying of a core are easier. The advent of cores has therefore greatly increased the safeguards that vendors must consider when selling their products. Contracts must be created to ensure that designers do not copy or distribute the IP. Some vendors use encryption techniques to limit the actual exposure to the IP that designers can achieve. Techniques known as watermarking are being developed to help vendors determine whether a particular instance of a processor in an IC was copied from the vendor and whether this copy was authorized.

These challenges, of course, come with benefits. One key benefit to core providers is that they can eliminate manufacturing from their business entirely. Many processor manufacturers, both general-purpose and standard single-purpose, have gone to a core-only business model.

## New Challenges Posed by Cores to Processor Users

The advent of cores also poses new challenges to designers seeking to use a general-purpose or standard single-purpose processor. These include licensing arrangements, extra design effort, and verification.

Licensing arrangements are more complicated for cores. A designer purchasing a core typically cannot just order one as easily as purchasing an IC. Contracts enforcing pricing models and IP protection must be drawn up and signed, perhaps requiring legal assistance.

Extra design effort will likely be necessary, especially for soft cores. A soft core must still be synthesized and tested. Even minor differences in synthesis tools can yield problems.

Verification requirements have become much more difficult. One increased difficulty is that soft cores that are synthesized must be tested extensively to ensure correct synthesis output. Furthermore, soft and firm cores mapped to a particular technology must again be

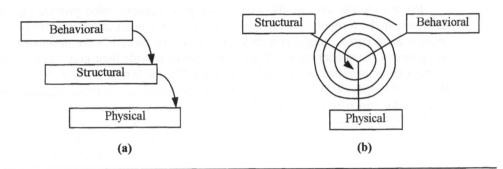

Figure 11.9: Design process models: (a) waterfall, (b) spiral.

extensively tested. Ideally, synthesis and physical design tools would generate correct implementations, but that is simply not the case today. In addition, even correct implementations will vary in terms of their timing and power.

A second increased difficulty in verification stems from the fact that there is no direct access to a core once it has been integrated into a chip. In the past, a system's ICs resided on a board, and those ICs could thus be tested individually by connecting a logic analyzer to the IC's pins. Today, a system's cores are buried inside of a single IC, so directly accessing a core's ports is impossible, requiring other means for scanning port values in and out. Furthermore, one cannot simply replace a bad core by another one, the way one could replace a bad IC in the past, thus making early verification even more crucial.

## 11.5 Design Process Models

A designer must proceed through several steps when designing a system. We can think of describing behavior as one design step, converting behavior to structure as another step, and mapping structure to a physical implementation as another step. Each step will obviously consist of numerous substeps. A design process model describes the order in which these steps are taken. The term *process* here should not be confused with the notion of a process in the concurrent process model discussed in an earlier chapter, nor should it be confused with the IC manufacturing process. Here, process refers to the manner in which the embedded system designer proceeds through design steps.

One process model is the waterfall model, illustrated in Figure 11.9(a). Suppose a designer has six months to build a system. In the waterfall model, the designer first exerts extensive effort, perhaps two months, describing the behavior completely. Once fully satisfied that the behavior is correct, after extensive behavioral simulation and debugging, the designer moves on to the next step of designing structure. Again, much effort is exerted, perhaps another two months, until the designer is satisfied the structure is correct. Finally, the physical implementation step is carried out, occupying perhaps the last two months. The result is a final system implementation, hopefully a correct one. In the waterfall model, when we proceed to the next step, we never come back to the earlier steps, much like water cascading down a mountain doesn't return to higher elevations.

Unfortunately, the waterfall model is not very realistic, for several reasons. First, we will almost always find bugs in the later steps that should be fixed in an earlier step. For example, when testing the structure, we may notice that we forgot to handle a certain input combination in the behavior. Second, we often do not know the complete desired behavior of the system until we have a working prototype. For example, we may build a prototype device and show it to a customer, who then gets the idea of adding several features. Third, system specifications commonly change unexpectedly. For example, we may be halfway done designing a system when our company decides that to be competitive, the product must be smaller and consume less power than originally expected, requiring several features to be dropped. Nevertheless, many designers design their systems following the waterfall model. The accompanying unexpected iterations back through the three steps often result in missed deadlines, and hence in lost revenues or products that never make it to market.

An alternative process model is the spiral model, shown in Figure 11.9(b). Suppose again that the designer has six months to build the system. In the spiral model, the designer first exerts some effort to describe the basic behavior of the system, perhaps a few weeks. This description will be incomplete, but have the basic functions, with many functions left to be filled in later. Next, the designer moves on to designing structure, again taking maybe a few weeks. Finally, the designer creates a physical prototype of the system. This prototype is used to test out the basic functions, and to get a better idea of what functions we should add to the system. With this experience, the designer proceeds to proceed through the three steps again, expanding the original behavioral description or even starting with a new one, creating structure, and obtaining a physical implementation again. These steps may be repeated several times until the desired system is obtained.

The spiral model has its drawbacks, too. The designer must come up with ways to obtain structure and physical implementations quickly. For example, the designer may have to use FPGAs for the physical prototypes, finally generating new silicon (a task that can take months) for the final product. Thus, the designer may have to use more tools, which itself can require extra effort and costs. Also, if a system was well defined in the beginning and if we would have created a first-time correct implementation using the waterfall model, then the spiral model requires more time due to the overhead of creating numerous prototypes. Nevertheless, variations of the spiral model have become extremely popular, both in software development as well as hardware development.

The preceding discussion focused implicitly on designing single-purpose processors, since we started with behavior, designed structure, and then mapped to a physical implementation. However, the discussion applies equally to using general-purpose processors. In the traditional waterfall approach illustrated in Figure 11.9(a), a general-purpose processor's architecture (structure) is developed by a particular company and acquired by an embedded system designer. The designer then develops a software application (behavior). Finally, the designer maps the application to the architecture, using compilation and manual design.

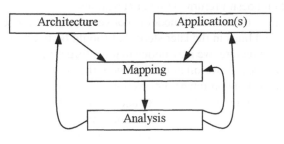

However, even this widely accepted approach is beginning to change. A spiral-like process model, illustrated in Figure 11.10, is beginning to be applied by embedded system designers. In this model, the designer develops or acquires an architecture, and develops an application or set of applications. The designer then maps the application to the architecture, and analyzes the design metrics of this combination of application, architecture and mapping. The designer can then choose to (a) modify the mapping, (b) modify the application to better suit the architecture, or (c) modify the architecture to better suit the application. This last step of modifying the architecture was previously too difficult to consider. However, with the maturation of synthesis tools as well as compilers that can generate code for a variety of instruction sets, this last step is much more feasible. Furthermore, as mentioned above, designers are increasingly obtaining the microprocessor architecture in the form of intellectual property, which can thus be potentially be tuned to the application. This is in stark contrast to the past, when an obtained microprocessor IC obviously could not be modified. By coincidence, the depiction in Figure 11.10 of this process model is referred to as the *Y-chart*, but has no relation with Gajski's Y-chart described earlier.

Refining to lower abstraction levels (whether behavioral, structural, or physical models) narrows the potential implementations, as illustrated in Figure 11.3(b). Such narrowing proceeds until a particular implementation is chosen.

## 11.6 Summary

Tremendous effort is being exerted to advance design technology, so that the gap between designer productivity and IC capacity can be reduced. Synthesis has made dramatic changes in the way that single-purpose processors are designed, making such design much more similar to software design. Increasing IC capacity means that software and hardware components coexist on single-chip SOCs, resulting in a design paradigm shift toward extensive reuse of predesigned cores. Simulating SOCs is beneficial but very hard to do quickly, and it is helped by co-simulation and emulation techniques. Whether designing software or hardware, a spiral design process model is a popular approach to design.

## 11.7 Book Summary

Embedded systems represent a large and growing class of computing systems, which some people believe will soon become even more significant than desktop computing systems. The nature of embedded systems has been changed dramatically by today's outrageously large chip capacities coupled with powerful new automation tools, but methods for teaching embedded systems design have not evolved concurrently. This book is a first attempt to remedy this situation. We started by introducing the view that computing systems are built primarily from collections of processors, some general-purpose, some single-purpose (standard or custom), which differ not in some fundamental way, but rather just in their design metrics like power, performance, and flexibility. We introduced memories commonly used along with processors and described how to interface processors and memories. With processors, memories, and interfacing methods, we could build complete systems, and so we gave an example of one such system: a digital camera.

During the first part of the book, we did not focus on the nitty-gritty internal details of any particular microprocessor, since modern tools greatly reduce the need for such knowledge. Instead, in the second part of this book, we focused on higher-level issues. We examined powerful higher-level computation models like state machines and concurrent processes, which enable the capture of more complex functionality. We introduced the basics of a large class of embedded systems, known as control systems. We summarized the key IC technologies available to implement embedded systems. Finally, we summarized the issues related to design technologies for mapping desired behavior to a physical implementation.

This book was intentionally broad in nature. It was designed primarily to serve as a starting point for students about to study the various subtopics of embedded systems in more detail, topics like VLSI/ASIC design, real-time programming, digital-design synthesis, control system design, and other topics. The hope is that the student pursuing those topics will have a unified view of hardware and software throughout their studies, and view embedded systems design not as a field comprising mostly low-level code hacking but rather as a unique engineering discipline demanding a balanced knowledge of hardware and software issues. We hope you have found the book useful.

## 11.8 References and Further Reading

- Balarin, F., M. Chiodo, A. Jurecska, H. Hsieh, A. L. Lavagno, C. Passerone, A. L. Sangiovanni-Vincentelli, E. Sentovich, K. Suzuki, and B. Tabbara. *Hardware-Software Co-Design of Embedded Systems: A Polis Approach*. Norwell, MA: Kluwer Academic Press, June 1997.
- De Micheli, Giovanni. *Synthesis and Optimization of Digital Circuits*. New York: McGraw-Hill, 1994. An introduction to the models and algorithms inside synthesis tools, ranging from high-level down to logic-level synthesis tools.

- Gajski, Daniel D. *Principles of Digital Design*. Englewood Cliffs, NJ: Prentice-Hall, 1997. Introduces combinational and sequential logic design, with a unique focus on synthesis and higher-levels of design in the later chapters.
- Gajski, Daniel D., Nikil Dutt, Alen We, and Steve Lin. *High-Level Synthesis: Introduction to Chip Design*. Norwell, MA: Kluwer Academic Publishers, 1992. A description of the methods and algorithms underlying high-level synthesis. Includes discussion of the Gajski Y-chart.
- Gajski, Daniel D., Frank Vahid, Sanjiv Narayan, and Jie Gong. *Specification and Design of Embedded Systems*. Englewood Cliffs, NJ: Prentice Hall, 1994. Introduces a top-down specify-explore-refine approach to design.
- Katz, Randy. *Contemporary Logic Design*. Redwood City, CA: Benjamin/Cummings, 1994. Describes combinational and sequential logic design, with a focus on logic and sequential optimization and CAD.
- Kienhuis, B, E. Deprettere, K. A. Vissers, and P. van der Wolf. An Approach for Quantitative Analysis of Application-specific Dataflow Architectures. In Proceeding of 11th Int. Conference of Applications-specific Systems, Architectures and Processors (ASAP 1997), pp. 338–349, 1997. Describes the Y-chart design process.
- A. C. J. Kienhuis. "Design Space Exploration of Stream-based Dataflow Architectures: Methods and Tools," PhD thesis, Delft University of Technology, The Netherlands, January 1999, ISBN 90-5326-029-3. Discusses advantages of working at a higher abstraction level; includes the abstraction pyramid and the Y-chart design process.
- Klein, Russ. Hardware/Software Co-Simulation. Mentor Graphics Corporation, technical white paper, http://www.mentorg.com/seamless. Describes the basics and some experiences with hardware/software co-simulation.
- Sommerville, Ian. *Software Engineering*. Reading, MA: Addison Wesley, 2000. A survey of the many different aspects of software engineering, including the spiral design process model.

## 11.9 Exercises

11.1 List and describe three general approaches to improving designer productivity.

11.2 Describe each tool that has enabled the elevation of software design and hardware design to higher abstraction levels.

11.3 Show behavior and structure (at the same abstraction level) for a design that finds minimum of three input integers, by showing the following descriptions: a sequential program behavior, a processor/memory structure, a register–transfer behavior, a register/FU/MUX structure, a logic equation/FSM behavior, and finally a gate/flip-flop structure. Label each description and associate each label with a point on Gajski's Y-chart.

11.4 Develop an example of a Boolean function that can be implemented with fewer gates when implemented in more than two levels (your designs should have roughly 10 gates,

Embedded System Design

not hundreds!). Assuming two transistors per gate input, and gate delay of 10 nanoseconds, create a single plot showing size versus delay for both designs.

11.5 Show how to partition a single finite-state machine into two smaller finite-state machines, which might be necessary to achieve acceptable synthesis tool run time. *Hint*: you'll need to introduce a couple new signals and states.

11.6 Define hardware/software codesign.

11.7 Write a small program that reads a file of integers and outputs their sum. Write another program that does not add the integers using the built-in addition operator of a programming language, but instead "simulates" addition by using an addition function that converts each integer to a string of 0s and 1s, adds the strings by mimicking binary addition, and converts the binary result back to an integer. Compare the performance of the native program to the performance of the simulation program on a large file.

11.8 If a simulation environment can simulate 1,000 instructions per second, estimate how long the environment would take to simulate the boot sequence of Windows running on a modern PC. Even a very rough estimate is acceptable, since we are interested in the order of magnitude of such simulation.

11.9 What is hardware/software co-simulation? What is a key method for speeding up such simulation?

11.10 Show the correspondence of the three types of cores with Gajski's Y-Chart.

11.11 Describe the new challenges created by cores for processor developers as well as users.

11.12 List major design steps for building the digital camera example of Chapter 7 assuming: (a) a waterfall process model, (b) a spiral-like Y-chart process model.

# APPENDIX A: *Online Resources*

A.1    Introduction
A.2    Summary of the ESD Web Page
A.3    Lab Resources
A.4    About the Book Cover

## A.1    Introduction

We intentionally designed this textbook to be independent of any particular microprocessor, microcontroller, programming language, hardware description language, FPGA, and so on. This decision was made largely because the growing popularity and complexity of embedded systems has been accompanied by tremendous diversity. The days when most courses on microprocessor-based design used a fairly standard microcontroller are quickly giving way to the situation of tremendous diversity in lab setups. Some setups emphasize 8-bit microcontrollers, while others emphasize 32-bit platforms using one of a variety of popular processors like Intel 80x86, Motorola 68000 variations, Sun Sparcs, MIPS processors, ARM processors, digital signal processors, multimedia processors (like TriMedia's), and so on. Furthermore, these processors come on a variety of development boards, each with unique features. Some courses focus mostly on hardware prototyping while others include extensive simulation too. Some courses integrate the use of FPGAs, which also come in diverse setups. New chips and platforms that integrate microprocessors and FPGAs are beginning to appear. This diversity, coupled with the evolution of embedded system design into a discipline, make the need to decouple lecture material from lab material quite evident.

However, we have not simply left the instructor and students entirely on their own with respect to lab setup. Instead, we have used the World Wide Web to supplement this book with extensive lab materials. In fact, using the Web, we can provide even more than a typical processor-specific textbook might be able to provide.

## A.2 Summary of the ESD Web Page

The Web site accompanying *Embedded System Design* can be found at: http://www.cs.ucr.edu/esd. It currently includes items like:

- Lab resources, including setup details and tutorials for the setup used at UCR, lab assignments, and solutions
- Links to related Web sites, data-sheets, and industry standards documents
- PowerPoint lecture slides

Of course, the Web site will continually evolve, so more items may be added in the future.

## A.3 Lab Resources

Because the lab resources are of great interest to many instructors, we provide a brief summary of the items on the Web site at the time this book went to press. The items are basically the items used at UC Riverside, generalized for use by other schools. Again, these items will likely evolve and expand. We encourage instructors to submit material that could be used to broaden the platforms that can be used in conjunction with the textbook.

For our lab setup, we chose to focus on the Intel 8051 and Xilinx FPGAs. For the FPGA side, we use VHDL as our hardware description language, and use Xilinx's Foundation Express for synthesis and mapping to FPGAs. For the 8051 side, we use the Keil C compiler, and emulators, programmers and chips from Philips. We also currently use a platform from XESS Corporation, consisting of a single board including both a Xilinx FPGA and an 8051 derivative.

We chose to use an 8-bit microcontroller, as opposed to a 32-bit platform, for two reasons. First, 8-bit platforms are typically quite simple, with no operating system, BIOS, or other more advanced features. Thus, we felt they are more suitable for an introductory type course. Second, we have found that students enjoy being able to build inexpensive standalone systems — many students have been quite creative in developing projects that they have then actually taken home and put into use. For a more advanced course on real-time embedded systems, we use a 32-bit processing platform.

The lab material is categorized by chapter, with a brief summary of associated labs.

### Chapter 2

- "Tutorial: Aldec Active-HDL Simulation." In this lab, code is provided for a 1-bit adder and a corresponding testbench. Code is provided for a 4-bit added built using the 1-bit adder previously used.
- "XS40 Tutorial: VHDL Synthesis." This tutorial shows students how to synthesize and download VHDL code onto an XS40 board. The tutorial gives steps showing how to synthesize the code provided using Xilinx Foundation Express to generate a bit stream.

- "XS40 Tutorial: Onboard Microcontroller (8031)." This tutorial shows students how to control the onboard microcontroller (8031) connected to the FPGA.
- "XS40 Tutorial: Sending Signals from the PC." This tutorial shows students how to inject signals from the PC into the XS40 boards.
- "Introduction to FPGAs with Schematic Capture." The purpose of this lab is to design a seven-segment decoder using AND, OR, NAND, NOR, XOR, and XNOR gates.
- "Introduction to FPGAs Using VHDL." This lab is a follow-up to the "Introduction to FPGAs with Schematic Capture" lab. The seven-segment decoder circuit draw in the previous lab is translated into VHDL.
- "Introduction to VHDL Simulation and Synthesis: Blinking LEDs Lab." This is the lab in which the student will implement a behavioral description of a 2-bit counter whose output is fed to a 2-to-4 decoder. The decoder is then wired to four LEDs.
- "Seven-Segment Decoder: Behavioral Description." This lab is a follow-up to the "Introduction to FPGAs Using VHDL" lab. In this lab the seven-segment decoder is rewritten so that it is a behavioral description.
- "ALU Design." The purpose of this lab is to build a 2-bit ALU. The ALU is written behaviorally.
- "2-bit Counter." The purpose of this lab is to write a VHDL description of 2-bit counter as a finite state machine (FSM).
- "FSM + D: GCD Calculator." The purpose of this lab is to write a VHDL description of a GCD (greatest common divisor) calculator. The calculator is divided into two parts — a controller and a datapath.
- "FSM + D: Parallel to Serial Converter." The purpose of this lab is to write a VHDL description of a parallel to serial converter as an FSMD.
- "FSM to FSM+D: Soda Machine Controller." The purpose of this lab is to implement a soda machine controller.
- "VHDL Calculator." The purpose of this lab is to implement a finite state machine in VHDL to perform simple calculations like addition, subtraction, and multiplication.
- "Watchdog Timer." In this lab, students will be designing a hardware watchdog timer.

In addition to the above labs, we include the following:

- "VHDL by Example." This Web site is designed to teach students VHDL through a set of increasingly complex examples, beginning with a simple logic gate, and ending with a microprocessor and a digital filter. We developed this site after observing that learning a hardware description language was too difficult for most students in an introductory course, primarily because VHDL textbooks go into too much detail regarding the language itself and don't spend enough time giving examples directly relevant to what the students need. We have used this Web site with great success. Students are able to write VHDL code for complex systems in much less time than before.

## Chapter 3

- "Microprocessor." The purpose of this lab is to implement a microprocessor in VHDL.
- "8051 Tutorial." This tutorial provides code to blink an LED using the 8051. The tutorial shows students how to compile the program using the c51 compiler, and then run the program using the PDS51 emulation software.
- "The 8051 Standalone Chip Tutorial." This tutorial provides code to blink an LED using the 8051 standalone chip.
- "Music Generator." The purpose of this lab is to design a peripheral device that plays musical notes.
- "Day of the Week." The purpose of this lab is to design a FSM when given day, month, and year will output the day of the week.
- "Prefix Length." The purpose is to describe, at FSMD level, an entity that will compute the length of the prefix of two 16-bit binary strings.
- "Virtual Clock." In this lab, students implement a software real-time clock (i.e., a virtual clock (VC)).
- "Instruction Set Simulator." The purpose of this lab is for the student to design and experiment with a simple instruction-set simulator.

In addition, we include the following:

- An 8051 instruction set simulator, provided as C++ source code.
- An 8051 synthesizable core, written in VHDL at the register-transfer level.

## Chapter 4

- "Implementing a 4-bit Counter and Interfacing it to an LCD." In this lab, students will learn how to write a simple C program for 80X51 microcontroller, compile it using the C51 compiler, emulate it on an emulator using PDS51, and learn how to use an LCD (Liquid Crystal Display).
- "Implementing a Calculator Using Peripherals." In this lab, the student will build a simple calculator using the keypad as an input and the LCD as an output peripheral.
- "A/D Conversion." The purpose of this lab is to be able to implement analog to digital conversion using the ADC0804LCN 8-bit A/D converter.
- "Stepper Motor." The purpose of this lab is to control a stepper motor, with instructions received from the PC via a serial communication link to the 8051.
- "4-Bit Counter with Seven Segment Display." Here, students implement a 4-bit counter using an 8051 and a seven-segment display.
- "Decimal Counter with Output Multiplexing." The purpose of this lab is to implement a decimal counter, which counts from 0 to 99 using two seven-segment display and an 8051.
- "Decimal Counter and Time Multiplexing." The purpose of this lab is to implement a decimal counter, which counts from 0 to 99 using two seven-segment display and an 8051. Unlike the previous lab, in this lab only one port is used so we must multiplex the output.

- "Keypad Scan." The purpose of this lab is to read input from a keypad and display the corresponding key pressed unto a seven-segment display.

## Chapter 5

- "Using EEPROMs," where the student connects an EEPROM device to a microcontroller and writes necessary code to complete the interface.
- "8051 External Memory." In this lab, the student interfaces an 8051 with an external memory device.

In addition, there are links to several memory datasheets.

## Chapter 6

- "Serial Communication." The purpose of this lab is to establish serial communication between the PC and the 8051.
- "ISA Bus." Here, students implement the ISA bus using VHDL.
- "$I^2C$ Bus." In this lab, students work on a VHDL implementation of the $I^2C$ bus protocol.
- "Bus Invert." In this lab students will implement a bus encoding scheme called bus invert.

In addition, there are links to numerous specification documents outlining major bus interfaces such as AGP, CAN, FireWire, ARM, $I^2C$, and USB.

## Chapter 7

- C/VHDL code for the Digital Camera example that is described in Chapter 7 is provided on the Web page.

---

# A.4   About the Book Cover

A quick look around our environment turns up embedded systems in a surprising number of places. This book's cover shows just a few such systems in common environments. A numbering of those systems appears in Figure A.1. A listing of those systems follows.

## Outdoors

1. Helicopter: control, navigation, communication, etc.
2. Medicine administering systems
3. Smart hospital bed with sensors and communication
4. Patient monitoring system
5. Surgical displays
6. Ventilator
7. Digital thermometer
8. Portable data entry systems
9. Pacemaker
10. Automatic door
11. Electric wheelchair
12. Smart briefcase with fingerprint enabled lock
13. Ambulance: medical and communication equipment
14. Automatic irrigation systems
15. Jet aircraft: control, navigation, communication, autopilot, collision-avoidance, in-flight entertainment, passenger telephones, etc.
16. Laptop computer (contains embedded systems)
17. Cellular telephone

---

Figure A.1: Embedded systems in common environments, numbered for reference.

18. Portable stereo (boom-box)
19. Satellite receiver system
20. Credit / debit card reader
21. Barcode scanner
22. Cash register
23. ATM machine
24. Automobile (engine control, cruise control, temperature control, music system, anti-lock brakes, active suspension, navigation, toll transponder, etc.)

25. Automatic lighting
26. Pump monitoring system
27. Lottery ticket dispenser
28. Cell-phone/pager
29. Traffic light controller
30. Police vehicle (data lookup, communication, sirens, radar detector, etc.)
31. Cell-phone base station
32. Handheld communicator (walkie-talkie)
33. Fire-control onboard computer

## Indoors

1. Cordless phone
2. Coffee maker
3. Rice cooker
4. Portable radio
5. Programmable range

6. Microwave oven
7. Smart refrigerator
8. In-home computer network switch
9. Clothes dryer
10. Clothes washing machine

11. Portable MP3 player
12. Digital camera
13. Electronic book
14. Trash compactor
15. Hearing aid
16. Dishwasher
17. Electronic clock
18. Video camera
19. Electronic wristwatch
20. Pager
21. Cell phone
22. CD player
23. DVD player
24. Smart speakers
25. Stereo receiver
26. TV set-top box
27. Television
28. VCR
29. TV-based Web access box
30. House temperature control
31. Home alarm system
32. Point-of-sale system
33. Video-game console
34. TV remote control
35. Electronic keyboard/synthesizer
36. Fax machine
37. Scanner
38. Wireless networking
39. Telephone modem
40. Cable modem
41. Printer
42. Portable video game
43. Personal digital assistant
44. Portable digital picture viewer
45. Phone with answering machine

# Index

## A

accelerator, 11
actuator, 247
adder, 33
address space, 57
aliasing, 264
allocation, 50, 294
ALU, 34, 56
analog-to-digital converter, 102
application-specific IC. *See* ASIC
application-specific instruction-set
      processor. *See* ASIP
arbitration, 160
ASIC, 13, 276
ASIP, 12, 74
assembler, 71
assembly-language programming, 61
asynchronous, 36

## B

battery-backed RAM, 120
baud rate, 91
behavioral description, 285
behavioral synthesis, 294
benchmark, 76
binding, 50
bit, 57
Bluetooth, 174
bridge, 165
buffering, 153
bus, 138

bus-based I/O, 145
busy-waiting, 232
byte, 57

## C

cache, 125
cache block, 59, 126
cache hit, 59, 126
cache line, 126
cache memory, 59
cache miss, 59, 126
cache replacement policy, 128
CAD, 43
CAN bus, 171
CCD, 180
cell-based array, 277
checksum, 169
clock cycle, 57
closed-loop control, 248
CMOS transistor, 30, 270
codesign, 21, 295
combinational logic, 33
communicating process model, 208
comparator, 34
compiler, 71
computation model, 209
concurrent process model, 223
condition variable, 233
consumer-producer problem, 228
control system, 245
control unit, 57
control-dominated system, 208

Embedded System Design

Printed in the USA/Agawam, MA
November 20, 2020

764881.005